D1798645

Sixteen Years In Chile And Peru: From 1822 To 1839

Thomas Sutcliffe

SIXTEEN YEARS

IN

CHILE AND PERU

FROM 1822 TO 1839.

BY

THE RETIRED GOVERNOR OF JUAN FERNANDEZ.

Thomas Sutcliffe

"But thou Defoe, o'er that lone isle has thrown
A spell so potent, who hath felt it not?
Unto my boyhood 'twas a fairy spot;
Yet to my fancy so familiar made.
I seem'd as well to know creek, cave, and grot,
Its open beach, its tangled greenwood shade.
As if I there had dwelt, and Crusoe's part had played."

BARTON.

FISHER, SON, AND CO.

NEWGATE STREET, LONDON; RUE ST. HONORÉ, PARIS.

1841

LS

DEDICATION.

THIS WORK

IS INSCRIBED, AS A TOKEN OF RESPECT,

TO THE NOBILITY, CLERGY, AND GENTRY,

WHO HAVE HONOURED IT WITH

THEIR PATRONAGE,

BY THEIR MOST OBEDIENT,

AND VERY HUMBLE SERVANT,

Thos Sutcliffe

PREFACE.

Captain Basil Hall has published a sixth edition of his work, entitled "Extracts from a Journal written on the coasts of Chile, Peru, and Mexico, in the years 1820, 1821, and 1822," in the advertisement of which we find the following allusion to the momentous scenes passing at that period :—

"A similar work, or one executed on the same plan, at the present moment, after an interval of nearly twenty years, would unquestionably afford matter for one of the most interesting, and perhaps useful, comparisons between promise and performance that the political world has ever witnessed.

"Such a task, however, could be executed only by an eye-witness, who, with equal opportunities to those which I enjoyed, and no less fidelity and diligence, should unite higher powers of observation, and greater capability of giving them effectual expression. For the describer of the present state of things in South America would be required, not only to relate what he should actually see, as I have attempted to do, but to trace and expose the causes as well as the probable consequences of the dreadful state of confusion—amounting in some places almost to anarchy—which, to the sorrow of every lover of political freedom and of social improvement, too deeply characterises the society of that magnificent continent.

" Nevertheless, when preparing this edition for the press, I set on foot some inquiries—not indeed with a view to any change in the text—but to the introduction of such explanatory notes, as might help to throw light on the progress of those stupendous events of which I saw only the commencement. But I soon discovered that, so far from these researches enabling me to furnish information to others, they only tended still further to mystify my own notions ; at last I gave up the inquiry in perfect despair, resolving neither to touch a word of my original narrative, nor to add anything new."—*London, March,* 1840.

Encouraged by these remarks, I have ventured to write the following work, presenting my readers with a narrative of sixteen years' residence in South America ; in the course of which I have described, in detail, the manners and customs of the natives of Chile ;—their struggle for independence,—and the unfortunate political convulsions which have occurred, since their final emancipation from Spain, up to the period of the establishment of the government now in authority, and which tolerated the following display of ingratitude.

" At the commencement of our political emancipation, we committed *the error* of admitting into our service various adventurers of the old world, who, if they were *allowed* to assist us in that epoch, a time ought to arrive when their services would not be required by us; but to our misfortune, many still remain with their respective grades, and who, if *tolerated* till now, we have at present sufficient motives to separate them entirely from the service. It is our wish that government would take this into consideration, and ordain it so, that in the service of the republic, we may only observe Chilians, for it is those that at all times have given to it honour, and unfading glory."—*El Cura Monardes; Santiago, March,* 1838, *by Portenos de Valparaiso.*

What other *eulogy* could be expected from the creatures of a faction, composed of the partizans of Spain ?

The following reply, however, from the pen of an eminent citizen, proves that the Chilian patriots were perfectly incapable of depreciating our services. Extracts from " El Valdiviano Federal," Santiago, March, 1838.

" Let it be the editor of the ' Valdiviano Federal,' that is supported *by government,* [*ironically,*] that will take it upon himself to contradict these new publications.

" During the first years of our emancipation, the government invited foreigners to come and establish themselves in this country, and in the meantime offered to them the most generous hospitality. A number have emigrated; it is a pity that they have not been more numerous—and what benefits have we not received from them? They have taken part in our war of the independence, and in proportion as our dangers increased, so did their zeal and endeavours in favour of American liberty.

" The following is a notorious, and an interesting anecdote; whilst we were assembled in the municipal hall, on the very day that the news of the dispersion and defeat of our army in Cancharayada arrived, and when every one had abandoned all hopes of being enabled to save their country, twelve Englishmen entered; and one of them, Mr. James Barnard, (an eminent merchant,) spoke as follows :—' The Patria is in danger, therefore we have come to offer our services, and are ready and willing to sacrifice our lives and fortunes in its defence.'

" This generous offer induced other foreigners to imitate their example, and awoke the fond hopes that the *Patria* might be saved, which were soon realized.

" Messrs. Barnard and Haigh (Mr. Samuel,) armed themselves, joined the cavalry as volunteers, and acted their part in various brilliant charges that were made, which decided the battle of Maipu.

And in what battle have we not seen foreigners running the same risks, and not with less enthusiasm than the natives of the country, to defend it?

" It is only the basest ingratitude, only the indifference, or, I should say, aversion to ' La Patria,' that can make them disown such eminent services.

"Generous foreigners—preserve for ever that love and the zeal which you have shown for your adopted country, whose soil you have assisted to irrigate with your blood, and to give it that independence which we now enjoy.

" All true Chilians, who are friends of liberty, do not forget your services, but constantly preserve the esteem you are worthy of.

" Countrymen—see in the foreigners who are your fellow-citizens, the best co-operators towards your prosperity, and who have contributed to deliver you from the abjection in which you were held by Spain."
—*El Doctor Don Jose Miguel Infante.*

This impugnation has induced me not only to be circumstantial, but to introduce extracts from the works of uncontroverted authors, who have detailed the " res gestæ" of the American patriots, the coadjutors of our gallant tars, who sealed the independence of Chile and Peru, so that the progress of those events may be traced from the first struggle for liberty, down to the period when the rulers of Chile opened their ports to the Spaniards.

Unaccustomed to literary pursuits, I have aspired to no elegance of style—solicitous only to state the simple facts with all their original freshness ; and I am willing to hope, that a plain, unadorned account of a country, which, notwithstanding the unforeseen and dreadful calamities by which it has been distressed, still posseses the elements of prosperity, and is important to England, were it only from the amount of British capital invested there, may not prove wholly uninteresting or unprofitable to my countrymen.

Ashton-under-Line, 1st June, 1841.

CONTENTS.

LIST OF PLATES.

JOURNAL

OF

A RESIDENCE IN CHILE,

&c. &c.

ON the 8th of August, 1822, I embarked on board the brig Bruce, Captain Greig, bound from Liverpool to Valparaiso and Callao.

The vessel lay opposite the powder magazines; she had eleven steerage passengers on board, principally young men, going to seek situations in mercantile houses in South America; besides a Mrs. Frederic, with her son and daughter, going to Valparaiso, where she expected to join her husband, an Italian settled in that city.

Getting under weigh, we rounded the rock with a good breeze from the north-east; our pilot left us near the north-west buoy, bearing information to the friends of nearly all on board, that we had bid adieu to England.

Sailing with a fair wind, we were, however, becalmed near the coast of Ireland, off Kinsale, and made no progress for three days; during this time, we caught a quantity of fish, principally gurnet and hake; a breeze from the

B

northward now carried us as far as the latitude of Madeira, where we were overtaken by bad weather, which continued for several days.

The passengers were all sea-sick, and very uncomfortable: having engaged their berths in Scotland, at forty pounds each, under the false impression that they would be cabin passengers, and provided with every thing necessary, they brought neither small stores nor bedding, therefore their case was most pitiable; and the distress of some, who had been delicately brought up, was greatly increased by their being reduced to live in the steerage on " ship's allowance," and to eat their victuals out of a " kid ;" an arrangement so different from their previous habits, that they could not reconcile themselves to it.

We saw the Salvages, and passed near to the Canaries, and the weather being remarkably clear, the lofty Peak of Teneriffe remained in sight during three days.

Arriving off the Cape de Verde Islands, and coming to anchor in Porto Praya, in the island of St. Jago, I went on shore with the captain, to call upon the governor. The American United States consul, who also acted as English consul, met us on the beach at our landing, and took us to the house of the governor, who received us politely, and treated us with the greatest hospitality. As I understood the Portuguese language, I had some conversation with him, which convinced me that he was a well-informed man; he introduced us to his wife and family, told the captain that he was welcome to his port, and that he might ship what water and supplies he required; being invited to pass the evening with him, he apologized that he could not offer us any butter to our (cha) tea : the captain took the hint, and his excellency soon after received a crock of butter, some cheese, porter, and biscuit, which excited many pleasant looks during our stay. The governor now made me his guest, and I took several shooting excursions wth him; quails and guinea-fowl are rather plentiful in the island. In one of our rambles I observed an enormous, tree, on the trunk of which many individuals, who had visited the place, had inscribed their names.

In several small plantations I found the sugar-cane, sweet potatoe, yam, cassada, cotton, and other tropical productions. Where they have water to irrigate the soil, it appears fertile, but the greater part of the island, or at least of what I saw, seemed arid and barren: goats of a very large size are numerous here; and, whenever we engaged in field-sport, we returned loaded with game.

The sailors obtained water from a well at some distance from the beach; and, soon after our arrival, there was a regular market established, at which our passengers and sailors disposed of their old clothes, and received in exchange spirits, fruit, and other products of the island.

A celebrated personage called upon us at the consul's residence, she was a black woman, known by the appellation of English Mary; she showed us certificates from several captains, who had left their recommendations with her, and to whom she had been purveyor of fowls, vegetables, and fruit. We gave her ladyship a good order, which pleased her exceedingly, and she fulfilled it to our entire satisfaction.

The troops in Porto Praya were, without exception, the most ragged and miserable I ever beheld; their arms and accoutrements seemed entirely unfit for service, and some of the sentinels were nearly naked.

The batteries, from our anchorage, had a very formidable appearance, but the few guns I was permitted to see were badly mounted; I approached to what I considered the principal battery, but a black sentinel ordered me to retire, so that I was deprived of the opportunity of saying any thing respectful of the garrison.

On the third day after our arrival, a vessel anchored, bound from London to the Cape of Good Hope; I went on board, but did not descend to the cabin, as she had several lady-passengers on board, who did not wish to be seen by strangers; they had freighted the whole of the cabin, and possessed therefore a right of exclusion.

Porto Praya is a miserable place, inhabited by unfortunate beings, principally Portuguese convicts. A Frenchman who was confined here, and who had formerly been a jeweller, occupied the only comfortable dwelling in the town, with the exception of the governor's and consul's houses.

Having remained six days in port, during which time our rigging was set up, our water filled, and the ship supplied with fruit, vegetables, fowls, and other stores; we weighed anchor with a good breeze from the northeast, which carried us to the Line, where, as a matter of course, such of the passengers and seamen as had never been so far southward before, were introduced to Neptune; however, the sports of the day were not too severe, and all passed off in good humour.

I was very fortunate when fish came near us, and caught several albicore, boneto, dolphin, and porpoises; but what is still more remarkable, for three days successively, about the hour of dinner, I caught a dolphin with a towline.

In the latitude of Rio Janeiro we spoke the Vulture,

American whaler, a full ship from the Pacific, bound to
Nantucket; the captain informed us that a British vessel had been taken on the coast of Chile by pirates, and
the crew murdered; on hearing this, as a means of
employing our time, and that we might be prepared if
we were attacked, I amused myself by drilling the passengers, and teaching them the broadsword and manual
exercises.

We next made the Falkland Isles, and passed close
to Beauchain, where I struck and caught a porpoise; it
was beautifully striped with black and white, and all we
saw afterwards were similarly marked: we also caught
numbers of Cape pigeons; when first taken they were
disagreeable, on account of discharging an oily matter,
but when kept for some time, and fed with biscuit, they
were esteemed by the sailors as a pleasant article of food:
I shot an albatross, and got it on board; it measured
fifteen feet between the tips of the wings, and was five
feet high. I also caught several with a hook and line
baited with pork skin.

When we made Staten Island, we had remarkably
fine weather; we ran alongshore with our top-gallant
stud-sail set, until within about seven leagues of Cape
Horn; here the wind headed us, and in an hour we were
under close-reefed topsails: for eighteen days the weather
was dreadful; our carpenter fell overboard, and all
attempts to save him were in vain, so we had to lament
his fate; we also lost a hencoop, containing a quantity of
fowls, which was thrown overboard at the time.

Off Chile we were spoken by the Chilian ship of war
Independencia, Captain Wilkinson; Lieutenant Granville boarded us, and said they were cruising in order to
intercept a Spanish brig; they had only been out from

Valparaiso four days, when the city was destroyed by an earthquake. We anchored in the bay of Valparaiso on the 30th of November, having been one hundred and fourteen days on our voyage.

I went ashore in the guard-boat with Lieutenant Wilson, son of Sir Robert Wilson, who politely gave me a passage; I also called on board the flag-ship, but his lordship, Admiral Cochrane, had left for Quintero.

The appearance of the city of Valparaiso was interesting, approached from the port; but, on landing, the sight that presented itself was distressing in the extreme; wherever I turned my eyes, I beheld only desolation, the buildings that were spared seemed terribly shaken, whilst great numbers were thrown down, and their ruins lay mingled together.

On the nineteenth of this month, (November,) about three-quarters past ten o'clock at night, a severe shock of an earthquake was felt throughout this part of Chile, especially to the northward of the capital; the greatest part of the churches, houses, and other edifices in Valparaiso, Casa-blanca, Quillota, Illapel, and other towns, were destroyed, and many lives lost; in Santiago the churches and other public edifices were much injured, but none fell; fortunately it happened at an early hour, when, on account of its being about full-moon, the greatest part of the inhabitants were up, and walking out, otherwise the results would have been still more disastrous.

The supreme director, Don Bernardo O'Higgins, was with his staff in the government-house at the time of the shock, and was just enabled to escape into the street before the building fell in.

The terror of the inhabitants was greatly increased by the conduct of some evil-disposed persons, whose object was plunder; these scoundrels gave out a report that the sea was rising, and threatened to overwhelm the town; fortunately they failed in their object, and many of them were afterwards found buried in the ruins, with their booty upon their persons. Lord Cochrane sent a party of seamen and marines on shore, and the merchants formed patroles, which kept the place in order: many of the ships in the harbour were converted into receptacles for the families of the foreigners, and they were fortunate in having such a home, for the rain poured down in torrents; such were the horrors of the scene, that language is inadequate to their description.

When I landed, scarcely a house could be found which was habitable, and numbers of temporary sheds had been erected.

I called upon the governor-general, Don Ignacio Zenteno, who lived in a log-house in the dock-yard, and was received kindly; I then informed him that I came to Chile with the intention of joining the navy: he forwarded my letters to the capital, and proposed to facilitate my being conveyed there, by supplying me with horses; I preferred, however, seeing Lord Cochrane, previously to my waiting on the supreme director in Santiago.

I met several old acquaintances in Valparaiso, some of whom were in the Chilian navy; there were three Chilian ships of war in the bay, also his majesty's ship Aurora, Captain Prescott, and United States' 74, the Franklin, Commodore Stewart, and about forty sail of merchant vessels.

Having procured a lodging, earthquake-proof, (being built with wood,) I left the Bruce, bag and baggage, heartily tired of being penned up in a small cabin; and to make up for the inconveniences suffered during a long passage, I bought a good horse, which only cost me about half the sum that I paid for a common saddle; and amused myself for a few days in riding and shooting in the neighbourhood of Valparaiso.

The appearance of the females, such as a new-comer generally sees, did not speak favourably of the Chilian belles, for at first sight I fancied they were all smokers, having noticed them in the evening sitting with what appeared to me to be a pipe in their mouths; but they were only taking "matte," of which they are very fond: this is an infusion of the herb of Paraguay, to which they add sugar and milk; it is taken out of a bowl of ornamented silver, cocoa-nut shell, or calabash, into which they introduce a silver tube, or reed; strangers at first find it difficult to sup matte, and many manage to burn their lips, before they acquire this Chilian accomplishment: a great quantity of this herb is consumed in Chile, but many of the natives drink tea and coffee.

On one of my excursions, about two leagues from the port, I met with a family, who were living in a shed, (ramada); their dwelling having been destroyed by the earthquake; it was the Carrera family, who had an estate called Vina-dela Mar: I remained with them two days, and was entertained in a most hospitable manner; the young ladies were amiable, handsome, and accomplished, and my prejudices against the Chilian matte-drinkers were entirely dispersed in their interesting society.

As soon as Lord Cochrane had returned from Quintero, I waited upon him on board the O'Higgins, a frigate that bore his flag; he received me kindly, and invited me to spend the next day with him; I accepted the invitation, and was introduced by him to his officers, after which he invited me to visit him at Quintero, where he proceeded that night, in the schooner Montezuma.

His estate is situated about fifteen leagues to the north of Valparaiso on the sea-coast, and has a small port called the Herradura; the houses on his property had fallen during the earthquake, and his lordship and his guests lived in sheds and tents; here I met with an old acquaintance, a colonel in the Spanish army, Don Fausto Hoyos, who had been governor of Valdivia.

Unfortunately for me, I arrived in Chile on the eve of a revolution formed against his excellency Don Bernardo O'Higgins, the supreme director, to whom I had strong recommendations. I had anticipated the honour of serving under Lord Cochrane, but his lordship decided upon relinquishing the Chilian service, and taking command of the Brazilian navy: before I was informed of his determination, I had forwarded my letter of recommendation, and received an invitation to visit the capital from his excellency Don Bernardo O'Higgins, and only waited the conclusion of a little business in Valparaiso.*

I amused myself with several officers in shooting and riding about the estate, during my stay with Mr. Macfarlane who had the management of it.

Here are several lagoons, on which are immense flocks of ducks of many varieties, also a great number of swans, and amongst them two of the black species from New South Wales, which had been presented to his lordship; the Chilian swans have black necks, the

---

* His lordship, Mrs. M. Graham, Colonel Don Fausto Hoyos, Captain Crosbie, Lieutenants Sheppard, Grenfelt, Cluley, and the nephew of Captain Graham, late commander of His Majesty's ship Doris, embarked on board the Colonel Allen, that the admiral had freighted to carry them to Rio de Janeiro.

rest of their plumage being white : the partridges here resemble an overgrown quail, they are very numerous, and fly singly, but feed in pairs.

As I sauntered along the beach one day, I found part of an American naval uniform coat, hung upon a bush, near to which a cross had been erected; on making inquiry I was informed that some North American officers, belonging to a ship of war, who had come out to Valparaiso on a shooting excursion, were drowned near the spot, with the exception of a midshipman, a native of Nantucket, who, being an excellent swimmer, saved himself; the bodies were buried underneath the cross.

From Quintero, I proceeded to Quillota, a large town about fifteen leagues from Valparaiso, where I took up my residence with a Mrs. Grimshaw, the sister of the curate; her husband, who was an Englishman, was then on his way to his native land.

The governor of this place, Mr. Faulkner, (or Fulner,) who, I had been informed, was an Englishman, sent for me to show him my passport, as the revolutionary troops from Coquimbo were in the neighbourhood. When I called upon him, he was assembling the militia to defend the town ; he inquired whether I belonged to the Chilian service, and on my stating that I was only a traveller, visiting Quillota for curiosity, he seemed anxious to break off the conversation. I then inquired if he was an Englishman, but he replied, I am from the United States, a native of Rhode Island ; adding, that he was then too much engaged to converse with me any longer ; I therefore took my leave, and returned to quarters. In the evening the troops entered Quillota, after having a slight skirmish with Fulner, whose soldiers deserted him, loading him with imprecations; it seemed that he was not a favourite. It is generally the case that governors of provinces, or petty states, have many secret enemies to encounter, especially if they do their duty ; but the outcry raised against Fulner had no reference to his official capacity —" I could a tale unfold."

A new governor was elected instead of Fulner, and, to celebrate the change of affairs, a dance was got up, to which myself and several other foreigners were invited. As it was the first that I had seen in Chile, I was greatly amused ; the company consisted of about two hundred persons ; there were two minuets, three country-dances, and a few waltzes; but the "bayles de golpe," a kind of dance peculiar to this country, in which there is no lack of agility or humour, formed the principal part of the entertainment, and was continued to a late hour: the punch-bowl passed quickly round amongst the military personages who had headed the revolutionary troops, and who seemed greatly exasperated against the supreme director Don Bernardo O'Higgins, and the governor of Quillota.

The bowels of the earth seemed also to join in the revelry of the night, for I had scarcely laid my head upon my pillow, after leaving the dance, when my fears were considerably awakened, and I scampered into the public street without any covering but my shirt, a poncho, and part of my bed-clothes; I had frequently wished, after my arrival in Chile, to feel the shock of an earthquake, but had no idea of being so much alarmed; the ground seemed threatening to open and engulf us, the buildings rocked, and tiles were falling from the roofs in all directions ; some of the houses were razed to their foundations, and the streets and squares were filled with the inhabitants who had fled in dismay from their dwellings, many of them kneeling and praying in a state of complete nudity; in fact, though the moment was by no means befitting, I could not refrain from laughing at the droll sights which I witnessed; the sensation which I felt from the shock, setting aside the fear which I had of the houses falling upon me, was, as nearly as I can describe it, similar to that which would be experienced by a person standing on a drawbridge whilst a loaded coach was driven quickly over it. The shock was preceded by a strange rumbling noise, and lasted about thirty seconds; we had several repetitions of it, but the first shock was the most severe; the churches and houses had been greatly injured by the earthquake of November, and the late shock rendered the latter nearly uninhabitable.

The vale of Quillota is very fertile, producing chirimoyas, plantains, and other tropical fruits, besides sweet potatoes in abundance; hemp is also cultivated, of which a superior quality of cordage is made. This valley is the "market garden," from which Valparaiso is supplied with fruit and vegetables; the river Chile, which gives its name to the state, waters it, and empties itself into the sea at Con-Con. I returned hence to a cottage, which I had hired at Con-Con, where I had left my dogs, gun, &c.

The troops created no small alarm as they advanced towards the port of Valparaiso, seizing any horses they thought fit, and even dismounting the riders in some instances, to "por ratto" their horses, a term used here by the military, when they press the horses of civilians. An English gentleman, Mr. Miers, with his lady and sister, resided at Con-Con. I rode into Valparaiso, and found that the late supreme director, Don Bernardo O'Higgins, had arrived there, having resigned the command; I waited upon him at the governor's; he

received me kindly, and blamed me for not having visited
the capital whilst he held the command, as he might
then have fulfilled my wishes, and given me a suitable
employment.

He informed me, that he was about to take the command of the Chilian army then in Peru, and that he would
get me appointed his aide-de-camp; and, on my expressing a wish to accompany him, he promised to write by
the next post for my appointment.

I left him, and went the next day to Con-Con, to give
up my cottage, and, having remained there a few days,
returned to Valparaiso.

Con-Con is a small village, inhabited principally by
fishermen, who supply the capital and inland towns with
excellent fish; they employ small canoes and balsas, (floats
made of two seal-skins joined together and inflated,)
on which the fishermen venture out to sea, and cross
and recross, with perfect safety, over breakers in which
no boat could live; the skins are well sewn, and the
seam is always above water; a small tube is fixed to a
hose, through which they blow at intervals, to inflate
the balsa, and make it more buoyant. There are great
numbers of penguins in this neighbourhood, here called
" paxaros ninos," from the plaintive note they utter, which
is not unlike the cry of an infant; the women in the
valley are better-looking than those I first saw when in
Valparaiso, but they use a profusion of carmine and
soliman, (c. sublimate,) which destroys their teeth, and gives
them a very haggard look when they arrive at twenty-five
or thirty years of age.

The huassos, or country farmers, are almost always on
horseback, and are reputed to be excellent riders; they
wear a kind of garment called poncho, which is a square

piece of woollen or cotton cloth, worked fantastically; it has a hole in the middle, generally bound with a silken riband, through which they slip their heads, and the garment hangs in folds upon their bodies; their saddles are composed of a number of sheep-skins, generally dyed blue; they have large wooden stirrups, and their heels are ornamented with enormous spurs, generally made of silver, the rowels of which are very remarkable.

Most of the foreigners residing here imitate the huassos, and keep their own horses; even the beggars follow their occupation on horseback; it is diverting to see the sailors at Valparaiso on liberty, riding along the beach, and frequently measuring their length on the ground; on Sundays a toll-gate was placed near the Almendral, and all that passed on horseback had to pay a small sum, to defray the expense of repairing the streets.

A few days after my return to Valparaiso, several vessels entered the bay, and amongst them, the Chilian ship of war Independencia; this occasioned some confusion, for no signal of their approach had been given; as soon as they neared the beach of the Almendral, a number of boats filled with soldiers put off, and landed, these formed themselves into a close column, and a party was detached who surrounded the dock-yard, and made the late supreme director a prisoner; they were under the command of General Don Ramon Freyre, who had come down to aid the party against Don Bernardo O'Higgins. A short time after they had landed, my servant came to inform me, that my horses had been taken from the stable by an officer; I went immediately to ascertain the fact, and found one of them with a military saddle upon it, the other had been taken to La Mereed, a convent, where the troops were quartered, or rather bivouacked, under some olive trees; I accordingly had my own saddle transferred to my horse, and rode to the camp, where I had an interview with General Freyre, who ordered my horse to be returned to me; he treated me politely, and on being informed that I had just arrived from England, for the express purpose of joining the Chilian service, he offered me an appointment in his corps of artillery. Finding that Don Bernardo O'Higgins was not to proceed to Peru, I obtained his recommendation to General Freyre, and put myself under the orders of Lieutenant-Colonel Don Ramon Picarte, who commanded the artillery. Colonel Beauchef, a Frenchman; Captain William Tupper, an Englishman; Doctor Green, an Irishman; Lieutenant Arrangren, a Swede; and an Araucanian casique, Benancio, accompanied by a party of Indians, came with General Freyre. The infantry marched on the third day, and the artillery on the day following; the division was composed of a part of two regiments, and a detachment of artillery.

The Indians were powerful men, about the middle size; their weapons were, a lance of great length, which they seemed to wield with the greatest ease; they had also bolos and lassos; their dress was a poncho and a chiripa, a piece of cloth wrapped round them, descending to their knees, and not unlike to a Highlander's kilt; they are said to be a brave set of men; their casique wore a scarlet coat embroidered with gold lace, and a laced cocked hat, the remainder of his dress was appropriate: I was informed that he was a severe scourge to the old Spaniards.

Colonel Picarte provided mules for my baggage, and we left Valparaiso about seven o'clock in the morning;

General O'Higgins gave me letters to his mother and sister, and I had several others for some of the most respectable inhabitants at Santiago. The road from Valparaiso, for about three leagues, was very tedious, being exceedingly hilly; the first post-house at which we rested, is situated on an extensive plain called Peñuellos; after continuing our march until night, we halted about two leagues from Casa Blanca, and ten from the port; during the march I shot several partridges, which description of game appeared to be plentiful.

About midnight we were greatly alarmed by some men riding up to our sentinels at full speed; they had been sent by the governor of Casa Blanca, to request assistance from us, as he had been forcibly deposed by the inhabitants; the next morning we met him, in the custody of some soldiers, on the road to Valparaiso, and he told us that he had been wounded, and treated harshly: when we came to the place where the town of Casa Blanca had stood, we found nothing but a mass of ruins, not a house having escaped destruction by the shock of the earthquake; here we were met by the new governor, accompanied by the people, who rent the air with cries of " Viva Freyre!" We next passed over an immense hill, called the Cuesta de Sapata. The greatest part of the road that we had traversed was in good repair, it was made by Don Ambrosio O'Higgins, father to the late director, who was formerly president of Chile ; he was a native of Ireland, and his name is still venerated by all who recollect him, in consequence of his benign character, and the many improvements made by him in Chile.

The view of the country from the summit of the Cuesta was very fine, and the troops, artillery, &c. winding up the zigzag path, would have been a good subject for a painter. We halted at the house of a widow, Doña Madalena Prado, who entertained us in a hospitable manner: marching at daylight, we passed the valley of Curicabe; the bed of the river only remained, to denote the course in which the torrent flowed during the rainy season; here we saw an old church, and several houses in ruins: we halted at Bustamante, and in the evening crossed the Cuesta de Prado, which is higher than the Cuesta de Sapata; the road over it is in excellent repair; at the foot of the hill we found a travelling cart (or coach) capsized, which proved to be the stage from Santiago to Valparaiso, (the proprietor was an American, named Moss.) We passed the night at the post-house, kept by a Chileno, who was surnamed "Judge Prevost," on account of some curious adventure, of which he had been the subject.

At sunrise we marched, and halted at the Hacienda of El Espejo, on the banks of the river Mapocho, which was nearly dry; there we joined the rest of the division, and General Freyre received a deputation from the junta; the result was, that he had to remain a few days longer previously to entering the capital; in the mean time I obtained permission to visit Santiago. The entrance to the city was by no means inviting; the suburbs, with the exception of a few quintas, (country houses,) consisted of nothing but miserable huts and cottages; the principal entrance, Calle San Pablo, is a shabby street for an approach, but the appearance of Santiago improves near the centre, or Public Square: I took up my residence at the English hotel, kept by a Mrs. Walker; we had an excellent table d'hôte, and the daily charge for bedroom, &c. was twelve

c

reales,* which was very reasonable, as half a bottle of claret was allowed to each person at dinner.

I had many letters of introduction to Chilenos and foreign residents, which I sent with my card; none but the natives did me the honour of calling upon me, and they were very kind, particularly the Marquis Don J. Torribio Larrayn, Don J. Antonio Rosales, Don Felipe Santiago del Solar, and others, who pressed me to take up my abode with them; and on my pleading an excuse, they seemed to vie with each other in their attentions, which, to me, a stranger, were of essential service.

The general and his troops entered the capital, and were quartered in the convent of La Merced, El Basural, and Maestranza, the military arsenal, where all the guns and warlike stores were kept and repaired.

The junta gubernativa lasted only a short time, for the provinces of Coquimbo and Concepcion would not agree to such a government, but named their plenipotentiaries; so that, acting with those of the capital, they might elect the person who would be most advantageous to the state, under present circumstances, as supreme director. On the 31st of March the election was made in the consular hall, (" el consulado,") where the plenipotentiaries met—Don Juan Egaña for the province of Santiago; Don Manuel Novoa, for Concepcion; and Don Manuel Antonio Gonzales, for Coquimbo: having examined their powers, and discussed the election of supreme director, they with one accord named for the charge, the Field - Marshal Don Ramon Freyre, who was then in the capital, and on the fourth of April he was installed in the hall of government, where all the corporations were assembled to receive and administer the

. * About six shillings.

customary oaths, with all the necessary ceremonies; after which the people evinced their joy by fireworks, &c.

I remained attached to the artillery, until several days after General Don Ramon Freyre had assumed the supreme command of the republic; and on account of my being a volunteer, and not entitled to pay, (officers in the Chilian service have no rations,) he desired me to send in a memorial, for unless I did so, he could not give me a commission in the Chilian service. I replied, that I thought it would be more honourable for me to receive my appointment from government, particularly as I had joined the division in Valparaiso, and since then had considered myself attached to the service, although I had not yet received a commission. I also stated, that General O'Higgins had applied to the junta, in order that I might accompany him, as his aide-de-camp to Peru. His excellency replied, that unless I acted conformably to the established rules, he could not serve me; at the same time remarking, that Captain Tupper, who had been serving many months under Colonel Beauchef, had to adopt this method. My friend Colonel Picarte introduced me to General Lastra and General Rivera, who had charge of the marine and army departments: I shewed them my certificates of service in his majesty's navy, a Waterloo medal, as well as the commission I had received in London from the Columbian agent in 1816, also that of " chef d'escadron,"* which I received previously to my capture and detention in the Havannah in the year 1817, with several other documents which I had presented to Lord Cochrane on my arrival in Valparaiso. The ministers were perfectly satisfied with my

* Lieutenant-Colonel of cavalry.

c 2

testimonials, and seemed decided on my serving in the navy; but Lord Cochrane had left for the Brazilian service, and as there were a number of meritorious officers out of active employment, and no more than two ships in commission, I requested to be employed where I should escape the envy and jealousy of the officers on half-pay, &c., until government could form a just estimate of my conduct and ability. His excellency accordingly gave me the commission of a captain attached to the liberating army in Peru, offering me at the same time the brevet rank of my Columbian commission; which I declined accepting, to prevent rivalry, &c.

Many of my friends were surprised to see me accept an inferior grade, but a little explanation soon satisfied them.

The pay of a captain of cavalry unattached is forty-eight dollars, and when in charge of a troop seventy-six; a major receives eighty; a sergeant-major of cavalry one hundred and eight; and a chef d'escadron, one hundred and fifty; so that I had a poor pittance to commence with, considering the rank that I had ceded.

A short time after I had joined the service, his excellency informed me, that he intended sending me to Peru, to take the command of the corps that formed the general's escort, which was then vacant, for General Pinto had superseded Commandant Ibañes and several of his officers: during the interview, I asked for permission to accompany the mother and sister of General O'Higgins to Valparaiso, where he was still detained. I was referred to General Calderon, the chief of the staff, who readily assented to my accompanying the family of *his friend,* for so he called General O'Higgins, and intrusted me with a packet containing the general's passport, to present to him on my arrival.

Colonel Borgoño, with his lady, Colonel Arriagada, and Lieutenant-Colonel Martines, accompanied us; the two first returned, after having ridden a few miles to show their attention; we halted at Doña Madalena Prados' house, near the Cuesta de Sapata, to whom I have before alluded; she treated us with the greatest civility and attention; on the next day, when within a few leagues of Valparaiso, one of the wheels of the carriage got out of repair, and became almost useless; to prevent delay, I galloped on towards the port, and had not proceeded far when I met General O'Higgins and Don Miguel Sañartu. I informed them of the disaster: the general went forward, and his companion returned with me, to procure some other conveyance; but before another carriage was ready, they fortunately arrived, having got a person to repair the wheel.

I remained some time with the general and his family; they resided in a comfortable house in the Almendral, and, notwithstanding the outcry that had been raised against the late administration, he was visited by most of the respectable families in the port, as well as by several individuals who were known to be determined enemies of the general during his government, but had now become his friends.

And here let me suspend my journal, while I present to my readers a connected account of the prowess of those patriots whose noble deeds consolidated the freedom of Chile, swept the Pacific, and carried independence into the heart of Peru:—

CHAP. II.

PROWESS OF THE PATRIOTS, UNDER GENERALS SAN MARTIN AND O'HIGGINS—CHILE
LIBERATED—GALLANT AFFAIR OF CAPTAIN O'BRIEN—SUCCESSFUL CRUISE OF COM-
MODORE BLANCO—CAPTURE OF LA MARIA ISABEL—LORD COCHRANE'S FIRST CRUISE
—SECOND CRUISE, AND IMPORTANT ACHIEVEMENT AT VALDIVIA—THIRD CRUISE,
AND EXPEDITION OF THE LIBERATING ARMY UNDER GENERAL SAN MARTIN—LORD
COCHRANE'S DARING AND BRILLIANT CAPTURE OF THE ESMERALDA, AT CALLAO—
LIMA AND CALLAO SURRENDERED TO GENERAL SAN MARTIN—LAST CRUISE OF LORD
COCHRANE, AND SUFFERINGS OF HIS CREWS—GENERAL SAN MARTIN ABDICATES
THE SUPREME COMMAND, AND QUITS PERU—HIS RECEPTION IN CHILE—LORD
COCHRANE LEAVES CHILE IN DISGUST—GENERAL O'HIGGINS DEPOSED, ARRESTED,
VINDICATED—HE LEAVES CHILE FOR PERU.

GENERALS San Martin and O'Higgins recrossed the
Andes with an army composed of Buenos Ayreans and Chilian emigrants, and defeated the Spaniards at Chacabuco,
on the 12th of February, 1817, upon which General
O'Higgins was elected supreme director of the republic.

General Ossorio invaded Chile with an army from
Peru, and routed the patriots at Cancharayada; but he
was finally defeated at Maipu on the 5th of April,
1818, where 2,000 of his troops were killed, and 3,500
taken prisoners; however, he escaped with a few to Talcahuano, and soon after fled to Peru.

General O'Higgins had conceived the gigantic idea of
disputing the navigation of the Pacific with the Spaniards,
whose vessels were blockading the ports of Chile; at a
time, too, when affairs were in a critical state, and when
the government had neither ships, mariners, arsenal,
money, nor any material for such an undertaking; which,
to many, appeared to be the maddest enterprise ever
projected. However, the general, although he had to
wade through many difficulties, as well as encounter a

strong opposition to his laudable designs, had, previous
to the battle of Maipu, managed to purchase the Wynd-
ham, of 44 guns, formerly an Indiaman; he commissioned her, with the name of a brave Araucanian chief,
Lautaro; and appointed an Englishman, Lieutenant
O'Brien, R.N. to be her commander; she was officered
and partly manned by foreigners, the rest of her com-
plement were Chilians, mostly landsmen; and such was
their patriotic enthusiasm, that many swam off to her, to
be enrolled amongst her crew.   The general having now
completely gathered the fruits of the victory of Maipu,
became desirous of raising the blockade of Valparaiso, and
Captain O'Brien was ordered to attack the Spanish frigate Esmeralda, of 44 guns, with the Pezuella, of 18 guns,
which was cruising off the port; and, in ten hours after the
Lautaro had sailed, she was engaged.   I shall here give an
extract from Miller's work, for, although I have received
various accounts from eye-witnesses of this brilliant
exploit, I prefer that given in his memoir, which I
have accurately extracted.

" The Esmeralda seeing a frigate-built vessel approach, mistook it for
H. M. S. Amphion, Commodore Bowles, who had before communicated
occasionally upon subjects relative to the blockade, with the Esmeralda;
which last, therefore, lay to, with her topsails to the mast, to speak the
supposed Amphion.   In that situation the Lautaro ranged upon the
weather-quarter of the enemy, when, having hauled down British colours,
and hoisted the Chilian, she discharged her foremost guns.   It was Captain
O'Brien's first intention to have laid the Lautaro alongside, but having
altered his mind, he ran upon the Esmeralda's quarter.   The Lautaro's
bowsprit caught the enemy's mizen-rigging, and hung her in a way so
inconvenient for boarding, that O'Brien jumped on board, with only thirty
followers.   The marines kept up a steady fire from the forecastle of the
Lautaro, which caused a heavy loss to the Esmeralda's crew, who, panic-
struck by the appearance of the boarding party, ran below, and the Spanish
ensign was hauled down by the assailants.   Unfortunately, it did not
occur to any one to prevent the two ships from separating, by lashing them
together, or to disable the prize by cutting her wheelropes and topsail-
halliards; a jerk of the sea canted the ships clear of each other, upon which

the Lautaro lowered her boats, to send a reinforcement, but before that could be accomplished, the Esmeralda's men, seeing but a handful of patriots upon deck, rallied, fired from below, and shot the gallant O'Brien, whose last words were, ' *Never leave her, my boys, the ship is ours !*' meanwhile, the Lautaro had incautiously left the main object, to take possession of the Pezuella, which had struck, but was stealing away.

" Upon perceiving the change of fortune on board the Esmeralda, the Lautaro gave over chasing the brig, and steered for the frigate; but before she could approach, the boarders were overpowered, and both the Spanish ships having rehoisted their own colours, escaped by superior sailing, Lieutenant Walker, (of the H. E. I. Company's service,) distinguished himself considerably, and, before the Lautaro returned to port, captured a vessel, having on board passengers who had fled from Concepcion to take refuge in Lima; upon them the Chilian government levied a contribution in the shape of ransom, which more than reimbursed the original purchase-money of the Lautaro."*

By this, the primary object of raising the blockade was carried into effect; and, as the routed Spaniards had taken shelter in Talcahuano, General O'Higgins posted down to Valparaiso, where, in a short period, he augmented the navy to five vessels, in order to blockade the port of Talcuhuano, which the Chilian army had already invested by land. The patriots of Chile came forward in the most liberal manner, and contributed largely' towards defraying the vast expenditure of the fitting out, arming, manning, and victualling the squadron, so that it was enabled to leave the port of Valparaiso on the 9th of October, 1818, under the orders of Commodore Blanco, to intercept the Spanish expedition, that had left Cadiz under convoy of the Maria Isabel, of 50 guns. This enterprise was crowned with success, for, on the 7th of November, the inhabitants of Valparaiso, "Porteños de Valparaiso," were gratified with the glorious spectacle of the following vessels and their prizes entering the port.

San Martin, of 56 guns, $\left\{\begin{array}{l}\text{Commodore Blanco,}\\\text{Captain Wilkinson.}\end{array}\right.$

* Miller's Memoirs.

Lautaro	... 44 guns	Captain W. Wooster.
Chacabuco	... 20 ...	Captain Dias.
Araucano	... 16 ...	Captain Morris.
Galvarino	... 18 ..	Captain Spry.

PRIZES.

| Maria Isabel ... 50. | Seven Transports. |

The frigate was cut out of the port of Talcahuano, where she had been run on shore close to the batteries, notwithstanding a galling fire which was kept up by the troops that had been sent from Concepcion; and the transports were taken as they came to their appointed rendezvous, (the island of Santa Maria); for, on account of a mutiny having taken place on board one of the convoy, she had been carried into Buenos Ayres, and from her the government got hold of the instructions, private signals, and rendezvous—which were remitted, with all possible speed, to that of Chile; and, luckily, they arrived in time for General O'Higgins to show the Chilians they were delivered from one of the greatest evils that could have befallen them, and that their independence was now consolidated through his exertions and the aid of a few foreigners, as the enemy's naval and military forces amounted to more than 3,000 men, and only three vessels escaped to Callao, two of which had landed their troops before the capture of the frigate.

General O'Higgins, in order to ensure to Chile the dominion of the Pacific, had invited Lord Cochrane, (afterwards Earl of Dundonald,) to whose fame he was no stranger, to take command of the navy, which, fortunately, his lordship not only accepted on the conditions that were offered, but engaged several naval and military officers of known experience, who had rallied around the Chilian admiral, desirous of distinguishing themselves under the command of a leader, whose

naval achievements had gained him so much honour;
—and in 1818, the names of the following distinguished
foreigners were, with that of their noble leader, enrolled in the Chilian service: Guize, Carter, Forster,
Charles, Miller, Spry, Esmonde, Cobbett, Freeman, Grenfelt, Granville, Simpson, Oseason, Wynter, Wilson, Hall,
Davies, Dean, and many others, who have assisted to
give days of glory to Chile, and in consolidating its
independence.

Lord Cochrane, his lady, and son landed in the port of
Valparaiso in November, 1818, and was received with
enthusiasm by all denominations of patriots, invested with
the chief command of the navy; and the plans of General
O'Higgins were now put in execution, in order to liberate Peru from the thraldom of Spain. The squadron
was fitted out with the greatest despatch, so that Lord
Cochrane might proceed to annoy or capture the enemy's
vessels, and at the same time sound the inclination of
the Peruvians

On the fourteenth of January, 1819, the Chilian squadron, composed of the following vessels, sailed for the
coast of Peru:—

Vice-Admiral Lord Cochrane.

O'Higgins . of .	50 guns .	. .	. Captain Forster,
San Martin . .	56 .	. . . .	. Captain Wilkinson,
Lautaro . . .	48 .	. . . .	. Captain Guize,
Chacabuco . . .	20 .	. . . .	. Captain Carter;

and on the twenty-eighth of February entered the
port of Callao, where his lordship had intended to have
carried the Spanish frigates Esmeralda and Venganza,
by boarding; these were moored close in under the batteries, and before they got near to the shipping the
wind fell, and his lordship's plan was frustrated; how-

ever, he anchored, with springs on his cables, within
gun-shot : the admiral withstood, and returned the fire
of the batteries and shipping for more than an hour;
the loss in killed and wounded did not amount to many,
but this proof of cool and undaunted bravery gave the
Spaniards a just idea of the men they had to deal with.
On the twenty-second of March his lordship made an
attempt to destroy the shipping by fireships, which proved a
failure on account of a ' brulot,' he had sent in, getting a
ground, and being destroyed by the batteries; the flag-ship
also sustained a heavy fire from the forts and shipping.

The enemy made an abortive attempt to disable
the squadron, but were soon forced to regain their
moorings under shelter of the batteries.   The Spaniards
had two frigates, two brigs, and twenty-six gun-boats.
The Chilian squadron were reinforced by two vessels that
Rear-Admiral Blanco had brought—the Galvarino of
22 guns, and Puyrredon of 16 : he hoisted his flag on
board the San Martin, and, with the Lautaro, remained
to blockade Callao. The admiral, with the rest of the
squadron, visited the ports of Huacho, Supe, Huarmey,
Paita, Huambacho, and all returned to Valparaiso in June.

Lord Cochrane sailed from Valparaiso on the twelfth
of September, and on the thirtieth re-entered the bay of
Callao, with the following vessels :—

O'Higgins . of 48 guns, Admiral Lord Cochrane.
San Martin . . 46 . . Rear-Ad. Blanco, Capt. Wilkinson.
Lautaro . . 46 . . Captain Guise.
Independencia . 28 . . Captain Forster.
Puyrredon . . 14 . . Captain Prunier.
Galvarino . . 18 . . Captain Spry.
Araucano . . 16 . . Captain Crosby.
And two fire-ships.

On the second of October the admiral made an attempt
to destroy the enemy's shipping by rockets, but on account

of the badness of their composition, it was unsuccessful; about twenty of his men were put "hors de combat" being burnt by the bursting of the rockets. It has since been ascertained that the Spanish prisoners in the capital of Chile, being very improperly employed in the laboratory of the military arsenal, had embraced every opportunity to mix neutralizing matter with the ingredients given to them to fill the tubes, by Mr. Goldsack, who had come out from England purposely to manufacture Congreve rockets. How could it be expected that these poor fellows would execute such a task with fidelity to the Chilian republic?

Another attempt was made to destroy the enemy's vessels by a fire-ship, which Lieutenant Morgel conducted in a gallant style; but the wind fellbefore she reached the shipping, and as she was sorely crippled by the fire from the batteries and vessels of war, that brave officer was obliged to fire and abandon her, but at such a distance that her explosion caused little damage to the enemy.

The Spaniards having their vessels moored close under the forts, and secured by booms and a flotilla of gun-boats, the admiral found it impracticable to destroy them, without endangering the existence of the Chilian squadron; and now, on account of a Spanish frigate La Prucba of fifty guns, having made her appearance off the port, and effected her escape to the northward, he altered his plans; and sailed for Pisco, where a detachment was landed under the command of Lieutenant-Colonel Charles and Major Miller. As this gallant affair has only been slightly mentioned in ' La Gazeta ministerial de Chile,' of the 18th of December, 1819, I beg to introduce here the following extract from the memoirs of an eyewitness.

" It was known that a strong detachment of regular troops had been stationed in Pisco, at the request of the royalist merchants and landowners, to protect their property in depôt there.   The patriots intended to land in the night, and take the garrison by surprise ; but the wind failing, the ships would not get near enough to disembark the troops until broad daylight on the 7th of November, 1819.   On landing, information was given that the Spanish garrison amounted to one thousand men.   It might, there-fore, have been prudent for the patriots to have re-embarked, especially as two-thirds of the marines were new recruits, who had not been even taught the platoon exercise ; but the remembrance of the disappointment before Callao, produced an unanimous desire to attack.   The Spanish force, consisting of six hundred infantry, one hundred and sixty cavalry, and four field-pieces, under the command of Lieutenant-General Gonzales, were drawn up to receive the assailants.   The field artillery, supported by their cavalry, occupied on their left a piece of rising ground, which commanded the entrances of the town, in the square of which their infantry was formed. Their right was strengthened by a fort on the sea-shore.   Lieutenant-Colonel Charles, with twenty-five men, filed off to his right, to reconnoitre the enemy's left, whilst Major Miller pushed on the town with the rest of the marines.   Captain Hind, with a rocket party composed of seamen, occupied the attention of the fort.   The Spaniards kept up a brisk fire from the field-pieces, and from the artillery in the fort, as well as from the infantry posted behind walls, on the tops of houses, and on the tower of the church.   Not a musket was fired, or a word spoken, in the patriot column, which marched with the coolness and steadiness of veterans, in spite of the loss it sustained at every step.   The silence, rapidity, and good order with which they advanced, struck a panic into the Spaniards, who fled when the patriots approached within fifty yards of their bayonets. The royalists were completely routed.   The gallant Lieutenant-Colonel Charles was mortally wounded whilst charging four times his own numbers outside the town.   The last volley of the Spaniards in the square brought down Major Miller.*

" They were conveyed on board the Lautaro.   The two friends, both apparently on the brink of the grave, took leave of each other in the most affectionate manner, as Charles was conveyed aft, through the fore-cabin, in which Miller was already placed by the kindness of Captain Guize.   In a few hours Charles expired, cool and collected to the last moment ; the manner in which he died would have done honour to any hero of ancient or modern times.   He was brave and talented, and his gentleness and suavity of manners had acquired for him universal love and respect.†

* A musket-ball wounded him in the right arm, another permanently dis-abled his left hand. A third ball entered his chest, and, fracturing a rib, passed out at the back.   For four days the surgeons considered it impos-sible for him to survive, and for the next seventeen, slender hopes were entertained of his recovery.

† Charles was educated at the Royal Military Academy at Woolwich. Having obtained a lieutenancy in the royal regiment, he went out to

" Captain Sowersby,*. who succeeded to the command of the marines, remained on shore for four days, unmolested, in which time all that was required for the ships was embarked.

" ' Two hundred thousand dollars' worth of brandy, lying on the beach, was wantonly destroyed by a party of seamen. Amongst the officers who distinguished themselves, besides those already mentioned, were Captain Don Manuel Urquisa, (severely wounded,) a Buenos-Ayrean; Captain Guitica, a German; Lieutenant Rivera, a Chilian; Lieutenant Carson, a North American; and Monsieur Soyer, a Frenchman (purser of the Lautaro), who acted as a volunteer."†

The squadron procured refreshments and other necessaries, visited and took the town of Santa, when the marines distinguished themselves again. Rear-Admiral Blanco returned to Valparaiso with the San Martin and Independencia, with the sick and wounded : the body of the brave and unfortunate Colonel Charles was preserved in spirits, and afterwards interred with military honours in the fort of Valparaiso.

Lord Cochrane proceeded to the river of Guayaquil, and captured two merchant vessels; but the object of his visit, La Prueba, had been lightened, and taken into

Portugal, in the year 1808, with a detachment of artillery, appointed to serve with the *Lusitanian Legion*, then raising under the orders of Sir Robert Wilson, who, perceiving the excellent qualities of Charles, appointed him his aide-de-camp; and throughout the service in the Peninsula, he distinguished himself on every occasion by his talents, activity, and intrepidity. When Sir Robert Wilson was sent to Constantinople, to assist in the negociations for peace between the Turks and Russians, Charles was again put on his staff, but his junction with Sir Robert was delayed till that general had been appointed military commissioner with the Russian army. Charles, during the whole of the campaign in Germany and in Italy, continued to do the duty of aide-de-camp to Sir Robert Wilson, and gained the affection and esteem of the allied commanders.

The sovereigns particularly distinguished him, conferring on him the cross of St. George of Russia, of Merit, of Prussia, and of Maria Theresa or Austria. There never perhaps was an officer, serving in foreign armies, who was more universally a favourite, and who displayed qualities which more entitled him, professionally and personally to estimation.

  * Killed at the battle of Junin.
  † *Memoirs of Miller*, Vol. 1, Pages 226 to 228.

shallow water, where she was moored close under a
fort : the squadron procured refreshments, and made sail
for Valparaiso ; but the admiral stood as far to the southward as Valdivia, where he captured a boat, and the
Spanish brig of war Potrillo of sixteen guns, that was sent
from Callao with specie and military stores for the garrison
of Valdivia.

The information which his lordship had obtained from
the officer and crew of the boat, (who being deceived by
the flag had left the port to pilot the frigate into Valdivia,)
induced him to enter the port of Talcahuana, and visit the
governor of the province of Concepcion, Colonel Don
Ramon Freyre, who received and entertained the admiral
in the most hospitable manner. His lordship communicated his information, and explained the possibility of
seizing the important fortress of Valdivia by a " coup de
main ;" and the colonel coinciding with his views, gave
him two hundred and fifty men, who, under the command
of Major Beauchef embarked on board the frigate, and
two small vessels that his lordship had taken up as transports.

" His want of effective officers caused him the greatest difficulties : he
had only two officers on board, and they were lieutenants ; one of these was
under arrest for gross disobedience of orders, and the other was utterly
incapable of performing the requisite duty of a lieutenant. Lord Cochrane
was, therefore, compelled to perform the several duties of captain and lieutenant, and to take turn in the watch with his only officer. On leaving the
bay of Talcahuano, the wind fell, and the ship was becalmed, under the
island of Quiriquina ; he did not leave the deck till after midnight, when
having given his orders, he went into his cabin to take a short repose. His
order to the lieutenant was, to call him up on the least stir of wind.
Scarcely had the admiral left the deck, when the lieutenant quitted his post,
leaving a young lad, a midshipman, in command of the vessel. A breeze
sprang up, and the lad, instead of calling the admiral, attempted to work
the ship himself, and ran her on a sand-bank close to the shore. The tide
was falling, but Lord Cochrane, ever ready with means suited to the emergency of the case, succeeded in getting her off the bank ; she was, however,

considerably damaged. Part of her false keel was knocked off, and the planking, called the garboard streak, was crushed; and she made water fast. Lord Cochrane still, however, resolved to take the ship to Valdivia, and accomplish his purpose. Notwithstanding the pumps were kept incessantly at work, the water increased to eight feet; she sailed badly, and every one except himself expected she would founder at sea. Finding that the water now no longer gained upon the pumps, he persevered, and, on the evening of the second of February, landed the troops in the most orderly manner at the landing-place of the Aguada del Ingles, outside of the harbour. The soldiers advanced to attack with spirit, while he went in his boat to reconnoitre the condition of the forts, so that by hailing he could more effectually animate and direct their operations, as he had the fullest confidence in the bravery of the military commanders. So admirably were the measures taken, and so promptly executed, that the fort of the Aguada del Ingles was taken before the garrison had time to give the alarm. San Carlos was then stormed and taken, the garrison flying in the dark to Chorocomayo Alto: so quick was the pursuit, that the conquerors in the dark entered pell-mell into the succeeding forts, which were open to receive the affrighted Spaniards, who cried out to their comrades to be received: in this way before midnight the strong holds of Aguada del Ingles, San Carlos, Amargos, and two Chorocomayos, and Coral Castle, fell into the hands of the conquerors. Lord Cochrane brought his ship into the bay next morning, under a heavy fire from the enemy's forts, and anchored in front of Niebla, at the same time embarking the military from the opposite side in boats, so as to land them in two divisions, the one to storm Niebla and Pioja, and the other to capture Manzanera: the affrighted garrisons having seen the patriot flags hoisted on the opposite fortresses, and observing the O'Higgins lowering her ports to open a fire upon them, and at the same time perceiving the approach of the patriot troops, fled from their guns with precipitation towards the city, abandoning these strong holds to the possession of the victorious troops. Thus with a single ship, and with less than half the number of troops which garrisoned these impregnable forts, did the well-judging, brave, and gallant sailor capture the important post of Valdivia; his loss was only seven men killed, and nineteen wounded: in the forts were captured the commander of the place, Colonel Hoyos, five commissioned officers, seventy-six non-commissioned officers and privates, besides a loss on the enemy's side of three officers and ten soldiers killed, and twenty-one wounded. This is one of the most splendid feats ever recorded in history. All the military stores of the Spaniards fell into his hands, among them upwards of a thousand cwt. of gunpowder, 10,000 cannon-shot, of which 2,500 were brass, 170,000 musket cartridges, and other stores in proportion. The troops, including those who escaped from the batteries on the south-side during the night, as well as those who fled from the north, retired with consternation to the town of Valdivia, whither Lord Cochrane followed them at the head of the soldiers, marines, and sailors: he marched to the plaza, or square, in the centre of which he planted with his own hand, the independent standard of Chile; he found here no opposition, as the affrighted Spaniards had retired to the woods among the Indians. Having arranged matters for the government of the town, leaving the troops in garrison, and the O'Higgins to be hove down in Coral bay, in order to repair the terrible damages she had sustained on leaving Talcahuana bay, he returned alone to Valparaiso in the little schooner Montezuma, which only mounted one swivel-gun, having his flag waving at the head of her small mast.

"On Lord Cochrane's return, instead of being hailed by the government for the services he had rendered, was annoyed by every possible vexation ; the minister of war declaring, that instead of reward, he deserved to have lost his life in the enterprise, as it was the act of a madman ! ! ! This minister secretly carried on a series of intrigues, the object of which was, to degrade the admiral, and lessen the glory which his brilliant services had so well deserved. This originated from motives of the most narrow-minded jealousy and the most unworthy prejudices. He did not even receive a public acknowledgment of thanks for this brilliant exploit, till, for his own indemnification in having acted without orders, and for the satisfaction of the officers and men serving under him, he was obliged, after a long delay, to solicit the boon; and even then, the payment of prize-money for the stores taken in the fortresses was actually refused to the victors ! It was only when Lord Cochrane's indignation was raised by the ingratitude of the government of Chile, and it was feared he was about to retire in disgust, that the requisite vote of thanks was conceded, that medals were distributed to the victorious troops, and that a mere nominal reward of the grant of an estate was given to Lord Cochrane as a compensation for his brilliant services."*

The following despatch from Lord Cochrane confirms the details already given :

"SIR,—I had the honour to inform you, from Talcahuana, that, taking advantage of the opportunity which presented itself of communicating with Colonel Freyre on the means most effectual towards expelling the enemy from the south of Chile, and freeing the country from future incursions, I availed myself of the assistance of that zealous and active officer; who supplied me, on the 28th ult. with the troops and other assistance I required. The O'Higgins, Intrepid brig, and Montezuma schooner, sailed with a fair wind, and on the 2d instant arrived at the preconcerted rendezvous, ten leagues to the southward of Valdivia. All the troops were then embarked in the small vessels ; and, leaving the O'Higgins outside, we stood in for the Aguada Inglesa, where we anchored at a moderate distance from the battery and fort of San Carlos. The troops were disembarked at sunset; but this was not effected before the castle commenced a fire upon us ; and in consequence of the heavy surf retarding the disembarka

* Miers.

[His Lordship has subsequently been deprived of this token of Chilian gratitude.—Author's remark.]

D

tion, the enemy gained time to collect a considerable force behind the precipices which line the beach.

" Nevertheless, the marines of the O'Higgins and Intrepid, with the military, having reached the shore, put the enemy to flight; and, pursuing them to the forts of Aguada Inglesa and San Carlos, immediately took possession of the first. The second was taken by assault after dark, in spite of all the efforts the enemy made to defend it. The rapidity with which we took the forts and batteries of Avanzado, Barro, Amargos, and Chorocomayo, can only be compared with the valour and resolution of the officers and men who entered the castle of Corral along with the enemy, whom they were pursuing to this last point that remained to them. In this manner fell all the batteries and forts on the southern bank, whose artificial strength is nothing when compared with their advantageous natural situation.

" I enclose you the letters of Major Beauchef, who commanded the brave detachment of 250 men, with which the patriot Colonel Freyre supplied me, and of Major Miller, who commanded the marines. Of the gallant conduct of these two officers, and that of Capt. Erezcous, who commanded the detachment from the Intrepid, as of all the rest, I can say nothing in praise adequate to their merit, and consequently I shall recommend them in expressive silence to the consideration of his Excellency the Supreme Director.

" I had almost forgotten to mention, that these forts and batteries mount seventy pieces of cannon, and that we have taken in the port the ship Dolores.

" On board the Montezuma,   (Signed)   " COCHRANE."
" Valdivia, 4th of February, 1820.

Lord Cochrane, with his 318 heroes, captured fifteen forts, that were garrisoned with 1,600 men, and the number of guns mounted upon their batteries when taken possession of were as follows :—

No. of Pounders.

Pounders	24	16	14	12	8	4	2	1	Total.
Brass ...	17	4	12	4	13	1	1	1	53
Iron ...	57	4			1	11		2	75
	74	8	12	4	14	12	1	3	128

The following is an extract from the Dumfries Monthly Magazine of November 1825.

" Another important acquisition was added to these by the capture, in the port, of the ship Dolores, which had formerly belonged to Chile, but which, in November 1819, had been treacherously seized by a part of her crew, and put into the hands of the pirate Benavides.

" After providing for the quiet and safety of the city and province, by establishing a provisional government, and leaving a part of his force to garrison the place under the command of Major Beauchef, his lordship proceeded with the Montezuma and Dolores—the Intrepid having recently been wrecked on a sand-bank within the bay during a strong gale of wind —to Chiloe, with a view to wrest that island also from the hands of the royalists. He departed from Valdivia on the 13th of February, and on anchoring off Chiloe, immediately landed a body of troops under the command of Major Miller, to attack the fortifications of San Carlos; but Miller, after taking and demolishing two batteries, was obliged to retire to the boats with considerable loss, the military, as also the natives, headed by several friars, having made a determined resistance. This convinced his lordship that the cause of Spain was devotedly adhered to upon the island; and his force being too small to attempt the reduction of the town, he returned, without having effected anything farther, to Valdivia. He then ordered the O'Higgins to be repaired, and, issuing such instructions as were necessary for the regulation of affairs until orders should arrive from the supreme government, he departed with the other vessels for Valparaiso on the twenty-eighth, carrying with him the stores taken at Valdivia, together with five Spanish officers and forty privates, prisoners.

" After the departure of Lord Cochrane, the patriot forces left in Valdivia were obliged to dispute the possession of their recent conquest with the royalists whom they had expelled, and who had taken shelter in Chiloe. Intelligence having reached Beauchef that the Spaniards were determined to return, and to attempt the re-conquest of Valdivia, he collected the whole force of the place, consisting of those troops he had brought from Concepcion, and such volunteers as had joined the patriot standard in Valdivia, which, when assembled, amounted to two hundred and eighty men; and with these he advanced from the city to engage the enemy at a distance. He met them near the river Toro, on the sixth of March, where the contest was soon decided; the Spanish officers having mounted their horses and fled, in about an hour after the commencement of the attack. Their men, left to the mercy of the enemy, instantly surrendered, and were made prisoners, to the number of two hundred and seventy. The whole of their arms and baggage was also taken; and with these trophies Beauchef returned on the 10th in triumph to Valdivia.

" The repairs upon the O'Higgins being finished by the 11th of April ensuing, she rejoined the rest of the fleet under Lord Cochrane on the 18th, in the harbour of Valparaiso.

" For the sake of despatch, the executive government had, some time previous to this, removed from Santiago to Valparaiso, the better to co-operate with San Martin in embodying the army, and making the necessary preparations for the invasion of Peru. The arrival there of the admiral, crowned with glory from the conquest of Valdivia, was hailed by all classes with unbounded enthusiasm. Medals were struck by government in commemoration of the event, and distributed among the officers, and ' Long live Cochrane, the hero of Valdivia!' resounded in every quarter. His lordship, on his arrival, immediately directed his views to the great object then in contemplation, and began to co-operate with the executive in repairing and recruiting the navy. But the funds of government were low, the seamen were tardily paid, and the prize-money promised them by Lord Cochrane was altogether refused. This at first occasioned secret murmurs of discontent; but at length complaint became loud and general, and his lordship, to whom the seamen looked for the vindication of their rights, found himself reduced to the necessity of proposing to government the alternative of either acceding to the request he had made, or of losing his future services. He therefore addressed to his excellency, the supreme director, a long exposition of his conduct since receiving the command of the squadron, and pointed out the manner in which his operations had often been retarded, and his measures counteracted, by the remissness or the wilful design of government. He reminded his excellency of the promises which had frequently been made to him, and which had been as frequently broken, regarding the pay and prize-money due to the seamen; he drew a ✎ vivid picture of the consequent distress of the crews, and the straits to which he was thus reduced in managing so heterogeneous a mass of materials as that of which the fleet was composed, consisting of men of all nations, and of all religions, whose characters were fierce, and their conduct ungovernable, excepting by appeals to the great leading principle of self-interest; he also justified his own actions and motives from the aspersions of his enemies, by a reference to incontrovertible facts; and concluded by begging the acceptance of his resignation in the following terms:—

" ' These circumstances, and many other similar ones, oblige me to adopt a line of conduct which my duty to your excellency, to the state, and to myself, most imperiously prescribes; this is, to solicit your acceptance of the important commission with which I have been honoured, and which I now beg leave to resign.

" ' I have detailed some of the motives which oblige me to abandon the service of a state in which I have been so highly honoured, particularly by your excellency; but my firm conviction is, that if I agree to the tardy and procrastinated measures of the government, I shall make myself tacitly instrumental in forwarding that ruin which cannot but be the result of the plans of the advisers of your excellency.

" ' Valparaiso, May 14th, 1820.'

" This high-spirited determination of Lord Cochrane was a result which his excellency, or rather his ministers, had not anticipated. His lordship's presence and services were indispensable to the success of the expedition; and therefore to soothe his resentment, and secure his farther co-operation, were acts of the first necessity. The justness of his lordship's complaints was accordingly acknowledged, and the most conciliating assurances were given of attention and good faith on the part of government in future; in consequence of which an agreement took place, and Cochrane consented to retain his commission. An estate had previously been offered him by government, of which he did not accept; and on the present occasion the offer was repeated, but was again respectfully declined. Yet, that his refusal might not be attributed to any other motive than disinterestedness, he purchased for himself an estate about eight leagues to the northward of Valparaiso, thereby to evince his attachment to the country, and his desire to be ranked among the number of its citizens. Shortly after concluding this purchase, he visited the estate, and having remarked the favourable situation of a bay which it contained, named Herradura, he gave in to government a statement of the advantages which it possessed over that of Valparaiso, and proposed that it should be resorted to in future by the vessels of war, as a much more convenient station; offering, at the same time, to grant a sufficient space of land for the establishment of an arsenal and marine depôt. But instead of receiving thanks for this gratuitous offer, he was informed that as the harbour of Herradura, and the estate of Quintero —the name of his lordship's property—were, in consequence of the advantages pointed out by his lordship, of the highest importance to Chile, he must desist from making any improvements upon them, as the state should not re-imburse his expenditure; and that the said estate should in future be appropriated by government; Lord Cochrane receiving back his purchase money, and being also remunerated for such improvements as he might already have made.—The chagrin and indignation of Lord Cochrane may easily be conceived, on the receipt of this information. He instantly demanded an explanation from the supreme director, of such unaccountable conduct, and received in answer a polite apology, attributing the whole affair to the officiousness of the attorney-general, who had founded the proceeding upon an old Spanish law which yet remained unrepealed. His lordship's devotion to the cause of liberty induced him to pass over this insult; but though he generously forgave such instances of mean jealousy, or childish policy, it was impossible that his proud and independent spirit could forget them. These little covert acts of baseness or ingratitude sting a lofty and generous mind infinitely more than the bold and open attacks of a dishonourable foe; and the recollection of these, no doubt, gave additional keenness to his lordship's feelings on many future occasions, when farther injuries called for a still farther extension of his generosity.

"Several circumstances, tending to subvert his lordship's authority, occurred also about this time in the navy, which again led to a remonstrance and a tender of his commission. He had made application to the minister of marine for the appointment of Captain Crosbie to the rank of flag-captain on board the O'Higgins, and on the eve of sailing with the expedition, he was astonished to learn that instead of Crosbie, Captain Spry had been promoted. On the order to ratify this appointment being transmitted to the admiral, he flatly refused to obey it, and answered that although no personal objection to Captain Spry induced him to adopt this line of conduct, he was determined that that officer should never tread the quarter-deck of his vessel as flag-captain, and that no such encroachment upon his own privilege as admiral, should be permitted by him so long as he retained the command of the fleet. This spirited reply had the desired effect; Captain Spry was continued in his former command, and Captain Crosbie was promoted according to his lordship's former request.

" The conclusion of this affair was followed by another of a much more serious nature. Captain Guize of the Lautaro, who had been guilty of neglect of duty, and of several acts of disobedience to his commander, was arrested by order of the admiral, and kept in confinement until government, which was immediately put in possession of the charges against him, should institute a court-martial to decide upon his punishment. The members of government, who seem never to have formed a just estimate of the bold and uncompromising character of Lord Cochrane, resisted this act of his authority in the most decided manner, until the following letter, which was received from his lordship by the minister of marine, restored them to a sense of their true interest : —

" ' Sir—The apparent determination of the supremacy to support a junior officer in the commission of the most outrageous breaches of his public duty, and of acting not only contrary, but in direct opposition to the orders communicated to him by his commander-in-chief, not only encourages his dereliction from duty, and is a precedent of the most pernicious character for the imitation of others, but brings my authority into contempt, and renders my exertions in the service of the republic nugatory. I have nothing to add at present to what I have already stated to you, except that you will place in the hands of his excellency, the supreme director, my resignation of the command of the squadron of Chile, and express to him my sincere wish, that whoever may be appointed to supersede me, his endeavours to serve the cause of liberty in the New World may be crowned with greater success than mine have been ; and that he may be better qualified to preserve that discipline in the squadron, which is not only essentially necessary, but indispensably requisite, for the honour of himself, the success of his operations, and the welfare of the cause he serves. I have to request you will inform me at the earliest period of the acceptance of my resignation, that I may order my flag to be struck ; as also, whether it would be agreeable to the present views of the supreme government that I should continue to reside as a citizen of Chile, among those persons who, after having exerted themselves in support of her sacred cause, have retired to enjoy the fruits of their labours ; if not, I request permission to leave the country ; and my passport constituting my ultimate request, I remain, &c.,

" Valparaiso, July 16, 1820.' " COCHRANE."

" On the following day, before any answer had been returned to the above communication, an anonymous paper was found upon the capstern head of the flag-ship, inviting all who felt themselves attached to his lordship, or who were aware how much the honour, safety, and interest, not only of the navy, but of the state of Chile, depended on his continuing in the command, to meet on board the Independencia, at one o'clock, for the purpose of taking into consideration what measures it might be most proper to adopt in consequence of his lordship's determination to resign. The events of the 18th showed that this invitation had been attended to. His lordship on that day received two communications, one from five captains of the fleet, and another from twenty-three commissioned officers, stating, that having heard with regret of his lordship's determination to abandon the service of a state from which he had received so ungrateful a return for his many splendid services, and being aware that he was the only man capable of commanding with effect the naval forces of Chile, they had come to the resolution of also abandoning the service with his lordship. They begged him, therefore, to forward their resignations to the proper quarter, and assured him at the same time of their devotedness to his person, and their esteem for his brave and honourable character. These documents were respectively signed by the five captains and twenty-three commissioned officers with whom they originated, and were answered by Lord Cochrane in the most obliging manner. He thanked them for this gratifying proof of their attachment; but he concealed the circumstance altogether from Government, that the determination of its members might not thus be biassed by a fear of such consequences, in deciding upon the subject of his own resignation. The secret, however, soon reached the ears of the Executive, by means of those—among whom were Captains Guize and Spry—who had not adopted with their comrades the resolution of sharing in the fate of their admiral. This momentous secret operated with so speedy an effect, that an answer to Lord Cochrane's communication was received on the 20th, of which the following is a copy:—

"'My Lord,—At a moment when the services of the naval forces of the state are of the highest importance, and the personal services of your lordship indispensable, the Supremacy, with the most profound sentiments of regret, has received your resignation, which, should it be admitted, would involve the future operations of the arms of liberty in the New World in certain ruin, and ultimately replace in Chile, your adopted home, that tyranny which your lordship abhors, and to the annihilation of which your heroism has so greatly contributed.

"His excellency, 'the supreme director, commands me to inform your lordship, which I have the honour of doing, that should you persist in resigning the command of the sqadron, which has been honoured by bearing your flag, the cause of terror and dismay to our enemies, and of glory to all true Americans; or should the government unwisely admit it, this would be indeed a day of universal mourning in the New World. The government, therefore, in the name of the nation, returns you your commission, soliciting your re-acceptance of it, for the furtherance of that sacred cause to which your whole soul is devoted.

"The Supremacy is convinced of the necessity which obliges your lordship to adopt the measures which placed Capt. Guize, of the Lautaro, under an arrest, and of the justness of the charges exhibited against this officer of the state; but being desirous of preventing any delay in the important services in which the ships and vessels of war are about to proceed, it is the pleasure of his excellency the supreme director, that the arrest of Capt. Guize be suspended, as well as his trial by a court-martial on the charges exhibited, which will remain in the archives of the marine department, to be postponed till the first opportunity which does not interfere with the service of the squadron, so important at the present epoch.

(Signed) " JOSE YGNACIO ZENTENO,

" Valparaiso, July 20th, 1820." Minister of Marine."

"Lord Cochrane, on receipt of this note, immediately set Capt. Guize at liberty, and returned to the various officers of the squadron their commissions, with the assurance that he duly appreciated so flattering a testimony of their personal esteem.

"It would require more minute and extensive information regarding the state of parties, and the characters of the various individuals composing the machinery of government in Chile during this period, to account in a satisfactory manner for so strange a system of alternate opposition and conciliation being thus persisted in towards Lord Cochrane. The amiable disposition of the supreme director O'Higgins, and his ardent devotion to the republican cause, go far to establish his freedom from active guilt in these transactions. But passively a considerable share becomes his due, in having permitted those over whom he exercised a direct control to exceed, the prerogatives of their office, and to destroy the balance of public justice by casting into the scale their own private feelings and interests. We have already seen the political evils to which he gave rise by creating the senatorial court of consultation, and endowing it with privileges imcompatible with his own supremacy, and the due subordination of parts in the scale of government. The uprightness of his motives no doubt disarmed the tongue of censure upon that occasion, while common sense taught the public to exonerate him from the direct odium of acts performed by a body of men, who had derived from him merely the power of performing them. Yet still he was adverted to as the remote cause of all, upon the same principle that we account for inherent depravity in moral nature, by referring to the unwary deed of a common progenitor. O'Higgins appears to have wanted that energy and decision in the cabinet which characterised his actions in the field ; he was incapable of overawing and binding to one common purpose the wills of those beneath him in authority; and thus, by giving scope to the passions and caprice of individuals, the general good became a frequent sacrifice, and measures of the last importance were either rejected or delayed until their rejection would have been the much safer course. Perhaps it is in this way, rather than in any other, that the cause of the treatment which Lord Cochrane experienced is to be explained. A ray from Mr. Stevenson's* pen has fallen amid the obscurity upon San Martin, and pointed him out as the author of the whole ; but this will not be admitted until it is distinctly proved that San Martin exercised an unbounded influence over the government, and that he studied his own interest more than that of the public. That government alone ought to be deemed culpable, is proved by the treatment which Lord Cochrane still continued to experience after San Martin had altogether forsaken its councils, and was exclusively occupied with the affairs of Peru. The same feelings were still retained in Chile which had formerly displayed themselves, and the same conduct was the result, until at length his lordship carried the resolution which he had so often adopted into practice, and quitted not only the service, but the precincts of a country which had proved itself undeserving of either his support or his presence. So illustrious and talented an indivi-

*Private Secretary to Lord Cochrane.

dual as San Martin would have possessed a weighty influence in any country, and under any political system, for such is the tribute which mankind involuntarily pay to superior merit; and if this tribute was awarded to San Martin in a more than ordinary proportion, the cause is explained by the circumstances with which he was surrounded. The unsettled state of society, the jealousy of superior merit among some in power, and the clashing of individual opinions among others, afford a more satisfactory answer to this problem. Ingratitude to public benefactors is a crime of frequent occurrence in revolutions, where the ascendant of to-day may be the slave of to-morrow, and where present expedience, more than maxims of general justice, form the motives of action with those to whom is committed the direction of affairs. The disputes which occurred between the government and Lord Cochrane are therefore nothing extraordinary; and I should not have dwelt so long upon their detail, did not every circumstance connected with the history of so romantic an individual, possess a degree of importance which ought to save it from oblivion."

Dumfries Monthly Magazine of November, 1835.

THE THIRD CRUISE AND EXPEDITION OF THE LIBERATING ARMY.

On the 21st of August, 1820, an army of near 6,000 men, well equipped, armed, &c. besides an ample store of arms, ammunition, and clothing, for the patriots in Peru, were embarked in twenty transports, mostly prizes, who sailed under convoy of the Chilian squadron, from Valparaiso, in order to liberate Peru; at a time when the treasury of Chile was in an exhausted state; and the greatest opposition had been manifested through the machinations of the enemies of liberty, who were still a powerful part of the aristocracy of Chile. Notwithstanding which, the indefatigable supreme director, Don Bernardo O'Higgins, with the co-operation of the commander in chief General San Martin, Admiral Lord Cochrane, and a few other distinguished patriots, had managed to surmount every difficulty, after having already paid 480,000 dollars for the following vessels of war: Lautaro, San Martin, Galvarino, Araucano, and Chacabuco.

On the thirteenth of August, the Supreme Director issued the following proclamation.

"In the tenth year of the South American revolution, and the three hundredth of the conquest of Peru, a people whose rank in the social scale has hitherto rated below its destiny, has undertaken to break the chains which Pizarro began to forge, with his blood-stained hands, in 1520. The government established in Chile since its restoration, having conceived this great design, deems it right that it should be carried into execution by the same person who, having twice promised to save his country, has twice succeeded. An expedition, equipped at the expense of great sacrifices, is at length ready to proceed, and the army of Chile, united to that of the Andes, is now called upon to redeem the land, in which slavery has longest existed, and from whence the latest efforts have been made to oppress the whole continent. Happy be this day on which the record of the movements, and the action of the expedition commenced! The object of this enterprise is to decide whether or not the time is arrived, when the influence of South America upon the rest of the world shall be commensurate with its extent, its riches, and its situation.   "O'HIGGINS."

The expedition arrived on the coast of Peru, and the vessels anchored in the bay of Tarapaca, three leagues to the south of Pisco, on the sixth of September; on the eighth a division landed and took possession of Pisco; on the twelfth the troops had all disembarked, and General San Martin established his head-quarters there, when, after having gained some advantages over the enemy, and sent General Arenales with a division into the interior, he embarked the troops, and proceeded to Ancon, leaving Lord Cochrane to blockade Callao.

The following are extracts of proclamations from the supreme director of Chile, and General San Martin, that were issued by the liberating army after it had disembarked at Pisco.

PERUVIANS!

"Behold the pact and condition on which Chile, in the face of the Supreme Being, and calling on all the nations of the earth as witnesses and revengers of a violation, faces fatigues and death, to save you. You shall be free and independent; you shall constitute your own laws by the unbiassed and spontaneous will of your representatives; no military nor civil influence, either direct or indirect, shall be exercised by your brethren in your social dispositions; you shall discharge the armed force sent to protect you, at the moment you choose, without any attention to your danger, or security: should you think fit, no military force shall ever occupy a free town, unless it be called in by a legitimate magistracy :· neither by us, nor through our assistance, shall any Peninsular or party feelings, that may have preceded your liberty, be punished : ready to destroy the armed force which resists your rights, we pray you to forget, on the day of your glory, all past grievances, and to reserve the most severe justice for future obstinate insults. " O'HIGGINS."

PEOPLE OF PERU !

"I have paid the tribute, which as a public man I owe to the opinion of others. I have shown what is my object and my mission towards you. I come to fulfil the expectations of all who wish to belong to the country which gave them birth, and who desire to be governed by their own laws. On that day when Peru shall freely pronounce as to the form of her institutions, be they whatever they may, my functions shall cease; and I shall have the glory of announcing to the government of Chile, of which I am a subject, that their heroic efforts have at last received the consolation of having given liberty to Peru, and security to the neighbouring states.

" SAN MARTIN."

His lordship being determined to humble the pride of the Spaniards, (who, vain of having frustrated his former attempts of capturing or destroying their vessels, had ridiculed them in every possible mode, even by representations in the theatre of Lima,) and after having reconnoitred the enemy's position, who were on the " qui vive,"he fixed the night of the fifth of November, for one of the most daring enterprises ever recorded ; and after having called out volunteers, and selected a part (for the crews of the shipping volunteered to a man,) he issued the following proclamation :—

" SOLDIERS and SAILORS !

" To-night we are about to give a mortal blow to the enemy; and to-morrow you will present yourselves with pride before Callao; all your comrades will envy your good fortune; one hour of courage and resolution is all that is required of you, to triumph. Remember that you have conquered in Valdivia, and be not afraid of those who have hitherto fled from you. The value of all the vessels that are captured in Callao will be yours, and the same reward in money will be distributed amongst you, that has been offered by the Spaniards in Lima, to those who should capture any of the Chilian squadron. The moment of glory is approaching. I hope that the Chilians will fight as they have been accustomed to do, and that the Englishmen will act as they have always done at home and abroad.

"Given on board the O'Higgins, Nov. 5th, 1820.

"COCHRANE."

Fourteen boats left the O'Higgins, at half-past 10 P.M. under the command of his lordship; they were formed in two divisions :—

1st. O'HIGGINS.	2d. LAUTARO AND INDEPENDENCIA.
Captain Crosby.	Captain Guize.
Lieutenant Esmonde.	Lieutenant Bell.
Lieutenant Brown.	Lieutenant Freeman.
Lieutenant Morgell.	Lieutenant Grenfelt.
Lieutenant Robertson	Lieutenant Gilbert.
Lieutenant Wynter.	Gardiner, Master of Lautaro.
Midshipman Delano.	Midshipman Hanower.
Midshipman Orello.	Midshipman Simonds
Well, surgeon	Midshipman Parker.
Tailor, boatswain.	Midshipman French.
Davies, gunner.	Midshipman Oxley.
Mullins, carpenter.	Michael, surgeon.
Captain Geron, artillery.	Frew, purser.
	Soyer, volunteer.
Lieutenant Romero, infantry.	Thompson, boatswain.
	Blasher, gunner.

And 240 seamen and marines.

The following is the order that was issued preparatory to the enterprise.

"Chilian States' Ship O'Higgins,
1st of Nov. 1810.

"The boats will proceed, towing the launches in the two lines parallel to each other, which lines are to be at a distance of three boats' length asunder.

"The second line will be under the charge of Captain Guize. Each boat will be under the charge of a volunteer commissioned officer, so far as circumstances permit, and the whole under the immediate command of the admiral.

"The officers and men are all to be dressed in white jackets, frocks, or shirts, and are to be armed with pistols, sabres, knives, tomahawks, or pikes.

" Two boat-keepers are to be appointèd to each boat, who on no pretence whatever, shall quit their respective boats, but are to remain therein and take care that the boats do not get adrift.

" Each boat is to be provided with one or more axes, or sharp hatchets, which are to be kept slung to the girdle of the boat-keepers. The frigate Esmeralda being the chief object of the expedition, the whole force is to attack that ship, which, when carried, is not to be cut adrift, but is to remain in possession of the patriot seamen, to ensure the capture of the rest.

" On securing the frigate, the Chilian seamen and marines are not to cheer as if they were Chilians, but, in order to deceive the enemy, and give time for completing the work, are to cheer ' Viva el Rey !'

" The two brigs of war are to be fired on by the musketry from the Esmeralda, and are to be taken possession of by Lieutenants Esmonde and Morgell, in the boats they command ; which being done, they are to cut adrift, run out, and anchor in the offing as quickly as possible. The boats of the Independencia are to busy themselves in turning adrift all the outward Spanish merchant-ships; and the boats of the O'Higgins and Lautaro, under Lieutenants Bell and Robertson, are to set fire to one or more of the headmost hulks; but these are not to be cut adrift so as to fall down upon the rest.

" The watch-word, or parole and countersign, should the white dress not be sufficient distinction in the dark, are ' Gloria !' to be answered by ' Victoria !'

(Signed)   " COCHRANE."

I will now give an extract from the journal of a distinguished naval officer who commanded his Majesty's ship Conway, at that period in the Pacific, and who, on account of the station he held, must have been an impartial historian.

" At midnight, the boats having forced their way across the boom, Lord Cochrane, who was leading, rowed alongside the first gun-boat, and taking the officer by surprise, proposed to him, with a pistol at his head, the alternative of ' Silence or death !'—No reply was made—the boats pushed on unobserved—and Lord Cochrane, mounting the Esmeralda's side, was the first to give the alarm. The sentinel on the gangway levelled his piece and fired ; but was instantly cut down by the coxswain, and his lordship, though wounded in the thigh, at the same moment stepped on the deck. The frigate being boarded with no less gallantry on the opposite side, by Captain Guize, who met Lord Cochrane midway, on the quarter-deck; and also by Captain Crosbie; the after-part of the ship was soon carried, sword in hand. The Spaniards rallied on the forecastle, where they made a desperate resistance, till overpowered by a fresh party of seamen and marines, headed by Lord Cochrane. A gallant stand was again made for sometime on the main-deck; but before one o'clock the ship was captured, her cables cut, and she was steered triumphantly out of the harbour, under the fire of the whole of the north face of the castle. The Hyperion, an English, and the Macedonian, an American frigate, which were at anchor close to the scene of action, got under weigh when the attack commenced; and, in order to prevent their being mistaken by the batteries for the Esmeralda, showed distinguishing signals: but Lord Cochrane, who had foreseen and provided even for this minute circumstance, hoisted the same lights as the American and English frigates; and thus rendered it impossible for the batteries to discriminate between the three ships: the Esmeralda, in consequence, was very little injured by the shot from the batteries.

" The Spaniards had upwards of one hundred and twenty men killed and wounded; the Chilians eleven killed, and thirty wounded.

"This loss was a death-blow to the Spanish naval force in that quarter of the world; for, although there were still two Spanish frigates and some smaller vessels in the Pacific, they never afterwards ventured to show themselves, but left Lord Cochrane undisputed master of the coast."*

General San Martin's Official Despatch to the Chilian Government.

"Head-quarters, Supe, Dec. 1st, 1820.

" Señor Ministro.—I have the honour of forwarding to you the despatches of ' El mui honorable Lord Cochrane,' vice-admiral of the squadron, relative to the heroic capture of the frigate Esmeralda, by boarding her under the batteries of Callao.

" It is impossible for me to eulogize in proper language the daring enterprise of the 5th of November, and by which he has decided the superiority of our naval forces, augmented the splendour and power of Chile, and secured the success of this campaign.

" I doubt not but that S. E. the supreme director, will render the justice due to the worthy chief, officers, and other individuals, who have had a share in that successful action. It is painful to record the loss of a few brave men, also to state that his lordship was severely wounded, but he is now happily recovered, and ready to confer new glories on the Chilian flag.

" I have not been able to send you the flag of Admiral Vacaro, of which mention is made in the despatches, on account of a mistake, and the great distance I am 'from the squadron, but it will be forwarded by the first opportunity.

" I beg you will honour me by congratulating S. E. on this important success, and principally on account of the influence it will have in the great object that occupies his attention. " Dios guarde a V. S. muchos anos."

" Al Señor Colonel Don Jose Ignacio Zenteno,
　　　　　Minister of war.　　　　　" JOSE SAN MARTIN."

* Captain Bazil Hall's Extracts.

" O'Higgins before Callao, Nov. 14th, 1820.

" Ex'mo Señor.—The efforts of the S. E., the supreme director, and the sacrifices of the patriots of the south, to acquire the dominion of the Pacific, have hitherto been frustrated, chiefly by the enormous strength of the batteries of Callao, which being superior to those of Algiers or Gibraltar, rendered every attack against the naval force of the enemy impracticable, with any class or number of ships of war. Nevertheless, being desirous of advancing the cause of rational liberty and political independence, which is the great object your excellency has in view, and to promote the happiness of mankind, I was anxious to dispel the charm which heretofore had paralysed our naval efforts. With this intention, I carefully examined the batteries, the ships of war, and the gun-boats, in this port; and being satisfied that the frigate Esmeralda could be cut out by men resolved to do their duty, I immediately gave orders to the captains of the Independencia and Lautaro to prepare their boats; and acquainted them that the value of that frigate, together with the reward offered in Lima for the capture of any of the ships of Chile, would be the recompense of those who should volunteer to take part in this enterprise.

" On the following day, a number of volunteers, including Captains Forster, Guize, and Crosbie, with other officers, offered their services; the whole amounting to a force sufficient for the execution of the project. Every thing being prepared, the boats were exercised in the dark, in the evening of the 4th inst., and the night of the 5th of November was chosen for the attack.

" Captain Crosbie had charge of the first division, consisting of the boats of the O'Higgins; and Captain Guize, of the second, which was formed of those of the other ships. At half-past ten, we rowed in two lines towards the enemy's anchorage, and, at twelve, forced the line of gun-boats guarding the entrance. The whole of our force boarded the Esmeralda at the same moment, and drove the enemy from the deck after an obstinate resistance.

" All the officers employed on this service have conducted themselves in the most gallant manner.

" To them, and also to the seamen and marines, I feel under extreme obligations for their activity and zeal in boarding the Esmeralda.

" I was sorry that the necessity of leaving at least one captain in charge of the ships, prevented my acceding to the wishes of the captain of the Independencia, who accordingly remained with the squadron

" I have also to lament the loss we have suffered, which is detailed in the adjoining lists.*

" That of the Esmeralda cannot be exactly ascertained, on account of the wounded and others who leaped overboard; but we know that, out of 330 individuals originally on board, only 204 have been found alive, including officers and wounded men. The Esmeralda mounts forty guns, and is not in

* O'Higgins, 3 killed, " El mui honorable Lord Cochrane," and 14 individuals wounded—Lautaro, 3 killed, 8 wounded—Independencia, 5 killed, 8 wounded.

a bad state, as was represented, but, on the contrary, very well found, and perfectly equipped. She has on board three months', provisions, besides a supply of cordage and other articles for two years. A gun-boat of four guns, which lay directly in the passage of our boats, was boarded and towed out on the following morning.

" I hope the capture of the flag-ship Esmeralda, secured by booms, batteries, and gun-boats, in a situation always before deemed impregnable, and in sight of the capital, where the fact cannot be concealed, will produce a moral effect greater than might be expected under other circumstances.

" I have great satisfaction in sending you the flag of Admiral Vacaro, that you may be pleased to present it to his Excellency, the supreme director of the republic of Chile.

" I have the honour to remain, Ex'mo S'or,

" Your excellency's most obedient servant,

" COCHRANE."

His lordship sent a more laconic epistle to S. E. the supreme director of Chile; and on the arrival of the news, the following eulogy was pronounced in the National Institution of Santiago in favour of the success of the maritime campaign of Lord Cochrane.

In order to preserve the originality of this document, I will not attempt to translate it.

" El elegio de Lord Cochrane, pronunciado en el instituto nacional de Chile sobre los succesos de la campaña maritima."

" Llega al Callao : este puerto se halla defendido por las mejores fortalezas de todo el pacifico, y coronado de baterias : 10 buques de guerra, y con gran numero de cañoneras presentaron una barrera formidable.

" El gallardo Almirante se apodera de la isla de San Lorenzo, ancla alli su escuadra emprende forzar la entrada del puerto y se adelanta con la O'Higgins, y el Lautaro : 300 piezas de artilleria vomitan la muerte al rededor de el y por tres costados vienen rayos à destruir sus buques ; pero el avanzo a un paso siempre igual par entre estos torrentes de fuego : asombra a sus enemigos, derama el horror y la muerte ; la maltrata sus buques y el terror llego a un extremo que se valian de arbitrios prohibidos, despidiendo balas rojas por todos los castillos.

·· Despues de escarmentarlos gravemente, vuelve sereno, y victorioso al resto de su armada.

" En este mismo punto y bajo de estos mismos fuegos despues de un año de preparacion para aguardar la Escuadra de Chile, y de dos meses de verla en sus puertos el virey, es quando se ha hecha prisionera la Esmeralda montada de los principales oficiales de la marina del Peru, y defendida de tanta tropa, que despues de una terrible mortandad hemos tomado 174 hombres.*

A series of success followed the expedition, and on the third of December, the regiment Numanica deserted the Spanish army, and joined that of General San Martin.

" On the 5th of July, the Spaniards abandoned Lima, and took shelter in the fortress of Callao; on the 12th, General San Martin, after various invitations, entered the city; on the 28th, the independence of Peru was proclaimed; and on the 21st of September, the castles of Callao surrendered to General San Martin, who had been elected Protector of Peru. Some misunderstanding had unfortunately broken out between the Admiral and Protector, who, it was said, had seduced Captain Guize and other officers to leave his lordship, and join the Peruvian Navy. " The admiral made a claim; 1st, for arrears due to the squadron ; 2nd, a bounty equal to one year's pay for each individual of the squadron, agreeable to the promise made before sailing from Valparaiso ; 3d, 50,000 dollars which had been promised to the seamen, in the event of their taking the Esmeralda; 4th, 110,000 dollars, the estimated value of the frigate. The protector contended that the Chilian government was alone responsible for the first and fourth claim. He admitted the justice of the second and third, but required to have time allowed him to liquidate them. The admiral was highly dissatisfied with the answer," and the breach being still widened with other circumstances, " the protector transmitted to Lord Cochrane a copy of that part of his private instructions from the Chilian government, which authorised San Martin, as commander-in-chief of the liberating expedition, to employ (*disponer*) the whole or any part of the squadron, as he may deem most expedient. In virtue of these powers, he ordered the admiral, and the vessels under his command, to leave the coast of Peru." " Lord Cochrane sailed in the month of October, 1821, with the O'Higgins, Valdivia, Independencia, and a small vessel, in pursuit of the Spanish squadron, and ascertained at Panama that it had touched there. This enterprising seaman proceeded in his leaky and inefficient vessels to the coast of California; but, learning that the Spanish frigates had not gone in that direction, he returned to the coast of Peru. The dangers and sufferings endured on this cruise have been seldom surpassed. The crazy ships were tossed about in a tempestuous and unfrequented sea, while the ill-paid, and discontented crews, suffering from great scarcity of fresh water and of provisions, were constantly obliged to keep working at the pumps. At one time, after a long calm, when ninety leagues from the nearest land, there only remained as much water as would fill a pipe, in the whole squadron. The crews were in a state of consternation at the horrid death which seemed to await them, and which no human effort could avert. Every eye was lifted towards

* Gazeta Ministerial de Chile.

E

heaven ; fervent ejaculations were uttered, for on such trying occasions there are no unbelievers. The crews were a medley of all religions ; but the same thoughts, the same fears, and the same hopes in the all-powerful Director of events, pervaded every breast. When the feelings of all were approaching to frenzy and despair, when they had arrived at that pitch of heart-rending agony, of which none, but those who have experienced similar calamities, can form any idea ; in this critical period, the sky assumed a threatening aspect ; the lightning flashed on the horizon, black clouds arose, peals of thunder resounded through the air, and every thing indicated an approaching storm. The drooping spirits of the sufferers revived, and one and all earnestly looked for the speedy approach of the tempest. Dangers which, at other times, would have been dreaded, in such shattered vessels, were now hailed with rapture. Torrents of rain fell, and, as if escaped from shipwreck, the men wept with joy. Every awning and sail that could be made available was spread.

" It rained in torrents for twenty-four hours, and every cask was filled. The wind, boisterous at first, soon moderated into a fair, steady breeze, and the trials and dangers of the sufferers were forgotten.

" In the mean while the Spanish naval commanding officer, Don Jose Villegas, fearing to come in contact with the patriot admiral, had made the best of his way from Panama to Guayaquil, where he capitulated to the Peruvian agents in that city, on the 15th of February, 1822. One of the frigates and the corvette remained in the river. The other frigate sailed for Callao, where she arrived on the 31st of March.

" All were delivered up to the Peruvian government. Lord Cochrane arrived in the bay of Callao on the 25th of April, and demanded the vessels as his prizes.

" The Peruvian government alleged he had no right to them, and refused to comply with the demand.

" Some altercations took place, and finally Lord Cochrane sailed for Chile on the 10th of May, 1822." *

The Chilian squadron anchored in the port of Valparaiso on the 13th of June, and his lordship sent the following official report of his operations to the Chilian government.

Admiral Lord Cochrane's official report to the Chilian government, on his return with the Chilian squadron in June 1822.

" The anxious desires of his excellency the supreme director are now fulfilled, and the sacrifices of the people of Chile are rewarded. The naval power of Spain, in the Pacific, has succumbed, it is now extinguished. The

* Miller's Memoirs.

following vessels having surrendered to the unceasing efforts of the squadron of this free state: the frigates, Prueba, of fifty guns; Esmeralda, of forty-four; Venganza, of forty-four; Resolution, of thirty-four; Sebastiana, of thirty-four . brigs, Pezuela of eighteen ; Potrillo of sixteen ; schooners, Aransasu ; Prosupina, and seventeen gun-boats ; the armed merchant ships, Aguila and Begonia, at Guayaquil, and others employed as block ships at Callao. It is highly gratifying to me, after labouring under such difficulties as were never before witnessed on board vessels of war, to announce the arrival of the Chilian squadron in Valparaiso, its cradle; where, owing to its constant services in the cause of the liberty and independence of Chile, Peru, Colombia, and Mexico, it is the object of admiration and gratitude to the inhabitants of the New World. .

" Cochrane."

Soon after the Chilian squadron and Liberating army had sailed for Peru, the Spanish party, who, unfortunately for Chile, were a wealthy and numerous class, headed by the Bishop of Santiago, who had great influence over the natives, began to exert their power of intrigue, and conspire to overthrow the patriot government, and regain the ascendency; but General O'Higgins, ever on the alert, frustrated their machinations, by exiling the prelate to Mendoza and Melipilla; others were punished by heavy contributions and imprisonment, besides which, their Spanish titles and dignities were annulled, until the court of Madrid deigned to recognize the independence of Chile. He gave freedom to the slaves, as well as to all who should enter the republic, and abolished that inhuman traffic. He invited foreigners to emigrate to, and settle in Chile; and as an inducement to such as were not Roman Catholics, he granted a boon that had hitherto been denied, viz., the rites of sepulture ! The first protestant that was publicly interred in the burial-ground allotted to them in the capital, (Santa Lucia,) was an English merchant, George Perkins, Esq. who had been barbarously murdered in his dwelling, and, what makes this circumstance worthy of notice, is the following fact:

E 2

The criminals were taken, tried, and led from their prison to the place of execution; at the same time the corpse of their victim was borne to the cemetery, and shot at the moment it was lowered into the grave.   This, and many other just and laudable acts of the worthy Director, gained him much popularity amongst the foreigners; but he did not escape the censure of those who strove to attribute such measures to sinister motives; and his secret enemies, finding that nothing could be done openly, strove to create dissension amongst the chiefs of the patriot army and squadron; and, unfortunately for the cause of independence, they were too successful, for no sooner had the party intrigues caused a rupture between the protector and the admiral, than the former found his popularity and power on the wane, which the following extract will fully explain :

"San Martin, now freed from the presence of a troublesome rival, began to carry into effect the arrangements he had so long contemplated regarding the maritime establishment of Peru.   The few vessels belonging to the republic were formed into a marine, and placed under the command of Captain—now created Admiral Guise, the personal enemy of Lord Cochrane, and such other European officers, among whom was Captain Spry, as had, like their admiral, left the service of Chile.   This marine was not less deficient in equipment than in number of vessels, for Lord Cochrane had already swept the Pacific, and gathered into the harbours of Chile almost all that remained of the Spanish fleets in that quarter of the world; but as, from that circumstance, no enemy existed to cope with them, it was, for the present, sufficient for the purposes of government.

"On the 8th of October, the protector issued a ' Provisional Statute for the Administration of the Free Departments of Peru,' in which he invested himself with the power of exercising, without control, all the various functions of the administration ; and also assumed to himself the sole command of the naval and military forces, with a right to increase or diminish their numbers as he might judge necessary, to impose taxes, contract loans, conclude treaties, and declare peace or war.   The assumption of this sovereign power he justified upon the plea of necessity, and limited its continuance to the declaration of independence throughout the whole of the provinces ; when he promised to constitute a general congress, for the purpose of establishing such a form of government as might appear best suited to the wishes and interests of the people.

" Previous to this, upon the 12th of August, a decree of a more liberal and gratifying kind emanated from the same quarter, declaring that all children born of slaves, on or after the 28th of that month, (1821,) should remain free, and be admitted to the same rights and privileges as the other classes of Peruvian citizens. This act of humanity and justice had previously been performed by all the other free states of South America— a transaction which sheds a redeeming lustre over many more questionable occurrences during their struggle for independence.

" The difficulties of the protector's situation were now beginning rapidly to increase, and to assume a very formidable appearance. The power which he had assumed was soon felt to be too weighty for the exercise of one individual: the working of the mines, commerce, and agriculture, were at a stand; and money and provisions were no longer to be obtained in sufficient quantities for his large army, which was crowded into the narrow limits of Lima and its immediate environs. The royalist army was also increasing in spirits and in strength, and extending its reconquests to the very skirts of the capital. In the beginning of 1822, it amounted to fifteen thousand men, in three divisions; one under General Canterac in Jauja, a second under Ramires in Arequipa, and the third under the Ex-Viceroy La Serna in Cuzco, where the latter had for the present established the seat of his government. Thus, superior both in numbers and in discipline, and in quiet possession of almost the whole country, these three commanders waited only a favourable opportunity to return and possess themselves of Lima.

" In this critical posture of affairs, San Martin adopted the expedient of negociating a loan in England, and caused, for that purpose, a number of proposals to be circulated through the medium of his agents in London. The terms which these held out were not deemed too unsatisfactory by some of the more speculative of British capitalists, so that but a short while served to fill up the list of subscribers. This, however, was but a temporary measure. The causes of his embarrassment lay deeper than in the mere financial wants of government; and perceiving all other resources to be unavailing, he at last determined to assemble a congress, but upon such a footing that it might prop and sanction rather than share his real power. For this purpose he reserved to himself the right of nominating deputies for those provinces which, being held in check by the enemy, were not likely to engage in the election; by which means a majority would be secured, upon whose support he could calculate for the furtherance of his measures. The 1st of May, 1822, was appointed for the opening of this legislative assembly, although, from intervening causes, it was ultimately postponed until the month of September following. But in the mean time, to give to his administration an appearance of popularity, the protector united to himself in the government a few of the leading men of his party, the principal of whom was the Marquis of Torre Tagle; yet as the spirit of his administration still remained unchanged, this step tended only in a small degree to allay the general discontent. San Martin was now regarded with suspicion by the great majority of the people, and, being well aware of this feeling, he exercised less caution in his public measures, than he might otherwise have been inclined to do.

" The poor Spaniards, who, according to his last proclamation, had remained in the country and sworn to the maintenance of its freedom, had the misfortune about this time again to experience his severity. From some unknown cause, most probably from jealousy, a tribunal of purification was erected, for the purpose of examining into the past conduct of those unhappy individuals, and as it was impossible that men who were bound by a thousand ties to the old government, could appear immaculate in the eyes of the new, the proceedings which took place in consequence were productive of much misery, but of little benefit. Among other restrictions imposed upon those victims of public contempt and hatred, it was ordered that no Spaniard should leave his house after the hour of sunset, under pain of having his property confiscated, and himself banished from the country; and some time afterwards, another decree followed the above, awarding a like penalty to such Spaniards as should wear a cloak in the streets, and also to any two who should be found engaged in private conversation. In this latter decree, the punishment of confiscation and exile was changed to that of death for the offence of appearing after sunset; and death and confiscation of property was ordained to all who should be known to retain in their houses any description of weapons, other than the knives used at their tables. From these provisions, the alarm and insecurity which prevailed in the capital may easily be conceived.

" Another cause of confusion and discontent was, that the regulations which had lately been made by the protector in regard to trade and commerce, had fallen very far short of the end proposed, for, by their differing only in a few instances from the late colonial system of commercial policy, they had increased rather than relieved the embarrassment of the country. The ports of Callao and Huanchaco were alone declared free; the coasting trade was permitted only in vessels belonging to the state, and limited to the ports of Paita, Huacho, and Pisco; while the embargo laid upon foreign vessels was such, that it amounted almost to a total interdict. Thus the hands of the industrious were bound up, and hope, the great motive to action, in a manner extinguished. It has been reserved for still more recent legislators to discover and act upon the important truth, that the only path to commercial prosperity is that of free competition.*

" With regard to foreigners resident in the country, a mode of legislation was adopted peculiar to the emergency of the times. They were invested with the rights of citizenship, declared amenable to the laws—and subjected, like native citizens, to all contributions which might be levied by government, as well as to the bearing of arms for the maintenance of public tranquillity. In one particular only, a slight provision was made in their favour—that they should not be called upon to march against the public

---

* The reader will scarcely require to be told, that the ministers of Great Britain—Liverpool, Canning, Huskisson, and Robinson—are here alluded to, whose names, like the snowball so frequently used as a simile by writers when speaking of fame, must still increase in popularity the further they advance into posterity, and the more ;their enlightened principles of policy are understood.

enemy. But the most arbitrary clause of the decree was, that they should no longer enjoy the privilege of complaining to, and claiming the protection of, the commanders of vessels belonging to their several nations;—a singular breach of that international law respecting subject and state, which is attended to even in the most despotic of governments. It is chiefly for the purpose of standing as a protector between the governments of foreign countries, and the subjects of their own, who may be engaged in commerce, that consuls are established abroad; and the principle involved in this regulation is held so sacred, that its infringement never fails to call down the vengeance of the offended upon the offending power. But as, previous to the recognition of the South American republics, no such officers could be established, the governments, whose subjects ventured within their territories, generally ordered a naval force upon that service; and had not then those governments by whom this policy was pursued, a right to consider themselves insulted when their officers were thus deprived of the liberty of interference?

" About the same time that these various decrees were issued by the protector, the liberty of the press was established; every citizen being allowed the right of freely publishing his opinions, uncontrolled by any act of censorship on the part of government. A conservatory junta was, however, instituted, to guard against all publications abusive of religion, or pernicious to morality, and also against all such as tended to disturb public tranquillity, or to injure the honour of private citizens; the penalty in such cases to be proposed and inflicted by the junta. How public writers were to avoid giving offence upon one or other of those points, in the eyes of a body of men who were permitted the utmost latitude of construction, might have formed a question of too much subtlety for common sense to determine. That tyranny is of all others the most insufferable, which makes a show of conferring some privilege, but at the same time accompanies it by so many restrictions, as amount to an absolute prohibition of its use. Imprisonment is rendered tenfold severe when our situation leads us to contrast it with the freedom of the world around us; and in like manner is our sense of oppression heightened, by being insulted with the empty show of liberality.

" Meanwhile an act of state policy had been performed, which has in all countries been found of much importance in conciliating those whose friendship or enmity depend upon trifles. This was the formation of a public institute entitled the Order of the Sun, for the purpose of rewarding civil and military merit, and composed of three different classes—Founders, Well-deservers, and Associates or Fellows. The badge to be worn by the first class was a white ribbon passing from the right shoulder to the left side, with two gold tassels and a gold medallion of the Order; the wearer to be addressed by the title of Honourable Lordship. That of the second was a gold medal, attached to a white ribbon suspended from the neck; the wearer to enjoy the title of Lordship. The third class was distinguished by a silver medal suspended from the left breast; no title being attached to the dignity of its wearer. The medals, which were afterwards changed to golden suns, bore each the arms of the state, with appropriate inscriptions; a pension was conferred upon the several members, all of whom, upon their admission, were sworn to defend the liberties of Peru, to maintain public order, to further the general welfare of America, and to devote to those ends both their lives and their properties, San Martin was nominated President of the Order, which at its first institution included within its list of members no fewer than two hundred and sixty-six individuals. Females were also declared eligible to the dignity, and of that sex one hundred and twelve additional members were added.

" All measures, however, were of no avail in effecting the object desired. The tide of popularity had turned against the protector, and no partial acts of this nature were sufficient to change its course. The disaffection of the citizens was now also spread to the army, and desertion, as a natural consequence, was every day diminishing its numbers. A feeling of jealousy had likewise been excited, owing to the partial conduct of the protector, between the Chilian and Puruvian soldiers; the latter of whom had been preferred in the service to the prejudice of the former, who regarded themselves as entitled to superior consideration, in consequence of having fought for Peru in the more magnanimous character of deliverers. This, combined with other subjects of complaint, had caused several officers to quit the service, and return to Chile; while the common soldiers, actuated by a similar feeling, chose to remedy and partly to avenge themselves by desertion. Partial evils have always a tendency to become general in their effects, and the protector, alarmed at the spread of this spirit throughout the army, issued strict orders for checking its tendency by severely punishing the offenders. To render their apprehension more certain, it was decreed that all persons who should be known to harbour or protect a deserter, were in the first instance to suffer a general confiscation of their property, and, should the offence be repeated, to be condemned to perpetual exile. For this purpose, also. slaves were invited to inform against their masters, with a promise of manumission upon the truth of their reports being proved.

" During this troublesome period, the only military operation of importance which took place, was the march of a division of the Liberating Army, amounting to two thousand men, under the command of General Don Domingo Tristan, a native of Arequipa, to possess itself of, or rather to retain, the valleys of Pisco and Ica, by which a communication might be kept up with the provinces of Upper Peru, and the rich districts along the coast protected from the incursions of the enemy. A part of the royalist army, under the command of Generals Canterac and Caratala, at that time held possession of Huamanga and the parts bordering on the position of Tristan; and having resolved to dislodge him, and reduce that district to its former obedience, they advanced on the night of the 7th of April, and surrounded his division without being resisted, or even perceived. Tristan, having thus allowed himself to be taken by surprise, was incapable of offering much resistance. By daybreak the whole of his troops, arms, ammunition, and baggage, together with a hundred thousand dollars, were in the hands of the enemy. He himself, with his staff, and a few of his officers, escaped to bear the tidings to Lima.

" Nothing could have been more unfortunate for the protector at so critical a moment, than the news of this defeat. His was truly an empire of opinion—an empire pleasant to contemplate in theory, but totally unsuited to the disjointed and untoward circumstances of real life. So many such circumstances had of late been occurring, that the exercise of an agent very different from that of opinion, had been rendered necessary to the maintenance of tranquillity ; and now that the charm of the army's invincibility was broken, the last prop of the protector's power might be said to be undermined. The news spread a general gloom over Lima ; and what rendered the disaster still more disagreeable was, that it led to fresh acts of oppression towards the already too much persecuted Spaniards. On the night of the 4th of May, the houses of those unfortunate individuals were broken into by parties of soldiers despatched for the purpose, and the inmates, without distinction of rank or age, were dragged from their beds and driven down to Callao, where they were placed on board a vessel then lying in the harbour. Clergymen, military officers—in short, all classes of Spaniards in the city, shared in common this act of unnecessary rigour. The greater number were not even allowed time to dress themselves ; several were hurried off almost naked, and all were forced to travel upon foot from the city to the shore. After being placed on board, they were left during two days without provisions, and deprived of all communication with their wives and families, who crowded round the vessel in boats, and implored, with unavailing tears, to be allowed the consolation of a last interview. On the first night of their confinement, two aged gentlemen perished from want of clothing and of food. Passports were at length offered them for sale, with liberty to embark in neutral vessels, in order to leave the country ; while those who were unable in this manner to purchase their freedom, were transported to Chile. Upon what grounds— excepting a suspicion that these people could not regard with feelings of perfect cordiality the new government—such proceedings were justified, remains yet to be explained.

" Previous to the defeat of Tristan, San Martin had entered into correspondence with with the Liberator Bolivar, with a view to procure from Colombia a reinforcement of troops for the prosecution of the war in Peru, and had also, for that purpose, solicited a private interview with the liberator at Guayaquil. To this Bolivar assented, and San Martin, having delegated the supreme authority to the Marquis of Torre Tagle, and appointed General Alvarado commander-in-chief of the army in his absence, departed for the place of conference about the end of June, 1822.

" The two chiefs met according to appointment at Guayaquil, and remained together for a few days, but of their conference no particulars were suffered to transpire. The result alone was explained to the people of Peru. by the return of San Martin without having effected any of the objects of his visit.

" During his absence, Lima had been the scene of much popular commotion. His secretary, or prime minister, Monteagudo, who had been appointed to the office about a year previous, had from the first been an object of detestation among all classes in Peru. The late arbitrary decrees and acts of cruelty enforced and sanctioned by the protector, were all traced to his contrivance and advice as to their first causes; and in this opinion the citizens were fully confirmed by the intolerable conduct of Monteagudo immediately upon the departure of San Martin for Guayaquil. The secretary then entirely threw off the mask, and, using as his agent the supreme delegate Torre Tagle, who either wanted firmness or authority to control his actions, he confiscated the property and exiled the persons of the citizens upon the most trivial pretences, and, by his open cabals, and through the agency of his spies, whom he had distributed through every part of the city, he in a few days, according to the language used in describing this period, converted Lima into a ' mansion of the most afflicting torments.' The inhabitants at last, goaded to desperation, assembled in a body, and demanded vengeance upon their oppressor. A meeting of the corporation was called, to examine into his conduct; at whose recommendation, the council of state, headed by the supreme delegate, deprived Monteagudo of his office, and placed him under an arrest. A committee of the council of state was to have been appointed for bringing him to trial; but so violent was the resentment of the people, and so great was their fear lest his influence with the Marquis of Torre Tagle should save him from punishment, that the corporation, to avert farther tumult, prevailed upon the council to convey him secretly on board a vessel, and decree his perpetual banishment from the country. Monteagudo was exiled accordingly, and the people dispersed in the quiet enjoyment of their triumph.[*]

" Immediately after the termination of this affair, San Martin arrived in the harbour of Callao. Astonished at the sudden proscription of his secretary, and afraid lest the condition of the capital might be even more dangerous than report had represented, he judged it most safe to remain on board, until fully assured of the fidelity of the army. He then ventured on shore, and proceeded to Lima, where, upon his arrival, he expressed in strong terms his displeasure at the proceedings against Monteagudo, and threatened to recall and reinstate him in office. But perceiving that the respect and awe which he formerly inspired, had in a great measure subsided, and not daring to push matters to an extremity, he suffered the decree of the council to remain in force, and, leaving the Marquis of Torre Tagle still to administer the affairs of government, he retired to his country residence near Callao.

" Orders had previously been issued for the convocation of the congress; and upon the 20th of September, 1822, the deputies from the various provinces assembled accordingly. An individual of their body, named Xavier de Luna Pizarro, was elected president, and after the necessary forms of instalment were gone through, a vote of thanks was unanimously passed, and

[*] In 1825, Monteagudo ventured again to appear in Lima, under the protection of Bolivar, by whom he expected to be reinstated in the ministry. But the recollection of his former crimes was still fresh in the minds of the citizens, and on the night of the 28th of February, some daring avenger of his country's wrongs, terminated the career of this obnoxious individual by assassination.

forwarded to San Martin, expressive of the deep gratitude which, as the representatives of the Peruvian nation, they felt for his services, and honouring him with the title of author of their political existence, and first soldier of their liberty. A deputation of members was at the same time appointed to wait upon his excellency, and solicit his acceptance of the supreme command of the army; but this honour he declined, as being incompatible with that perfect independence which he knew to be the general wish of the people. ' I am resolved,' says he, in his answer to the president, and after expressing his gratitude for the honour intended him— ' I am resolved not to betray my own feelings, and the great interests of the nation. Permit me, therefore, to observe, that long and painful experience has induced me to say, that the distinguished rank to which your sovereignty has deigned to elevate me, so far from being useful to the nation, should I fill it, would only oppose your just designs, by alarming the jealousy of those who desire a positive liberty; it would divide the opinions of the people, and decrease the confidence which you alone ought to inspire in the absolute independence of your decisions. My presence, sire, in Peru, considering that power which I have left, and the force which I should possess, is inconsistent with the *morale* of the sovereign body, and with my own opinion ; because no forbearance on my own part would defend me from the shafts of malediction and calumny. Sire, I have fulfilled the sacred promise that I made to Peru ; I have seen her representatives assembled ; the force of the enemy does not menace the independence of a people determined to be free, and who possess the means of being so. A numerous army, under the direction of chiefs inured to war, is ready to march in a few days to terminate the contest for ever. Nothing remains but to offer to your sovereignty the expression of my most sincere gratitude, and the firm assurance, that if at any time the liberty of the Peruvians should be threatened, I will dispute the honour of accompanying them as a citizen, to defend their freedom on the field of battle.'

" San Martin had already adopted the resolution of retiring from the country ; and on the same day on which the above communication was delivered to Congress, the following farewell address to the people of Peru was published and put into circulation :—

" PERUVIANS !—I have witnessed the declaration of the independence of the states of Chile and Peru. I hold in my possession the standard which Pizarro brought to enslave the empire of the Incas, and I have ceased to be a public man ; thus I am more than rewarded for ten years spent in revolution and warfare. My promises to the countries in which I warred are fulfilled ; to make them independent, and leave to their will the election of their governments.

" The presence of a fortunate soldier, however disinterested he may'be, is dangerous to newly constituted states. I am also disgusted with hearing that I wish to make myself a sovereign. Nevertheless, I shall always be ready to make the last sacrifice for the liberty of the country—but in the capacity of a private individual, and *no other*.

" With respect to my public conduct, my compatriots (as is generally the case) will be divided in their opinions; their children will pronounce the true verdict.

" Peruvians ! I leave your national representation established: if you repose implicit confidence in it, you will triumph; if not, anarchy will swallow you up.

" May success preside over your destinies, and may they be crowned with felicity and peace !

" Pueblo-libre, September, 20 de 1820.

(Signed)   "SAN MARTIN."

" Having thus wholly resigned his power into the hands of the congress, San Martin prepared immediately for his departure. His exit from the territory which he had visited to emancipate, differed widely in splendour from his entrance. The former resembled a sun-rise in a clear sky; the latter, a sun-set amid clouds and storms. The protector of Peru embarked and departed like a private individual, amid silence which sprung from other causes than regret and affection, and landed at Valparaiso on the month of October, 1822. His sudden appearance excited much surprise in Chile, where no one had entertained the slightest suspicion of his abandoning, at so critical a juncture, the state of Peru. An escort shortly afterwards arrived, to conduct him to Santiago, in which city he remained until the latter part of December, when, owing to the unsettled state of the Chilian government at that period, he crossed the Andes, and once more took up his residence in the town of Mendoza.

" Such was the departure of San Martin; an event which will in all likelihood prove a lasting subject of inquiry among the speculative part of posterity. Yet that inquiry, however ingenious, will end as all such inquiries must, the premises of which are founded upon human character. That is a book which, like the oracles of the Sibyl, is susceptible of many interpretations; and while one writer assumes as a position founded on fact, that San Martin owed only to unavoidable misfortunes the questionable light in which his patriotism was eventually placed, another may with equal plausibility assert, that those misfortunes alone prevented him from thoroughly establishing his character as a tyrant. So much for decisions drawn from the secret motives of human conduct. When we reflect how much even our highest virtues are indebted for their operation, if not for their existence, to causes directly at variance with their nature—how often charity is the result of self-love, religion of superstitious terror, apparent liberality of a secret wish the more surely to accomplish by that mean some object of oppression;—in short, when we reflect how much all men are given to conceal their true motives until their tendency has become irresistible, we will be inclined to regard only the ulterior consequences of conduct as affording safe ground for final decisions respecting it.

" Yet, in the case of San Martin, we are not left entirely without other and more certain grounds of opinion. His public proceedings while in Peru, however involved and contradictory, furnish a clue by which we may, with considerable precision, trace the progress of his dereliction from that fair and manly system which he originally followed, to that chaos of arbitrary measures into which, as if by unavoidable destiny, he latterly was so deeply plunged as to be capable of extricating himself only by a precipitate retreat from the scene of confusion. It has been the misfortune of every public benefactor, to have his character vituperated and his actions misrepresented, by that portion of the community whose interests are identified with the abuses which he has tasked himself to reform—by those whose ignorance or prejudices prevent them from perceiving and entering into his extended views, and by those whose envy is excited by the presence and triumphs of superior merit.   Of such enemies San Martin found a host in Peru. Instead of a people unanimous in sentiment, he found himself in the midst of factions that were severally eager to profit by his services, yet slow to reward him with their gratitude. He also shortly discovered himself to be an object of secret aspersion, and the disgust which he consequently felt, and the contempt which he must necessarily have entertained for the national character, so much more degraded than that of the other free states of South America, might naturally inspire him with the idea, that it was only with a high hand that the regeneration of the country could be effected. He appears, accordingly, from that period to have acted upon the specious but false reasoning so common in such cases—that the ultimate object would justify the means which might be used to accomplish it; and had he proved successful, perhaps the world, as it has frequently done by others, might, by its applause, have borne him out in the truth of his opinion."

General San Martin met with but a cool reception in Chile; but on his way to Buenos Ayres he passed a few days with General O'Higgins, at his country seat, where he was received with every demonstration of friendship and respect.   The worthy director could do no more; for he also had to contend with various factions, who, as each obstacle to the independence of Chile had been removed, the freedom of Peru nearly established, and a loan of one million sterling contracted in London in order to consolidate the liberation of both—the supreme director of the republic of Chile became an object of envy : and he who had steered the vessel for nearly six years through a tempestuous sea, was, when she arrived in a tranquil haven, ungratefully dismissed from his well-earned dignity, by the crew whose lives and liberties he had preserved— " Oh incultum vulgus !"

Such had been the exertions and intrigues of the malcontents, that in the short space of three months, those champions of liberty, San Martin, O'Higgins, and Cochrane, had ceased to command: thus Chile and Lima became the prey of contending factions. The legislature of Lima, considering that they were indebted for the freedom of that department to the efforts of Generals San Martin and O'Higgins, invested the first with the title of Generalissimo of the Forces of Peru; the second, Captain General of Peru; and forwarded the following decrees to the general and admiral of the liberating expedition.

DECREE.

" The sovereign constituent congress has resolved that his excellency the Generalissimo of the forces of Peru, Don José de San Martin, be distinguished with the title of " Founder of the Liberty of Peru;" that he retain the privilege of wearing the "bicolor cordon," which was the insignia of the supreme chief of the state; that in every part of the territories of the nation be paid to him the same honours as to the executive power; that, on the conclusion of the war, a statue be raised, on the pedestal of which to be engraved an appropriate inscription; in the mean time, his bust to be placed in the national library; that he shall enjoy his former pay; and that a pension for life, in imitation of that to Washington, shall be granted, in 'conformity to the decision of the committee.

" Sept. 22d, 1822.   Signed, &c.

Vote of Thanks from the Peruvian Congress to Lord Cochrane.

" The sovereign constituent Congress of Peru, contemplating how much the liberty of Peru owes to the Right Honourable Lord Cochrane, by whose talents, valour, and constancy the Pacific has been freed from our most inveterate enemies, and the standard of liberty has been displayed on the coasts of Peru, resolves that the Junta of Government, in the name of the Peruvian nation, do present Lord Cochrane, admiral of the squadron of Chile, expressions of our most sincere gratitude for his achievements in favour of this country, once tyrannized over by powerful enemies, now the arbiter of its own fate. The Junta of Government, obeying this, will command its fulfilment, and order it to be printed, published, and circulated.

Sept. 27th, 1822.   Signed, &c.

A pension of 20,000 dollars per annum was decreed to General San Martin; one of the finest sugar estates in Peru, (Montalban,) settled on General O'Higgins; and the amount of 500,000 dollars (confiscated property) was distributed amongst twenty general and field officers; but those of the Chilian squadron, whose daring prowess had freed the Pacific, and enabled the Liberating army to enter and invade Peru, were not only excluded from being participators of the Peruvian bounty, but had the mortification of being denied the prize-money that was due to them; and on their return to port, were paid their arrears in notes issued by a *Spanish speculator,** or in tobacco, by which they had to suffer a considerable discount, or sell the latter at an enormous loss: such treatment, and other flagrant acts of injustice, from the ministers, who were personal enemies of Lord Cochrane, caused him, and a few of his brave followers, to abandon Chile in disgust, rather than suffer a repetition of such indignities, or embroil themselves with the malcontents, whose chief had forwarded the following invitation to the admiral, which I now publish with a few other documents, that will throw a considerable light upon the subject of the revolution by which General O'Higgins was deposed.

MY LORD,   Concepcion, December 18, 1822.

" The province under my command being tired of suffering the effects of a corrupted administration, that has reduced the republic to a state of greater degradation than it was suffering when it made the first struggle to obtain its liberty; and when by means of an illegitimately created convention, without the will of the inhabitants, (pueblos,) they have traced the plans of enslaving them, by constituting them to be the patrimony of ·an ambitious despot, and when, in order to insure him in command, they have trodden underfoot the 'imprescriptible' right of the citizens, exiling them in the most arbitrary manner from their native country.

" Nothing now remains for us, but heroically to resolve, that we will strive to place the fruit of eleven years of painful sacrifices in the way of salva-

* Don Antonio Arcos.

tion; to which effect, I have deposited in the hands of its legal representatives who are united in this city, the 'problematica,' authority, that I have hitherto exercised; but, notwithstanding my want of merit, and sincere renouncement, that constituent power has deigned to place upon my weak shoulders this enormous weight, by again depositing the civil and military command in my person; which the adjoining resolution, I have the honour of remitting, will explain to your lordship. God preserve your lordship many years.

(Signed)　　　　　" RAMON FREYRE."

I never could learn what kind of answer his lordship returned to General Freyre, but he issued the following wholesome advice to the Chilians, at his departure.

" CHILENOS! You have expelled from your country the enemies of independence; do not sully the glorious act, by encouraging discord, and promoting anarchy, that greatest of all evils; consult the dignity to which your heroism has raised you; and if you must take any steps to secure your national liberty, judge for yourselves; act with prudence, and be guided by reason and justice.

" It is now four years since the sacred cause of your independence called me to Chile: I assisted you to gain it; I have seen it accomplished; it only now remains for you to preserve it.

" I leave you for a time, in order not to involve myself in matters foreign to my duty, and, for reasons concerning which I now remain silent, that I may not encourage party spirit.

" Chilenos! you know that independence is purchased at the point of the bayonet; know also, that liberty is founded on good faith, and is supported by the laws of honour; and that those who infringe them, are your only enemies—among whom you will never find,

(Signed)　　　　　" COCHRANE."

The provinces of Concepcion and Coquimbo refused obedience to the supreme government, and formed of themselves their independent assembly or form of government, and with one accord began to raise troops, to depose General O'Higgins; and on the twenty-eighth of January, some of the inhabitants of the capital assembled in the 'Consulado,' to treat seriously about the deposition of the supreme chief of the republic of Chile, who was cited before them by a respectable deputation.

General O'Higgins at first thought of compelling the respect of the people, but finding that the minions, upon whom he had heaped honours with the greatest prodigality, had tampered with the opposite party; after taxing them with their treachery, and with his own hands tearing off the badge of distinction from the commandant of his body-guard, in the presence of his soldiers, he responded to the summons, rather than cause one drop of blood to be spilled, or suffer further insults, and in the presence of all assembled, he dictated the following abdication to his secretary.

" Firmly believing that during the present circumstances I have it in my power to contribute to the tranquillity of my country by retiring from the supreme command of the state, and having well deliberated on the subject, I have finally agreed with the inhabitants of Santiago, who are here met, and are the only body with whom I can at the present crisis treat, that I hereby abdicate the supreme direction of the republic of Chile, and consign the provisional exercise of my authority to a junta gubernativa, composed of the citizens Don Agustin Eyzaguirre, Don J. Miguel Infante, and Don Ferdinand Errazuris, because there is not a national representation at present, unto whom I could verify my abdication; which representation the said junta gubernativa must procure to unite, and form, with the greatest brevity, in consideration, that if the present doubts are not settled by the provinces, the junta will cease, and the inhabitants of the capital will deliberate, as to what steps it will be most convenient to take ; and, in order that they may know what are or will be their prerogatives and faculties, a regulation, stating this, must be made by the committee, that are proposed by the inhabitants, viz. Don Juan Egaña, Don Bernardo Vera, and Don Joaquin Campino.

" Print, publish, and circulate,

" Given in Santiago, January 23d, 1823.

" BERNARDO O'HIGGINS."

" This act of abdication was read to all present, and General O'Higgins proclaimed the newly elected government himself; he then divested himself of the tricoloured scarf, which is the distinctive badge of the supreme command of Chile, placed it in the hands of the junta, and gave them possession of the elevated charge to which they had been called; and having

F

received from each of them the customary oath, he added that of fidelity to them, which was also given by the chiefs of the garrison, and the principal inhabitants of Santiago. A document, of which the following is a copy, was circulated in the capital on the 6th of February.

"What name shall we give to the memorable occurrence of the twenty-third of January? It was a movement of liberty, exercised in a generous and worthy manner, resisted with valour, and accepted with heroism at last. The sons of Arauco never belie themselves, commit base actions, machinate in darkness, nor act by surprise; neither do they expect aught from criminal acts.

"The northern and southern provinces are in a state of independence, and in actual hostility; the inhabitants of Santiago, united with the municipal authorities, have consulted the decorum and risks of the "Patria," and being conscious of the necessity, of a new pact with the provinces, of a new administration, new ministry, and, lastly, a new national representation, worthy of the name, that will produce and insure civil liberty by proper institutions; the inhabitants know their power, but desire nought by violence; they wish that their "majestad" may be known to be as pure as their intentions. The supreme director, the first sword of America, the terror of the enemies of Arauco thought himself insulted, but he respected those he had defended, and who had raised him to the supreme authority; the inhabitants and the director enter at last into the arena, as if to fight a duel, (combate singular) which could only be witnessed amongst a generous and magnanimous people, a fight of reasoning who can paint or describe such a new and interesting scene? What vigour! what dignity! what energy! united with so much moderation!

"The foreigners who were present proclaimed it admirable, and to ourselves it seemed that the Chilians appeared greater on that day, than when they defeated and confounded their enemies; the scene soon changed its aspect, and was compacted into a union of brothers, who, in common, deliberated and adopted measures for the quietude and welfare of all. The inhabitants elected, and the director proclaimed, the junta, who have begun to exercise their power.

"General O'Higgins, restored to the career of his genius (genio) that destiny has assigned to him, may still give days of glory to the 'patria.' The trumpet of war still sounds at a distance, and calls him to victory."

General Freyre's note to the Ex'ma Junta.

"Valparaiso, February 6th 1823.

"S. S. of the Junta Gubernativa of the capital of Santiago.

"On my arrival at this port, with the army of the province of Concepcion under my command, which acts in concert with that of Coquimbo,

ECMO SEÑOR DON BERNARDO O'HIGGINS

SUPREMO DIRECTOR DE LA REPUBLICA

DE CHILE.

Fisher, Son & Cº, London & Paris.

I have found the ex-director, Don Bernardo O'Higgins, about to march to
Peru, with permission of this government. As this person has exercised
the supreme magistrature, and as all the inhabitants of the republic have a
right to demand a just (residencia) account of his proceedings from him,
I have subjected his person to a decorous arrest, and the same measures
ought to be adopted towards the ministers and public magistrates of the
late administration, in the other towns as well as in the capital, because
the representation of your government is confined to the capital, and is
not sufficiently qualified to determine upon these and other objects, that,
from their nature and importance, belong to the ' representacion general '
of the state, that ought soon to be established.

" On this account, and making V. S. S. responsible for any contrary act,
I hope you will take every necessary measure concerning the object mentioned.

" God preserve V. S. S. many years.

" RAMON FREYRE."

General O'Higgins, as well as his ministers, suffered,
for the space of five months, the strictest examination.
How far he was culpable, the following note will
explain :—

" Conservative Senate,   " Santiago, June 30th, 1823.
" To His Excellency the Supreme Director-General Don Ramon Freyre,
    " Ex'mo Señor,

" The reasons specified by the fiscal of the tribunal, " de residencia,'
are so powerful; the good sense of your Excellency, upon the public
convenience of acceding to the solicitude of the Captain - General Don
Bernardo O'Higgins, is so respectable; and so evident is the maxim, that
particular interests ought to be ceded to the general welfare, and all
private considerations as usually occur in such cases, ought to be waived;
that the senate do not hesitate one moment in assuring your Excellency,
they find no objection against acceding to the solicitude of the general
but have taken into consideration, that the name of O'Higgins is blended
with the glories of this country, and is to be found in all the pages of our
glorious struggles. The general has, for a very long period, represented the
nation; therefore the senate cannot do less than charge your Excellency,
that the permission which is to be granted for him to leave this country, be
worded in the most honourable terms, that it may serve as a testimo-
nial of the high estimation and consideration of this country towards him,
when he arrives amongst those to whom he will be a stranger : the senate
proffer to your Excellency the votes of their highest esteem.

" AGUSTIN EYZAGUIRRE, President,

(It is a true copy.)   " CAMILO HENRIQUES,"
   " HENRIQUES."

F 2

On the receipt of this document, the supreme director remitted the following passport to General O'Higgins.

"To His Excellency, Captain-General of the Armies of this Republic, Don Bernardo O'Higgins.

"Ex'mo Señor,

"Only the repeated requests of your excellency, have been able to tear from me the permission I concede you to leave the country in which you are numbered amongst its distinguished sons, and whose glories are so closely entwined "estrechamente enlazados" with the name of O'Higgins; that the most brilliant pages of the history of Chile are monuments consecrated to the memory of your Excellency: in whatever part your Excellency may reside, you must hold the government of this country in your most ardent request. I urge also that your Excellency will never forget the interests of your dear country, and the consideration that your fellow-citizens deserve.

"I should be neglectful in my duty, which your Excellency knows how to appreciate, if I did not add the two following conditions: first, I circumscribe your leave to only the term of two years; second, your Excellency will advise the government continually in what part you reside.

"This same note will serve as a sufficient passport, and, at the same time, a recommendation to all the authorities of the republic, and the envoys, and other public officers, you may meet in foreign countries, in order that they may render all the attention due to your character, as well as the consideration of this government.

"God preserve V. E. many years.

"RAMON FREYRE."

On the thirteenth of July, His Majesty's ship Fly, Captain Phipps, arrived from England. I went on board her with Colonels Arriagada and Martines; she was a fine corvette; the commander and officers treated us in a hospitable manner, and on returning to the shore, whilst at dinner, I informed the general what a fine ship she was, &c. stating that, had he intended to go to Peru, a favourable opportunity offered; (I had previously understood that the general's intention was to leave for Europe:) he paid a marked attention to what I was relating, and as soon as we arose from table, his sister Doña Rosita, called me aside, and informed me, "that the general

wished to go to Peru." The general overheard her, and
began to chide her, on which I requested him to inform me,
if such was really his desire : he told me it was, but that
he intended to sail in an English merchant-vessel,
commanded by a Captain Wilson, with whom he had
made a partial agreement; I then went out, and was
about to mount my horse, when the general requested I
would not mention the subject to any of his countrymen.
I then begged leave to speak to Captain Phipps, requesting, at the same time, that he would lend me his passport,
to show that he could leave, on which the general gave
it to me, as well as instructions how to act in case he
could go down in the Fly. I went on board, and Captain
Phipps received my intimations in the most favourable
manner, but was afraid that, on account of the vessel
having to sail the next day, there would not be sufficient
time for the necessary preparation ; " but," said he, " let
us see Captain Maclean, who is senior, and then I can
tell how to act." We went on board his majesty's ship,
Blossom, and found Captain Maclean on the point of
leaving for Santiago ; and on being referred to, he, in the
most obliging manner, gave Captain Phipps leave to
remain twenty-four hours longer, that he might be
enabled to serve so distinguished a personage. We then
went to the Governor-General, Zenteno, who thanked
the captain for his kindness, and then accompanied him
to the general, to offer his services.

The general and family were overjoyed at having such
a favourable opportunity, and, after returning their sin-
cerest thanks to Captain Phipps, they informed him that
he would not be detained longer than the next day, and
at the time appointed I had the honour of conducting
General O'Higgins and his family to the port, where

Lieutenant Wynn waited upon them, to take them on board in one of the ship's boats, which was decorated in a handsome manner. We embarked at the custom-house; there were numbers assembled, who took leave of the general, and I had the honour of being the only one that accompanied them in the boat belonging to the Chilian service; the governor, and Don Felippe, Santiago del Solar, Colonel Arriagada, and Lieutenant-Colonel Martines, went off in other boats. Captain Phipps wished to honour the general by a salute; but on his seeing the preparations, he begged them to defer it.

I remained on board until the vessel left the port, and, previously to my taking leave, the general made me a present of a sword, a brace of pistols, his saddles, and other accoutrements: he also gave me a letter to his excellency the supreme director, as well as one of recommendation, besides a number of notes and cards to his friends in the capital, whither I went soon after my landing; next morning I waited on his excellency, who seemed surprised at the general having left for Peru. I also gave him the following letter of recommendation, and, " I believe, in an improper moment."

" Valparaiso, July 15th, 1823.
" E'xmo Sr. Don RAMON FREYRE,

" Respected Friend,

" Captain Don Thomas Sutcliffe, the bearer of this, is an officer worthy of your consideration; he is perfectly instructed in his profession, which is accredited by his having served in many campaigns in different parts of the world. He has also suffered a few years for the cause of freedom, (liberty.)

" These considerations have impelled me to recommend him to you, because I am sure he will be worthy of those honours you are accustomed to bestow on such as merit them.

" I hope you will continue to enjoy good health, and command your invariable friend,   " BERNARDO O'HIGGINS."

CHAP. III.

SHORTLY after General Freyre was elected to the supreme command, he entered into a treaty, by means of plenipotentaries, with the government of Peru; in which it was stipulated, that Chile should assist that republic to overcome the unexpected difficulties in which they were involved, in consequence of the recent successes of the Spaniards. An expedition was formed, composed of two battalions of infantry, a corps of cavalry, and the skeletons of two more battalions, and Colonel Don Jose Maria Benevente was named commandante-general.

As there was a want of military stores, instead of being sent, as I had been promised, to take the command of the general's escort, I was directed to hasten to Valparaiso, to await the orders of the government; and having remained there a few days, I embarked on board the brig Colon, with despatches to Peru. There were several passengers on board, and, after a pleasant voyage of twelve days, we made the island of San Lorenzo, and at eight P.M. on the seventh of September anchored at Callao. I passed the night on board His Majesty's ship Aurora, Captain Prescot, who greatly excited my surprise by informing me that General Don Simon Bolivar, and a division of the Columbian army, was in Lima. I landed early in the morning, and the governor of Callao, Colonel

Valdivieso, provided me with horses: as soon as I reached Lima, I went to the residence of Captain General Don Bernardo O'Higgins, who expressed much pleasure at seeing me, as well as at hearing from his friends in Chile, several of whom had sent letters to him.

I had scarcely been half an hour in the city, before an aide-de-camp of General Bolivar came in quest of me; but as my despatches were addressed to the president of Peru, I waited on that personage first: he had scarcely perused the correspondence, when another aide-de-camp of the Libertador, (for so General Bolivar was called,) came, and demanded the letters, &c. which I had brought. The president, Don Bernardo Torre Tagle, gave them to him, telling him to inform the general, that it was a most singular demand of the Chilian government, concluding with " ahi va este pastel" (here, take this nonsense)—he needed not to have made use of this expression, for so soon as General Bolivar had read the documents, he was so enraged, that he declared if it were not, that the step would expose the cause he was serving to the ridicule of our enemies, he would have the correspondence published.

The " Libertador" recognized me, and inquired why I had left the Columbian service; I informed his excellency that (according to the account I had received in England, from Don Francisco Zea, the Columbian envoy), all those who had joined General Mac Gregor after the retreat from Santa Magarita, or followed him to Florida or Porto Bello, had been cashiered, and that I was considered one of that class, although I had been captured previously to my getting to Amelia island, and sent to Havannah, where I remained until 1821.

The general urged me to return to his army, and

made me very liberal offers; but having joined the
Chilian service, though in an inferior grade, I begged to
be excused from changing again.

General O'Higgins informed me the next day, that
the despatches which I had brought, announced to
government that the expedition was nearly ready to
embark, but that it would be necessary to forward a
quantity of warlike stores to Arica, which could not be
procured in Chile; this accounts for the displeasure which
the Libertador expressed when he read them.

I had to pay four ounces of gold for my passage, as
well as fifty dollars for my horse; therefore, as the army
was much in arrears, and badly rationed, I should have
had to suffer many inconveniences and privations, but
fortunately General O'Higgins made me his guest; he
was highly respected, and was visited by the principal
inhabitants of Lima, as well as the chiefs of the Peruvian,
Buenos Ayrean, and Columbian armies. General Bolivar
was very affable at these tertullias, and often urged me to
return to the Columbian service; but as I preferred the
character of the Chilians, I declined his offers: notwithstanding which, he treated me with the utmost cordiality
and friendship, and, as an acknowledgment of my former
services, he recommended me to General Guido and
others.

I will now narrate the lamentable occurrences that
caused the patriots to solicit the aid of General Bolivar, in
order that what had been gained at the cost of such immense sacrifices might not be wrested from them by the
Spaniards, or, what was still worse, a few denaturalized
Americans, who were still devoted to their cause.

The Junta Gubernativa, that ruled Lima after the
abdication of General San Martin, only remained in

office five months and a few days, for on the 26th of Feb.,
1823, they were deposed by General Santa Cruz, who
headed a military movement, and obliged the sovereign
congress to elect Don Jose de la Riva Aguera president
of Peru. As the junta had been acused of apathy, in-
decision, and disloyalty, the new administration were
determined to act with energy, and at first gave general
satisfaction, so as to establish the credit of the government, and obtain the co-operation of the native and foreign
merchants, and negociate a loan in England. General
Santa Cruz was appointed commander-in-chief of the
Peruvian army, and sailed with an expedition of about
5000 men to the south of Peru, in order to draw the attention of the Spaniards from the capital; notwithstanding
which, the Spanish army of 9000 men, under General
Cantarac, invaded Lima, and invested the fortresses of
Callao. All the exertions and sacrifices of Chile and
Buenos Ayres, towards liberating Peru would have
availed little, had not that champion of liberty, General
Bolivar, been at hand, and who, foreseeing that the Spani-
ards were gaining ground in Peru, generously sent a
division of his army, with one of his best generals,
(Sucre), and who arrived in time to secure the fortress of
Callao.

General Bolivar had just sealed the independence of
Colombia, at the base of " El Chimborazo," for the last
division of the Spaniards were defeated, captured, or
killed, on the 24th of May, 1822, at Pichincha, and in
which affair a division of Peruvians, under Colonel Santa
Cruz, and Buenos Ayreans, under Colonel Lavalle, had
highly distinguished themselves.

On the approach of General Canterac, the president,
sovereign congress, and other employées, as well as

such as were addicted to the patriot cause, fled to Callao, on the 17th and 18th of June, after having publicly appointed General Sucre to the chief command of the troops, who took up a position outside of the castles; he had about 4000 Colombian and Buenos Ayrean troops, and 1000 Peruvians, mostly militia, and with which he engaged the Spaniards on the 20th, who advanced within gun-shot of the castles, but retreated to their position, after having suffered considerable loss.

On the 22nd General Sucre was invested with the supreme command by the congress, who had deposed El San Rivaguero, who left for Truxillo.

General Canterac, finding that nothing could be gained by beseiging Callao, levied heavy contributions on the Limanians; and after having committed a few absurdities, that served to depreciate the Spanish cause, he retired to the interior, and was followed by a division of Buenos Ayreans under General Martiner; and 3000 Colombians and Chilians were sent to co-operate with General Santa Cruz. General Sucre delegated the supreme power to the Marques de Torre Tagle, and after having appointed General Guido to be governor of Lima, he marched to join the last division, and act under the orders of the Peruvian commander-in-chief.

A revolution broke out in Truxillo, whither the ex-president Rivaguera had retired, for the congress had resumed their sessions there, and authorized him to levy troops, &c. &c. However, they had soon to repent their having restored the president, for no sooner had he organized a respectable force, than he dissolved the congress, and exiled many of its members.

Such was the state of affairs when General Bolivar's opportune arrival in Lima, on the 1st of September,

1823, dispelled the cloud that threatened the destinies of Peru, he was invested with the supreme authority; but El Marques de Torre Tagle still retained, although in a manner curtailed the nomination of employées and detail of the government.

General O'Higgins very kindly took me with him to repay visits, and to private parties, which gave me an excellent opportunity of being introduced to many of the first families in Lima; and, as far as I could observe, their manner and habits, &c. were far superior to what I had been led to expect; from what I had read and heard repecting the Limanians, I confess I had imbibed no small stock of prejudice. This, however, wore away as I became better acquainted with them; and, with the exception of a few peculiarities, such as the "saya," and "manta," "capa," and "sombrero;" " segar," and mode of riding on horseback, I found them the identical people I had met with in all the Spanish colonies I had hitherto visited; and I am confident, that, had the ladies of Lima the benefit of professional teachers, they have talent and vivacity enough, combined with a proper education, to compete with many of our European belles. The multitude of works that have been published in Europe during the grandeur and decadence of this once opulent metropolis, must have given such as have perused them a strange idea of its inhabitants; but many of these authors have only portrayed the characters of the black sambo, mulatto, and mixed population; in their description of the manners and customs of the Limanians, they have only "observed the dark side of the shield,"and forgotten that there are good and bad in London, Paris, and Madrid. Why not such in Lima?

In January we received information of the defeat of

COSTUMES OF NIMES.

Fisher, Son & Co. London & Paris

Fairland lith

General Santa Cruz, in Upper Peru; the division of General Sucre, Miller, and Pinto was also taken by surprise, at Arequipa; but they fought their way to the coast, and embarked for Callao: the schooner Montezuma, in which General Pinto embarked, fell in with the convoy that were conducting Colonel Benevente's division from Arica, whence they had been obliged to embark, after destroying their horses, (I lost two :) after a short conference, it was determined that the troops should return to Chile, the infantry to Coquimbo, and the cavalry to Valparaiso: the Colonels Aldunate and Sancher, who were at a distance, sailed to Callao, which was the rendezvous. On this occasion General Pinto had a narrow escape, a Spanish privateer, commanded by a daring Italian, " Martelini," engaged the Montezuma, but the intrepid Captain Wynter and her crew, mostly English, defended her with so much valour and success, as to oblige the privateer, a vessel of superior force, to sheer off, with the loss of many killed and wounded.

The infantry were thirty-nine days before they arrived at Coquimbo, but they who went to Valparaiso in a British ship, the Sesostris, made a good passage of twenty days, and did not suffer so much as their comrades.

Colonels Aldunato and Sancher disembarked their troops, part of which were quartered in the castle of Callao, and the rest in Bella Vista.

The squadron of cavalry to which I expected to have been commandant, arrived under the command of Major Latus, a Chileno, who held a commission in the Buenos Ayrean service; there were also two other captains who held commissions in the Buenos Ayrean service; Captain C. C. Wood, of the engineers, (an Englishman,) also arrived, and acquainted me that General Pinto had placed

Major Latus in command, in consequence of Lieut.-Col. Castañeda, an old Spaniard, who was the acting commandant, having been taken prisoner in Arequipa, therefore nothing could be done until I saw General Pinto; and being out of favour with some of the leading politicians in Chile, on account of the little service I had rendered to General O'Higgins, I visited the major and officers of the corps of cavalry, as one appertaining to the Chilian army, and passed muster with them as such, until Colonel Sancher embarked with them for Chile, leaving me with Colonel Aldunato, to procure and prepare a transport to conduct the rest of the Chilian troops to Valparaiso. I hired a Liverpool brig, the Laurel, Capt. Gill, which was soon got ready, and provided with water, provisions, &c.

However, General Bolivar was in want of soldiers to quell a revolution which General Rivaguera had raised in the province of Truxillo, and to meet the Spanish army who were approaching to Lima; he, therefore, ordered our troops to be detained; but Colonel Sancher, who had his detachment on board, and was out of the reach of the batteries, thought proper to sail for Chile; this march exasperated the Libertador, who was compelled to send troops, and go in person to quell the insurrection; this revolt was soon put down by Colonel La Fuenta, a Peruvian, who acted in concert with others against General Rivaguera.

On account of the fear that was excited by the Spaniards, who were often reported to be within a day's march of the city, a party of cavalry went out to reconnoitre, and marched upwards of forty leagues, without seeing, or even hearing of the enemy, excepting a detachment of cavalry, that were at "El Tambo de Cañete" under the command of a Spanish colonel; and in order to dispel the fears of the Limenos they sent them intelligence every four hours until they were recalled.

The state of Lima being so disturbed, General O'Higgins removed to Callao, and took a passage for himself and his family in an English brig to Truxillo. The following is a copy of the passport given to him by the president "El Marques de Torre Tagle :"

Seal of Office].—" EL CUIDADANO, PRESIDENT OF THE REPUBLIC BY THE CONSTITUTION PERUANA.—His Excellency Captain General Don Bernard O'Higgins passes to " Huanchaco," with all his family, by sea, in what vessel soever he pleases ; or by land, if he should think it convenient.

" The eminent services that he has rendered to Peru, imperiously demand, not only that no embarrassment be placed in his way, but that he shall be assisted in the most advantageous manner with whatever shall be necessary.

" The Government will make all the authorities responsible for the smallest omission " en el particular" (with regard to this), for Peru ought highly to respect his excellency, and treat him with consideration, as a just recompense for the stupendous efforts he has made for its liberty.

" Given in Lima, December 23rd, 1825.   " TAGLE.

.   " By order of His Excellency,

" JUAN DE BERINDOOJA."

As soon as the general and his family were ready to embark, he gave me his passport, which I took to the Governor of Callao, and to the port admiral: the first offered a guard of honour, which the general declined in a suitable manner; the latter, General Vivero, called upon the general, and conducted us to his barge, which was decorated for the occasion; and whilst taking us off to the vessel, he expressed the highest satisfaction, in having the honour of conducting the son of his old friend Don Ambrosio O'Higgins, who had been the viceroy of Peru. Several of the principal Peruvians, as well as a number of foreigners went off, to take leave of the general.*

I need scarcely remark that I felt extremely pained to see the general and his family so much buffeted about, particularly now, when all their fortune was at stake, in consequence of the Spaniards having taken possession of their only dependence, " El Hacienda de Montalban," which the Peruvian government had given to the general, as a recompense for his having been the founder of their independence.

I learned from a letter that I received, that they had reached Truxillo in safety, and that the general had rendered important services to two of his countryman, Las S.S. Novoas, who had involved themselves by aiding General Rivaguera, notwithstanding his scanty means, and he supplied them with pecuniary aid, and successfully interceded with General Bolivar for their liberty.

I here insert a copy of a letter which General O'Higgins gave me when we separated, addressed to General Pinto.

> " Lima, December 24th, 1823.
>
> " My esteemed friend, Captain Don Thomas Sutcliffe, will be the bearer of this. He was sent here by Government, to continue his services in the army under your command. I recommend him to you, because I know he is a good officer, and will merit those marks of distinction which you always confer on patriots of his class.
>
> " I remain your unchanging friend,
>
> " BERNARDO O'HIGGINS."

---

* I then bid farewell also to a chief, who, if he had remained in command, or even continued in the republic, he had almost freed from the " Godos," I am confident would have secured to me at least a higher grade in the Chilian service after fifteen years' honourable connexion with it, than that which I held previously to my entering into it: however, I feel unmingled satisfaction, in having, from a sense of duty, made sacrifices, that I might serve those who were worthy, whilst others were mingling in the internal broils that have taken place in Chile, from no other motive but their own aggrandizement; it will be seen in the sequel, that every new government, at the beginning, has treated me as a partisan of the fallen one.

The Buenos Ayrean, with a few Peruvian and Columbian troops, remained with the detachment of Chilenos, to
garrison Lima and Callao; a part of the former showed
symptoms of dissatisfaction on account of want of pay,
(during the few months that I was in Peru, I never saw a
pay-day,) and they were unwisely sent to the castle of Callao; for General Bolivar had sent for the Columbian troops,
and about this time Colonel Valdivieso was superseded by
General Alvarado; besides Colonel Aldunate, on account
of the detention of his troops, stopped the preparations
for embarking, and paid Captain Gill, of the Laurel, for
the time his vessel had been delayed.

It was concluded that I must leave for Chile by the
Laurel, with despatches; and, on my departure, General
Guido gave me the letter, of which the subjoined is a
copy.

"Lima, February 3rd, 1824.
"S'or Don Francisco a Pinto,*
"My dear Friend,

"The captain of cavalry, Don Thomas Sutcliffe, returns to Chile, to
continue his services in the army to which he belongs. I have been informed that the services of this officer to the interests of America are distinguished, and that his conduct has not ill deserved (demerecido) our
confidence and protection; permit me to recommend him to you in the
strongest manner, because I am sure he will be worthy of your esteem—
'porque confio que correspondera al pais como un caballero patriota no
menos que á las atenciones que tenga la bondad de dispensarle.'

"Your commands will be attended to with satisfaction, at any distance
by your affectionate friend.
"TOMAS GUIDO."

On the fourth of February, I received my passport,
and went to Callao, along with Major Cavareda† who
was to have a passage to Chile with me; but the
brig not being ready until the next day, the major
returned to Lima, and I took up my quarters with
Colonel Morla, who commanded the Chilian artillery,

* Published in my Manifest. † Now minister of war.

G

and resided in the castle. I supped with the governor, who put his signature to my passport about midnight, and gave me several letters for Chile and Buenos Ayres; he was a native of the latter state: the colonel returned with me to his house, and I had scarcely retired to rest, and begun to doze, when I was roused by a confused noise, as if from a multitude of persons engaged in a warm dispute; I arose and went to the door, but a soldier, the servant of the colonel, told me not to go out, for there was a row, "bochince," amongst the Peruvian and Buenos Ayrean soldiers; this alarmed myself, the colonel and the rest of his family; he was immediately seized with a fit of trembling, being upwards of sixty years of age, and said, "Sotaliffe es asunto de los Godos, estamos, perdidos!" (Sutcliffe, it is an affair of the Spaniards, we are lost!)—I bade both him and his wife to be quiet; and in order to discover what was really the matter, I secreted my papers and money about my person, disguised myself in one of the soldiers' great coats and cap, and went out by the backway. I soon found that it was only a second edition of what had occurred in Lima: the soldiers had made General Alvarado, Colonel Estomba, and other chiefs, prisoners, and prevailed on all the detachments to join them: the Chilian artillery respected their colonel, and, on that account he was not imprisoned with the rest. Of this act of violence Sergeant Moyano, of the battalion No. 11, was the ringleader; he had formerly been an officer, but had been reduced to the ranks for misconduct.

Returning to the colonels, I found a corporal's-guard at the door; I then recollected that a number of English and American sailors had been arrested for smuggling, whom I had been endeavouring to release; at this moment the guard had left them, and they were standing in a group,

near to the place of their confinement: at first they did
not recognize me, but as soon as I made myself known,
I readily obtained from them a pair of trousers, a red
shirt, and pea-jacket, which, with a hairy cap, completely
disguised me, particularly after having my mustachoes
shaved off; my own uniform was packed up amongst
their clothes : here we remained without molestation until
eight o'clock, when all were set at liberty.

No sooner had I obtained my freedom than I went to
Captain Fisher's, who kept a tavern, and had been a
passenger with me in the Bruce; here I procured a fresh
disguise, and hastened to the mole, but found that no
shore-boats were allowed to take passengers off to the
shipping: whilst I was considering what to do, Captain
Brechard, a Frenchman, who commanded a Peruvian
corvette, La Santa Rosa, came down to the mole; his boat
was there, but one of the men was absent, upon whom he
began to bestow some hearty curses; seizing the opportunity, I stepped forward, and offered to take the man's
place, which was immediately accepted; I pulled the after-
oar, until we came alongside his vessel; he gave some orders
to an officer, and then took us alongside a French ship,
L'Amerique, of Havre, Captain Haselin, a friend of mine;
he had no sooner got on board, than I jumped off the
gangway upon the quarter-deck; he inquired what the
d—l I was after; I answered by thanking him for having
been the means of my escaping from shore ; the captain
shook hands with me, and welcomed me on board his
vessel, but Captain Brechard took the affair in a serious
light, and began to talk about compromises. I then
hailed the brig Laurel, and requested the mate to send
her boat for me, telling Captain Brechard, that if the flag
of the ship I was on board could not protect me, I would

leave her; he then desired me to give him my hand, and begged of me to keep the affair secret from the new rulers on shore; we then all sat down to breakfast; and Captain Haselin, his surgeon, and officers, heartily enjoyed the narrative of my escape.

The mutineers seized the port-admiral General Vivero, the harbour-master, and all the chiefs and officers they could find, and confined them in the castle.

I had a few articles of my equipage on board, but the greatest part of my property, amongst which was my horse, remained in the castle; I had sold the horse to a friend for 200 dollars, but Moyano appropriated it to his own use, which made my losses considerable; however, I regained my liberty, and therefore was pretty well satisfied.

The merchants in Callao suffered greatly, for they were not only deprived of all the articles of provision that were in their stores, but had also to pay a contribution to supply those in the castle with pay, &c. However, the disorders that were committed were not very great.

On the sixth, several detachments came from Lima to Bella Vista; the castles fired upon them, and killed many. General Martines, who commanded the Buenos Ayrean army, and other chiefs, came with a flag of truce; and the mutineers allowed General Correa, who was a favourite, to enter the castle; here the leaders, Moyano and Parejas, had a conference with him, which lasted above two hours. They demanded the arrears of pay due to them from the Peruvian government, and insisted on being sent back to Chile. The soldiers cheered General Correa as he returned to Lima.

No satisfactory answer being returned at the time appointed, and as there were not wanting agents, or spies, of the common enemy, it was strongly rumoured that if the terms were not complied with in twenty-four hours, the castle would be given up to Casa Riego, a Spanish chief, and other officers who were then in confinement in Casas Matas.

In the evening, the castle opened a heavy fire upon Bella Vista; and, fearful lest I should be made a prisoner, I went on board a Buenos Ayrean brig, the Protector, Captain Neeson.

About ten o'clock at night the batteries opened a heavy fire upon the shipping, on account of two vessels—the Mirror, an American ship, and a Chilian schooner, the Sea Serpent—having got under weigh, and made their escape: many of the ships had their hulls damaged, and the Santa Rosa received five shots in her bows; but no lives were lost.

On the seventh, I went on shore with an officer of H.M. ship Fly, and Captain Gill, who procured his vessel's papers from the harbour-office, for she had been cleared out before the mutiny took place. An old Spaniard, Gonzales, had got into office as harbour-master, and, although I was in disguise, he taxed me with being an insurgent; I produced my passport, in which I had fortunately been described as a civilian, on account of the Spanish privateers that were fitted out in Chiloe, and boldly presented it to him for his signature; he then appeared satisfied, and sanctioned my embarking.

Shortly after we got under-weigh the forts began to fire upon us; we, therefore, stood towards H. M. ship Fly; they still continued to fire; and as the shot might have endangered her, we stood straight out of the bay, and though we ran the gauntlet of the three castles, which expended a few dozen shots upon us, none of them hulled us. The harbour-master's boat at first gave chase to us, for which we

were prepared, having on board plenty of muskets and
ammunition, as well as a few deserters, who had taken
refuge with us. Although Captain Gill was advanced in
age, both he and his mate, who had formerly been master
of H. M. ship Blossom, seemed determined to act upon
the defensive. The brig belonged to Mr. Gladstone, of
Liverpool, and the captain, mate, and crew richly deserved
a recompense for saving her, for as she had been taken up
as a transport, she would eventually have been captured,
and perhaps condemned. After we got out of reach of the
batteries, we hove-to, got in our boats, and made all snug
on board,* and after a pleasant passage, we anchored, on
the 4th of March, in the bay of Valparaiso.

The moment I disembarked, I waited upon the Governor-General Zenteno, and acquainted him with the
events that had occurred: he was thunderstruck at the
intelligence, and informed me that General Freyre had
left for Concepcion, to take command of an expedition
against Chile, whither I sent all the particulars; I also
communicated the facts to General Miller, who was at
the baths of Colina. The governor did not pay my passage,
but told me to make out a memorial to government, that
they might authorize him to remunerate Captain Gill for

* What a providential escape! The fortress was given up to the
Spaniards on the 10th, and such of the patriots as were not shot, or transported to the island of Chucuito in the lake of Titicaca, had to suffer
the horrors of famine; for about 8,800 individuals, prisoners, refugees, and
garrison, perished in the most miserable manner, amongst whom were
the Marquis Torre Tagle, ex-president, with all his family, the Conde de
Lurigancho, ex-vice-president, and a number of wealthy Peruvians, who
had proved themselves traitors to the patriot cause. The Spanish governor,
General Rodil, withstood a blockade and siege for eighteen months, and,
after having consumed every horse, mule, ass, dog, cat, or anything that
could be made available to support life with, he made an honourable capitu-
lation on the 19th of February, 1826, and embarked on board H. M. S.
Briton, Captain Sir Murray Maxwell.

having brought me, and several articles, such as arms, provisions, &c., belonging to the Chilian detachment, that was to have sailed for Valparaiso.

Some of the "wiseacres" in Valparaiso would not give credit to my statement, because they said I was an " O'Higginista;" however, their own experience soon convinced them of what they were unwilling to admit upon my evidence; for many of them being merchants who traded to Peru, suffered severely.

My friend, Don Felippe Santiago del Solar, invited me to accompany him and his family to the capital, and offered to supply me with horses, &c. In this case I realized the truth of the proverb—"A friend in need is a friend indeed."

The information I brought was highly important, both to government and the merchants, as there was a number of vessels ready to sail for Callao and other parts; but, as no one seemed to credit my statements, I obtained no thanks for the exertions I had made. I may here remark, that government never remunerated Captain Gill, although I sent in a memorial, according to General Zenteno's directions.

I had expended all my money in Callao to assist Captain Gill to provide a supply of fowls, vegetables, and other necessaries, so that I had not a dollar in my pocket when I landed ; and, as the governor could not supply me with any of my arrears of pay, I was in an awkward predicament. However, Don Felippe Solar performed the needful, and I arrived in Santiago the next day, and presented myself before the acting supreme director, Don Fernando Errazuris, who was so much taken up, at the time, with the pope's nuncio, El S'or Mussi, who had lately arrived from Rome, that he could not attend to my relation respecting Callao,* On the day following, however, I had a short audience with his excellency, and the minister of war, and hacienda : they seemed so incredulous as to my story, " that my feelings became greatly excited, and I expressed myself in terms that did not at all please his excellency," in consequence of which I received orders the same day to march to Coquimbo. I called upon the minister of war, Don Diego Benavente, to whom I was unknown, and stated my inability to proceed for want of money, horses, and even uniform ; upon hearing which he ordered me to make out a memorial, and request two months' pay, which I received ; he also gave me a sword, which he had as a sample, together with an order to the intendente, General Lastra, to supply me with two horses and a mule—all which were attended to; to these he added a document authorizing me to demand others from the magistrates or governors to whom I should have occasion to apply during my march to Coquimbo.

General Miller, whom I had previously met in Lima, having come in from the baths of Colina, I called upon him ; he resided with General Blanco, the chief of the staff; he was very particular in his inquiries, and seemed satisfied that my account " was too true."

* The nuncio did not remain long in Chile, but government obtained from him a diminution of the feast-days, and abolition of other ceremonies. He gave license also to the friars to secularize themselves.

CHAP. IV.

I COMMENCED my march in the evening of the 15th. Don Felippe Solar gave me letters to his friends on the road, and to his relatives at Coquimbo; these enabled me to take up my first night's lodgings with one of them, who resided a short distance from Santiago; he treated me with great attention, and furnished me with a better horse, which was very acceptable to me, as those which I had were both " sore-backed," without ears, and scarcely able to carry me—(such were the " caballos del Estado.")

Passing the village of Colina, we halted at the foot of the mountains of Chacabuco. Here Generals O'Higgins and San Martin defeated the Spaniards. I strolled over the field of battle, where the bones of the slain " lay bleaching in the sun;" my soldier and the guide, who had both been in the battle, stopped to show me the places where the " godos " held out, when they were overcome. We passed the night at an " alojamiento;" a small " ramada" (shed) had been erected near to some shady trees; here two women, one of whom was a musician, sold eatables and " chicha." I ordered a " casuella," a stew of fowls and potatoes, which these road-side cooks understand how to prepare, and is the best article to be obtained on a march in this part of the country.

I listened until a late hour to the masculine voice of the songstress, who accompanied herself with a cracked guitar;

my men related to her some stories of the prowess of the
Porteños and Chilenos, and sung a few patriotic and
popular songs, until sleep overcame us all; the loqua-
cious party had taken "quantum sufficit" of "chicha
molla," (a kind of beer made from a berry not unlike the
juniper;) I believe they deemed this beverage to be highly
necessary, as a great deal was said next morning about
"animos" spirits, of which the Chilenos have strong
apprehensions.

At eight o'clock we crossed the Cuesta de Chacabuco,
and had a beautiful prospect down the vale of Curimon.
The roads over the mountains were almost impracticable,
and in many places two horses cannot pass each other,
which often creates disputes between travellers and muleteers.   There are many crosses erected on the road-side,
in memory of individuals who had been launched into
eternity; the sight of these alarms the solitary traveller:
but there are few instances of highway-robbery, especially
to the north of Santiago.

On descending the valley, the road to Mendoza
branches off to the right through Santa Rosa, which is
the nearest Chilian town to the pass of the Cordillera,
and is about three leagues distant therefrom; after
traversing about four leagues through this fertile valley,
I crossed the hanging-bridge of "El Rio de Aconcagua,"
and arrived at the city of San Felippe, about twenty-five
leagues from the capital: I called upon the governor,
Lieutenant-Colonel Perez, he received me coolly; and
although it was his dinner-hour, he told a soldier to
conduct me to my quarters, which was a room, full of
fleas, adjoining the (cabildo,) municipal-house: fortunately I met with Mr. Plumb, an Englishman, who
made amends for the governor's "hospitality," and who,
I was informed, had given me the "sobriquet of O'Hig-

ginista." I staid one day with Mr. Plumb, and examined the town; it was neat, laid out in squares, with several churches and convents, besides a handsome "alameda," ornamented with poplars; nearly all the buildings and walls were whitewashed,

The population of the valley exceeds 14,000; it is very fruitful, and has many fine haciendas, well stocked with animals, besides many rich mines, mostly of copper.

Next day I halted at Putaendo, six leagues distant, and remained there more than a week with my friend Don Tomas Vicuña; his family were with him, and I enjoyed their amiable society.

This is also a verdant valley, sustaining about 5,000 inhabitants; the river Chile passes through it, and waters a great number of haciendas; the Cordilleras are here infested by what the natives call leones, or puma, a species of animals about the size of a Newfoundland dog, and not much unlike to a huge mountain-cat; they play havoc amongst the cattle, but are seldom known to attack men, except when they are closely pursued; they are hunted by dogs trained for the purpose;—my friend Vicuña had several of their skins stuffed, and hung up about his outhouses, as trophies of the sports of his herdsmen; besides these animals, there is another species about this locality called guanacoes, and vicuñas, which in winter, when the snow drives them from the mountains in numbers, are hunted, and easily caught.

The gold and copper mines here are numerous, there are also excellent gold-washings, especially at the Cuesta de Minillas.—I left my friends on the 28th, and had not proceeded above four leagues before I was overtaken by two gentlemen, who informed me that a vessel, La Minerva de Valparaiso, had also escaped from Callao on the night of the same day that I left, and that I had

been sent for by government, on account of the captain
not being able to state the particulars. They also informed
me that the confirmation of the news I had brought had
excited a great sensation in the capital, and they advised
me to return to Santiago; but on account of the treatment
I had received, I thought proper to continue my route.—
I now changed the course I had intended to have taken,
for the romantic one nearer the Cordilleras: after passing the Cuesta de Garillas, I halted at the hacienda of
Alicagua, fifteen leagues from San Felippe, where
I remained two days, and partook of the hospitality of Don
Pedro Marcoleta. There are several valuable gold mines
in this district; from one called Lepilco, I was informed
that gold had been cut with the chisel: I here witnessed
for the first time the process of grinding and washing
gold ore.

On the 31st of March I left Alicagua, and passed
the Cuesta de Por Cura, which took me four hours; at
noon I arrived at Petorca, twelve leagues; this is a
mining district, and well populated; great quantities of
gold, of a superior quality, are procured from the numerous mines that are constantly at work here.

This is a small and neat town, and I have to acknowledge the urbanity with which I was treated by the
governor, El Sor Silva, who procured me several specimens of rich ore. I remained here two days, marched on,
and passed the village of Fierro Viego, two leagues; and
halted at Pedegua, seven leagues; next day I crossed the
Cuesta de las Palmas, over a very bad road; this mountain is studded on the west side with a countless number
of palm trees, producing small nuts, which, with the
syrup that is extracted from the trees, brings in a very considerable revenue to the proprietor; at three I halted at
the village of Tilama, eight leagues.

April 4th, I passed La Cuesta de Naranga, a very high mountain, and at three halted at the village of Pupido, a mining district, seven leagues; next day I passed the Cuesta de Pupido, which occupied me more than three hours in crossing. I saw a puma that had just been killed, it was a large one; the Guasos were skinning it; they informed me that it had been a great annoyance to them, and "muy lobo" very cunning and shy; at ten I passed the river Chuapa, and halted at the Hacienda del Peral-lillo, famous for its copper mines; I here saw upon the surface of the earth a small vein of pure copper; next morning I passed La Cuesta de los Cristales, and at twelve arrived at the town of Illapel, thirty-five leagues from Petorca; the governor, Don Miguel Irrisabal, made me his guest, and treated me with great attention; I continued with him several days; during which the funeral ceremonies of his father, the late Marquis de la Pica, were celebrated; all the relatives of the deceased that could attend, besides a great number of the neigh-bouring gentry, were present; it lasted two days, and was conducted with all the "rango," grandeur, that the place afforded.

The governor took me to visit the neighbouring haciendas, and I was much pleased with my "jaunt;" we also visited the famous gold-mine of La Vaca, belong-ing to El Señor Montes; I descended more than two hundred yards, but the heat and inconvenience expe-rienced in this kind of research, made me abandon my intention of visiting "los labores," the place which was worked; there was a great deal of water in the mine, and a number of Peones kept ascending and descending, who had to carry it out in sheep-skins, as well as others who carried the ore; in consequence of this I was a pretty figure when I emerged from the adit of the mine, my clothes being completely saturated with dirty water and my own perspiration; besides which, I was heartily laughed at for my pains; however, " I had descended a gold mine," and made a promise that I would never make so foolish an attempt again, unless I became interested in one: I procured a few fine specimens of ore.

Having witnessed the mode of operating, I will here endeavour to describe the process of procuring, and of grinding gold ore. The ore when brought from the mine is ground in a mill, which is erected near to a stream of water, often at some leagues distant; and generally belongs to an individual who receives payment for the use of his "trapiche," and whose profits are surer than those of the miner, especially if his mill be kept going. The ore is put into a trough, in which a large round stone is forced to revolve by a water-wheel; a small stream of water runs into the trough, which carries away the earth and light particles of gold, that have to pass over several shorn sheep or goat skins, to which the gold adheres; these are afterwards washed in a wooden trough, and the antimony and gold are diffused by water over the skins; again, these are washed, and then a quantity of quicksilver is introduced in the trough, which adheres to the particles of gold; then all is put into a piece of linen cloth, and strained until nearly all the quicksilver has been separated from the gold; this residuum is then placed under a retort, and the rest of the quicksilver is evaporated, when there remains a lump (pella) of pure gold: the earth is sometimes worked four or five times, and as often as it yields sufficient to repay them for their labour, the process is repeated.

The valley of Illapel is well cultivated, and there are

several large haciendas.   Some of the best horses in
Chile are bred here, and their hoofs are said to be the
hardest, especially those in the neighbourhood of Chuapa;
a great quantity of wheat, barley, Indian corn, beans,
wine, and brandy, is produced.   There are mines of all
kind of metals, but principally those of gold and copper
are worked; of the latter about 6,000 quintals are sent
annually to Valparaiso from this district.   The gold is
generally sent to the mint in Santiago, or smuggled; and
no exact account can be given of the quantities produced.
The town of Illapel has, with the exception of the Plaza,
a shabby appearance, being nothing else but a long
straggling street, with small thatched houses, that seem
to have suffered from the earthquake of 1822, and to
have undergone but little repairs.   I found the inhabitants
very hospitable; the females are reputed handsome; and
the town has the " sobriquet" of " Sal si puede," (leave
me if you can :) I here witnessed a strange sight, called an
" angelita," or wake :   the owners of dancing-houses,
" chinganas," of which there are no scarcity even in the
smallest villages, no sooner hear of the death of an
infant amongst the poorer class, than they hurry to apply
for it, and the highest bidder carries off the prize : they
then dress it in a gaudy manner, paint its face, and fix
its eyes open; then it is put up in a conspicuous place in
the dancing-room, and surrounded with candles; a few
rockets are let off, to warn the neighbours, and the room
is soon filled with revellers, who eat, drink, dance, and
sing to the tunes of a harp, guitar, and ravel, (a fiddle
with three strings,) for several nights and days, so that no
small profit is derived from the exposure of a dead child,
or, as they call it, " an angel."   I have been informed
that many of the chinganeros have been known to pre-

serve the body in spirits or vinegar, " en escaveche," so as to be enabled to continue their saturnales, or hire it out to others.

An Englishman of the name of Carter, who resided in this district, called upon me, and invited me to accompany him to his "chacara," which was a short distance from the town: I was surprised at the neatness of his house; and the appearance of everything I saw reminded me of an English farm: he was married, and his wife was reputed to be very industrious; she had a flour-mill under her own management. Carter was an excellent horseman, and managed his "lasso" as dexterously as the natives: he had been many years in Chile, for he was cabin-boy on board of the ship Scorpion of London, a vessel that formerly traded on the coast of Chile, whose captain was enticed on shore, and murdered in a barbarous manner by a set of villains, accompanied by a person that Captain Banker had raised from indigence, and who had acted as his agent. The ship was captured by boats that had been manned and sent from Valparaiso, to aid those who on shore represented themselves to be some of the principal gentry in Chile, wearing crosses or badges of condes, and marquesses, they had borrowed to carry on their infernal plot; however, they were all hated and stigmatized by their countrymen; and few of them, with the exception of the villain who betrayed the captain, ever prospered with their ill-gotten booty. A merchant of Coquimbo warned Capt. Banker to avoid the snare; but he lost his life and ship by putting too much confidence in an ungrateful wretch. I left Illapel on the 9th, and halted at the foot of the Cuesta de los Hornos, ten leagues, and passed the night in a miserable-looking hut; and, what surprised me was, although there

was neither a door, (a loose hide served as such,) or
window, or even a chair to sit down upon; all the dishes,
plates, forks, spoons, and even other utensils, were of
silver; these articles, a decent and clean bed, with
a few pictures of saints, three pair of Chinese trunks,
and several country saddles, with a rug that covered
half of the floor, and a large copper chafing-dish, "brasero"
filled with cinders and charcoal, completed the furniture of the habitation of one of the principal miners, who
made me his guest; and although there were no more
than seven persons, a supper was placed before us sufficient for forty. I cannot but say that I admired the good
cheer, &c. of this hospitable miner far better than the
appearance of his dwelling; however, such is the case in
many of the mining districts, for they have a good house in
the town, and content themselves with a " rancho," whilst
they attend to their mining occupations. The governor
of Illapel, no doubt ashamed to see a cavalry officer
obliged to march on horses belonging to the state, sent
me a fine black horse as a present, which, on account of my
recent losses in Callao, was a valuable acquisition. April
10th, I passed the Cuesta, where there are many valuable
copper mines, several of which are open close to the road,
so that it would be dangerous for a traveller to pass during
the night, besides which it is one of the worst mountain
passes I had yet seen; at noon I passed the river Pama,
and at two I arrived at the town of Combarbala, ten leagues;
this is also a mining district, and has a population of about
5,000; here are several good gold mines, and washings,
and many copper mines, the produce of which is sent to
Valparaiso. I saw little cultivation, except in the neighbourhood of the town, which is small, and has a neat
parish church; I took up my quarters with an old

H

acquaintance, El S'or Salas, who treated me in a hospitable manner. Next day I passed the rivers Combarbala and Cogoti, halted for a few hours at the village of La Ligua, and took up my quarters for the night at an hacienda near St. Marcos; here there was a very fine house, and I obtained leave to stay, and was shown into a "quarto," an empty room, which I soon found was infested with fleas, however I managed to make up a bed of my saddle geer under the "corridor;" and as I had marched twenty leagues, I soon fell asleep. About midnight I was aroused to take my supper, which I at first declined, but the landlord and his chaplain, a portly friar of the Franciscan order, were so importunate, that I accompanied them, and sat down to a splendid supper, where there was an ostensible show of plate, and good cheer. There were about fourteen persons present; the landlord, his lady, and daughters, inquired after several officers I had known in Peru, and I dare say would have prolonged their conversation to a late hour, had I not pleaded an excuse. I confess I thought it strange to leave such an entertainment, to occupy my miserable lodging; however I soon learned that travellers in Chile must take their "almofrez," (bedding) or a good supply of sheep skins with them, or they will often have to fare so, even at the wealthiest houses, for beds are seldom offered to any, except such as go on a visit, and know that they will be provided with them. There are no inns on this road, so that travellers are of course entertained by private families, and the service is repaid with answering questions, and telling the news of the part they have come from. Even the poorest inhabitants give a hearty welcome, and share their repast with such as choose to stay with them for the night, without accepting or receiving any emolument.—Twelfth, I passed the village of Guatemala, on the banks of the Cogoti, and at eleven at Yañillo, where I found the Marquis of Monroy on his death-bed. I had a letter to him, but on account of the distress his family were in, I continued my march, and halted for a few hours at a farm, La Punta de Guano, where I purchased an enormous copper stirrup that weighed several pounds, and served for a bell, that had formerly belonged to El Cura Monardes, an original, and of whom I had heard many curious anecdotes. I passed Rio Grande, which was not fordable at this season, over a small wooden bridge at Monte Patria, and at four I halted at the village of Sotaki, fifteen leagues, and took up my quarters with the curate, who treated me in the most hospitable manner. The valleys of Sotake, Monte Patria, and Yañilla, are well populated and fertile. Thirteenth.—I went next day to Guamalata, the estate of Don Bernardo Soler, uncle to my friend Don Felippe, who had given me letters of introduction. Here I halted two days, and spent the time agreeably with the old gentleman's sons, who had charge of a copper-smelting establishment. On the sixteenth, after having been supplied with good horses by the SS. Solers, I traversed the plains of Kitayaco, and about three o'clock in the afternoon saw the sea, and port of Coquimbo, and shortly afterwards I entered the city of La Serena, the capital of the province; twenty-two leagues. I called upon Commandant Boyle, for, the Intendente, General Don Francisco A. Pinto, had left the day before to meet his lady, whom he expected from the province of Cuyo; and, as he had left no orders respecting me, I called upon Don Gregorio Cordoves, who was acting intendente. He, also, had not received any instructions; so, on presenting my

H 2

passport, I was attached to the squadron of cavalry I ought to have commanded in Peru, "as a supernumerary," and on half-pay. However, the hospitality of Don Bernardo Soler, and the rest of his family, who made me their guest, placed me in very comfortable circumstances. I had the satisfaction of receiving a letter of thanks from the supreme director, General Don Ramon Freyre, for the service I had rendered him, by informing him, previous to his sailing for Chiloe, of the affair of Callao, "which unhappily made the expedition prove an abortive one," for the Spanish governor, Quintanilla, had received succour and encouragement to hold out, on account of Lima and Callao being again in the power of the Spaniards. It now may be seen, that had the proper authorities paid attention to my information, and taken the necessary precaution, they might have blockaded Chiloe, and perhaps have intercepted the vessel that was the conductor of the despatches, money, warlike stores, and officers, to relieve that place. General Pinto, on his return complimented me on my escape, and shortly afterwards I was put in command of the first company of the squadron of the Granaderos Lanceros, vacated by the death of Captain Molinares.* I remained nine months in Coquimbo, and received the greatest attention from the natives, as well as the foreign residents. La Serena is

* General Pinto was called to be minister of state in the war department, and Colonel Don Jose Maria Benevente succeeded him as governor-intendant of the province. Shortly after we had arrived, government finding that most of the convents had been nearly deserted on account of so many friars having secularized themselves, decreed that all the convents should be taken possession of at the same hour throughout the republic, and their effects, ornaments, and treasure, registered and deposited in the hands of commissioners that had been named for that trust. This would have been a death-blow to the Spanish faction; but commiseration to a few old friars, some of whom had powerful relatives and friends, impeded this salutary reformation from producing the effects that had been anticipated.

nearly surrounded by a mud wall. It has six churches, four belonging to the convents of San Francisco, Santo Domingo, San Agustin, La Merced; the others are La Matrix, parish-church, and that of the hospital of San Juan de Dios. There is a fine view of the port and bay, for the ·town is delightfully situated on three tables (mesetos), rising above each other, the streets are laid out at right angles, the houses are built of "adobes," bricks dried in the sun, and of one story, they are spacious, have a court-yard and garden, so that eight or twelve occupy a square of about 18,844 yards; the streets are paved and irrigated, and each house has an " asequia" to supply their gardens, &c. with water, which tends to the salubrity of the climate, for in this province they have little rain, and that only during a few days in June, or July, which is their winter season. During my stay I observed that there was little need of medical men; surgical aid, owing to accidents, or quarrels amongst the lower classes, was frequently required.

The Coquimbanos live to a good old age; I knew many who had passed their 70th year and were hale and active; also there are instances of people passing 100. They marry very young; it is common to see men of 15, and women of 13, commence the matrimonial state, so that it often happens that a couple that marry so young, after having brought up a numerous family, are, before they attain their 40th or 50th year, not to be recognized as their parents. At a party I have actually met with females, differing so little in apparent age, that in more than one instance I have taken the daughter to be a sister, and on one occasion to be the mother.

The residents of the capital are generally Haciendados and Habilitadores, the first are wealthy landholders, and the latter are merchants or store-keepers, who are the purveyors of the miners, and in reality reap all the real benefits of their labourious and improvident customers. I have known very few operative miners, excepting such as were so fortunate as to discover or possess a good silver or copper mine, realize any thing handsome, whilst the habilitadores, some of whom began with a very insignificant capital, have often in a few years become very wealthy. By what I have seen of the miners in general, their habits of extravagance is proverbial, for few toil harder for their money, and none lavish, or throw it away with more prodigality. Molina says " they are extravagant in their expenses, and passionately addicted to gaming, in which they pass almost all their leisure moments, and instances are not unfrequent of a miner losing one or two thousand crowns of a night. Losses of this nature are considered by them as trifles, and on such occasions they gaily console themselves with a professional proverb—' that the mountains never keep accounts.' Nothing is more abhorrent to them than frugality, and whenever they find one of their companions who has amassed a sum of money by his economy, they leave no means untried to strip him of it, observing that avarice is a vice peculiarly degrading to the character of a miner ; and so addicted are they to ebriety, that those who on first joining them are remarkable for their abstemiousness, are soon led from the influence of example, to participate in the general intemperance. From these causes none of them acquire property, and they generally die in the greatest poverty and distress, while the profits of their labour are wholly absorbed by those who supply them with provisions and liquor."

The dress of the miner is different from the other classes of labourers. They wear a cap made of uncut scarlet velvet sewed up in such a manner that when placed upon the head, it has the appearance of a boat when capsized, one point of which touches the lower part of the forehead, and the other the back of the neck. The dress is a shirt which is worn loose over a pair of short trowsers that are very wide, generally of a coarse blue cloth, and only reach to the knee, under which may be observed two or three pair of drawers of the same length and magnitude. They wear long stockings, mostly of white worsted, over which they use socks that just cover their ancles. These are of red worsted; and over them they fasten sandals, made of hide, that have a peak upwards at the toes. They tie their stockings with black or blue garters, which are ornamented with tassels that hang below the calf. Round their waist they wear a broad coloured sash, to which is attached their knife, and a curious leathern pouch, made from the entire skin of a kid, which is fantastically ornamented. In this they carry their money, tobacco, and implements for striking a light. They have also a curious leathern girdle which almost covers their posteriors, and is ornamented with a fringe of thongs. They have generally one or two waistcoats, no jacket, but wear their poncho thrown in a careless manner over their left shoulder. Their wives and daughters dress in a gaudy and extragavant manner, and wear the most expensive shawls and trinkets.

The natives of Coquimbo are very hospitable, and fond of giving balls, tertulias, and pic-nics, or excursions to the port, or other favourite resorts, where sheds are erected of myrtle, or other evergreens; and the entertainment often lasts for several days, which are passed in feasting, gaming, and dancing. There is an annual feast held about twelve leagues from the city, at an Indian village, Andacol, where there is an image of the Virgin that is said to have performed many miracles, and pilgrimages are made to its shrine, by devotees from every part of Chile, and even from the provinces of Rio de la Plata. I, with several of my acquaintance, visited this festival, and was greatly amused to observe the manner in which the devotions, or, I may say, saturnalia, were carried on. In the morning several masses are performed, and a sermon is preached, in which the Virgin is lauded extravagantly; after which, cock-fighting, gambling, racing, dancing, eating and drinking, are carried on until the ensuing morn, and continued so long as the feast lasts. I knew a friar, Padre Concha, who was a noted gambler, gain from 12 to 15,000 dollars, and nearly lose it all again at this feast: many have cause to rue the effects of their visit to Andacol. A lady, the wife of a friend of mine, had been elected the patroness, and was indulged so far as to be allowed to provide and entertain the principal guests, for they have a free table; and as everything necessary has to be brought from the city, it cost her a considerable sum. There are good gold-washings at Andacol, and whenever it rains numbers of the natives are employed in washing the earth, and many pieces of pure gold (pepitas) have been found that weighed several pounds, and of the best quality (twenty-three carats). I have been credibly informed that a "pepita" of an extraordinary size was once found in this neighbourhood, and the finder was so overjoyed with his success that he gave a feast, and during the entertainment he unwisely placed the gold in a large bowl of punch; unfortunately for him the splendid prize vanished, and is said to have soon found its way to the royal museum at Madrid. Molina quotes the following instances :—

" A person, on opening a water-course to an estate in the plain of Huilquilemu, discovered, with much surprise, a vein of gold dust, which produced more than fifty thousand dollars, without the least labour. The same good fortune occurred to another in ploughing a piece of land for grain. These instances are not unusual, and naturalists have given the name of ' montas' to these kind of casual mines, which are always of small extent."

I could cite many other corroborating facts that are recorded in Chile; but the above afford a fair sample of the
golden treasures that have been found before my visit to this
province, which has since been enriched by the discovery
'f the silver mines of Arqueros and Copiapo, where veins
and lumps of pure metal have been met with, that have
made the fortunes of many of the lucky proprietors.

The port of Coquimbo is about two and a half leagues
from the city, in lat. 29° 55′ S. long. 73° 35′ 45″ W. In
1824 there were only two decent houses, some stores,
a dilapidated barrack, and ruinous fortifications, in fact,
everything seemed to be in a poor state; there were
seldom any vessels at anchor; now and then a whaler,
or casual vessel to take in copper, or a coaster,
arrived; and during my stay H. M. ship Fly, and the
U. S. sloop, Peacock, and schooner, Dolphin, arrived; the
latter came from Callao, and brought me several articles
which I had left in the castle when I escaped; a Spaniard,
whom I had treated with attention, Casa Riego, had preserved my writing-desk and sword, and sent them to me.

The Chilian squadron, under Admiral Blanco, put in to
refit, for he had fallen in with a gale that disabled his
vessel; he had been on the look-out, for the Spaniards
had a line-of-battle ship, the Asia, and a brig, El Aquilles,
in the Pacific, and others were expected; but shortly
afterwards, these vessels being seized by their crews, the
Asia was delivered up to the Mexican government, and
the Aquilles to the Chilian.

The port of Coquimbo is well sheltered from the prevailing winds, and vessels may anchor near to the shore.
Good water cannot be procured, except from a rivulet
that enters the bay about two miles distant from the city;
and in fine weather vessels may either anchor near it, or
raft the water to the port.

Fish is abundant and good; the pechihuen, camerones, and ostions are celebrated. Game is also plentiful on the neighbouring hills, and water-fowl are plentiful in the lagoons.

The province of Coquimbo is the most arid and uncultivated in Chile; yet I have a statistical account which represents it to produce 90,000 fanegas of wheat. (a fanega is 150 pounds;) 5,000 of barley; 13,000 of beans; 14,000 of Indian corn; 10,000 of figs; 150,000 gallons of wine; and 27,000 of brandy; and its population is estimated at about 90,000.

The following treasury statement will show the imports of provisions from the southern provinces, by sea:—

"La Serena, July 30th, 1832.

"CUSTOM-HOUSE AND TREASURY OF COQUIMBO.

Wheat	32,297	Fanegas.
Meal	2,809	do.
Flour	26,397	do.
Beans	6,549	do.
Wallnuts	470	do.
Potatoes	550	do.
Galvanzes	93	do.
Aniseed	70	do.
Charqui (dried beef)	4,684	Quintals.
Tallow	2,462	do.
Cheese	508	do.
Butter	69	do.
Almonds	49	do.
Fat Jars	7,442	
Hams	1,065	"Jose Novoa."

The prices of provisions in the year 1834, were as follow:

Charqui	from 6 to 7½	per quintal.
Wheat	from 3½ to 5	per fanega.
Beans	(Frijoles) 5 to 6	do.

which are considerably dearer than in the other provinces, with whom a carrying and coasting trade is carried on.

Wheat varies every year, according to the crops; still, the average is from four to six shillings a fanega, in the southern, and from twelve to twenty in the northern districts. There is a great deal of manœuvring and speculations in grain. Corn laws have been established in order to protect the landed proprietors, viz.—When the Chilian flour does not exceed the value of four dollars the quintal, 100lbs., flour that is imported, pays two dollars per quintal: or, as follows :—

PRICE IN CHILE.			DUTY ON FOREIGN FLOUR.
4 dollars per quintal	.	100lbs. .	2 dollars per quintal.
4 to 5	do.	. . .	1 to 4 do.
5 to 6	do.	. . .	1 do.
6 to 7	do.	. . .	4 do.
7 upwards	do.	. . .	Free from Duty.

All the wheat and flour that is imported into Chile, can only be allowed to enter the port of Valparaiso. There are many ports in this province, but only two besides the principal one are frequented, Huasco and Copiapo. The Cordilleras are low, and nearly all are passable during the summer, which facilitates the trade with the Buenos Ayrean provinces.

On the 21st of January, 1825, the first squadron of the Granaderos Lanceros, my company No. 1, and Captain Bascuñan's No. 2, received orders to march with all possible despatch, towards the capital.

I took leave of my friends in Coquimbo with regret; on the eve of my departure I was sent for by the governor-intendente, who informed me that he had recommended me to government, and, as a further proof of his friendship, gave me two letters, the one to his brother, who was minister of state, and the other to his friend General Rivero, governor intendente of the province of Conception.

" Mi Diego,   " Serena, January 28th, 1825.
" Captain Sutcliffe will deliver this. I hope thou wilt distinguish him with thy friendship, and that thou will introduce him to thy friends, for his conduct and morals make him accredit thy distinction.
" Adieu, my Diego, be as happy as is the desire of thy
                                         " Jose Maria."
" S'or Don Juan de Dios Rivera,   " Serena, 28th January, 1825.
" My good Friend, Captain Sutcliffe, of the Lancers, is to deliver this letter. The honourable conduct of this officer has made him worthy of my recommending him to thee; the knowledge you have of him, and this re-commendation, may, I hope, make him merit thy friendship.
" Dispose as you wish of your friend, who kisses thy hands.
                                 " Jose Maria Benevente.
" Al Señor General y Governador Intendente de la
  provincia de Concepcion S'or Don Juan de dios Rivera."

As the lancers had no horses belonging to the corps, the intendente made a requisition, or porrato, from the neighbouring villages and estates, which had to provide us with all that were required, as well as baggage animals, until these were exchanged for others, which the governors of the several departments we had to pass through, would, previous to our arrival, have collected for us. The cavalry of Chile do not keep their horses in stabling; all, with the exception of the president's guard, are sent to graze in fields that belong to the state, or are rented, and when wanted they are collected ,in a pen, and each soldier throws his lasso over any horse he may choose for the day. Currycombs, and brushes, or even wisps, are seldom, if ever, seen in the army; nor are veterinary surgeons required. This accounts for the maltreatment and destruction of so many of those useful animals during a campaign, or a long march.

We marched from La Serena on the 29th, for our preparations had detained us longer than was expected. The second squadron remained under the command of Major Latus: and Commandant Boyle accompanied us; we were two troops of 100 men each, and about as many women accompanied them, most of whom were obliged to walk. Each soldier in Chile has a wife, or companion, most of whom are "Chinas," (half Indians). These are very useful, generally preceding the corps when on a march, and having a comfortable meal ready, and often a small shed erected for the weary soldier at his journey's end. They are hardy and indefatigable women; and I have seen them ford deep and rapid torrents, and make their way through apparently impassable sloughs.

We exercised the soldiers an hour each day on horseback, whenever we came to a suitable spot. This was highly important, as we had no opportunity of doing it in Coquimbo for want of horses; and several of our soldiers having been miners, were unaccustomed to riding, and would have been unfit for service, had they not passed through a course of regular drilling.

We returned by the same route that I took when going from the capital to Coquimbo, and entered the capital on the 16th of February. We halted in the principal square, where his excellency General Don Ramon Freyre, the supreme director, and General Don Louis Crux, the chief of the staff, reviewed us.

We performed various evolutions, and went through the lance and broad-sword exercise. His excellency was pleased to pass a public commendation on the troops, in regard of their general appearance, and the state of their discipline. He shewed a particular mark of attention to Commandant Boyle, and the officers of our squadron, by ordering all the other corps of cavalry to observe the tactics we had adopted, " La Moderna Española," which had been reprinted in Lima.

Previously to this time, the Chilian army was a complete medley, in respect of its discipline, each commandant of a corps using what tactics he thought proper; but it was now ordered that all must adopt the same manoeuvres, which secured uniformity.

Soon after my return to the capital, I made an excursion to view the field of battle on the plains of Maipu, with two officers belonging to the Lancers, and we were hospitably entertained at the Hacienda del Espejo, about three leagues from Santiago; my companions galloped over the ground in high glee, and amused me by relating the particulars of the glorious 5th of April, 1818.

As this victory sealed the independence of Chile, I will

present my readers with a brief account of the prowess of the patriots, and add an extract from General San Martin's official despatch relative to the battle of Chacabuco; and also that of the crowning victory of Maipu.

Chile ought only to date its freedom from the battles of Chacabuco and Maipu, for, although the first popular commotion occurred in 1810, when the President Carrasco, was deposed by the inhabitants of Santiago, and a provisional government, or junta was elected, their title was only that of " Preservers of the rights of the king during his captivity." This new order of affairs caused a series of revolutions; and, as those who were denominated patriots, were contending factions, the Spaniards and their adherents got hold of the reins of government again. Generals O'Higgins and Carrera were, after a gallant defence, and sanguinary conflict of thirty-six hours, defeated at Rancagua; and, with the rest of the patriots, men, women, and children, forced to fly across the Cordillera de los Andes, and, as many had to leave on foot, the hardships and sufferings they had to undergo are not to be described ; whilst the Spanish generals, Osorio and Ordonez, on the 9th of October, 1814, made their entry, and were received by the inhabitants of Santiago with every possible demonstration of joy and gladness—(con cuantas demostraciones pueden hacerse de jubilio y alegria.*) And Chile might have yet remained in the kind and paternal possession of Spain, had not the sufferings of the patriots, who emigrated to Mendoza and Buenos Ayres, raised the sympathy of the chiefs of that republic, Los SS. Alvares, Puerredon, and General San Martin, who promised to aid in liberating

* Gurman's History of Chile.

that country; and, whilst the emigrants were enjoying the hospitality of their neighbours, and those less fortunate enduring the taunts of their enemies, in Juan Fernandes and Quiriquina, the Buenos Ayrean army was recruited, organized, and prepared for the invasion of Chile. General Don Jose San Martin marched from Mendoza on the 17th of January, 1817, and crossed the Andes, with an army of about 5,000 men, 10 field-pieces, 2 howitzers, 1,600 horses, upwards of 9,000 mules, and 700 head of horned cattle. The artillery and heavy baggage cost a deal of fatigue and loss of cattle in the march; and although every possible precaution that could be devised, was put in practice whilst crossing, above 500 horses and 4,000 mules perished. An extract from General San Martin's despatches to the president of Rio de la Plata, will give the details of the battle of Chacabuco—

"On the 28th of March the army was in the best condition, and united at Los Mananteales on the road to Los Patos, from which station I commenced to combine and direct my movements, so that I could command the four passes of the Cordilleras, and break through any obstacles the enemy might oppose to me in the defiles of those I penetrated.

"The army was divided into two divisions—the vanguard, under the command of General Don Miguel Soler, and the second was led by General O'Higgins and Colonel Sapiola, with two squadrons of cavalry. The artillery and artificers followed after.

"I sent Major Don Antonio Arcos on our left with 200 men, and ordered him to penetrate the defile of Valle Hermosa, and attack one of the enemy's posts, then mount the Cumbre del Cusco, and leaving the Cordilleras de Piuquenes in his rear, open those passes, and march on to Los Achapayas, take possession of that position, and put it in a state of defence, so that he could return to the army, and debouch in Putaendo.

"This officer entered Achapayas on the evening of the 4th, and attacked the military commandant of San Felippe, who, with about 100 soldiers, and all the militia he could collect, opposed him, but they were routed and pursued by the brave Lieutenant Lavalle, and 25 horse grenadiers; and the towns of Putaendo and San Felippe were abandoned, as well as their baggage, horses, &c.

"General Soler made forced marches, and advanced rapidly with the infantry; on the 6th he mounted the artillery, and united all the corps of the vanguard above Putaendo, leaving Commandant Negochea with 80 of my escort, and 30 of his squadron, on the heights, and Commandant Melian occupied the small town of San Antonio; and on the same day he encamped and established the head-quarters of his division at San Andres del Tartaro. The enemy received considerable reinforcements on the evening of the 6th, passed the river of Aconcagua, and before day-break took up a position in front of Commandant Negochea, with 400 cavalry, 300 infantry, and 2 field-pieces.

"This gallant officer, without vacillating a moment, called in his advanced-guard, and without firing a gun, allowed the enemy to approach within 60 yards; and having given the right to Captain Don Manuel Soler, and the left to Adjutant Don Angel Pacheco, he charged them in such a gallant style, that he routed and pursued them to the heights of Coimas, where, after having left 34 killed and 4 wounded, they sheltered themselves under cover of their infantry. These, however, abandoned their position, as well as the town of San Felipe, and recrossed the river.

"In the mean time Colonel Las Heras, who had taken the road of Huaspallata to Santa Rosa, obtained great advantages and brilliant success for his vanguard, under Major Don Henrique Martines, attacked and carried the post of the Andes with the bayonet, after an hour and half's resistance, and took 47 prisoners, arms, ammunition, and other articles.

"This division was ordered to enter Santa Rosa on the 8th, and remain in communication with the vanguard of the army that had occupied San Felipe, which was executed within an hour's interval.

"On the night of the 7th, the enemy abandoned the positions of Aconcagua and Curimon, leaving their baggage, &c., and began to accend the Cuesta de Chacabuco; on which I resolved to follow, and march upon them and the capital with all possible rapidity, and attack them on every opportunity that offered, notwithstanding my field-artillery had not yet arrived.

"On the 9th, the bridge of Aconcagua was repaired, and Commandant Melian marched with his squadron, to reconnoitre the enemy. The army followed after, and Colonel Las Heras having joined us, we halted at the entrance of the ravine.

"The enemy's intentions were now visible; the position they had selected on the heights, and the resolution with which they appeared disposed to defend themselves, shewed they were decided upon sustaining their ground,

"Our advanced parties halted within a musket-shot of theirs, and the necessary information was procured during the night, and a plan of the position taken, so that at daybreak we would be able to attack the enemy.

"Your excellency will see in the plan I have sent, our movements delineated, as well as the enemy's position.

"I gave the right to General Soler, who, with No. 1 Cazadores; companies of Granaderos-holteadores of 7 and 8, in charge of Lieutenant-Colonel Martines No. 11, 7 field-pieces, my escort, and 4 squadrons of Granaderos a Caballo. in order that he might attack their flank, and throw them into disorder, whilst General O'Higgins, who had charge of the left, attacked them in front, with the Bolteadores Nos. 7 and 8, and 1st, 2nd, and 3rd squadrons, and two field-pieces.

" The result of our first movement was just as I had expected, for the enemy had to abandon the position they had taken on the heights, and the rapidity of our movements did not allow them sufficient time for the troops that were in the houses of Chacabuco to arrive and dispute our gaining the heights.   It was necessary to consider that their infantry marched on foot, and had to retreat across a plain of four leagues, and although they were covered by a strong column of cavalry, experience had already taught us that one squadron of Granaderos a Caballo were sufficient to throw them into disorder, and put them to the rout.

" Our position was the most advantageous ; for General O'Higgins could continue his attack in front, whilst General Soler remained always in a situation of throwing them into disorder, in case they attempted to rally before they descended to the plain.   So I ordered Colonel Zapiola to march with the 1st, 2nd, and 3rd squadrons, to charge and detain the enemy until the Bolteadores Nos. 7 and 8, got up.   This piece of service crowned my expectations, for the enemy were obliged to take up a position, marked in the plan.   General Soler continued his movement on the right with judgment, decision, and combination, notwithstanding he had to ascend and descend the most rugged and almost impracticable precipices.   The enemy did not observe this manœuvre until the general had command of their position, and menaced their flank.   They now made a desperate and tenacious resistance for more than an hour amidst a horrid fire.   Above 1,500 infantry, the flower of their army, disputed the victory with the greatest ardour.   They were supported by a respectable body of cavalry. Notwithstanding, the decisive moment presented itself, and the brave General O'Higgins, with the Bolteadores 7 and 8, Commandants Cramer and Conde formed close column of attack, and charged the enemy's left with the bayonet, Colonel Sapiola, with Commandants Melian and Molina, broke the right—all was the effect of an instant.   General Soler fell upon their position.   The enemy sent 200 men to defend an elevated part, but Commandant Alvarado arrived in time with his Cazadores, and detached two companies with Captain Salvadores, who charged the enemy with the bayonet, and to rout them was the work of an instant.   Lieutenant Soria of the Cazadores distinguished himself in this affair.

" In the mean time the cavalry, led on by their commandant, charged in the bravest manner ; the enemy's infantry were broken and routed ; the slaughter was terrible, and victory complete and decisive.

" Commandant Negochea, who, with the 4th squadron and my escort, fell, on the right, (marked in the plan ;) made terrible havoc, and the cavalry pursued the fugitives to the Portznelo de Colina.

" Thirty-two officers, many of superior rank, and above 600 rank and file, were made prisoners, about as many slain, all the artillery, military stores, baggage, were taken, and the first trophy of the day were the colours of the regiment of Chiloe."

I

The general—after recommending the valour and particular services of Generals Soler and O'Higgins, the staff-officers, and his aids-de-camp, Don Hilarion de la Quintana, Don Jose Antonio Alvarez, Don Antonio Arcos, Don Manuel Escalada, and Don Juan O'Brian, Captain Aldao and El Patrioto Ramirez, who took the president General Marco and his party prisoners at San Antonio, where they had fled to in order to embark—concluded his despatch with the following article: "Lastly, El Commandant Cabot upon Coquimbo, Rodrigues on San Fernando, and Lieutenant-Colonel Freyre on Talca, have each had equal success; in one word—the echo of patriotism resounds at the same time in every part; and to the army of the Andes ever remains the glory of saying—' *In twenty-four hours we have concluded our campaign, passing the most elevated Cordilleras in the globe, concluded with the tyrants, and given liberty to Chile.*'

"JOSE SAN MARTIN."

The Chilians, willing to show their gratitude to General San Martin, offered him the supreme command of the republic, which he declined accepting; so General Don Bernardo O'Higgins was elected supreme director on the 14th of February; and, having appointed his ministers, and placed confidential patriots in command of the provinces, his first endeavours were to liberate the unfortunate captives, who had so long suffered confinement, and other vexations, in the depôts of the islands of Juan Fernandez and Quiniquina. In this enterprize his efforts were so well seconded by an intrepid Englishman, Captain Morris, who had been an officer in the royal navy, that in a few days above one hundred of the most respectable citizens, some of whom were of an advanced age, had the unspeakable satisfaction of re-entering their homes, and receiving the embraces and welcome of their families and friends, who loaded their deliverer with every possible demonstration of gratitude and respect. The following is one of many of the letters the general received from the liberated captives, and one who had been opposed to the new order of things at the commencement of the revolution, on account of his titles and dignities.

"Valparaiso, April 4th, 1817.

"S'or Don Bernardo O'Higgins.

"My esteemed Friend,

"Hope maintains the end of all things, and makes persecution tolerable. We have suffered distinctly, and are now happily reunited by the heroic services which you and your brave companions in arms have rendered; by which, affliction has disappeared from this country, and more than one hundred citizens have been restored to their families and homes, that had been so long suffering a cruel banishment.

"You have manifested so much interest in our behalf, that no one can doubt but that your constancy has gained our eternal gratitude.

"To testify which, as well as my constant regard towards your person, I for my part assure you, that I shall consider myself for ever beholden to you, and feel it indispensable and satisfactory to solicit your commands, so that I can accredit my profound gratitude, and obligation to manifest it to the satisfaction of the best regard, with which,

"I remain your affectionate and obedient servant,

"MARTIN CALVO ENCALADA"

The General next turned his attention towards liberating the southern provinces; for the enemy had garrisons in Talcahuano, Los Angeles, Valdivia, and Chiloe. The troops that had fled to the southward were pursued by the brave Colonel Las Heras, who on account of the reinforcement that General O'Higgins had sent, was enabled to oblige General Ordofies to take refuge in Concepcion. Las Heras encamped on the heights, and, on the 5th of May, General Ordofies made a sortie; but he was beaten, and obliged to return, with a considerable loss, to his entrenchments. The patriot army, commanded by General O'Higgins, who had left the capital in charge of General Don Luis Cruz, then named supreme delegate, remained during the months of May, June, and August, in front of Talcahuano; and, although it was the winter season, it was constantly employed in harassing the enemy, recruiting, and disciplining the army. During this period, a French general, Brayer, who had distinguished himself under Napoleon, arrived at head-quarters, accompanied with several officers, who had served in the French army. Through the recommendation of General San Martin, he became not only a welcome visitor, but was appointed major-general of the Chilian army; however, his discipline and tactics were not suited to the patriots; a circumstance which caused some bickerings, and led to his retirement from the service.

The independence of Chile was sworn to, and proclaimed in the capital, on the anniversary of the battle of Chacabuco, (12th of February;) therefore, this spot will for ever be a memorable monument of the services of Generals San Martin, O'Higgins, Soler, the brave Buenos Ayrean and Chilian patriots.

The viceroy of Lima being determined on the conquest of Chile, sent another expedition, commanded by his son-in-law, General Ossorio, of more than 3,500 men, who disembarked, with a respectable train of artillery, at Talcahuano, where he soon formed an army of about 6,000 men, with which he advanced towards the capital, and succeeded in routing the Patriots at Cancharayada. The particulars of this action are detailed in the following official despatch.

" BUENOS AYRES GAZETTE.

" Wednesday, 22d April, 1818.

" *Despatch of his Excellency the Captain-General of the Andes to the Supreme Government.*

" MOST EXCELLENT SIR,

" The unlooked-for events which took place on the night of the 19th ult., at Cancha-rayada, threatened to annihilate the liberties of Chile. It was certainly a spectacle in the highest degree alarming to see an army, composed of valiant, disciplined, and veteran soldiers, completely dispersed without fighting.

" Ever since the opening of. the campaign, as I had been perfectly confident of success, all my movements had for their object to render the victory complete and decisive. The enemy, in fact, from the moment he abandoned Curico, never occupied a position in which our troops did not harass and threaten to turn their flanks.   Thus circumstanced, both armies encamped at the same moment in the neighbourhood of Talca, and in such a position that it was impossible to recross the river Maule.

"Our situation was the most unfortunate possible, and was rendered disastrous by the most unlooked-for incidents.   Our infantry did not reach their position till sunset; and as I found it impossible to commence the attack at that hour, the army was formed for the time in two lines, while a reconnoissance was made in order to ascertain which was the most advantageous ground to take up.   On further examination, I decided upon occupying a position on the left, and directed that wing of the army to move upon it; but the troops were scarcely in motion when a vigorous attack was made by the enemy, the effect of which was to throw the baggage and artillery into confusion.   This was about nine o'clock in the evening, and the disorder soon spread to the left wing of the army, which, after a brisk fire of half an hour, was dispersed likewise.   The enemy, however, lost many men; and on our side we had to lament that the gallant General O'Higgins was wounded.

"Aided by the officers, I did everything in my power to rally the troops on a neighbouring high ground, and this was presently accomplished under the protection of the corps de reserva.   An obstinate contest now took place; but our people became stupified and confused in the darkness, and there was nothing for it but to abandon the post.

"The right, meanwhile, had not been nearly so severely pressed, and Colonel Las Heras had the address to retire with the infantry and cavalry under his orders.   This was the only point we had to trust to when I reached Chimbarongo.   I immediately took steps to establish a communication with our scattered forces, especially in the narrow pass or gorge of Regulemu.   The head-quarters were at San Fernando.   Here we continued for two days; and I can assure your Excellency our situation was embarrassing enough.   All the baggage, and the whole of the materiel of the army, was gone; everything had been taken from us; and we were left absolutely without the power of facing such a superior force, flushed as they were with victory.   In this predicament, there was no alternative left but to fall back with all speed upon Santiago, and to put every possible means in requisition to obtain supplies, which might enable me to save the country.

"Your Excellency will scarcely believe it possible, that, at the end of three days, the army was once more organized and encamped on the exercising ground, at a league's distance from this city.   Their spirits were completely revived; and within thirteen days of their dispersion, and after a retreat of eighty leagues, were again in condition to face the enemy. The zeal, energy, and perseverance, with which the commanding officers, and indeed every individual of the army, co-operated to re-establish order and discipline, is beyond all praise.   It must be confessed, however, that our force was still greatly inferior to that of the enemy : many corps were reduced to mere skeletons, and some battalions could hardly muster two hundred men.

"Meanwhile our opponent came on rapidly; and on the 1st instant

I received certain information, that the body of his army, having crossed the Maipu by the fords of Longuen, had marched in the direction of the pass of Calera; but his position was neither secure nor skilfully chosen. On the 2d we marched and took post near the aqueduct of Espejo. During the 3d and 4th there was a good deal of skirmishing between the sharp-shooters, and the troops continued under arms on both these nights.

"On the 5th the enemy drew still nearer to us, evidently with the design of turning our right flank, intending thereby to threaten the capital, as well as to cut off our communications with Aconcagua, and open for himself the road to Valparaiso. As soon as I discovered this movement, I conceived the fit opportunity was come for attacking him; and I therefore placed myself directly in his front by a movement to the right, which was preparative to all the succeeding operations. I placed the whole of the infantry under the command of General Balcarce: the right flank under the immediate orders of Colonel Las Heras, the left under Lieut.-Colonel Alvarado, and the reserve commanded by Colonel Hilarion de la Quintana. The right division of the cavalry was placed under Colonel Don Matias Zapiola, with his squadrons of grenadiers, and the left division under Colonel Don Ramon Freyre, with the body-guard of his Excellency the Director of Chile, and the mounted chasseurs of the Andes.

"The enemy, upon seeing our first movement, immediately occupied a strong position in front of our line, and detached a battalion of chasseurs to a small knoll on his left, in order to maintain a four-gun battery established about half way up the hill. These dispositions were most judiciously conceived, as they completely secured his left, while his fire protected the whole front of his position.

"Our line, formed in close column, marched to the right of the enemy, offering an oblique face to their attack. The reserve fell back at the same time, to be ready to cover and support our right. A battery of eight guns, commanded by Captain Blanco Ciceron, was advanced towards our right, and another of four guns occupied nearly the centre of our line, which soon commenced playing with great effect on the enemy's position.

"Things being thus arranged, our columns descended the side of the rising ground which formed our position, and charged the enemy's line. We were received with a furious fire, but continued our march, although their flanking battery of four guns annoyed us excessively. At this instant, a considerable body of the enemy's cavalry, placed behind the hills, came forward and charged our mounted grenadiers, who had formed in column by squadrons considerably in advance. The leading squadron was under Captain Escalada, who, the instant he saw an attack was intended, dashed forward, sword in hand, upon the enemy, and Captain Medina followed immediately. The enemy turned about, and galloped off to the little hill, where, aided by the grape-shot from the four-gun battery, and the fire of the infantry, they rallied and drove our troops back again. These squadrons soon formed anew, and, leaving the fortified hill to their right, pressed forward in pursuit of the enemy's cavalry, who retreated to a height in their rear; where, being speedily reinforced, they attacked Colonel Zapiola, who withstood this new charge with great steadiness. At last the enemy gave way, and were finally driven entirely from this point. Meanwhile, a most vigorous and destructive fire was kept up between the enemy's right and our left. His best troops were stationed in that quarter, and presently they were advanced in close column, accompanied by a body of cavalry.

" Captain Borgoño had by this time gained the summit of the hill forming our position, with eight field-pieces, which he was carrying to our extreme left, with the intention of raking the enemy's line. He very promptly, however, availed himself of the opportunity, and opened such a fire of grape upon the enemy's advancing columns, that he very soon threw their cavalry into disorder. Notwithstanding this advantage, and the gallant efforts made by Captains Alvarado and Martinez, our line began evidently to falter. At this critical moment I gave orders for the reserve, under Colonel Quintana, to charge the enemy ; a service which was performed in the most brilliant manner. The troops employed consisted of the first and third battalions of Chile, and the ninth battalion of the Andes, under Captains Ribera Lopes, and Conde. This energetic charge, and one by Captain Tonson of the Coquimbo regiment, gave a new impulse to our line, and the whole fell upon the enemy with more decisive effect than ever.

" The squadrons composing the body-guard, and the mounted chasseurs under the intrepid Colonel Freyre, charged at the same period, and were in turn repeatedly attacked by the enemy. It is difficult to give an adequate idea of the numerous feats of bravery which distinguished the troops on this day. I speak not only of bodies of troops and commanding officers, but of individual soldiers. It may, however, be safely asserted, that a more daring, vigorous, or well-supported attack, never was made ; neither, it ought to be allowed, was there ever a more determined resistance. At last, however, the perseverance and gallantry of our soldiers succeeded, and the position was wrested from the enemy at the point of the bayonet.

" These important successes alone, it might have been thought, would have given us the victory ; but it was not in our power to break the enemy's columns completely. Our cavalry, indeed, hung upon their flanks and rear, and harassed them excessively. Still, however, they retreated in a compact body, till, on reaching the narrow lanes near Espejo, they obtained posses-sion of a hill, where they commenced a new action, which lasted above an hour. On our side, this was maintained by the third regiment of Arauco, the infantry of Chile, and other detachments, which were successively engaged. Eventually, however, the gallant 1st and 11th battalions of Coquimbo, which had already borne the brunt of the action on our right, attacked the enemy so briskly, that they entirely overthrew them, and put them to rout. The gates and lanes being occupied by our cavalry, only the commander-in-chief Osorio, and two hundred horse, escaped ; and it is probable that he will not long evade the pursuit of the troops which are in search of him. All the enemy's generals have fallen into our hands ; and, up to this date, we have taken 3,000 men and 190 officers ; and on the field of battle lie 2,000 killed. All the artillery and ammunition, the hospitals and stores, the military chest, and every article it contains— in a word, everything appertaining to the royal army, is either dead, or prisoner, or safe in our power.

" Our own loss amounts to one thousand killed and wounded. As soon as the returns of their names are received, they shall be transmitted to your Excellency, together with those of the officers most distinguished on this occasion.

" I have to acknowledge the greatest obligation to Señor General Balcarce, whose talents have materially sustained the army since the very first moment of the campaign. To Adjutant-general Aguirre I may give the same praise ; and the other individuals of my staff, including Don Diego Paroissiens.

" I am also highly satisfied with the conduct of the chief engineer, Dalbe, and my aides-de-camp, O'Brian, Guzman, and Escalada; the secretary of war, Zenteno, and my own private secretary, Marzan. My only regret is, that I cannot do adequate justice to all parties, as it is to their united valour and exertions that the country is indebted for so glorious a day.

" I entreat that your Excellency will permit the names of the officers who have assisted in this severe and honourable campaign, to be inserted after this despatch.

" I am aware that it will hurt the modesty of our gallant supreme director, Don Bernardo O'Higgins, but I feel it right to mention that his Excellency, notwithstanding his being severely wounded, having insisted upon being placed on horseback, actually rode to the field, and was in the battle at its conclusion. I grieve, however, to add, that these exertions have aggravated his wound.

" God protect your Excellency many years,

"Jose San Martin."

" P. S. The action commenced at nine in the morning, and ended at sunset. The force of the enemy was 5,300 men ; ours was 4,900."

During the panic which had been created by the advance of the Spaniards, the government of the capital decreed, " that a part of the immense plain, then uncultivated and without water, should be divided amongst the chiefs and officers of the Patriot army;" which has not yet been attended to. I met with an accident on this plain, which I am sure it would offend some of my Chilian friends, if I were to omit describing here.

I had been on a shooting excursion with two Americans, who were officers in the Chilian service, Captain Delano, of the navy, and Major Ross, of the marines ; and, on crossing the plain of Maipu, we observed several whirlwinds of an unusual magnitude, one of these came in the direction of our road, and made the dust fly about so as to form a dense column. I was determined to try what effect the discharge of my fowling-piece would have, and, notwithstanding the intreaties of several Chilians who accompanied us, and strove to dissuade me from the attempt, I dashed into it, and discharged both barrels; the report of which, with the effect of the whirlwind, frightened my horse, and on account of one of my stirrup-leathers breaking, he threw me, and I remained for some time senseless on the ground. On recovering from the effects of the fall, I inquired of Major Ross where I was, and he replied in a jocular manner, " You are here now, but a short time ago you were dancing upon the top of the whirlwind;" the joke, as well as the bruises I had received, put me out of humour; this made matters worse, for, on nearing the city he galloped forward; and on my arrival, and for some time after, I was so jeered about the adventure, that I made a resolution to let the whirlwinds alone for the future.

We remained nearly two months in the barracks of San Diego.

During my stay in Santiago, Don Felippe Santiago del Soler made me his guest, and I passed my time very agreeably; his amiable lady, Doña Mercedes Rosales, together with his family, and the rest of my Chilian friends, treated me with the greatest kindness.

On the 3rd of April we marched, and were obliged to ford the river Maipu, the bridge being out of repair; the bed of the river was full of large stones, and the torrent very rapid, which made it difficult to pass; some of our horses fell, and their riders narrowly escaped drowning.

We halted for the night at the Hacienda of Doña Concepcion Xara, from whom we received the greatest kindness. On the next day we passed the beautiful vale of Maipu, and the pass of Angostura, and halted at the Graneros, houses belonging to the estate of La Compania, and next day entered the town of Rancagua, where we took up our quarters in the convent of San Francisco.

Rancagua is about twenty-two leagues from Santiago; it is the capital of the department, situated near the river Cachapaul, which fertilizes the beautiful plains of Rancagua, Mendoza, and El Olivar.

Rancagua had suffered greatly by an attack from the Spanish army. Here Generals O'Higgins and Carrera furnished their enemies with a proof of the gallantry of the Chilian troops. The marks made in the tower of San Francisco by the cannon and musket balls, still remain a monument of the defence of Rancagua.

We ought to have been supplied with horses at this place, but as they were not collected in time, we left an officer to wait for them, and conduct them after us.

We marched the next day, April 6th, and crossed the river Cachapaul, which was deep and rapid, in consequence of the melting of the snow on the mountains; we suffered no farther damage than getting our baggage wet.

The squadron halted at the Hacienda de Apalta, on the plains of Mendoza. This place belonged to Don Valentin Valdivieso, who treated the commandante and officers hospitably. I passed the greater part of the night with Captain Bascuñan, at the Requingua, the estate of Don Francisco Valdivieso, who was there with his family and several visitors; and, as they were an agreeable party, we passed a few hours pleasantly, and joined our troops at daybreak, as they were preparing to march. We passed the village of Rio Claro, which lies in a valley of that name; and at sunset entered the city of San Fernando, the capital of the province of Colchagua.

Here we halted a few days, and obtained several re-cruits, and some horses belonging to the state, of the most miserable description, worn out, with sore backs, and without ears, (the national mark), Pilones.

San Fernando is a populous town, but has a shabby appearance, and suffers at times from the inundations of the Tinderedica.

On the 15th of April, we were summoned to defend the town of Curico, which was menaced by Pincheyra, a noted bandit, who, with a few old Spanish officers, de-serters, robbers, and a party of Indians, infested the Cordilleras, and struck terror into the inhabitants, by sacking all the towns and estates that lay near the Andes.

We passed the river Tinderedica, over the hanging bridge, and halted at the convent of Chimbarongo. On the next day we passed the Serrillos de Teno, a place noted for robberies; we then crossed the river Teno, halted at Curico, and took up our quarters in the con-vents of San Francisco and La Merced.

We found the inhabitants in the greatest alarm ; the governor and his family, with several others, had left the place, and the rest were preparing to emigrate towards the coast, for they had reason to fear a visit from Pin-cheyra, who had been seen in the neighbourhood.

Curico is only three leagues distant from the Cordil-léras, and, as it was about the time of full moon, our arrival inspired the people with confidence; the acting governor, El S'or Labra, and a worthy citizen, Don Francisco Merino, did all they could to supply us with

horses, as well as to put a stop to the emigration, and
assemble the militia; the latter were without discipline,
and in want both of arms and accoutrements. We obtained a few of their horses, as well as some from the
governor; and other resources were afforded, by which
our men were better mounted, and rendered fitter for
service.

Three days after our arrival, we were informed that
Pincheyra had surprised Don N. Pavez and his family,
who were on their way to Mendoza, and that the forces of
Pincheyra were marching towards Curico.

We set out to meet them, accompanied by Don
Francisco Merino, and about 150 militia, who were armed
with carbines, others with lances, the rest with swords
and clubs. The main body halted in the Hacienda of
Guaico, and a division was sent to reconnoitre. About
nine at night they had a skirmish with the advanced
guard of the robbers, who fled on the approach of our
troops; and before we could overtake them, they had
ascended the Cuesta del Planchon, where it was impossible
to follow, for the defile was exceedingly steep, and by
rolling down stones they could have destroyed us. Nor
would it have been wise to pursue them further, as we
should then have given them an opportunity of selecting
another pass, and entering Curico, whilst there was
no force to protect it. Two officers remained with a
party of men to guard the pass; the rest returned
to the Hacienda del Guaico, and on our arrival there
we found that all the militia had absconded during the
night, along with their officers; but El S'or Merino
remained with us to the end of the pursuit. We
killed several of the robbers, took nine prisoners,
and might have captured more, had our soldiers paid

as much attention to the men as they did to their horses and booty.

However, we rescued the female part of Pavez's family, and he himself made his escape, but his brother and several of his servants were most cruelly butchered. We saw their bodies, which were literally cut in pieces.

Pavez recovered the greatest part of his baggage, and we recaptured a quantity of cattle, some of which had been hamstrung. If we had been supplied with better horses, and conducted by proper guides, we should doubtless have destroyed this foraging party; one of the leaders, a Spaniard, Captain Godet, received a severe wound in the head.

By our timely arrival, this department was spared the horrors of a visit from these inhuman desperadoes. The prisoners were lodged in the gaol of Curico, from which they were allowed to escape through the connivance of their partisans, and thus avoided their merited punishment. Our commandant kept a strong party in the Cordilleras for several weeks; and, on one occasion, we were shut in by a heavy fall of snow, which confined us twenty days; and so great was our destitution, that we were obliged to kill several horses for our maintenance. Horse-flesh, without salt, bread, or vegetables, is poor food for an European; but the Chilian soldiers, especially those from the frontier of Concepcion, are said to be partial to this food, and mares are often given them when short of other provisions.

I found campaigning in Chile to be much more harrassing than I had ever experienced on the Peninsula, or in Flanders. I also learnt that we had to expect no quarter from our barbarous enemies, should we have the misfortune to fall into their hands, and there was little honour to be gained in fighting with a horde of robbers. However, the kind treatment of the Chilians acted as a stimulus to exertion in their defence.

We remained in Curico seven months, and experienced the kindest treatment from the inhabitants; and I am proud in being able to say, that our soldiers gave them no occasion to complain of their conduct during that period.

Whilst we remained here, we broke up and captured several gangs of marauders who had infested the Serrillos de Teno, and rendered the roads almost impassable.

On the 22nd of October I received orders to march with my troop to Talca, to relieve part of a regiment (No. 4), that was on its march to Valparaiso; my orders were, to get to my station without halting.

We marched at sunset, and passed the river of Lontue and Rio Claro in the dark, and arrived at Talca early on the next day, distance 22 leagues.

I relieved Major Gana, who marched the same day after his regiment.

Commandante Boyle arrived five days afterwards with the other troops; he came to my quarters at midnight, and, after some preamble, informed me that a revolution had broken out in Santiago, and that General Freyre had been deposed. He showed me an official despatch, in which I saw that Colonel Sanches of the 4th regiment was supreme director. My commandante was named Coronel, and had orders to take the military command of Talca, and to place me in command of the squadron of Lancers; this news surprised me, but knowing my commandante to be a great friend of General O'Higgins, and that the revolution was brought about by his partisans, I concluded that they thought

Commandante Boyle to be a person in whom they might safely repose confidence. Under such circumstances, however, he thought it prudent to await further news from the capital; and it was well that he was persuaded to do so, for on the next day I received an official communication from government, authorizing me to take command of the squadron; and Commandante Boyle received another to deliver it up to me, with all the documents belonging to the military chest and stores, for order had been restored in the capital.

Twenty-four hours after the revolution, Colonel Sanchez, Don Felippe Santiago del Soler, Colonel Biel, and several others, were made prisoners, and exiled.

Government was rather severe with Commandante Boyle, for he was dismissed from the service, though he had taken no part in the revolution; and the governor of Talca, with the most respectable part of the inhabitants, offered to give their testimony in favour of the conduct of Commandante Boyle.

I had scarcely gone through the ceremony of receiving the command, the papers, &c., when an officer, Captain Bascuñan, commander of the 2nd troop, arrived with an order from the minister of war, to take the command from me, as the order did not come from the general-in-chief, "Commandante General de Armas." I did not obey it, and informed Captain Bascuñan, that as I could not act without orders from the chief of the staff, he had better join his troop and take charge of the Archives, and receive the military chest from Commandante Boyle, until I should have further communications.

I forwarded the minister's order to the Commandante General de Armas, and stated the particulars.

Commandante Boyle, on leaving, gave me the following certificate :—

"Don Jose Maria Boyle, Lieutenant-Colonel of the Chilian army, and Commandante of the squadrons of Granaderos Lanceros,—
"I certify that the conduct of Captain Don Tomas Sutcliffe, during the time he has served under my orders, has been irreprehensible; and, that in the fulfilment of his duty he has given general satisfaction. With respect to his private conduct, all I can say in this matter is, that he has always acted with the strictest honour, which has ever been his guide.
"At the request of the bearer, and for his own particular ends, I give this in Talca, this 30th day of October, 1825.
"JOSE MARIA BOYLE."

I soon received a communication from Santiago, in which the general informed me that I had acted in accordance with the rules of service. He gave me orders to retain the command until a new commander should arrive.

A few days after, a Major Zimenes, an officer of infantry, who had lately joined the squadron in Coquimbo as captain, arrived; he went directly to the barracks, summoned the officers together, and on hearing that I had not obeyed the order that Captain Bascufian had brought, he began to call me an " O'Higginista," and told them that he was major of the regiment, for the corps had just been raised to a regiment.

After he had produced his commission, the trumpeters assembled to welcome their new chief. This coming to my knowledge, I went straightway to the barracks, called the adjutant, and inquired why the band had been playing without my knowledge; he informed me that "his major" had arrived. I ordered him to sound parade; he did not obey me, but went to the major, who came out and inquired if I had ordered that call. I replied that I did, and I requested the adjutant to bring me the standing orders of the corps. Major Zimenes informed me that he was "my jefe," and shewed me an order from the minister of war, empowering him to take command of the squadron, until the commander of the regiment should arrive; on this, I told him that I was sorry he had adopted such proceedings without first seeing me; and on all the officers assembling, I took the book of orders from the adjutant, and gave him into custody of the officer on guard; after which I read the standing orders of the army, and my correspondence with the chief of the staff relative to Captain Bascuñan. I then informed Major Zimenes that he was welcome to take up his quarters with me until I should hear further from government; at the same time requesting that he would not interfere with the troops, until he was properly installed as major of the corps: this he did not seem to relish. However, during our controversy, Lieutenant-Colonel Don Ambrosio Acosta happily arrived and delivered an official note from the Commandante General, in which I found that he had become commandant of the regiment of Lancers.

This officer was a Spaniard, who had embraced the patriot cause, and had married a sister-in-law to General Zenteno, who was related to General Blanco. He was a good cavalry officer, and had the manners of a gentleman. However, I felt hurt at the conduct of the minister of war, Don Jose Maria Novoa, because, though the corps had been raised to a regiment, and augmented to three squadrons, he had not only deprived me of the majorship to which I was justly entitled, but had also ordered me to serve under a junior officer; in consequence of this, on Captain Bascuñan's arrival, I sent in a memorial complaining of such usage, to which I received the following answer through the medium of the new com-

K

mandant, and which was also inserted in the general
orders of the army :

"Santiago, November 10th, 1825.

"DECREE.

"The Supreme Government have had no cause to detract from the credit
(concepto), that Captain Don Tomas Sutcliffe has gained; the orders of
which he complains were dictated in a critical moment, and when despatch
was necessary, with the equivocal belief that he was not the senior captain of the squadron. The commandant-general of the army will make this
public, and return the original document into the hands of the said Captain
Sutcliffe,

"A rubric of His Excellency,

"NOVOA, Minister of War."

Finding it impossible to preserve harmony with Major
Zimenes, I sent in (previously to Lieut.-Colonel Acosta
taking the command,) another memorial, requesting my
removal on half-pay.

My friend, Colonel Benavente, having received the
command of the regiment of Casadores a Caballo, and all
the troops in the canton, came from Coquimbo, and, on
my visiting him, he prevailed upon me to remain until
the campaign was over; his head-quarters were at
Quelchedeguas, and we received orders to march to
Serro Verde, a league distant.

His Excellency General Freyre, notwithstanding his
want of success during the last expedition against Chiloe,
felt determined in wresting that hold from the dominion
of the Spaniards; who, whilst they held possession,
fostered the hopes of their partizans in Chile, and, with
the few friars that remained, were using all their
influence and energies in order to gain their ends; for,
ever since the secularization of the friars, and the seizure
of their wealth, they had propagated the grossest
calumnies against the administration, and accused it of
having destroyed the religion of their forefathers, in order

to introduce the licentiousness of the foreigners who had been tolerated to enter and reside in the country; and devised every art to agitate and alarm the consciences of the Chilians. No sooner had the supreme director sailed with the expedition against Chiloe, than the bishop of Santiago, El Doctor Don Jose Santiago Rodrigues, a Chilian, who was the oracle and leader of the Spanish party, with his auxiliaries, began to bestir themselves, in order to persuade the people, who had received their lessons at the "confessional," to rise, and purge the country from its heretical rulers; but their intended enterprize was frustrated by the vigilance of the government; and the acting director, Don Jose Miguel Infante, put a stop to the proceedings of the "Spanish faction," by arresting the bishop of Santiago* on the night of the 23d of December, 1825, and sending him directly to Valparaiso, from whence he was transported to Acapulco.

On the 15th of January, 1826, the war of independence was at last terminated by the valour and constancy of the Chilian arms, and that of Peru ended eight days afterwards: for by the perseverance of Generals Bolivar, O'Higgins, Sucre, and other eminent patriots who had united in the common cause, the armies of Spain were defeated at Junin, Ayacucha, and in Bolivia. These were decisive blows, for, after the two first, the viceroy, General La Serna, capitulated, and on the 19th of January, 1826, General Rodil delivered the important fortress of Callao to the Peruvian government.

Previously to our leaving Talca, some Indians arrived, from whom we received information that Pincheyra was

* This prelate was particularized on his arrival at Madrid by the marked attention of his sovereign, Ferdinand VII., and was entertained at court as a distinguished exile !!

K 2

meditating an attack on that city, which prolonged our stay, and preparations were made to defend the place. A corps of cavalry was formed of volunteers, and the militia were placed under discipline, and bivouacked every night in the principal square, which was intrenched.

One night we received information that Pincheyra had left the Cordillera, and was on his march towards "El Astillero," an hacienda, distant about ten leagues from Talca, in the direction of the Cordillera; we marched towards the place, and on approaching the houses of Don Fr. Salcedo, we found that Pincheyra had plundered them, and killed two peones; but, hearing of our approach, had made off with his force towards the Cordillera, taking with him a young lady about sixteen years of age, who was sister to the owner of the estate, and who had a brother, Captain Don Mateo Salcedo, in the second squadron of our corps, that lay in Coquimbo.

This information was a powerful stimulus to our exertions, and incited us to make all possible haste in pursuit of the robbers, who unfortunately gained the pass of the Cordilleras before us; we took several prisoners, and obliged Pincheyra to relinquish his booty; and when we returned to "El Astillero," we had the unspeakable pleasure of hearing that the young lady was restored to her family, and in Talca.

The robbers came upon them so suddenly, during the night, that the females of the hacienda had only time to escape into the vineyard, whence they were dragged, and placed on horseback by the Indians, who galloped off to the Cordillera, where they thought themselves safe for the night; but our advancing upon them sooner than they expected, put them to flight; during

the confusion that ensued amongst them, the young lady
escaped into a thicket, where she remained concealed
until daylight; she heard the firing, but could not distinguish friends from foes; when they had all passed by
the place where she lay, she ventured out, and turned
towards home; but, having lost her shoes, her feet were
so much lacerated, that she was compelled to seat herself
by the wayside, in a situation where she could see all who
passed by, without being observed herself: fortunately
one of her brother's servants who had been sent to look
after cattle, passed near her; she hailed him, and he bore
her proudly to his master.

I called upon her with Captain Bascuñan, when she
returned us many thanks, telling us that she should ever
feel grateful, for we were her deliverers.   Poor girl!
she was never seen to smile after this disaster, and refused
to be seen by any, except her family; before she had
returned home, she made a vow to take the veil, and is
now a nun in the convent of Trinitarias in Concepcion.

I am not able to describe the sufferings of Doña Trini-
dad Salcedo, in language adequate to convey a proper
impression of their severity; my friend, Don Maurice
Rugendas, to whom I related the affair, gave me a beautiful oil-painting to commemorate it, which is an accurate
and striking picture of the ferocious savages who committed such atrocities.

On the 17th of February, we marched to our station
at Serro Verde, three leagues from the pass of Rio Claro;
a few days after our arrival, the wife and daughter of
Don N. Maturano, and a peon, arrived, and informed us
that Pincheyra had attacked Rio Claro, and that they
had escaped with difficulty; we informed Colonel Benevente, and made every preparation to march; he had

previously been advised by El S'or Maturano, who had escaped on a bare-backed horse, to Quelchedeguas. He accordingly sent an order for us to march; and on our joining the " casadores," we halted, and passed the night in front of the hacienda.

On the next morning we entered the village of Rio Claro, and found that great havoc had been made; all the houses were completely gutted, and five dead bodies lay under a shed. We advanced about seven leagues in the Cordillera; but the robbers had one day's start of us, and got off with more than a thousand head of cattle, which they had collected before they attacked Rio Claro.

We returned to our station, and on the 28th of February I received my discharge from the regiment, and was attached to the staff of the war-office on full pay; so I gave up my troop to the first lieutenant; and, after having obtained a receipt and certificate from Commandante Acosta, I marched to the capital.

General Freyre had just returned after taking the islands of Chiloe, and he seemed surprised at the usage I had received; a few days after I was appointed adjutant to General Don Jose Manuel Borgoño, who was made chief of the staff.

REDUCTION OF THE CHILIAN NAVY.—General Freyre reduced the army and squadron. Three ships were sold to the Buenos-Ayrean government; one, a frigate of 44 guns, foundered at sea, and all on board perished. Captain Cobbett commanded her; he was a nephew to the politician, a brave officer, and his loss was sincerely regretted by all who knew him. I am ignorant of the names of the other officers, therefore I can only say, that many of the brave patriots who performed such acts of gallantry under the orders of Admiral Cochrane went down in her.

The Estanço was established, whereby a monopoly of teas, tobacco, foreign liquors, and cards, was given to a company, who had to remit the proceeds to the bond-holders, in order that the debt might be redeemed, and the interest paid. Don Diego Portales, Zea, and Company were the proprietors.

Also several estates belonging to the convents were sold, as well as lands appertaining to the state, in order to raise funds to meet the payments of contracts, and other expenses incurred during the expedition of Peru, and the two expeditions of Chiloe; as well as the war occasioned by that horde of bandits, called a Spanish army, that was ravaging the province of Concepcion and Maule.

General Freyre renounced the supreme command on the 4th of July, 1826, and General Don Manuel Blanco Enclada was elected president of the republic on the 8th.

An attempt was made in the provinces of Chiloe and Valdivia, at this time, to restore General O'Higgins to the supremacy.

Colonel Don Jose Antonio Aldunate was deposed, and sent to the continent, by those troops which, with the acting governor of San Carlos, had declared themselves favourable to General O'Higgins; after having solicited a court-martial, which was granted, he justified himself, and was sent back with troops, by means of which he restored order in the province.

As General O'Higgins had been " dado de.bajo," (dismissed the service,) for having exceeded the terms of his leave of absence, General Freyre was promoted to the rank of captain-general, and Colonel Acosta was promoted and placed in command of the canton of Maule.

CHAP. V.

GENERAL BLANCO was soon tired of the supreme command, and sent in his resignation to the congress, in which
he stated very powerful motives that had induced him to
take this step.

On General Blanco's resignation being accepted, the
vice-president of the republic, Don Augustin Eyzaguirre
succeeded him on the 10th of September, 1826, as president. The election of this citizen, whose patriotic services
are often recorded in the annals of the emancipation of
Chile, did not please a few, who could not bear to see any
one occupying the post of president of the republic, who
had not obtained military rank in the army during the
war of Independence.

They did not bear in mind, that he was one of the few
citizens that had always been the firmest and most per-
severing supporters of liberty, of which the republic could
boast; who had, on more than one occasion, been safely
entrusted with the public confidence, when it was hard to
tell where that confidence could with advantage be re-
posed, and who suffered for his attachment to the cause
of freedom in Juan Fernandez.

I am extremely sorry that I cannot do justice to my
worthy friend, for such he was as long as he lived; but

EXMO. SEÑOR DON MANUEL BULNES PRIETO.

PRESIDENTE DE LA REPUBLICA

DE CHILE.

Fisher, Son & Co. London & Paris.

with the few documents I have been able to save or collect, I will show, that during the short period of his
government he devoted himself, without reserve, to the
work of improving the state of the republic, particularly
in the southern provinces, which were almost ruined by
the incursions of Pincheyra; mischiefs that were tolerated
to an incredible extent.

He made an appeal to his fellow-citizens to aid him
during the almost exhausted state of the treasury, in pro-
secuting his laudable plans; and, that he might secure
an energetic agent, he named General Don Jose Manuel
Borgoño to be the general-in-chief of the army.

With the advice of this general he strove to ameliorate
the condition of the soldiers, by increasing their pay from
six to seven dollars; and in order to lessen the abuses
that had crept into various corps, he issued decrees for
better regulating punctuality in the payments.

This gave umbrage to several commandants of corps,
one of whom refused to pay the customary honours to
his excellency.

He named General Freyre commandante-general-de-
armas and inspector-general of the army and militia; he
protected foreigners from extortion; and besides other
beneficial acts, he made many new regulations with respect to the standing army, the militia, and other different
branches of the administration; he sent General Borgoño
to the south with all the disposable forces, adopting every
proper expedient to raise funds for their armament and
maintenance during their campaign against Pincheyra;
and, lastly, he dissolved the regiment of Granaderos
Lanceros, which was totally unfit for service, and, according to the statement of their commander, "falta de moral,"
without discipline.

I shall now proceed to relate the particulars of the campaigns of General Borgoño, who had honoured me by appointing me his aid-de-camp.

November 15th, we marched in company with the regiment No. 8, Colonel Beauchef, and on the 24th entered Talca; the general took up his quarters in the house of Doña Maria Antonia Donoso, mother to his lady, and one of the most respectable matrons in the city. Shortly after our arrival, the regiment of Granaderos Lanceros was disbanded.

Colonel Acosta, after having been promoted and made commandante-general of the Canton del Maule, had entrusted the management of the corps of Lancers to Major Zimenes.

The 2nd squadron, Commandante Don Manuel Latus, Captains Salcedo and Rodrigues, had just arrived to join the regiment; and I was sorry to see them and other meritorious officers thrown out of employment. My comrade, Captain Bascuñan, retired from the regiment in disgust shortly after I left it; he married and took up his abode in Talca. The non-commissioned officers and privates, with the exception of a very few, were drafted into the corps of infantry, and thus the regiment of Granaderos Lanceros, which only a few months before had been held up as a model to the army, ceased to exist, at a time when called upon for active service. So much for intrigue. Government and the general attached the blame to the proper parties.

The expedition intended for the Cordillera being nearly ready for action, I was sent to the capital on the 18th of December, and returned with an ample remittance in specie on the 24th instant. On dismounting at the general's house I met with a cool reception, and before I could recover from the surprise I was thrown into by the general stating that " I had deceived him," or even before I could explain myself, we heard the trampling of the escort, and the soldiers crying out " Plata, Plata, ahi veine la Mosca ;" and on their entering the court-yard, the general said " Que Plata." On my answering that it was what I had brought from the capital, he embraced me, and the opinion was soon changed in my favour.

The general had been informed only two days before by an officer, that I had remained some time in Curico, and that he had seen me at a dance there. This circumstance, connected with my appearance so many days before they had any reason to expect my return, led them to conjecture, when they saw me arrive, that I had not fulfilled my errand, never supposing that I could march 160 leagues in less than six days, and bring treasure from the capital, where it is no easy task, after a decree is made out by government for the commissary to issue the money, to be able to obtain it without the delay of some days ; but through the exertions of the president, Don Augustin Eyzaguirre, I was despatched in twenty-four hours: so the soldiers received a month's pay ; and as the general had got every thing that was necessary, he despatched Colonel Beauchef and his division to the Cordillera.

On the 3rd of January, 1827, the general marched ; we passed the river Maule at the ferry, and halted at the hacienda of Longomillo, on the banks of a deep and navigable river, that entered the Maule from the southward ; on the next day we halted at Linares, about fifteen leagues from Talca ; this is a small town, but the country around it is populous and fertile, wearing a very different aspect from all that I have seen north of the Maule ; here the woods are numerous, and there is less need of irrigation; we here found a troop of dragoons, from which the general took an escort.

The day following we crossed the rivers Putagan and Achygueno, which were deep and rapid, and halted at the hacienda of Longabi, where we found a squadron of cavalry. The houses of this hacienda were fortified. Pincheyra had once made an attempt to attack and plunder this estate; Commandante Jourdan was stationed with a squadron of dragoons to defend it, and on Pincheyra's advancing from the Cordillera, he marched against him rather too hastily; for there were troops on their march from Talca, and a squadron of dragoons from the neighbourhood of San Carlos, intending to operate jointly with him; however, he considered his force sufficient; but, on charging the maurauders, he fell, his horse being entangled by the "bolos;" only one officer and a few of his soldiers escaped. Poor Jourdan's body was found cut to pieces, with several others, and afterwards interred with military honours in the chapel of Longabi; he was a good officer, and his fate was much regretted; he left a widow to deplore his loss.

In the evening we marched, and passed the river Longabi, which is fordable, and halted at El Parral, about fifteen leagues distant.

This is a small town surrounded by a ditch, or pallisades; there is also a kind of fort; the place has been visited by Pincheyra, and the Governor Commandante Urutia, and his lady, with a few resolute men, defended their house, and obliged the villains to retire, after losing several of their number; a friar, Padre Gomes, accompanied the robbers, and strove to stimulate them in their efforts to storm the house of the governor; he was seen to sit astride a gun that had been taken, in order to reanimate them: he was chaplain to the followers of Pincheyra.*

We found a troop of dragoons stationed here; we passed the night at the governor's; and, next morning, just as we were preparing to march, we received intelligence that Pincheyra was on the road we had to pass. It was well for us that we did not leave at daylight, as we were informed that they had been in ambush until after sunrise, and decamped after murdering six paysanos.

At six in the evening we halted at the town of San Carlos, about twelve leagues.

January 7. Halted; the general visited the military station of Gauna, where a corps of cavalry is generally fixed; it is an elevated situation, and has an observatory, which commands an extensive view of the surrounding country; there is a tower in San Carlos capable of containing two companies of infantry.

January 8. We marched, passed the river Nuble at the ferry, and halted at Chillan, eight leagues; this is the head-quarters of the army of the south, and the capital of the department: shortly after our arrival, the general sent Commandante Godoy, and Lieut.-Colonel Tupper, with a reinforcement, and provisions; they marched by the pass of Alico. The worthy promoter of this campaign, Don Augustin Eyzaguirre, was obliged to abdicate the presidency of the republic, on the 26th of January, by a military tumult, and the congress elected Captain General Don Ramon Freyre to be his successor.

General Borgoño, Colonel Biel, chief of the staff, and several other chiefs and officers, left the head-quarters on the 5th of March, and after passing the rivers Chillan, Diguillin, Itata, Lavendaño, and Bermejo, arrived at

* Now much respected and revered in Chile.

Yumbell, about twenty leagues; the road was, for the most part, sandy and heavy; but the country fertile. We passed several large haciendas, the blackened ruins of which, marked the ravages that had been committed by the royalists, the Indians, and other marauders that had joined the remnants of the Spaniards, during the latter part of the struggle for the independence of Chile, under the command of Neira, Pico, Benevides, and Pincheyra. From Chillan to Yumbell we did not see a single house that had escaped their ravages. We were met and conducted to our quarters by the military governor, Lieutenant-Colonel Don Juan de Luna, Commandante Ukiso, of the Casadores, and his officers, with several others.

Yumbell, as a military station, is a miserable place; it contains two barracks, a church, and about ten or twelve decent houses; the rest of the habitations are miserable-looking straw huts : it is surrounded by a mud wall, open in various parts, stands upon about eight acres, and is commanded by hills within musket-shot. The Bermejo, a small river, passes close by the town ; but the water is bad, and what is generally consumed is brought from Rio Claro, distant about a league.

From the neighbouring height, La Sierra de la Centinela, there is a delightful view of the country ; the Cordillera is seen at about twenty leagues distant ; the volcano of Antuco is situated bearing by compass E. ¼ N., its top was covered with snow, and smoke issued from it, which was propelled to the northward ; its irruptions are frequent, and are sometimes visible to a great distance ; near to it there is another volcano, which has for many years ceased to emit its smoke, the name of it is Serro Veludo, and sulphur is collected from it.

A neighbouring elevation is called Serro Quintana, in honour of a patriot chief, who defended himself and his detachment successfully there against a superior force of Spaniards and Indians; the country southward and eastward has a wild appearance; but in the neighbourhood of Yumbell there are excellent vineyards, which produce the best grapes and wine in Chile; those of Serro Parra are the most famed.

During our stay in Yumbell, Commandante Bulnes arrived with his squadron of cavalry from the Cordillera, and was quartered in the neighbourhood; the general received favourable communications from Colonel Beauchef. Whilst we were here, a cacique, and a few Indians arrived from Marilaun, an Indian chief, with whom the general had entered into correspondence; the general dispatched him with presents, and invited the caciques to meet him in Los Angeles, or Chillan.

A French gentleman, Don Bertran Matieu, who had resided for some time on the frontier, wrote to the Spanish officers, Sinosain and Sanchez, (who had left Pincheyra,) and were at this time with Marilaun, accelerating their delivering themselves up to government, which had promised to give them passports, enabling them to return to Spain, if they would quit the Indian territory.

The general marched on the 20th; we passed Rio Claro at the "Salta de Agua," a beautiful cascade, and crossed the river Laxa, at the ford of the islands, (Vado de las Islas;) this is the broadest river I have seen in Chile; the river Claro enters it about half a league from the ford, and the Laxa enters the Bio Bio, about four leagues lower. The governor of the district met us here, accompanied by a party of militia on horseback, and at

eleven o'clock we arrived at his hacienda, " La Palma ;"
here we found large and well-built houses; for, during
the war it had sustained no injury from the Indians, in
consequence of the respect entertained towards the owner.
El S'or Armasa was a Spaniard, and his conduct towards
the Indians, and all others with whom he came in contact,
was such, that he obtained the name of " Taita," father.

Whilst we were here, two Indians came to inform the
general that Marilaun could not meet him at the time
appointed, because it was the " chicha" season: this is a
drink these people are very fond of, and much resembles
our cider ; it is extracted from apples.

On the 24th, we marched, accompanied by El S'or
Armasa, and his chaplain, El Doctor Ruis; we crossed
the river Guanque, about a league from its confluence
with the Bio Bio; here we were met by a cacique and
his followers, who began to harangue us in the Indian
language; but as they were settled on the north bank
of the Bio Bio, we soon dismissed them. And at eleven
o'clock came to Bio Bio, and crossed at the ferry, about
a quarter of a league from the foot of the fort of
Nacimento; we took up our quarters in a shed that
had been prepared for the general in the fort; all the
buildings had been destroyed by the Indians.

When the fort was attacked, the governor of El
Parral was one of its defenders, and lost his left hand ;
the walls and edifices of this fort were brick and stone ; it
occupies a commanding situation near the confluence of
the rivers Bergara and Bio Bio.

The Bergara is a deep and rapid river, and runs from
the Indian territory in a northern direction; there is a
ferry close to the fort: I took up my quarters outside the
walls; and the owner of the house at which I staid, enter-

tained us with a " bayle;" the party, a mixed assembly
of Indian and Chilian extraction, were gay and cheerful;
the harp, " ravel," and guitar were played until a late
hour; but there was more drinking than dancing; I was
astonished to see the women drink such quantities of raw
spirits, " blanco toro," and " peelque." Our beds were
made on the floor of a room, and, shortly after I had
fallen asleep, I was suddenly awakened and alarmed;
and when I opened my eyes, found myself nearly smo-
thered with onions, a long pole on which a great many
strings of onions were suspended, having either been
pulled down by some of the party inteptionally, or fallen
by its own weight. It was well for me that I escaped
without serious injury, for the end of the pole had made
a hole in the floor, near my head. Shortly afterwards,
a woman in the next room began to cry out in a dreadful
manner, and was in a few minutes delivered of a female
child; our chaplain, Ruis, was with us, and previously to our
leaving Yumbell, he baptized the child, and I stood godfather to it. During the night, one of our party lost his
horse, and after some search the bones and offal were
found; it had been killed, and perhaps the owner, who
complained greatly of the rascality of the Indians, had
eaten his share of it at supper. It is always advisable for
travellers on the frontier to take particular care of their
horses.

March 25. We again crossed the Bio Bio, and had
a pleasant ride of about eleven leagues over the most
fertile part of Chile: we passed many farms, but all the
houses were in ruins; not a living animal was to be seen,
except wild horses and foxes.

We passed El Pangal, where Lieutenant-Colonel
Don Juan Maria O'Carrol, commandante of dragoons,

L

a brave and excellent officer, was barbarously murdered,
having been taken prisoner. A cousin of his, Major
Don Miguel O'Carrol, accompanied us, who with sorrow
recollected his relative's death.

We halted in a beautiful orchard of fruit trees, where
we dined, and regaled ourselves; the peaches were ripe,
and of an excellent quality; this farm, which contained
about 600 quadres, 2,400 acres, had formerly belonged to
a private soldier, who was orderly to the general; he had
been obliged to emigrate with his family, and was reduced
to beggary: such was the fate of thousands that once
peopled the Island de la Laja.

At 4 o'clock, we entered Los Angelos, once the principal city of the frontier, but now a heap of ruins; sheds
had been erected by El S'or Armasa for our reception;
but the rain compelled me to seek drier quarters, and, in
company with Lieutenant-Colonel Tupper, I took my
night's lodging in an oven, which luckily had remained
entire, amongst the ruins of a house that once belonged to
General O'Higgins.

This city, and the surrounding country, had contained
30,000 inhabitants about seven years before we visited it;
but the Spaniards, on their retreating to the Indian territory, had destroyed it; and their cruelties, in conjunction
with those of the marauders who accompanied them, reduced it to a desert without an inhabitant. Here was an
extensive fort in ruins, the ditch of which was nearly filled
up; a numerous garrison might have been quartered here.

The city had been well and regularly built; the streets
being formed at right angles; it contained an extensive
square, and almost all the ruins were of brick: we visited
those of the principal church, and I went with Colonel
Viel to see the tomb of one of his countrymen, an officer

who had been killed and interred there; he was the son of the French Admiral Brueys, who was with the fleet at the battle of the Nile, where he fell.

We visited Los Angelos, in order to place a corps of cavalry to protect it, and to repopulate it, by recalling the emigrants who were scattered in the northern provinces, and bore the appellation of " Arrivanos." El S'or Armasa, and several others from Yumbell, had brought peones to commence this laudable enterprise; and his chaplain, who was a patriot, became the curate, he and his patron, were the " restauradores" of this city.

I will now show what a horde of monsters the predecessors of Pincheyra were—and who had commenced their career of desolation, and unheard-of barbarities, in their native province, and on their defenceless countrymen, under the plea of serving the cause of " Ferdinand the Seventh, and the Spanish Nation;" by giving the following translation of a document that was published on the very day that their leader, Benavides, was executed in the capital of Chile, and subsequently in a work published by El Doctor Don Juan Ascencio, in Lima, 1833. Pages 103 to 110.

VINDICTA PUBLICA.—Chilians, who are interested in the glory of your country, and all others who observe the conduct of the Americans—know that the execution you have this day witnessed, does not in the least offend the delicacy with which Chile has observed the laws of nations, in the war she has so vigorously sustained against the tenacious endeavours of the usurpers.

Vicente Benavides, son of Torribio, the gaol-keeper of Qurihue, in the province of Concepcion, a de-naturalized Chilian, was a soldier of the Patria, and rose to be a sergeant of grenadiers during the first epoch of our revolution; he deserted to the enemy, and in the memorable action of

L 2

El Membrillar, gained by General Makenna, he was taken prisoner, and brought to the town of Linares, whence, during a dark night, and whilst the army were preparing to make a vigorous attack on the enemy, he escaped to them, after having set fire to some ammunition.

He continued with the serviles of Ferdinand, and was again taken prisoner on the glorious 5th of April, at Maipu, tried by a military tribunal, and sentenced to be shot as a deserter; but, having escaped in a most extraordinary manner, he presented himself to the general-in-chief of the army of Los Andes, who had interested himself in his behalf, in order to save his life. He made an offer of his services, showing that it would be easy to dissuade the Indians, and, inhabitants on the southern frontier, or on the margin of the Bio Bio, from being deluded by the Spaniards, who were striving to engage them in a desultory war, and against the laws of nations. His offers being accepted, he received his instructions and passport; and, after having arrived at the city of Los Angelos, he passed over to the fort of Nacimiento, where he convinced the commander of the enemy's forces, Don Juan Francisco Sanchez, that he was qualified to carry on a desultory war; so that on this chief's retiring to Valdivia, he confided the command of the frontier to Benavides, who renewed his services to the king, by one of the most scandalous acts, and in open violation of the usages of war. He attacked and took the fort of Santa Juana, where, after a sanguinary conflict, an officer and fourteen soldiers were taken prisoners; he proposed to exchange the officer for his own wife, who was in the city of Concepcion. Lieutenant Forres was sent, with a flag of truce, by the general of the army, who had acceded to the proposals of Benavides, but this barbarian .detained the officer and sent Riveros alone, as soon as his wife had passed the fort of San Pedro; and that very night he consummated one of the most unheard-of acts of ferocity in the present age, for, no sooner had the poor lieutenant, who had borne the flag of truce, taken his supper with Benavides, than he was murdered along with the fourteen prisoners captured in Santa Juana.

His instructions to his officers seemed to be written in characters of blood, for he imposed no gentler punishment than that of death on every insurgent. These orders were scrupulously obeyed by the vile instruments of his cruelty; for each of the monsters who had been so authorized, dealt death and destruction around him, and in order to augment their forces, offered the terrible choice to their peaceful countrymen— "to follow them or die." In order to conceal their route, or place of ambush, when on their marauding parties, they did not scruple to murder both children and aged persons. [In the month of June, 1820, General Freyre met a woman in the Hacienda del Tortoral, whose husband had been murdered a few days before by one of these commandants of guerillas, because he had mentioned his having been in his house. Innumerable acts of this kind might be cited, and are notorious in the departments of Chillan and Rere. In the valley of Palomares, a party of the enemy finding a man, sixty years of age, his wife, son, and three grand-children asleep in their houses, robbed and murdered them, and all the inhabitants of the city of Concepcion saw their bodies interred, in April, 1821.] They had commenced this kind of warfare in 1819: and at times the general-in-chief of the army of the south had been obliged to retaliate, although with the moderation that characterizes him, and in obedience to the instructions he had received from the supreme government, in order to put a stop to their barbarities; he also used more conciliatory measures, by issuing general pardons, which were most religiously observed, even with the most abandoned, when they presented themselves; he further prohibited and impeded the officers and soldiers from wreaking their vengeance upon such as had been instrumental in the murders of their companions in arms; but nothing could mitigate the insane fury of Benavides, and his barbarous satellites. Lieutenant-Colonel Don Carlos Maria O'Carrol was taken prisoner in El Pangal, on the 23rd of September, 1821, and shot in cool blood, along with Captain Bourne, for Benavides said he had orders from the king to shoot all foreigners.

On the 26th, he attacked a detachment of the battalion, No. 1., of Coquimbo, 300 men, on the banks of the river Laja, near the ford of Tarpellanea; and next day he sent them an offer of quarter, which General Don Andres Alcara received at a time when the worthy old veteran had expended the whole of his ammunition, and his soldiers were nearly exhausted with fatigue and hunger. He capitulated, but no sooner had the soldiers surrendered their arms, than they were inhumanly butchered, and the officers shot, even without the consolations of religion; and what was still more atrocious, the poor general, Major Ruir, and about 300 families that had been collected in the Isle de la Laja, were given up to the Indians, who accompanied Benavides, in order that they might be lanced to death. He also burnt and destroyed the towns of Los Angelos, Nacimiento, Huelqui, Talcamavida, Santa Juana, San Pedro, and Arauco, as well as all the haciendas of the departments of Rere, Puchacay, Chillan, and San Carlos.

On the 27th of November he sent in proposals to capitulate, in order to cover his perfidy; yet, whilst his emissary, a clergyman named Ferrebur, was enjoying the immunities of a flag of truce, Benavides pushed forward a detachment

of cavalry to continue hostilities. Finally, he threw off the
mask of the king of Spain, when General Don Joaquim
Prieto communicated notice of Peru having fallen, and upon
which he depended (for the viceroy had promoted him to
be a colonel of the Spanish army); he sent an answer protesting that he would make war against Chile with his last
soldier, although the king and the Spanish nation should
acknowledge its independence.

From one crime he precipitated himself into another.
Or, was it because he had dared to trample upon the laws
of nations? for his government could never tolerate acts
of piracy.

He armed a vessel, and sent her to cruise off the coast of
Chile, with orders to respect no flag, and his instructions
were, to put the crews of every insurgente, or other suspicious vessels, to death; orders which were strictly obeyed:
for the situation of Arauco, on account of being so near to
the island of Santa Maria, where vessels entering the
Pacific were accustomed to touch for refreshments, &c.,
made the capture of the following vessels easy to them:—
The ships Perseverance, Hero, and brig Arsella, were
taken, as well as several boats belonging to other vessels.
The captains of the vessels were shot, and the son of that
of the Hero perished with his father. I cannot name them,
but Sub-Lieutenant Sanchez, who witnessed their execution, said that he and others shed tears over the fate of the
innocent and unfortunate youth who was shot with his
father. The vessels were English and North Americans.
He has since exulted that he has caused damage and
destruction to the amount of millions of dollars.

At last he was reduced to offer terms of surrendering
himself to General Prieto; and during the negociation, he

embarked with a few others in a boat in the port of Lebu, and tried to escape for the coast of Peru, and rejoin the royal army; but being obliged, on account of want of water, to put into the bay of Topocalma, in the province of Colchagua, a soldier, who was sent on shore, and tired of his associates, informed two patriots, Los SS. Hidalgo, and Fuenrelida, who, with others, captured the boat, and remitted Benavides to the capital, where he has been tried according to the laws of this country, and sentenced to be executed—for, as a deserter to the enemy, he ought to die; and as he has violated the laws of nations, he has lost all pretences to military honour due to prisoners of war; as a pirate, as the barbarous destroyer of many towns, &c., it has been found necessary to inflict that kind of death which will avenge humanity, and terrify others from having the audacity to imitate him; therefore he was, on the 21st of this month, sentenced to be dragged on a hurdle to the gallows, at the tail of a mule, and after he had been hung up till dead, his head and hands were to be cut off, and fixed upon pikes, to decorate the towns of Santa Juana, Tarpellanca, and Arauco. He has had three days allowed him to make his peace with his Creator, so that he has received all the necessary aid and consolation of religion, although this faithful vassal of the Catholic king denied such indulgence to General Alcarar, Lieutenant-Colonel O'Carrol, Major Ruis, and the other unfortunates who fell into his clutches.

March 27th, we left Los Angelos, and on our way over the plains, crossed several patches of wild strawberries and roses; at twelve we halted near a small lake, Caugui, where there was an abundance of wild ducks. The woods in the

Montaña, a range of above four or five leagues, were on fire, and nothing but rains could stop the progress of the flames. We saw a party of Indians hunting horses at a distance, but they took to the woods. We halted an hour at the Hacienda of Cantera, belonging to General O'Higgins. There is a remarkable hill here, from which I took the bearings of Los Angelos, Nacimiento, San Carlos, a ruined fort on the Bio Bio, and Serra de la Centinela Yumbell, to correct others which I had taken on my march, in order to make a croquis of our route. The houses on this hacienda had been lately burnt, and the vineyard destroyed by some spiteful enemy of the general.

At seven o'clock we arrived at the village of Antuco, about twenty leagues from Los Angelos; the inhabitants of this village were delighted to see us; they had not seen a priest for many months; and when they were informed that our chaplain, Ruis, was intended to be the curate of Los Angelos, they were overjoyed; but I cannot adequately describe the effect that was produced among them when they found that the general-in-chief of the army was with us; he was soon beset with persons lodging complaints against the military commandant, who seems to have been a petty tyrant. The general referred them to Don Pedro Palazuellos, the auditor of war; and Colonel Viel, the governor, was put under arrest, and ordered to Chillan, and another officer was appointed in his place; this appointment gave general satisfaction.

A large entrenchment serves to fortify this place, and two companies of infantry are stationed in it.

Near the village is a small solitary rock, of a conical form, about twenty yards high, where, some time ago, a brave officer, named Arkinigo, with a few soldiers, withstood an attack from the marauders, until he was left alone;

on being promised quarter, he surrendered himself, but the villains no sooner got hold of him than they butchered him in a most barbarous manner.

The morning after our arrival, we visited the fort of Antuco, situated near the base of the volcano, of which we had a fine view: there is a large lake at the foot of the hill, called Laguna de Antuco; and what is remarkable, it is said to ebb and flow like the sea; there are no fish in it, neither do any birds approach its waters.

This pass of the mountain is such, that it is said a carriage may be driven across from Chile to the province of Mendoza; an entrenchment crosses the valley near to what is called the fort, which is a small house capable of containing forty men, built upon a hill near the centre of the valley, where the road passes; it was without either palisades or loop-holes.

The ride in the Montaña, before we reached the Cordillera, was very romantic.

We here met a detachment of infantry returning from the expedition; they had with them about forty Chilenos, whom they had rescued; also a number of prisoners, amongst whom were the sisters of Pincheyra and their families.

The general wrote to Colonel Beauchef, who was in Trapa-Trapa, collecting Chilian captives and treating with the Indians.

The houses of Antuco are well built, and generally of wood. The apartments are separated by partitions made of cane. The inhabitants are cleanly, very industrious, and of a fair complexion. We saw several handsome women here, one of whom attracted general notice.

We left Antuco on the 29th, crossed the river De la Laxa at a ford distant about a league from the village, and halted at the Laguna Tupan; here were immense flocks of ducks, and they afforded us some profitable sport. Whilst traversing the Montanna, we were all at once surrounded by a party of armed men, whom we at first took to be robbers, but to the unspeakable joy of some of us, they proved to be a party of mounted militia from Tucapel, who, on hearing our firing, had marched to reconnoitre; their commandante, El S'or Salvo, was complimented by the general for his promptitude; we were accompanied by them to the fort, a distance of about ten leagues, where we took up our quarters.

Tucapel is a straggling village, the houses are built in a manner nearly similar to those at Antuco; the fort is extensive, and surrounded by a deep ditch. Major Vidaurre was there with a detachment of the battalion No. 6. The source of the river Itata is near this place.

March 30th, we left Tucapel at daylight, and crossed the rivers Itata, Trillalen, Damcalque, Pemuco, and Nequillen; halted at noon at Pemuco: here were two or three houses, and a church, the only one that remained on the south-east frontier save that at Yumbell; the curate had been tutor to General Borgoño, to whom he gave a hearty welcome. One of the released captives gave birth to a female child on the march, and, immediately after it was born, she immersed it in a torrent of melted snow—how chilly !!!

At sunset we arrived at Chillan, after a march of nearly twenty-six leagues.

The governor and principal inhabitants of Chillan, called to compliment the general on the happy result of the expedition against Pincheyra, and all with the exception of a few who considered Pincheyra to be the champion of their " rey y religion," church and king, expressed their satisfaction at being almost freed from such a plague.

. The captives who had been rescued, were restored to their friends, and such as were so young when taken as to be unable to describe their place of residence, or family name, were taken and adopted by others.

The sisters of Pincheyra, with their families, were delivered to my landlord, Don Gregorio Moreno, who offered to support them in his hacienda, on account of their kindness to his niece, whom he had ransomed from Pincheyra.

Colonel Beauchef returned with the rest of the expedition to Chillan, or their cantonments; and such had been their success, that if it had not been for Commandante Carreno, a Spaniard, deviating from his instructions, neither Pincheyra nor any of his followers would have escaped.

The cacique, Don Nicolas Marilaon, his son, and four other caciques, Lieutenant-Colonel Zinosain, and El S'or Sanchez, who had left the Indian territory under the safe conduct of an escort sent for them; sixty Indians well mounted, armed with lances, lasso, and bolas, and preceded by a band of music that had been sent to meet them; a guard of honour, and cortege of the staff officers, and a number of persons who had collected together out of curiosity—made their entry into Chillan. The general and his aids met them, and on the commandant of the frontier presenting the cacique and his followers to the general, the Indians were conducted, with their caciques, to the quarters which had been prepared for them, and regaled according to custom; for no business was attended to until three days after their arrival, during which time they enjoyed themselves, in eating, drinking,

and listening to martial music, which they desired might
be played during their entertainment; nothing seemed to
delight them more than the band of trumpeters, and they
often called for the instruments to be sounded close to
their ears.

The sheep that were given them were killed in the
following manner: the throat of the animal is first cut,
after which a quantity of salt is thrust down the wound,
and the blood, heart, liver, and lights are generally
devoured raw, the rest was given to the women to cook;
some of them had as many as four wives.

Some of the women did not appear to be above twelve
years of age, and, on account of their youth, had rather an
agreeable appearance; but the more aged had a forbidding
look; their hair was put up in numerous plaits, to which
were attached glass beads of various colours, and thimbles,
which made a jingling noise like so many bells; they had
also a profusion of beads round their necks, arms, and
ankles. They generally wear a short woollen petticoat,
"chiripa," and a piece of red or blue cloth, or baize, which
is thrown over their shoulders, and fastened in front, or on
one side, by an enormous silver pin, called a toupa; some
of these are more than a pound in weight: they also wear
large silver ear-rings of several ounces weight, called
eupellas. The women with their children kept apart from
the men whilst they were feasting, and always managed to
secure their weapons, for during the "borracheros" drinking bouts, they are continually relating or singing their
traditionary stories, or songs, and often work themselves
into a frenzy, and frequently vent their rage on each other:
as these were strange and novel sights to me, I enjoyed
them, and often repeated my visit during the time they
lasted.

On the fourth day, Marilaon, accompanied by his caciques, his son, Fermin, and his "mosetons," warriors, made his appearance at the general's residence, who with the staff-officers were ready to receive them.

Marilaon was dressed in an old embroidered scarlet coat and cocked hat, and cut a droll appearance; although he could speak the Spanish language fluently, for the Spaniards had him educated in the college of Chillan, yet in the presence of the Indians he had his interpreter, and spoke to the general in the Araucanian language; there were several interpreters on both sides, to prevent mistakes. The " parle" or conference lasted nearly two hours, and was concluded by Marilaon, declaring himself a patriot; and to consolidate the peace that he and his allies had made, he gave up his youngest and dearest son, Fermin, as a hostage, charging the general to educate him. The general satisfied the cacique that he would take the greatest care of the youth; and also gave the cacique a Chilian uniform. After receiving numerous presents, the Indians departed from Chillan, accompanied about a league by an escort, similar to that which led them into the city.

April 25. The general sent me to the capital with despatches, on my way I halted at Tango, where I visited the ex-president, Don Augustin Eyzaguirre, and gave him several letters; he received and treated me in the most friendly manner. It was past eleven o'clock at night when I arrived, and as his servants were retired to rest, he placed some refreshments on the table; but on observing me smile at the circumstance, he begged of me to excuse the cold supper, and to pardon his awkward service. Whilst doing honour to his viands, for I had rode nearly forty leagues that day, he seemed to devour the contents of the

letters, and every now and then the ejaculations, "Graciosa
a Dios," thanks be to God, escaped from his lips; we conversed until a late hour, he was well satisfied with the
operations of the army, and more so with General Borgoño, and that he himself had been the promoter of the
expedition, and had thus facilitated the re-populating of the
southern provinces.

The following is an unvarnished and impartial statement of the eminent and patriotic services of his Excellency Don Augustin Eyzaguirre, up to the date of his
abdication, extracted from official and authentic documents.

In the year 1810, he was elected alcalde of the city of
Santiago; and, on the installation of the first junta gubernativa, which after the deposition of the president, Carrasco,
were put into power, on the ever memorable 18th of
September, he refused being one of the members; although
he was elected by the unanimous vote of his fellow-citizens,
on account of his having displayed such energy in creating
a patriotic government on the eve of the aurora of the
liberty of Chile, to avoid being accused of interested
motives.

He afterwards, with the same disinterested motives,
rendered various important services to the state, until the
disastrous epoch of 1813-14, when the viceroy of Peru,
Aboscal, sent an expedition to invade Chile; and, whilst
the chief of the republic marched against the invaders,
El Senor Eyzaguirre was elected president of the junta
that had been put in charge of the supreme government, at
that time surrounded with innumerable difficulties and
dangers. All the true patriots of Chile well may have
cause to recollect the termination of that unfortunate campaign; for the country was again enslaved, and El Senor

Eyzaguirre was exiled, with many other illustrious patriots, to the island of Juan Fernandez, where they underwent the greatest hardships and sufferings, until the glorious restoration of 1817.

He was afterwards usefully employed in various commissions, and gained the esteem of all his fellow-citizens. In 1823, he was once more placed in charge of the republic, as president of the junta gubernativa that succeeded the supreme director, Don Bernardo O'Higgins. He was subsequently elected the representative of the province of Santiago, and member of the conservative senate, where he exercised the functions of president. On the 9th of July, 1826, that hazardous period in which the public order was subverted, he was elected vice-president of the republic; and afterwards, on the renunciation of his Excellency Lieut.-General Don Manuel Blanco Encalada, El Señor Eyzaguirre reassumed the supreme magistrature, where he acted in such an energetic and impartial manner, that he displeased a few, who revolutionized the troops stationed in the capital. An armed force, led on by an adventurer in the Peruvian service, Don Fro. de P. Latafriatt, proceeded to, and invaded, the precincts of the Hall of Congress, where the national representatives were holding their sessions, and, in the most insulting manner, strove to disperse the deputies, by ordering his soldiers to prepare their arms; but a spirited member rose, and by a short and well-directed harangue, caused the fanfaron to be ashamed of his temerity, and the troops to retire; the congress then issued a decree, in which they strove to throw a veil over what had occurred; and after having admitted the resignation of his excellency, and elected his successor, he retired to his estate at Tango, where he passed the evening of his life in quiet peace, and pleasing enjoyment of ease, rest, and freedom of body, as well as mind, agreeable to the practice and sentiments of the wise senators of Rome, who, on like occasions, used to retire to their rural seats, as given us by one of their own poets :*

> " How blest is he, who, tired with his affairs,
> Far from all noise and vain applause prepares
> To go, and underneath some silent shade,
> Which neither cares nor anxious thoughts invade,
> Does, for a while, alone himself possess,
> Changing the court for rural happiness."

* This worthy patriot departed this life in his 70th year, on Wednesday, July 19th, 1837 ; and the ministerial paper of the 28th of July, 1837, says as follows :—

" The republic has to regret a great loss in the person of Don Augustin Eyzaguirre, one of the founders of its independence, and one of the individuals that has most signalized himself by his private virtues, as well as his ardent zeal in favour of the public good, and for his accredited integrity and purity in the various public employments he owed to the confidence of his fellow-citizens." (Here followed an enumeration of his services, &c. nearly the same as I have already stated.)

El Araucano, No. 361.

Doña Ana Josepha Guzman de Larrayn, widow of the Marquess de la Cassa Larrayn, and mother-in-law to the late Don Augustin Eyzaguirre, sent me the following letter in answer to the one of condolence. ,

" S'or Don Thomas Sutcliffe,

" Santiago, August 12, 1837.

" Esteemed Sir,

" I have received yours of condolence for my loved and departed Eyzaguirre.

" I am sure it would be a great loss to you, for he professed a true regard for you, and you have maintained his constant friendship.

" You may well suppose how afflicting our loss has been ; it was a severe blow for me, and all his family ; for although he was long an invalid, his respectable presence served to console us.

" I return you my sincere thanks for your kind attention, and hope you may continue in health, and that you will command, S. A. S.

" Q. B. S. M.   " ANA JOSEFA GUZMAN."

M

Whilst I remained in the capital, H. E. Captain-General Don Ramon Freyre retired from the supreme command, and he was succeeded by General Don Francisco Antonio Pinto, who soon despatched me with a considerable remittance for the army. During the remainder of this campaign, I was sent on various duties to the Cordilleras and frontier, and made use of this opportunity to survey the country, so as to make a plan; for we had no other mode of ascertaining the distances on marching from place to place, but under the direction of guides, and these were not always to be depended upon. At the latter end of May the army retired to their cantonments for the winter; and the general and his staff left Chillan on the 12th of June: we had a fatiguing march, for it rained almost incessantly until we arrived, which was on the 25th. On the 2nd of July, General Borgoño, who had been appointed minister of state, took charge of the war department; and did me the honour of retaining my services, and making me his guest. I will now subjoin an official account of the campaign against Pincheyra, which was published in the Government Gazette.

OFFICIAL DOCUMENTS. —" War department, March 1st, 1827. Head-quarters, Chillan, February 20th, 1827.

" Señor Minister.—On the 24th of January, I informed V. S. of the plan of the campaign I intended to undertake against the hordes of bandits that infested, and found shelter in, the Cordilleras, and the measures I had adopted to insure an entire execution. Now I have the honour to detail to V. S. the movements of each division, and the results up to the 10th of this month.

" According to the orders I had imparted to Colonel Beauchef, he marched with his division from the Invernada de los Girones, on the 23rd, taking the road that leads to the Cajon de Roque, where on the 28th he was joined by the governor, Antical de Malalqui, the cacique, Leviman del Campanario, and two hundred Indians from each reduction.

" On the 29th, he continued his march to the Barancas, where he was met by various caciques, who, with one hundred and fifty warriors were in readiness to follow him.

Colonel Beauchef well knew the importance of making the Indians act so as to compromise themselves at the commencement of the campaign, and in order to take advantage of the good disposition they manifested; he resolved, and ordered Captain Ruiz of the Cazadores, with fifty soldiers of his corps, and one hundred Indians, to march on the 30th, to take a party of the enemy that were situated in the Cordillera del Saco.

" On the 31st, this officer met and captured seven out of nine in the Cajon de las Palmas; besides fifteen families, amongst which there were two sisters of Pincheyra, one hundred horses, and forty head of horned cattle.

" On the 1st of this month, Captain Ruiz joined Lieut.-Colonel Bulnes, in the Cuesta del Saco; this chief had, two days previous to his leaving Longabi, attacked and routed a strong detachment which Pincheyra had sallied out with on a maurauding party. They were obliged to fly, abandon the cattle, and suffer three of the party to be taken prisoners.

" On the 2nd, Colonel Beauchef made a forced march of sixteen leagues, and by which he joined Lieut.-Col. Bulnes, in order that, at daylight on the 3rd, they might both fall upon the encampment of the bandits, which was situated in Casa Trama; but on account of having anticipated their flight to the opposite bank of the Nieuquen, they paralyzed the effects of our divisions. Our auxiliary Indians,

with twenty-five Cazadores, were ordered to follow them;
but not having sufficient resolution for the enterprise, they
returned the same day. It was then necessary to appoint
Captain Ruiz, with seventy-five soldiers; in this much time
was lost; and in the pursuit of the enemy, we did not
obtain the success we expected; notwithstanding which,
the Indians, by taking another route, captured twelve
families, and killed six of the bandits, one of whom was
Paulino Arquiero, adjutant of Pincheyra, who was formerly
a serjeant of the battalion Chacabuco, and was the " caudillo" of the mutiny of the grenadiers, at San Carlos: on the
5th Captain Ruiz returned, and on the 6th the division
halted on the right of the Nieuquen.

" Commandant Carrero,[*] who, according to my orders, was
to have marched on the 28th from the foot of Antuco, in
order that, on the 3rd, he might arrive at the Juntas de
Daquegue, and from thence pass the Nieuquen, where he
would remain in aptitude to cut off the retreat of the
bandits, when they would be attacked on their front by
Colonel Beauchef, found it necessary to vary the direction
of his march on the 29th, and take the road that leads to
the Lagunas de Epulauquen, instead of that to the Juntas de
Daquegue. He sent me information that his motives for
taking this determination were, the unexpected and sudden
separation of the Indians of Trapa-Trapa, Queo-Queo,
and Guayli, who, to the number of one hundred and fifty,
had joined him; their desertion was occasioned by their
having been informed by a messenger, that Marilaon was
preparing to invade their territory, for the assistance they
were giving us, besides other exaggerated reports,[†] that
they through fear came to the determination of returning.
On which Commandant Carrero thought it prudent, under

* A Spaniard.   † All this was false.

such circumstances, to avoid a disadvantageous encounter on the other side of the Nieuquen with the Indians, who, according to the account of the same messengers, were waiting to attack him, and embraced the alternative of marching to strengthen the main body of the division to the northward. Through this incident our combinations were all frustrated; and these would, according to the information of Colonel Beauchef, if properly conducted, have produced a decisive result.

" Commandant Carrero joined the division on the 7th, which marched to the Vado de la Invernada, and next day continued to the south, passed the Daquegue, and on the 9th arrived at Rarinleubre, from which place Colonel Beauchef forwarded his communications to me relative to his operations. and remitted to head-quarters some sick, as well as part of the baggage, &c., to facilitate his movements, so as to be enabled to follow Pincheyra into the territories of the Mulatto.

" The bandits have lost twenty-two killed; six prisoners and six deserters have given themselves up to Colonel Beauchef, more than forty families, besides two hundred horses, and one hundred head of cattle.

" The operations on this side of the Cordillera have been reduced to send a division under the command of Lieut.-Colonel Godoy, by the Boquete de Alico, composed of three companies of his corps, battalion of Chacabuco, and one hundred dragoons, under the command of Lieut.-Colonel Tupper, in order to occupy the Vega de Roble Guacha, a necessary station, so as to be enabled to maintain our communication with Colonel Beauchef, and afford protection to the convoy of provisions remitted to the division. On the 4th, they took possession of this port, after having left a stockade, with forty men on the summit of El Caracol, to put an entire stop to the bandits passing by that road. On the 10th I sent a convoy of seventy loads, which, with some cattle, reached Roble Guacho on the 14th, all safe.

" The light detachment of infantry that were destined to beat and scour the woods, have by various surprises taken forty horses, twenty-five of them saddled; some muskets, pistols, and swords; but on account of the intricacy of the thickets, they have not been able to capture a single prisoner.

" Do me the honour of placing this in the hands of S. E., the president of the republic, and receive the sentiments of my greatest consideration and esteem.

" JOSE MANUEL BORGOÑO."
" To the S'or Minister of War," &c.

" Yumbell, March 19th, 1827.

" Señor Minister.—Although on account of not being able to verify the movements of the southern division, according to the plan of operations which I have remitted to V. S., I may not be allowed to expect a decisive result of the campaign; still there are some hopes, for by the · communications I have just received from Colonel Beauchef, Pincheyra will either have to surrender or perish; he informs me from the valley of Las Damas, date 7th of March, that a cacique, in company of many more from the territory of El Mulato, have presented themselves in his name, offering security of friendship and assistance, as well as to deliver up Pincheyra, and his "secuases," begging only to be allowed time to negociate in a secret manner the defection of Neculman, the only cacique that still accompanies the enemy; they also offer to leave in hostage any of those present as a security of their promises, stating at the same time, that the cacique Mulatto could not visit the colonel on account of a complaint in his eye-sight.

"This success is almost equal to a decisive one, for it deprives our enemy of his best ally, and will subject him to a cruel persecution, where he had thought to find an asylum, and from whence he has no means of escaping, for he has neither provisions nor horses. I am told to believe at the same time, that some movement is about to take place amongst the fugitives, for, according to what intelligence I can get from the deserters that arrive daily to incorporate themselves in our division, the greatest part of them are quite discontented, and are only waiting for the surety of a pardon, to reunite themselves.

" Some of Marilaon's messengers have paid me a visit here, whom I have dismissed with the interpreters " capitanes de amigos," who are charged to unite all the Indians, and offer in my name a " parlamento," where peace will be made, and for which they seem to manifest the most cordial desire; but I will take care that it will not be established without taking good precautions to insure its observance.

" All of which I hope you will do me the honour to instruct his excellency the president of the republic, and protesting towards the person of V. S., the sentiments of my most distinguished consideration.

" Jose Manuel Borgoño."

" Señor Minister, War Department, &c."

———

" Head-quarters, Chillan, April 18, 1827.

"Señor Minister,—I have the satisfaction to inform V. S. that the Cacique Don Francisco Marilaon, governor of the plains, with three more caciques of Butalmaipu, have arrived at Yumbell, on the 15th, according to advices I have received from the commandant-general of the frontier, Don Juan de Luna, in consequence of the invitation this chief has made in order to celebrate peace.

"Lieutenant-Colonel Don Miguel Zinosain, and Don Tiburcio Sanchez of the Spanish army, have abandoned the asylum they had found with the Indians, our enemies, and are in Yumbel under the security of the pardon which has been offered them. They will be shortly presented to me at my head-quarters, by the chief of the frontier; and I doubt not that the renewing of our friendship with the inhabitants of the plains, being supported and secured by a respectable force that is now situated in the Isla de la Laxa, which will not only consolidate the peace on our southern frontiers, but also notably influence the conduct of the Pehuenches with respect to the rest of the bandits that have found shelter in their territory, under the orders of Pincheyra. Do me the honour, &c.

"JOSE MANUEL BORGOÑO."

"Señor Minister of War, &c."

———

"Head-quarters, Chillan, May 30th, 1827.

"Señor Minister,—On leaving the command of the army of operation, and the campaign where I was destined being concluded, I have considered it my duty to make known to his excellency, through the medium of V. S. the excellent conduct of the chiefs, officers, and troops that composed it.

"The happy results which have been obtained are owing to the constant endeavours of all, who have fulfilled their duties in the most satisfactory manner. Colonel Beauchef, who was in charge of the command of the three

divisions destined to act in the Cordilleras, by the activity
that characterizes himself, and by his decision in over-
coming all the obstacles that seemed to frustrate a
march of more than one hundred leagues in the most
difficult and rugged part of the Andes, has recommended
himself.

" Commandantes Puga and Bulnes, who served under
his orders, and Commandante Godoy, have equally given
proofs of their zeal in maintaining good order and regulated
discipline in their corps; and although, after that fatiguing
and painful expedition had been terminated, it was
found necessary to destinate these same troops to operate
in the woods, where the bandits had their hiding-places,
they succeeded on various occasions to take them by
surprise, and chastise them, until possessed of that terror, that so tenacious a persecution ought to inspire
them with, they were at last obliged to look for security in the most distant, retired, and hidden recesses of
the woods.

" Lieutenant-Colonel Luna, commandant of the frontier,
has, in the performance of his duty, conducted himself
with the prudence and propriety that only could have
insured the success of the participation of the Indians;
his loyal and frank conduct has inspired them with sentiments of the greatest confidence.

" I ought, above all, do justice to the merit of the chief
of the staff, Colonel Viel, who, by his laborious, energetic
mind and knowledge, manifested in the fulfilment of his
duties during the operations of the campaign, in the
branch of his administration, made himself worthy of the
good reputation he enjoys. I feel it an honour in recommending him to the consideration of his excellency, the

vice-president, as well as the whole of the army, who have omitted no sacrifice for the termination of the horrors and evils that have afflicted those departments. I have the honour, &c.,

"JOSE MANUEL BORGOÑO."

"To the Minister of War, &c."

CHAP. VI.

On the 9th of July I was promoted to the grade of major of cavalry, which when effective with my gratification of ayudante de campo, gave 124 dollars per month. This, and the general's hospitable table, with little duty to perform, made my situation respectable and agreeable, and quite independent of the foreigners who were residents in Chile ; for although my relatives and friends had, previous to my leaving England, procured me many letters of introduction to my countrymen who were settled in South America, I am sorry to say that in only one instance, Alexander Miller, Esq., I did not receive even common civility; and several expressed their reasons to be so, on account of having to maintain a strict neutrality. This was illiberal, for, had it not been for the patriots, and a few adventurers like myself, they, nor any other foreign merchants, would have ever found their way to South America, or the means of gaining wealth, or the importance they displayed ; and many who, I knew, had few pretensions to affect such dignity. On more than one occasion, on account of their pointed remarks against the poor " pat-riots" as they called us, I had to call to their memory certain epochs which were not over agreeable to them, and prove that my memory was too retentive: and I could relate many anecdotes, from which I will select the following :

"On passing through the town of Casa Blanca, I dismounted to take dinner at Ferroni's Hotel, (an Italian who had settled there); he informed me that there were three foreigners who had arrived before me, and with whom I could dine, if I chose to do so : wishing to proceed on my journey as soon as possible, I assented ; but my host soon returned and informed me that they objected dining with a patriot officer. This did not at all surprise me, but I was curious enough to inquire who they were, and recognized the individual who had been the spokesman, the others were perfect strangers. I could not help smiling at the importance of this man of consequence, and soon exposed his motives for shunning my company.

"On my arrival at the capital, I met a person who had just arrived, and had made a beautiful collection of shells, and who put many questions to me relative to some rare specimens he showed to me : I informed him I had never studied conchology, although I had made many collections myself ; but as he was going to Valparaiso, I could refer him to a scientific conchologist and artist, who could paint shells admirably. This pleased him, and he was still more so when I gave him the address of the gentleman alluded to, for he was acquainted with an intimate friend of his. I then informed him that Mr. B. was very backward at acknowledging that he had ever painted shells, except to such as myself, who was an old aquaintance of his; but I would give him a talisman, in case he could not succeed in acquiring his assistance as an artist. I then gave him my card, on the back of which I put— ' at Colin Mitchell, Esq., Havannah, 1820.'

"Some days after the gentleman had left for Valparaiso, a friend of mine arrived from the port, and on meeting

EL SEÑOR DON BENJAMIN BIEL.

MAYOR GENERAL DEL EXERCITO

DE CHILE.

Fisher, Son & Cᵒ, London & Paris.

with me, said, ' Sutcliffe, you are the d—l at finding people out, for there is poor B. has been terribly roasted on your account;' and he informed me that Mr. B. and a friend had been invited by Mr. C. to see his collection of shells, thinking he had made a valuable acquisition, but he had found that Mr. B. knew nothing about painting small shells, for it turned out that he had only been employed by a Mr. Nichols, superintendent of the foreign burial-ground in the Havannah, to daub coffins and shells, in which he often crammed two dead bodies. This and a few other laughable affairs were the cause of some amusement; and the following circumstance put a stop to all speculations relative to my travels, &c., previous to my visit to South America:

The French government sent out consuls to Chile and Peru, who, with the captain of the French vessel of war that brought them out, visited the capital; Monsieur La Forct was consul for Chile, and Monsieur Chaumet de Fosse, consul for Peru: shortly after the first had been acknowledged by government, Colonel Don Benjamin Biel, a native of France, gave them a dinner, to which the ministers of state and several other personages were invited. I had also the honour of being one of the party, and a circumstance took place which caused some surprise and admiration; Monsieur Chaumet de Fosse had travelled a deal, and was extremely fond of relating passages of what he had seen; so after dinner he strove to entertain us with an account of the Morea, and the Black Sea. Now, as I had, whilst serving in the navy, visited the Levant, I entered into the conversation, which seemed to annoy two or three foreigners attached to the Chillan service, who were present; and who, as they had never served in Europe, seemed to doubt my ever

having been in the Mediterranean, and made some such
remarks to Colonel Biel and Monsieur de Fosse, who, as
it were, to turn the laugh against me, mentioned having
visited a part where he was the fourth stranger who had
resided there since the Turks had taken possession of the
country : this remark caused several at the table to smile,
and I inquired where the secluded spot lay ; on which he
informed us it was Yannina, the capital of Albania.   I
then asked him whether his visit was previous to the
latter end of 1809, which question rather surprised all at
table ; he said he went there in 1810; on which I replied, I
had visited Albania before him, and that I knew a French
consul, Monsieur Poqueville, his secretary, and several
Englishmen, who had visited Ali Pasha in 1809, one of
whom was Dr. Holland, who had been sent from Malta
to assist him during his illness ; next Captain Lake, of
the Engineers, who went to erect a fort for him ; besides
which, two officers of my ship, the Kingfisher, Mr. Weeks,
the purser, and Mr. B. Festing, midshipman, went to
Yannina, whilst the Kingfisher was lying in the port of
Prevesa : this and a little " romaic" conversation with
Monsieur de Fosse, convinced all at table that I had been
in Albania.   General Borgofio was so well pleased with
the occurrence, that he not only congratulated me, but he
made me the warmest proffers of his friendship.   I then
claimed the attention of all present, and after pulling out
my watch, and taking a paper out of it, I showed them
a drawing of a boat, with a solitary individual in it at
sea, with an oar for a mast, boat-hook for a yard, and
a French flag for a sail, which was handed round : I sent
for one of my Journals, and, when my servant brought
it, I read them the following extract.

" We had just arrived on our station off Corfu, after having accompanied the expedition that had, under the command of General Oswald and Commodore Spranger, captured the islands of Zante, Cephalonia, Itaca, Santa Maura, and Cerigo, when we fell in with several vessels from Brindisi, and Ancona, bound to Corfu, laden with wheat and assorted cargoes. I was sent with one as prize-master, with orders to take her to Cephalonia. I left the Kingfisher on the 28th of October, off Fanu, and, on the 30th, when in sight of the port I was bound to, it began to blow a gale from the S. E. I had the misfortune to lose my rudder, and during the gale to be driven in among some small islands near to Corfu, where I had every expectation of being wrecked; luckily, as we neared the coast, the wind changed, and, to prevent my being driven on some rocks that were still to leeward, I let go both anchors, which brought us up close to the small island of Melira. Next day it became more moderate, and I began to prepare a temporary rudder; but just after sunrise, one of my men informed me, that two boats were approaching us from Fanu. I soon observed they were full of soldiers, and immediately lowered down my boat, secured my clothes, and some provisions, &c., scuttled the prize before I left her, and pulled into a small creek, where we landed, for I fancied the island had been uninhabited; however, we were made prisoners by some Greeks, who were hid amongst the rocks; they treated us well, and did not deprive us of a single article we had brought on shore. I had the satisfaction to see the prize sink before the boats got to her; so they had only a few such articles as floated, to repay them for their trouble and disappointment. We were taken next day to Fanu, and delivered up to the French commandante, who ordered my men to be put into confinement, and treated me with attention. On the 7th of November, his Majesty's ship, Leonidas, Captain Griffiths, came with a flag of truce, and landed a number of prisoners, who had been taken from the prizes; and on hearing we had been captured, demanded us in exchange, which not being acceded to, he got permission to send us a little money. On the 9th, we were sent to Corfu, and landed at Cassope, the north-west point of the island. I had a horse provided me, and we arrived at the citadel, at four P. M. The governor, General Donslou, sent the men on board a vessel of war, and politely gave me a seat next him that day at dinner. I passed a few days very agreeably, although a prisoner of war, until a messmate of mine, Mr. E. Barnard, who had been cast away during the gale, and made prisoner, with several seamen and marines, near to Parga, on the Albanian coast, were brought in, and with whom I was sent on board of the French brig of war, San Felippe, Captain Colounne. Mr. B. and myself messed with the officers, and our men with the crew; and on the whole we were treated with civility, and at times had permission to go on shore with the officers. Another prize's crew, that had been commanded by a quarter-master, were also brought to join us. They had also been wrecked. It was reported that we were to be sent to Italy by the first opportunity, which made me very uneasy, and I began to form a plan of escaping. There were two frigates, the Flora, and Danæ, of forty guns each; the brig we were on board, of ten guns; the Joubert ketch, of four guns; and several gun-boats. The frigates lay close under the island of Vedo; the ketch and gun-boats in the Mole. Our brig lay on the

Quarantine grounds, and we were at least two miles and
a half from the harbour, or any battery; besides which,
there was an island between us and the frigates. There
were eight officers, and a crew of forty men on board,
mostly Italians and Greeks; several of whom were dissatisfied; and had informed me that they would aid me,
if I would attempt to take the brig. I refrained from
giving them any encouragement, fearful that it might be
only a snare laid to entrap me, although I longed for an
opportunity to seize her, with my own men, for we were
in all twenty-two prisoners on board, but could not prevail upon my companion to join in the enterprize. I was
also informed that eleven men, and nearly all belonging
to the same watch, were determined to embrace the first
opportunity of deserting. Most of the officers were daily
on shore, some of whom often remained all night; and
when the men had determined to put their plan into execution, I was advised, and intended, to accompany them,
with several of my men, but one of them, Handsford, an
American, whom I had invited, informed the commander
of my intention; luckily he did not know that any of the
crew were concerned, and I was conducted under a guard
on shore to the office of the Commandante de Marine, and
underwent a strict examination; after which I was taken
on board of the Joubert ketch, which was fitting out in
the arsenal, in order to be sent over to Italy. On the
same night of my arrest several of the crew made away in
one of the San Felippe's boats, and got safe to Previsa.
On the 27th of December, the crew of the ketch received
their pay, and liberty for twenty-four hours. Monsieur
Martin, the commander, took me along with him, and
his officers to the opera. Previous to my leaving the
vessel, he enjoined me not to stay on shore all night; on

which I answered, that I would return on board before midnight. I spent a pleasant evening, and on the conclusion of the first act, I had occasion to leave the opera-house, and went to the landing-place. On seeing several boats lying there, an idea occurred of the facility of escaping in one of them, to the Albanian coast; but having given my promise to return on board, I felt a certain qualm of conscience, so I went into the citadel, answered the queries of the sentinels, descended to the arsenal, and got on board the ketch, which lay alongside the Mole. There were only three men and a boy on board, the last was servant to the captain, and in order to amuse myself, I had begun to teach him to write; the men were below, and, to keep the boy employed, I set him a copy, and informed him I had returned on board on account of an indisposition which made it uncomfortable to remain on shore. I placed my linen, &c. which was in a bag, near to the cabin-window, also a French flag, and a fishing line; these I fixed so, that I could get at them from the outside; then taking a small lantern, and a cane with a hook fixed to it, I went on the Mole to fish for polipuses, as I had often done before. I caught one, and leaving the boat close under the stern, I returned on board; after giving the fish to the boy, I entered the cabin, and opened the window. I then wrote the following on the boy's copy-book:—" Mon Captaine, je me suis sauvez apres d'avoir retourne abord."—I then told the boy I would go and fish again, and should the officers enquire for me, he might tell them I was on the Mole fishing. I watched my opportunity, got my bag and the French flag in the boat, and began to scull alongside of the Mole, and got out unnoticed, although I had to pass close by the guard-vessel.

I then took two oars, and pulled out towards the island
of Vedo, and when I got a considerable distance past the
frigate and the island, I heard the sound of oars; I then
placed the lantern on a loose thwart, and I left it there,
and, changing my course, I pulled directly towards the
Albanian shore. I soon saw the lantern lifted up, and the
light extinguished; so I happily escaped my pursuers.
The wind being fair, and blowing fresh, I made a sail of
the French flag, mast and yard of an oar and boat-hook,
and stood out towards Fanu, in hopes of falling in with
some of our squadron. I remained twenty-four hours
beating about; and on account of having no provisions,
nor water, I was compelled to bear up to the island of .
Sasno, and got there, after having been out three days
and four nights. I then procured water, but had the
mortification to see the squadron nearly hull down to
windward; so I was obliged to put into Avlona, a port
in Albania, where I arrived nearly exhausted by fatigue
and hunger. After I landed, I was taken to the palace
of Ibrahim Pasha, the Turkish governor, who received
me kindly; and on hearing I was an English officer,
gave orders I should be supplied with food and lodging,
until I had an opportunity of rejoining the squadron.
The Albanians treated me well, and entertained me a
fortnight; I then embarked on board a small Greek
vessel, bound to Cephalonia, and had the boat towed
astern; when we neared Corfu, I found that the vessel
would have to pass inside the island, and as there was
a probability of our being examined by the French guard-
boats, I came to the determination of taking to the boat
again; so, after procuring some provisions and water,
I took leave of the Greek captain and crew, who gave me
a most hearty " callo-catif-odio," (good voyage.) A short

time after I had left her, a large boat put off from shore towards me. I was soon overtaken, and interrogated; they secured my boat astern of theirs, and began to search me, and ransack my bag; they took my watch, and some trinkets, also twelve sequins; and afterwards pulled into a small creek, where I certainly believed they would have murdered me, had it not been for a party of horsemen, who luckily approached us. One of the villains showed me his pistols, and bade me be quiet; but expecting the worst, should they be left to themselves again, I sprang up; and called out as loud as I could, " Aman, aman !" (mercy, mercy !) in the Turkish language. The horsemen compelled the villains to land me; by good luck, it was the " Billibash" of Ajio Seranda, a port close by. I soon informed him who I was, how I had been treated, and how sensible I was that he had saved my life. He then ordered four of his men into the boat, and gave them orders to conduct her to the port where he resided. When he arrived he made them restore the plunder, and had them punished. I here met with a Greek merchant, who took me to his residence in Ajio Seranda, where I was introduced to a son of Ali Pasha, called Mouctar Pasha, who ordered a boat to be manned, in which I was sent to Panorma, a port opposite Fanu, and close under the mountains of Strada Bianca; and in the course of a week I was put on board of his Majesty's brig, Imogene. The captain gave the boatmen one hundred piasters on my account, and I made them a present of the boat, besides sending my watch to the Billibash, for his kindness and attention.

The French captain, who had accompanied the consuls, seemed to pay great attention to my narrative; and as soon as I had concluded, he gave me his hand, and informed the party present, that he was lieutenant on board of the frigate Flora, which was lying in Corfu at the time, and recollected the circumstance of my escape, as well as most of the particulars I had just related; which caused a general feeling in my favour, and did away with the impression of many, who had been, through their jealous disposition, biassed against me. The president of the republic, General Don Francisco Antonio Pinto, did me the honour to invite me the next day to dine with him, and complimented me on the manner in which I had entertained the company at Colonel Biel's, for he had been informed of every particular; and Monsieur La Foret, the French consul, was so well pleased at the eclaircissement, that he invited me to be his guest until I should return to the army. Sometime afterwards, in Valparaiso, whilst in company with Captain Simpson, of the Chilian navy, in the store of an American, E. L. Scott, Esq., a French officer, who had been a midshipman on board of the Joubert ketch at the time I made my escape, recognized me, and the by-standers were greatly amused at the Frenchman's mode of relating the occurrence of my leaving them in the lurch.

General Pinto had travelled in Europe, and was conversant in the English and French languages: he was unprejudiced and tolerant, and strove to establish a liberal and paternal government, and every encouragement was given to promote public education; scientific professors were invited from Europe, in order to illustrate the Chilians. A military college was founded for the education of cadets; and boarding-schools for young ladies and gentlemen were for the first time established in Chile. A Philharmonic society was formed, under the direction of Los S.S. Masonni y Drewicke, that served

to enliven the winter of 1827; however, these and many
other laudable undertakings were of short duration, for
the enemies of independence, aided and abetted by those
friars, who, through the commiseration of government,
had been allowed to remain in possession of part of their
cloisters even after the reformation of the monasteries,
managed to keep the republic in constant agitation, for
to these may be traced all the disorders that had occurred
ever since the Pope's Nuncio had opened the way to the
secularization of the friars, and subsequently the exile of
the Bishop of Santiago. The friars and a few fanatical
priests had redoubled their energies, so as to gain many
proselytes, and to whom they incessantly inveighed against
the wickedness and immorality of a government which
had dared to promote so many heretical innovations. I
have heard some of these fanatical orators preach, and
strain every nerve in order to induce their hearers, and
especially such as had placed their consciences under their
paternal care, to beware of foreigners and their pernicious books, for to these they attributed the cause of
earthquakes, inundations, and every other judgment.
During the passion-week of this year there were groups
of penitents parading the streets of the capital and other
towns, flogging themselves with armed disciplines, and
sprinkling the by-standers with their blood; others
were crawling about with heavy beams attached to their
shoulders and arms. However, government, to put a
stop to their fanaticism, prohibited such exhibitions, but
this only tended to make them more violent; many of
the former nobility and rich proprietors, who still
longed to regain their lost titles, and restore the
aristocratical government of their beloved Ferdinand,
assisted these revivals of their holy cause by private con-

tributions, and held "missiones and exercicios" on their estates,* and used every species of intrigue, in order to discredit the administration of General Pinto, so as to effect a change. Such was the state of affairs when General Borgoño, after having entrusted the war department in the hands of his secretary, left, in December, 1827, for the army of the south. We had a pleasant march, and reviewed the troops at their different stations, previous to their marching to the Cordilleras. Pincheyra had been kept in the Indian territory; and since General Borgoño had taken the command of the army, that commenced its operations in 1826, not a single town or estate had been plundered by the marauders. In order that the frontier might be properly guarded, and the troops kept in readiness to act at any given point, the general had several forts and stockades put into repair and constructed, one of which was in the pass of Alico, a port of importance.

Shortly after our arrival at head-quarters, the general visited the Cordillera; I accompanied him; we were a party of sixteen. We halted on the first night near the Montaña, and bivouacked under some shady apple-trees. There are immense woods of this fruit, and they were then ripe; no sooner had we halted than our soldiers set to work, and we had plenty of good cider. There we found two large troughs (canoas), near which were several calabashes and clubs, the latter to bruise the apples to a pulp, and the former to preserve it in: our soldiers knew how to manage them admirably well, and I was amused at their dexterity. The Indians generally, when the fruit is in season, assemble to hold their borracheros (drinking bouts), which I have heard described in the following manner:—A quantity of apples is collected, put

* Penitential devotions.

into the canoa, and then beaten and bruised until the mass is reduced to a pulp, a little water is added, after which it is pressed and the liquor poured off into calabashes, which are shaken and passed from hand to hand, until it ferments; it is then drank, and a fresh supply made; and so the process is repeated as long as the chicha season lasts.

Next morning we passed by several haciendas, two of which belonged to my old friends, Colonel Arriagado and Lieutenant-Colonel Matines, they were both in ruins; near to these was one, the vineyard and outhouses of which were in good repair, but the principal houses seemed to have been recently burnt. On inquiry I learned that the estate belonged to Doña Crux Arraos, " who was a staunch adherent to her king and all his faithful followers," for as such she had often entertained the gentlemen who accompanied Pincheyra. This came to the ears of a patriot officer, who, not liking to get the ill-will of this lady's connexions, managed to take a party of Pincheyra's followers, who were in the neighbourhood, and got the report circulated, " that one of this lady's attendants had informed where they where;" this exasperated their comrades so much, that, forgetting " the pasteles* of Doña Crux Arraos," they set fire to her houses.

We found that the marauders had too many allies and friends in the neighbourhood, some of whom actually supplied Pincheyra with arms, and the earliest intelligence of our movements, for we never could despatch a party from Chillan but the robbers were informed of the fact before we could surprise them; however, Colonel Biel devised and adopted a plan to prevent this, and he sent the soldiers out singly to different places, with orders

* Pastry.

to unite themselves into one party at a stated point; by
this mode he succeeded in capturing several of the worst of
the marauders.   One of them, a desperate villain, named
Chauketta, who often came to plunder even in the suburbs
of Chillan, was taken, and brought, with two of his comrades, where they were all shot on the next day in the
" plaza."

Colonel Biel had at this time an Indian captive, who
had lately come from the interior of Arauco, named
Cañime; this man went, out of curiosity, to witness the
execution of the robbers, one of whom was an Indian;
after he returned, the colonel ordered him to fetch a looking-glass out of his trunk, that he might shave himself.
Shortly afterwards he heard Cañime rush out of the room,
uttering a dreadful shriek; not knowing the cause of his
alarm, the colonel sent a soldier to bring him in, but he
had hard work to accomplish his task, for Cañime fled
into the stable, and tried to hide himself in the straw;
however, when he was brought in, his countenance
expressed the greatest alarm, and the perspiration was
running from his face in streams.   When questioned as
to the cause of fear, he roared out " Chauketta longo
Chauketta," and pointed towards the room, meaning
that Chauketta's head was in the trunk.   The colonel, at
once surmising what had occasioned his terror, went and
fetched the glass, and, on placing it before the Indian, he
broke away from the soldiers and ran out into the street;
it was a long time before he could be convinced that it
was the reflection of his own face which he saw in the
glass; for he had never seen a looking-glass before;
and the belief in witchcraft and ghosts is universal
amongst the Indians, although their bravery is proverbial.

I have often amused myself at their expense with a phosphorus bottle and lucifer matches; and whenever they saw my quadrant, compasses, or theodolite, they proclaimed me a " machi," and often have I overheard them calling me " Machi huinca," European sorcerer.

On one occasion I really gave them motives to believe that I was one: some Pehuenche Indians had arrived, and had their " parla" and presents; but on their leaving the town, they were informed that the general had not treated them so well as others, and that their presents were not so numerous and valuable; on which they returned to Chillan; when they came to the general's, he was engaged preparing despatches, and ordered me to detain them for a short time. I then asked some of them into my apartment, and gave them bread and wine; they seemed very curious, and made several attempts to purloin a pair of spurs and a bridle, which I had to order my servant to take from them, and to keep his eye upon their movements. After they had finished their repast, one of them took a knife and attempted, in a very deliberate manner, to cut my uniform buttons from a coat that was hanging up; I told him to desist, but he still persevered, on which I got up, in order to take the coat away, the man still persisted, and put me into a rage; I suddenly spoke to him in English, and pulled off my wig, which he no sooner perceived than he cried out " longo, longo,"* and both he and his companions scampered away as fast as their legs could carry them, until they came to their horses, which they immediately mounted and rode off without seeing the general, who was highly amused when he heard of the occurrence.

The failure of the expedition in accomplishing the

* His head, his head.

total ruin of Pincheyra was brought about by the agency
of the Godos, the name given to the Spaniards, and those
who were the enemies of emancipation, for Mariloan
never intended to attack our allies, and Fermin, his son,
with whom I had a great deal of conversation on this
subject, told me that when his father and Pincheyra were
allied, not a week passed without his receiving information of our movements; he also told me that great interest had been made to persuade him to distrust the
offers of General Borgoño, and to remain in his own
territory. Pincheyra sent his secretary, Vallegos, accompanied by Lavandero, to communicate with General
Borgoño; I had some conversation with both of these,
and Vallegos, a long-headed fellow, who was a native of
Cauquenes, told me that his chief, Colonel Don Antonio
Pincheyra, served the cause of El rey Fernando, and had
many friends in Chile; he stated that the reason of the
atrocities and cruelties that were committed, was our not
regulating the war; for he said "you hang and shoot your
captives, and we act as we do only in revenge."

Lavandero, whose mother resided in Florida, thought
better, and was persuaded by some of our party to accept
the general's offer of pardon, and to desert the cause of
Pincheyra.

The general had to contend with many difficulties in
this expedition, not only from the intrigues of the godos,
and of the faction who were opposed to the present
administration, but also from several officers in the army,
particularly on the frontier, who were known to be
the fomentors and instigators of disturbance, by means
of which they enriched themselves; these were discharged, and their places filled up by others more worthy
of the trust.

On our entering the Montaña, we passed Naguel Toro, where a squadron of cavalry was stationed; we then traversed the woods to the distance of about eight leagues, and halted at the fort which was erected on the banks of the Nuble, near to where a rapid stream enters the river; the fort was merely a large stockade, in which barracks and huts were erected, capable of holding one hundred and fifty men.

Here were great numbers of tall trees, with the names of which I am unacquainted; beside cypress, cedars, apple, canela, mayten, peumo, and avellanos, the fruit of the last is not unlike filberts, but the shells are soft: this forms a part of the food of the Indians; they also eat the piñon, which grows on the southern mountains.

Whilst we were here, we captured a party of Pincheyra's followers, and amongst them several women; we then returned to San Carlos, and thence to Chillan. The general sent me to the capital for the arrears of the money due for the maintenance of the army; and on this occasion I received 15,000 dollars. Whilst in Santiago, I was introduced to a French gentleman, Monsieur St. Roman, who being desirous of seeing the country, accompanied me: this time I narrowly escaped being robbed at a place called Chimbarongo; but I fortunately caught the villains attempting to steal the soldiers' arms, and next day drove them on foot three leagues, and on entering the estate of El S'or Armasa, who was a judge, they were punished for their temerity.

We had very heavy rain during our journey, and my companion remained in Talca, with a countryman of his, to whom I had introduced him. I was only thirteen days absent from Chillan, and my return was a welcome one, on account of the specie I had brought.

General Borgoño visited General Freyre at his estate, Cucha-Cucha, near to Chillan, where he stayed three days; General Rivero, and others, were there also; this is a fine hacienda, and produces the best wine in the province, not much unlike port wine.

When we returned to head-quarters, the general gave me leave to visit the frontier, and different parts of the province, in order to finish my survey; during which time I had a good opportunity of amusing myself, and of observing the manners and customs of the inhabitants.

I first visited the hacienda of Niken, belonging to a gentleman in whose house I resided whilst at Chillan, and with whom I enjoyed myself in fishing and shooting. The rivers Niken and Perquilauquen abound in fish, such as perch, cauque, and pexerey; the country around is visited by immense flocks of peoquenes, a species of geese that migrate from the Cordillera; there are two kinds of them, the grey, and the variegated; their weight is generally from six to eight pounds, and they are a good article of food; like our geese they feed on grass; after having been on the plains for some time they get fat, and find great difficulty in raising themselves completely from the ground, to effect which they always have to run a little.

The Huassos kill numbers in the following manner; they first fix a number of stakes, or bushes, so as to form a crescent, near the centre of which they make a pen, where the stakes are placed closer, so as to prevent the birds from running; then three or four men on horseback begin to drive the birds toward the enclosure, for they seldom fly, even when within gun shot; after this the rest of the party close round the space where the birds are confined, and as soon as they have forced them into the pen, they commence an attack upon them with sticks, and by these means generally secure an ample reward for their trouble.

There are also numerous flocks of peroquetts of various size and plumage; besides partridges, ducks, and different kinds of doves.

This hacienda was once visited by Pincheyra, during the celebration of a feast; and whilst the guests were at mass, he murdered several, robbed the church and houses, and carried off several women, one of whom was the niece of the owner, Don Gregorio Moreno; this gentleman fortunately escaped into a morass, but his poor old mother was beaten so unmercifully, that she died shortly after; this treatment was used to make her tell where the plate was secreted. Don Gregorio afterwards ransomed his niece for three hundred dollars; and on account of the kind treament she received from the sisters of Pincheyra, he brought them to his estate, when they were taken prisoners; but they no sooner collected a supply of provisions, than they decamped to the Cordillera, and joined their husbands.

After leaving Niquen, I visited all the different passes from that of El Parrall to the Bio Bio; I also revisited Los Angeles, and found many settlers, and that the new buildings had begun to make a show amongst the ruins.

I next visited San Carlos, and saw my " commadre" at Nacimiento; I found my god-daughter in good health, and received a quantity of piñones from her mother; and at my departure gave her a suitable present.

I there re-passed the river, and visited Rere, returned to Yumbell, and went to see the neighbouring lakes, one of which, Avendano, produces pearls of a good colour, but of a very small size.

After three weeks' absence I returned to head-quarters, highly delighted with my tour.

On the 12th of February, a ball was given to celebrate the anniversary of the battle of Chacabuco and which was kept up two days.

The females of Chillan and the southern provinces are good-looking, and reputed to be very industrious; excellent carpets, ponchos, bed-quilts, and various kinds of course cotton, and woollen cloths are made by them; they dye these by means of a coloured matter which they extract from roots and plants of various kinds. Some of these colours are bright, and do not fade; the women are amiable, and seem to be good housekeepers, and from the little observation that I could make, I should judge them to be good wives.

The Chillanejos are also an industrious people; their farms are well cultivated, and the land is very fertile; wheat produces from eighty to one hundred fold, and the ground requires very little preparation. Notwithstanding the distress which prevailed in these provinces, provisions were very cheap; good wines are produced here, particularly the Cucha-Cucha and Carlon wines; potatoes, French beans, and frigoles, which are the principal articles of provision amongst the labouring classes, grow in abundance.

The locusts are often very destructive here, laying waste and sweeping away whole crops; their devastations bring no small emolument to the friars, or clergy, who are often called out to " conjure" them, and get well paid for performing the ceremony; but I have never known the locusts obedient to their charms: I once tried an experiment with a mixture of gunpowder and sulphur, which during one morning destroyed more of these insects than all the "conjuration" of the priests will do in an age; this action gained me the ill-will of a noted "conjurador;" so that I never attempted to spoil his trade afterwards; recollecting that it is well to allow every one to have his own ideas—"for without faith we are not to be saved."

. A manufactory of woollen cloths was once established in Chillan, by El S'or Lantaño; where, I have been informed that excellent cloth was made; this was burnt by the Spaniards, and is now superseded by a good tannery, which supplies excellent leather.

On account of the missionary convent being in Chillan, the men are generally well-informed, and some of the best counsellors, or lawyers in Chile are natives of this city; nearly all that I knew were what are there called "Tintirrilos." I was amused during the election of their municipal corps, particularly at the desire each manifested to become a member, and at the quarrels that ensued, frequently the candidates came to blows with each other.

General Borgoño once sent an officer with a party of soldiers to preserve the peace, on which both parties set off to the city of Concepcion, to lay their complaint before the governor-intendente, nor did they return until a person was sent to pacify them; they then brought an order for the governor to retire ten leagues from the city; but General Borgoño having received ample instruction, on finding the umpire to be partial, ordered him to return to Concepcion, which of course gained the ill-will of the fallen party towards the general.

A short time afterward, there was an election for a president and vice-president of the republic, but this caused no alteration at all in the course of affairs, because here they had no private interest at stake; for in Chillan,

and nearly all the provincial towns in Chile it is well to
be a " Cabildante," for then they have justice in their
own hands, which in some cases is quite necessary.

Chillan was once a large and populous town, but it
was greatly injured by an earthquake; and afterwards it
suffered severely by the ravages of war.

During the time that General Carrera besieged the
Spaniards,who were shut up here, the friars, among other
inventions, made the image of the Virgin open and shut
her eyes, and nod her head; and on General Sanchez presenting his baton, she received it, and returned it to him;
this being pronounced a miracle, animated the beseiged;
the priests also strove by various illusions to terrify the
besiegers; but General M'Kenna* soon exposed their
tricks; and by taking some of them, who went out at night,
with the intention of alarming the outposts, he made the
rest desist.

Sanchez, in order to reward and gain proselytes, made
several of the ladies of Chillan colonels, lieutenant-
colonels, majors, &c.; some of these, with whom I became
acquainted, have shown me their badges.

The missionary college was destroyed by a Buenos
Ayrean officer, Pastoriso, who it is said set fire to it on
the retreat of the patriots, to deprive his enemies of the
good quarters it afforded. This was both a wanton and
unnecessary action; judging from the ruins, it must have
been a noble edifice; it was built of stone; the church is
still in good repair; the ruins of the convent have been
in part cleared away, and are converted into barracks
for cavalry; and a few sheds have been added.

The other convents and principal buildings are partly
in ruins; but lately there has been a spirit of renovation,

* A native of Ireland.

O

for whilst I was in the south, eight or ten good houses were built, some of which had two or three chimneys—a novel sight in Chillan.

On account of the disturbances created by the disaffected, we suffered the greatest necessities, through the exhausted state of the treasury; and as the remittance for the purchase of rations for the month of February had not arrived in due time, General Borgoño despatched me to the capital, where I was detained a fortnight, and then did not receive more than 4,500 dollars; and this was when the congress had awarded the proceeds of the " Estanco," that had been created for the payment of the foreign debt. The following letter that was published by a zealous patriot, El Doctor Don Jose Miguel Infante, and that of El Padre Guzman, will explain matters better than I can do, relative to the exhausted state of the treasury, &c.

ARMY OF OPERATION OF THE SOUTH.

" CHILLAN, April 6th, 1828.—Major Sutcliffe has arrived at last, with 4,500 dollars, to pay for the rations that correspond to the month of February, and another officer leaves to bring the sum that corresponds to the month of March. Now, if this aid be sustained, all will prosper, for it is now time to put a *stop to sedition;* and the manner in which it may be accomplished is, not to be deprived of what is absolutely necessary for our maintenance; then we may have good order and discipline, and the republic may depend upon the co-operation of an army, which, although a small one, may serve its urgency, without becoming a *tool of faction,* or the *instrument of anarchy.*

" When such epistles are sent from a military encampment, *who does not perceive the unhappy state of affairs?*

" The proceeds of the ' *Estanco,*' jointly with the 4,500 dollars that have been remitted from Santiago, scarcely cover two-thirds of the monthly pay, &c., but we may deduce the consequences, by having the above *extract from the army of the south before us.*

" The ' *Estanco*' was created to pay the interests of the *(emprestito de Londres)* foreign loan; and congress *have taken it from the contractors in the year* 1826, and placed it under the control of the treasury, with the proviso that the proceeds should be applied to the payment of the *bondholders.* It was then to be feared that government would apply the whole or part of this capital to other purposes: and in a short time after the decree of its translation was issued, the legislature was requested to subministrate the whole proceeds of a year, *under the protest*, that it would only be expended in paying the arrears of the army, and other debts, in order to regulate the treasury department, &c., which was granted; therefore, by this means, the receipts of the ' *Estanco*' were placed at the disposition of government, for the term *of one year*, after which it was to be expected that those funds would of course re-assume their natural application ; *but it was not so*, for government applied to the National Commission, in order that they might continue receiving the proceeds for the period *of four months longer;* and the commission prorogued it until the day the congress should be installed : I have not made this statement merely to demand how it has happened, that after these two concessions have been made, the army and civil officers should be still in arrear. No, that is a matter of little importance. But to speak properly, I should state, that from the 25th February, in which the congress was installed, the products of the ' *Estanco*' ought to have reassumed their legal application—that is, to be employed in the payment of the interest of the English loan ; *instead of their having since been destined to pay the army.* This appears to be a controvertion of the laws. Can it be justifiable, even if the impoverished state of the treasury be alleged? No: Because, if it were in such a state, why did they not apply to congress, *the only authority that could alter the laws ?"*—*Valdiviano, Federal, May 22nd*, 1828.

An extract from El Reverendo Padre Fray Jose Javier Guzman's work, published in Chile, in the year 1836, under the auspices of His Excellency General Prieto, and in the government press.

" No sooner had General Pinto been invested with the supreme command, than the direful effects of the Reformation of the (*Religiosos*) Friars, decreed in the year 1824, [*General Pinto was Minister of State at that period,*] was made manifest, but more especially during the latter part of his administration, not only on account of the penury and sufferings that the few who had retained their cowl had been reduced to, by being deprived of their revenues, and confined to a reduced locality in their convents ; but on account of the demoralization of the people, which arose principally from the want of operatives to assist the curates in the administration of their religious duties.

" Yes, at this period many of the subaltern rulers of the provinces took possession of the convents, treated the friars as the most abject and despicable people, and persecuted them in such a furious manner, that many were obliged to secularize themselves and abandon their holy vestments which they loved so dearly ; thus passing, as if it were by force, from the clerical state.

" Yes, the immorality and depravation of the manners of the people, had risen to such a pitch, that the former *religion* of Chile was unknown.

" The want of a bishop to ordain the clergy, and above all, the introduc-

o 2

tion of a multitude of immoral and pernicious books, which were publicly
sold, and read without any shame by those who purchased them, to their
families, was, in my opinion, the principal cause of so much *libertinism*
being introduced into Chile.

" Amidst such lamentable circumstances, in which it appeared, that im-
piety had established its throne in the republic, the incomprehensible
power of our benign God was exemplified; and who, in the midst of our
afflicting troubles, heard the clamours of his servants; and several pious
and zealous clergymen and friars, dedicated themselves with the greatest
interest to practise public and private devotions, in order to put a stop to
the rapid progress of iniquity, and restore piety, devotion, belief, and the
religion we now happily see re-established and prosper throughout the
republic."

On the rainy season setting in, our army retired to
their cantonments, having taken about twenty-eight of
the robbers prisoners, with some horses, during the campaign; beside keeping Pincheyra pent up in his hiding-
place, without having had an opportunity of making a
" malone" (foray.)

Had it not been for the intrigues of his allies and
secret friends, this war of " brigandage" would have
ended with the campaign.

We left Chillan in May, and had a wet and wearisome
march; we were detained twice on account of the rivers
being impassable; this season was more severe than any
other that I had seen during my residence in Chile.

The large and populous village of Rio Claro (Rengo)
was nearly destroyed, and many lives lost; numbers of
houses were thrown down; trees torn up by the roots,
and cattle swept away by the impetuous torrent; the
banks of the rivers were filled with the trunks of trees
that had been swept from the Cordillera; and several of
the rivers and streams had changed their course; in fact,
the ruin and devastation that had taken place on our line
of march cannot be fully understood, or conceived by
any who have not beheld such scenes for themselves.

When we arrived at the capital, we found that it had been threatened with an inundation; and had it not been for the " taja-mar" (parapet,) which was erected as a defence, and government taken the precaution of causing part of the river to take its course to the south of the city El Aguado, much more damage would have been done.

A great number of houses and mills were washed away in the suburbs of La Chimba; besides an assemblage of huts belonging to the poorer class, who had formed a settlement, called Guangali, on the bank of the river. A subscription of considerable amount was raised, to which government not only contributed, but assigned a site for the people to rebuild their huts upon.

The general reassumed his functions as minister of war, and still retained me in his service.

A revolution broke out in the province of Colchagua; the battalion, No. 6, stationed in San Fernando, had been corrupted by two dissatisfied persons, Señores Silva and Urriola, who with a few others of their party, were striving to revolutionize the rest of the army.

General Borgoño, with the battalion No. 7, Colonel Rondisonni, marched from the capital, and were joined in Rancagua by two companies and a squadron of militia.

On our march we halted at the Requingua, an estate belonging to the father-in-law of Urriola; here an attempt was made to steal or disperse our horses.

Next day, hearing that Urriola was on his march, we went to meet him; but finding that he had taken up a position at Pelequin, a narrow pass, where the road was rendered almost impassable by the heavy rain that had fallen; and knowing that an engagement could not take place there without great loss of life, which the general wished to avoid, as his object was simply to re-establish the power of government in the province; and besides this, expecting to be joined in San Fernando by a regiment of dragoons that had been ordered to meet him; he took another route by the Cuesta de Cuenca, and left the battalion, No. 6, without molesting them, intending, on his arrival at San Fernando, to send Lieut.-Colonel Tupper, with a division of cavalry and infantry, to bring them to their duty, or attack them; but all his plans were frustrated, for no sooner had our advanced-guard entered the city, than they were attacked by a party of dragoons belonging to the regiment that was to have joined us; they were soon repulsed, leaving one dead, and several wounded in the "plaza." Lieut.-Colonel Tupper took up a position, and awaited the arrival of the rest of the troops, who, on hearing the firing, made all possible haste to join him. On account of the firing that was kept up from the convent of San Francisco, the general thought that the dragoons had possession, so he ordered No. 7 to form close column, and attack it; we marched, and on silencing their fire, discovered that the regiment of dragoons had carried away all our baggage and spare horses, and continued their march to join Urriola.

In the midst of this disorder, the colonel of the regiment of dragoons arrived, and informed the general that his major and subalterns had revolted, and made him a prisoner; the general sent a letter to the major, who would not answer it; but continued his march to join Urriola and Vidaurre, who then commanded No. 6.

Major Bosa, Captain Rivera, and several soldiers of our party, were badly wounded, and two killed.

The general marched after the dragoons; but they and the revolted battalion made forced marches, and by fording the Maipu, during the night, got considerably ahead of us; we were also deceived by the intelligence that we received, which led us out of our direct route; indeed all seemed combined against us.

When we were passing the Maipu, we heard the firing, which announced that they had been attacked by the troops which remained in the capital: on hearing this, the general halted at the Hacienda del Espejo, where we heard Vidaurre had routed the troops which had been sent to oppose him, and that the president and his ministers had fled; so the general determined to march to Valparaiso, where the congress had met, to place himself under the orders of the legislative body.

As I was about to march with an official despatch to Valparaiso, an aid-de-camp of the president arrived at the Cuesta de Prado, to call the general to an interview with his excellency at the Hacienda del Espejo, who immediately set out, accompanied by Lieutenant-Colonel Tupper, two aids-de-camp, and orderlies. Shortly after we had reached the Espejo, an officer, Captain Soto, arrived, and gave the general a particular account of all that had transpired, and mentioned the fact that Urriola, Lattapiat, Vidaurre, and others, were in the "maestranza," military arsenal; and that when he left, they were aware that the general was alone in the hacienda; this information made us feel that our situation was rather a critical one; and as the night advanced, we took some precautions to prevent surprise; whilst at supper, conjecture being on the wing, we began to surmise who would be most likely to disturb us; and the general impression was, that none of the rebels was more

fitted to such a commission than Lattapiat; he had
already immortalized himself by attacking the legislative
body; and we thought it very likely that he would now
attempt by a midnight dash, to make prisoners of the
president and minister of war, and thus gain the applause
of those who were opposed to government: such conversation as this by no means tended to allay our apprehensions of a nocturnal visit; we, therefore, determined
to keep watch, and those of us who retired to rest, had
not been long asleep when we were aroused by a violent
knocking at the gate; we all jumped up in haste, and
after arming ourselves, proceeded to examine the cause
of the alarm; on challenging the disturbers, and enquir-
ing who they were, the reply was, " La Tapia." We now
prepared for a fight; but only observing two persons, we
opened the wicket, when, to our surprise, it was a
" Latapia," who had come to inform the general that our
commissary had arrived safely in the neighbourhood.*

This unnecessary alarm served to furnish us with
a source of merriment, and then we all retired to rest;
this was highly necessary, for as we had been continually
drenched by the rain, and our baggage and bedding
having been taken by the enemy, we had neither the
means of repose, or of changing our raiment for several
days.

I had just closed my eyes, when we were again disturbed, and one of the president's aid-de-camps arrived to
call General Borgoño and his troops nearer the capital,
as there seemed to be a diversion in favour of government.

* The family name of Lattapiat is La Tapia; but on his going to Peru,
in company with a foreign officer, S'or Margutti, who had begun to teach
him French, he altered his name to Lattapiat.

I was ordered to march to the Cuesta de Prado, to Colonel Rondsionni, and had to pass the Mapocho, which was considerably swollen; I had also to go through several thick woods, which, on account of the darkness of the night, and the heaviness of the rain, was by no means pleasant; but the calls of duty were imperative, and I was not therefore at liberty to consult my own ease.

Shortly after my arrival the troops marched, and after enjoying three hours' rest, which the general had authorized me to take, I followed them: they halted until night in the Chacara de la Merced, and then after passing through the city, took up their quarters in the powder magazines.

Whilst we were in La Merced, Urriola formed his troops in the principal plaza, and there made an attempt to organize a new government; but in this he was disappointed, and both he and his partisans were loaded with execrations by the inhabitants of Santiago.

General Pinto sent for Major Vidaurre,* who on entering the palace, was interrogated as follows: — "What cockade is that which you wear? Answer, The Chillian. What troops have you under your command? Anwser, Chillian. What has brought you to act against government? Answer, We were called by El Pueblo. What co-operation have you received? Do you not see that you have been led astray, and have acted improperly? Return with your troops to your duty, and I will grant you my pardon." To this Vidaurre made a short reply, left the palace, and soon evacuated the plaza; and then, in spite of the exertions of Urriola and his partisans, order was restored. The dragoons marched to Apoquindo, and the battalion, No. 6, to the Chacara de la Merced.

* This officer was shot in Valparaiso, July 4th, 1837, by those he had aided during the disorders of 1829 and 1830.

A general pardon was issued; and all the officers, excepting myself, were promoted.

By this mad enterprize, the "moral" discipline of the army was almost destroyed; for there had been several attempts made to revolutionize the battalion, No. 7, and Captain Briceño was caught attempting to seduce the soldiers: several lives were lost, and many were severely wounded; amongst whom, Captain Winter, aid-de-camp to his excellency, and Dr. Buston, the staff surgeon, were two of the greatest sufferers.*

A short time afterwards, the dragoons again revolted, and were carried to the south by two subaltern officers, but were intercepted by Colonel Bulnes, who obliged them to capitulate; after this the regiment of dragoons, and the battalion, No. 6, were disbanded.

About a month after this, Urriola made another attempt, and the palace was attacked at daybreak: but a part of the battalion, No. 7, arriving at the time, dispersed the rebels, and compelled them to take shelter in the convent of San Pablo, from whence they were dislodged, routed, and several of them taken prisoners, tried, and shot.

General Borgoño had sent me to inform his excellency, that although he was an invalid, he might command his services; but the president told me to remain with the general, at the same time stating, that he would not send for General Borgoño, unless some more serious circumstances should require his attendance; the general sent me to the palace in the evening to await orders, and I with several other chiefs and officers bivouacked there, that we might be ready to act, if necessary.

Next day all was quiet; but Urriola and several others

* Sir Harry Verney, a major in the English army, was on a visit at Santiago, and he went out to see the fight.

escaped the pursuit of Colonel Tupper, who dispersed the remainder of the disaffected troops at Colina.

General Borgoño suffered so much fatigue by the affair at San Fernando, that he was obliged to retire from the ministry; and previous to his giving up office, he appointed me field-adjutant of the army, and retained me still in his service.

CHAP. VII.

REVOLUTION OF 1829 — GENERAL PINTO RESIGNS — DON FRANCISCO RAMON VICUÑA
ELECTED PRESIDENT OF THE REPUBLIC—GENERAL PRIETO'S DEFECTION—BATTLE
OF OCHAGAVIA—THE PRESIDENT DEPOSED, AND A JUNTA NOMINATED.

THE REVOLUTION OF 1829.—General Pinto was obliged to retire on account of ill health, and the president of the senate, Don Francisco Ramon Vicuña took charge of the government during his absence; several of the partizans of the late revolution were taken, tried, and executed; which, in place of deterring others from joining the malecontents, strengthened their party; and on General Pinto's resuming his avocations, he, on account of General Borgoño's illness, appointed General Don Joaquin Prieto to the command of the army of the south; I had been on friendly terms with this gentleman, who was a decided O'Higginista, and he invited me to accompany him, as his aid-de-camp, to which I acquiesced; but government ordered me to remain with General Borgoño, and allowed me my pay and gratification, just as if I had been serving at the head-quarters of the army.

The general went to reside with his family in the country, until he recovered his health; and I obtained leave to visit the estates of Los S. S. Toros, at Huachun. I also made an excursion with my friends, Don Jose Antonio Rosales, his brother, Don Manuel, and Don Felippe Santiago del Solar, to their gold mines, at El Chivato, near Talca, and I had intended visiting General Prieto with El S'or Solar: but on passing the town of Curico, a friend

of the general, who thought I was his aid-de-camp, informed me that there was a defection in the army—which
was soon manifested; for those soldiers who, under the
command of General Borgoño had hitherto withstood the
machinations of the factious, were at last induced to act
against government. On my return to the capital I applied to be included in the military reform that was established by congress, whereby a national credit of 600,000
dollars was effected, and six per cent. allowed for it, in
order that all the chiefs and officers, who were not actively
employed, might receive a remuneration for their services,
and retire from the army, which, it had been calculated,
would materially reduce the annual expenditure.—Numbers of these officers, although they had been remunerated
by government, joined the malecontents, and were placed
on full-pay, as soon as their party obtained power; and so
remained. I was not allowed to participate in this indulgence, on account of my services being required.

The following extract will exemplify the manner in
which General Prieto commenced his operations against
the horde of Pincheyra.

"GENERAL PRIETO.

"Ambition is the mania of the day, but as no one dares to confess this
defect, it must be covered with the mask of *patriotism*.

"Also, the desire of living at the expense of the public treasury is pre-
dominant, a system that is commonly preferred to labour and industry, and
from which has resulted a bad interpretation of the word *disinterested*.

"Let us speak of General Prieto. . . . . The president,
Don F. A. Pinto, whose generous protection extends to all such as have
been unfortunate; whether it has been through his own deliberation, or
the insinuation of others, took pity of the situation of General Prieto, and
to the surprise of every one, has confided the command of the army of the
south to him. Much has been said on this subject, and its consequences
have been calculated by some who imagined that he would be grateful to his
benefactor, and others that he would act contrary. These have judged right,

for a few days after he had arrived in the south, were sufficient for him to trace his plans, and began by ridding himself of a chief, (Colonel Biel,) who might have retarded his progress. . . . .

" In the conduct of General Prieto, *speaking as seriously as the case demands*, we see the development of a plan projected in Santiago, and which ought to be executed in the south, by the very person who had received a nobler charge from his benefactor.

" *El Verdadero Liberal, No.* 76, *July* 11*th,* 1829."

The situation of government became every day more and more alarming; placards of the most inflammatory kind were stuck up in different places, and seditious papers publicly distributed; and what made things worse were, the legislative and executive bodies being at variance; so General Pinto sooner than compromise his own honour, and that of the nation, sent in, on the 29th of October, his resignation to the congress, in which he stated his motives in a frank and honest manner. This was acceded to, and they named Don Francisco Ramon Vicuña, president of the republic. Shortly afterwards, General Prieto detached the cavalry, and a party of mounted militia towards the capital, and when they had advanced part of the way, a corps of cavalry that was in Santiago, commanded by Lieutenant-Colonel Baquedano, and another in San Fernando, left their commandant, Uquiso, and joined Colonel Bulnes, who being thus reinforced, continued his march, until within a short distance of Santiago. Colonel Don Benjamin Biel was first in command of the troops in the capital; he had three battalions of infantry, a squadron of cavalry, and a park of artillery; these were commanded by Colonels Rondisonni and Tupper, Lieutenant-Colonels Castillo and Amunategui, and they were marched out of the city to the neighbourhood of Tango, nine leagues distant.

On the 7th of November, government issued a decree for the nomination of an electoral body, to assemble on the 15th of March, 1830, to appoint a president and vice-president, on account of the national congress having admitted their renunciation. The same day, the malcontents in the capital met in the "Consulado," and extended an "acta," by which they deposed the vice-president, and elected a "Junta Gubernativa," which was made known to the president by a deputation, but he received them coolly, saying "he acknowledged no authority in those who had united to usurp the command," and ordered them to disperse, and at the same time, that the "Consulado" should be closed. They then met in the national institute, where about five hundred persons signed a paper, in which all the inhabitants of the province were called upon to acknowledge the provisional junta; but the troops that were stationed at Tango, under the command of Colonel Biel, would not acknowledge them, and sent in an "acta," dated November 9th, signed by the principal chiefs and officers, stating "that they would support the national authority." His excellency, the president, in order to relieve himself from the personal inconveniences he and his family had to experience, left on this night for Valparaiso, in company with the ministers of state, taking the government seal, and every requisite to fulfil the duties of his charge, and gave ample instructions to Colonel Biel, "advising him upon no account, if it could possibly be avoided, to come to blows with the opposite party.

On account of the illness of General Borgoño, I might have remained quietly with him, but I considered it my duty to act with the government and legislative body, and presented myself to the minister of war, Colonel Don

Jose Antonio Cotapos, who gave me orders to attend his excellency the president, which I did, until he left for Valparaiso; as I had no previous intimation, and on account of his leaving at midnight, with the ministers of state, I was unprepared to march with them, but on inquiry I was ordered to remain with General Borgoño, until I should hear from his excellency, who thanked me for my services. I then retired to my quarters, resolved to take no further part in the civil broils, unless my general should be actively employed; for, as a foreigner, I considered it the best policy to let the Chilians end their domestic quarrel without my voluntary co-operation, and was thankful that I could do so, without compromising myself for the sake of promotion, as hitherto I had only acted in favour of government, although at times against my own interest.

Colonel Biel's division returned to the capital, when on the 12th they agreed to acknowledge General Freyre as commander-in-chief, in order to put an end to the disorders that menaced the republic, and preserve the moral discipline of the army, without separating themselves from the obedience they had sworn to the supreme executive, which they acknowledged and would only obey, until the nation had resolved by the unanimous vote of the provinces to elect another. But unfortunately, the very next day General Freyre, accompanied by General Blanco and others, proceeded to the barracks of the battalion, No. 8, and strove to persuade the corps to obey and acknowledge the junta; Colonel Tupper was absent at the time the generals entered, but on being advised, he rushed forward to the place where the troops had been put under arms by the orders of the commander-in-chief, and spoke to the soldiers in a spirited and undaunted manner,

as follows:—"Soldiers, the general has led you to victory;
I also have led you to victory. Whom do you obey?
your colonel, or the general;" he was instantly answered,
"We obey our colonel—"Viva el Colonel Tupper!" on
this the generals, and those that had accompanied them,
finding their plans were frustrated, thought proper to
retire. A mob had collected outside the barracks, which
was soon dispersed, and all the troops in the capital put
themselves again under the command of Colonel Viel,
and declared in an acta dated November 13th, signed by
all the chiefs and officers, that they had withdrawn themselves from under the command of General Freyre, on
account of his having refused to act in accordance with
the legitimate government, and placed themselves under
the command of Colonel Biel as commandante-general.
This was a severe blow to the opposite party, who, in
order to make the division unpopular, called it "El
Exercito Frances," the French army.

The cavalry from the south, under the command of
Colonel Bulnes, had taken up a position in the Chacara
de Ochagavia, about one and half league from the capital,
and Colonel Biel marched out to a Chacara in the neighbourhood; and then General Don Francisco Lastra was
appointed chief of the division, in order that the army
might become "a national one," and Colonel Biel remained second in command.

His excellency, the president, had installed the government in Valparaiso, and the ministers carried on their
communications with the legitimate authorities as usual.
The governor of Santiago, El S'or Bilbao, with the municipal body, did all they could to supply the division
of General Lastra with men, horses, and resources, and
summoned the militia: however, only a small corps that

P

were brought by El S'or Colonel Romo, obeyed the order.

On the 15th, Lieutenant-Colonel Amunatigui marched from Valparaiso with two companies of artillery, but were intercepted on the 18th whilst passing the Cuesta de Prado, by Colonel Bulnes and five hundred cavalry, and were obliged to capitulate; after which the greatest part of the soldiers and two officers joined the vanguard of the army of General Prieto. Previous to General Prieto's arrival at Ochagavia, two deputations from the governor-intendent of Santiago, met him on the 30th, at Codegua,* when the division of Colonel Bulnes was ordered to suspend hostilities, until the chief of the division in Santiago, and the government, sent a deputation properly authorized to treat, which was to be on the 5th of December, on which day the Colonels Don Manuel Bulnes, Don Antonio Villagran, on the part of General Prieto; Colonels Don Benjamin Biel, and Don Pedro Godoy, on the part of General Lastra, agreed, that a suspension of hostilities should take place until two P.M. of the 6th, at which time two persons, named on each side, should conclude a treaty of peace, before the specified hour, in order that an end might be put to the political quarrel. General Lastra named on his part General Don Manuel Borgoño, and the minister of the supreme court Don Carlos Rodrigues, with Colonel Don Pedro Godoy, as secretary; and General Prieto named El Sargento Mor Don Jose Antonio Vidaurre, and El Doctor Don Jose Antonio Rodrigues Aldea, but nothing definitive took place on account of various informalities, so the armistice ended, and hostilities recommenced.

On the 8th, the Aquilles, brig of war, was taken out to

* El S'or Don Javier Rosales, now the envoy of Chile, was on this deputation, for he belonged to the liberal party,

sea, by two mutinous officers. She had a considerable
quantity of specie and government documents on board,
that had been placed in security; so government applied
for the assistance of Captain Bingham of his majesty's ship
Thetis, who having his excellency, the president, and the
vice-admiral of the Chilian squadron, C. C. Woorster,* on
board, got underweigh, went in pursuit of her, and, after
exchanging a few shots, brought her into port again. This
affair nettled the opposite party, and augmented their
hatred against foreigners. General Prieto took up a position in the Chacara de Ochagavia, and General Lastra in
El Olivar, close to the city; he had the principal square
fortified, and frequent skirmishes took place between each
party. General Borgoño used to visit General Lastra
daily; on the 13th of December he staid late, in order to
prevail on General Lastra, and the other chiefs, to refrain
from attacking General Prieto, but in vain, for next morning they marched at daybreak; on our hearing that they
had commenced hostilities, the general ordered me to
ascend the hill of Santa Lucia, and report to him what
should occur. I observed the division of General Lastra
attack the left of General Prieto's, and dislodge him from
the Chacara de Ochagavia, after which General Prieto's
cavalry made several charges, but still General Lastra's
division continued their march till near to the Chacara de
Eyzaguirre, which had been on the right of General Prieto's
army; then the firing ceased, and General Lastra's division
halted nearly on the same ground as that on which General
Prieto's army had been formed.

Before the battle ended, a party of mounted ragamuffins
denominated " La Partida del Alva," (break-of-day boys,)
entered the city, and committed various depredations, and

* The following government annulled his commission of vice-admiral.

P 2

entirely gutted the house of Mr. La Foret, French consul, situated in the Chimba, who, with his family, managed to escape to a friend's in the neighbourhood, and afterwards remained, concealed for two days, in the house of General Borgoño. Both parties claimed the victory, and in my humble opinion they were right, for what General Lastra had gained by fighting was lost; for in the end he was completely outwitted by General Prieto, the particulars of which are well known in Chile. An armistice was agreed upon for forty-eight hours, during which time General Freyre was appointed commander-in-chief of both armies, and plenipotentiaries were named, who cele-brated a definitive treaty of peace, by which the com-mands of both generals were to cease, and the division of General Lastra to leave the capital. A provisional junta, composed of Don Jose Thomas Ovalle, Don Isidoro, Errazuriz, and Don Jose M. Guzman, was appointed to govern until a president should be elected. General Freyre was acknowledged by both divisions on the 17th, and on the same day General Borgoño and Don Santiago Antonio Perez protested against the mal-inter-pretation of the treaty. On the 18th it was publicly pro-claimed; on the 19th the militia of Aconcagua, and other districts that had joined General Prieto, were ordered to return to their places of residence; and on the same day the newly raised corps of Carbineers of the Constitution, belonging to General Lastra's division was disbandoned, and the general gave up the command of his division; both of the contending parties met at Ochagavia, and the troops celebrated the peace by a fraternal embrace. I presented myself to General Freyre, to receive his excellency's orders, in company with Lieutenant-Colonel Ross; he made the latter his aid, and ordered me to remain with General

Borgoño. The troops of Colonels Rondissoni, Tupper, and Castillo, were sent into cantonments at Quillota, and General Prieto, who, disregarding the treaties, had still kept the command of his division, entered the capital, and was received by his partisans as a conqueror. Soon afterwards a rupture commenced between General Freyre and General Prieto, which the following documents will elucidate.

"OFFICIAL DOCUMENTS.

No. 1.

"Head-quarters of the Liberating Army, at Ochagavia, December 17, 1829.

"To his excellency Capt. General Don Ramon Freyre,

"In conformity with the definitive treaty of peace, ratified yesterday afternoon, your excellency has been recognized by this army. The soldiers, who fought so ardently in the war of independence, are the same who wish to augment their glory, serving as protectors to the liberty and rights which Chile acquired in its emancipation: this emancipation would have been useless without the enjoyment of these, and, for this reason, the army of the south believed themselves justified to undertake new labours, not to lose those they had consecrated to their country against their old oppressors. The chiefs and soldiers of the army of the south, without other designs, without other aspirations than the most laudable, to cause to be respected the fundamental laws, and the freewill of the country, feel a double pleasure in seeing their desires realized, without more shedding of blood, through the happy intervention of your excellency; and, in the nomination of you, as their plenipotentiary, they feel more and more satisfied. They hope, and have reason to hope, that under the orders of your excellency, they will never be converted into instruments of oppression, but rather that they may be the shield of the will of the country, which your excellency has known how to respect always: this consideration has contributed, without doubt, to the joy with which the liberating army has submitted to your excellency.

" On this occasion, I assure your excellency of my sentiments of esteem and respect.

(Signed)   "JOAQUIN PRIETO."

No. 2.

" Captain General of the Army, December 19, 1829.

"Having informed myself of the contents of your esteemed note of the day before yesterday, in which you were pleased to communicate to me, the recognition made to the army of my person, as general in chief, by virtue of the definitive treaty of peace; I have to assure you, with every effusion of my heart, that the blood we so prodigally shed in twenty years of war, to gain our independence, must be economised in the contests for liberty, which, if it is the more difficult to acquire, ought only to be protected by the soldier. That army, which under your command, has constantly proved these sentiments; I doubt not, being as brave as it is generous, it will sincerely embrace our old and common companions of so many glories, with that noble generosity, which is emblematic of the Chilian character. I glory in commanding an army as virtuous as it is brave, and I have an especial satisfaction in signifying to you my distinguished esteem.

(Signed)   " RAMON FREYRE."

" To the Señor General of Division, Don Joaquin Prieto."

No. 3.

" Captaincy General, December 19, 1829.

" DECREE.—Desirous that the evils should cease, which until now the republic has experienced through military preparations, which the circumstances have occasioned,· and being prejudicial to agriculture and the arts, that the citizens destined to these various occupations should remain any longer away from their homes. I decree the following:—

" 1st. The division of national guards from the province of Aconcagua, and others of this class, who may be found incorporated in the division of the south, shall return to their homes, from whence they came, in charge of their respective chiefs.

"2nd. It is hoped that their zeal for order will give no cause for complaint from their fellow-citizens during their transit, but rather that they will continue, as they have ever done, to show an example of discipline and morality.

"3rd. The major-general of the army will charge himself with the execution of this decree.

(Signed)   " FREYRE."

"OBEJERO, Secretary."

No. 4.

" Captaincy-General, December 19, 1829.

"DECREE.—Having augmented the corps in the army, owing to the critical circumstances of the republic, and out of which danger· it has now, happily escaped, and there being no object for the continuation of the squadron lately created, I decree the following:—

" 1st. That the squadron denominated Carbineers of the Constitution is disbanded.

"2nd. The chiefs and officers that composed it, will return to occupy the destinations they held previous to their incorporation in it.

" 3rd. The major-general of the army will see that the arms and other things that have belonged to the

said corps be received into the government stores, under
the most ample inventory, as also to the due compliance
of this order,—let note be taken of it, communicated, and
printed.

(Signed) "FREYRE,
"OBEJERO, Secretary.

No. 5.
"The Captain-General of the Army.

"Soldiers,—After having given to the republic the in-
estimable treasure of internal peace, it is requisite that
you manifest to your pacific fellow-citizens, that in the
generous breast of the Chilian soldier the ignoble passion of
resentment is not harboured; and that if military ardour
made you interrupt, by a fatal casualty, the happy harmony
with which you knew how to distinguish yourselves in the
glorious epoch in which you fought for the national independence, already you are reconciled with the sincerity
which distinguishes true brothers.

"Soldiers,—The days of bitterness, which political
circumstances brought upon our dear country, have disappeared for ever—erase them from your memory, and let a
mutual embrace be the bond to distinguish the sons of the
republic. This is the wish of your general and companion
in arms.

(Signed) "RAMON FREYRE."

No. 6.
TO THE NATION.
"Santiago, January 18th, 1890.

"To the Most Excellent Governing Junta,
"I have exhausted all the means dictated by prudence,
in order that the excellent S'or Captain General Don
Ramon Freyre should co-operate in sustaining the cause

of the people, as he appeared to do previous to the signing the treaty of peace, in which I manifested to him an unlimited confidence; but, unfortunately, the suggestions of men interested in disunion, and a never stifled predisposition against me, have opposed themselves.

"That treaty was signed, and when we hoped that he should seek all his support in the army under my command, because the three battalions that covered the garrison of the capital had given him a terrible lesson of disobedience, I began to discover that not only was he surrounded by chiefs belonging to those battalions; and even the very man who menaced him with the preparation of arms in the barracks of St. Augustin, but that he was taking measures to diminish the effective force of the army under my command, always postponing it in the armaments and whatever succours were required.

"I sought the important mediation of your excellency, to induce the S'or Captain-General to adopt another line of conduct; and there was a meeting in the very palace, where bases were laid down and stipulations made, which, for the future, should produce frankness and mutual security. Nothing was accomplished by the captain-general and the most excellent junta found itself likewise crippled in its operations, because its powers were disputed, and I was denied the character with which I am invested as general of the army of the south. The evil had now no remedy in negociation. The reports respecting my destruction, and that of the army of the south multiplied; and yet notwithstanding I passed to his excellency the letter No. 1., which I annex in copy, in which I recapitulated a part of my just complaints. In reply I received that of No. 2, and with it the official communication No. 3, in which he wants to dispossess me of the command of the army.

" The captain-general affects to be ignorant, that by the treaty of peace, I only ceased to be general-in-chief of the liberating army; which was composed of that which I held for the government, and of the forces from the provinces of Colchagua and Aconcagua, and from the departments of Melipilla and Rancagua. There was not, nor is there now a national government: for this reason, I was an independent general, and authorised by the provinces to re-establish the constitution, and protect the free opinion of the country. By the treaty, perhaps ceding my powers, I sacrificed all to peace and union; and I divested myself of that character, returning to that position and state that I held previously to the provinces taking up arms; the same did General Lastra, he remained without any command, as he was before; but I retained that of the army of the south, as so charged by the government and by the provinces of Concepcion and Maule.

" Even the captain-general found himself in a similar position to that of mine in 1823; he was then intendent of the province of Concepcion named by the government, and he submitted to that honourable assembly, and in this character came to the capital, where General O'Higgins had been already deprived of the command, and a governing junta was already installed with general applause; such as the whole population have shown in the installation of your excellency. Even in order to take at that time command of the republic, the captain-general had to resort to the honourable assembly of Concepcion, soliciting leave and consent.

" In fine, reflections, convincing arguments, and mediations, deserving the greatest respect, have not sufficed; and now in this position, true to the trust which the people have put in me, and seeing so many violations against the treaty of peace, and the representations of the army under my command, I have felt it incumbent on me to place it in safety, so as to cause its rights, and those of the country to be respected. The steps I am going to take, have this object, with this view I shall go and encamp myself out of the city, where I will always be at the disposal of your excellency. As soon as your excellency, or any other citizen, may be nominated for the general government, by the plenipotentiaries of the provinces, or recognized by these, I and my troops will give proofs of disinterestedness and obedience, laying down my command with pleasure, if I am so ordered.

"I hasten to impart to your excellency this inevitable resolution, that your excellency may take measures of safety with the civic corps of your command, and on this occasion I reiterate the homage of my high consideration and respect.

(Signed)   "JOAQUIN PRIETO."

No. 1.

" Santiago, January 17, 1830.

" My Esteemed General,

" I have often sought you out that we might agree to opportune measures for the tranquillity and happiness of the country, and I have done so because in all my public conduct I have not proposed to myself any other object, nor have I other views than the welfare of my country, and because you also have manifested to me on several occasions your desires, and the expediency for these interviews, but I have the sorrow of observing that they have not produced, up to this day, the beneficial effects we had believed they would, and I apprehend, as does the public, that far from advancing in the great work which I thought to accomplish with your consent and co-operation, it is getting worse from day to day; the fatigues and laudable efforts of good and distinguished patriots, who have sacrificed themselves to destroy the order of things which was carrying the republic to its complete ruin, and to substitute another which should conduct it to the happiness of which it is worthy, are frustrated.

"As all that we have resolved upon verbally between ourselves, and in the presence of several respectable inhabitants, has unfortunately remained without execution; and, as a state of things that appears to result from a want of confidence, and in which the apparent object is to persecute me, is already perceived; the occasion has arrived that we act in this matter frankly, if more frankness on my part were possible, that this be in writing, so that in any case my reputation may not suffer; and, moreover, to vindicate myself before the people who have done me the justice to believe in the sincerity and good intentions with which I have resolved to suffer for them. Exhausted of the legal resources, with which the majority of the populations of the republic solicited the remedy for the violations that our fundamental code, and that of the electoral laws suffered, the provinces of Concepcion and Maule raised the cry against the infractors, certain that they would be seconded, as we have seen, by the rest of the provinces; and, as the vote of that of Colchagua and Santiago was stifled by armed force, I was called upon to remove the obstacle which impeded its free utterance. The country demanded of me this important service, and I did not hesitate in affording it, exposing myself to the risks and sacrifices from which others wanted to fly. You and all the Chilenos have been witnesses of the approbation which the movement merited, at the head of which my fate and my ardent desires for the public good placed me. You

were the first to justify my resolution. You have gone
on in consonance with my sentiments, and have repeated a
thousand times that you would not take command of the
oppressive force, which the fallen government offered you,
because the resistance that was intended to oppose to the
army under my command, which army reclaimed the fulfilment of the law supported by the general vote, was revolt-
ing to justice and your own heart. In fine, the entire nation
has expressed itself, and its expression justifies but too
well the enterprize which patriotism made me undertake.

" By the true republicans, by the real lovers of their
country, I was invited long since to move from Chillan, to
celebrate with you an intimate alliance and friendship,
which should form the column and irresistible support of
the rights and liberties of the country given to it by law.
On the first suggestion I showed myself disposed and ready
to sacrifice on the altar of the country minor resentments,
which must be silent when the public cause speaks; and
sincerely did I decide upon that union, which I looked upon
as the rock on which would be shattered the miserable
aspirations, the anarchy, and the invasions against the
liberty and rights of Chile, and of the Chilenos. Scarcely
had I put myself in contact with your friends, and with
mine who have influence more particularly in the public
affairs, than I declared to them my most sincere desires to
strengthen that union indirectly entered into, and 1 offered
them to avail myself of every opportunity which might be
presented to give to you and to all, proofs of my good faith.

" In fact, on the 14th of last month, when the victory
over the forces that oppressed the people, was about to
secure completely their liberty, I was invited by the chiefs
who commanded them to a negociation; which, economizing
Chilian blood, might produce the same happy results as a

triumph. Then did, I believe, arrive the opportunity to prove the good faith with which I had lent myself to your friendship, and I did not hesitate to deposit in your hands my fate, that of the faithful and virtuous army I commanded, and that of the whole of the republic, naming you plenipotentiary on my part to adjust that treaty; that treaty was verified, and in its ratification I wished to give you another new proof of confidence, hoping that it would oblige you to give me yours.

"The day after the treaty of peace was sealed you presented yourself in the encampment of Ochagavia with two pretensions which were fatal to the treaty. The first was to explain article eight, with an addition, which left in existence the local authorities, of whose nullity the country had repeatedly complained; and the second was, that I should withdraw myself from the command of the army in the south by virtue of article three of the treaty. Your friends made you perceive that the commissioners had not the faculty to explain, nor add to the treaties after their ratification; that for such a proceeding new powers were necessary, and all the formalities which are used in such conventions; that the interpretations which you suggested were equivalent to a defeat on our part, because it was wanted to oblige the city of Santiago to groan under the yoke of null and despotic authorities; that they should continue arbitrary, disposing of the persons and rights of the citizen, without you or any other having the power to prevent them, because, by the treaty, neither was given, nor could be given to you the attribute to interpose in the resolutions of those authorities. In the same manner they persuaded you that I complied with said article three, ceasing to be general-in-chief of the liberating army, ceasing to be an independent general, to submit myself to you as the sole chief of both divisions, until the necessary means were prepared for me, and the general government of the republic established, so as to return to my appointment as intendant of the province of Concepcion, with the command of the army of the south, which a general power had confided to me. You yielded to the conviction, and 1 could not but attribute your solicitudes to a surprise or equivocation, and the more so when I found you rationally decided to seek your security, and that of the people in the army under my command, which sustained it, rather than in the corps of the garrison of Santiago, which had repeatedly disturbed its tranquillity. The character and pretensions of the general of the army of the south, and that of the persons about him, inspired more confidence than the character and pretensions of the chiefs who commanded the garrisons of Santiago, and that of the persons who surrounded them, and indeed it was blinding myself much, not to discern which of the two divisions offered the best guarantees. Satisfied on the point, sundry persons supplicated you in my presence, not to separate one single soldier from the army under my command, until the battalions commanded by General Lastra were cantoned, so that it might calm the inquietude in which their presence put the inhabitants, and the apprehension of a reaction which would not be difficult, considering that already on another occasion they had failed in their engagements, and in the obedience which they had promised to you, and considering likewise that the suggestions of the persons with whom you were in intimate friendship might have their effect; the chiefs and officers of those corps declared that you would yield to that supplication, founded in the same treaties, because, if the article 1st places under your orders both armies, and empowers you to canton them as you may consider convenient to the better service of the state, its security and public tranquillity, neither that nor any of the other articles authorizes you to diminish nor augment the strength in which the divisions were found, and in which they were delivered up to you. Nevertheless you thought proper to decree under date of last 19th December, ' that the division of national guards from the province of Aconcagua, and others of this class, who may be found incorporated in the divisions under my command, do return to their homes, from whence they came in charge of their respective chiefs;' and although I might have objected to this disposition, on account of its being contrary to the tenor of the treaty, I allowed it to take effect, giving up the militias of Aconcagua, and those of the cavalry of Rancagua; and I caused a person, of whom you could entertain no suspicion, to write to you, informing you that the decree referred to, tacitly extinguished the battalion of Maipu, which in its greatest part was composed of the militias of Rancagua; and you replied through Don Manuel Gandarillas, that you were ignorant of this information, and that it would be better not to comply with that part of the decree amicably objected to. I confided in the good faith and remained tranquil, until I knew that after your reconciliation you complained of me, as if it had not taken place, for having left in the Maipu the militias of Rancagua.

"In a few days you ordered that the one hundred artillerymen of Valparaiso, who on the Cuesta de Prado, passed over to the vanguard of the army of the south, should return to Valparaiso; then it was that I submitted to you in a friendly manner, through Don Fernando Errazuriz, a representation that these artillerymen formed part of the Maipu, and that their return to Valparaiso would weaken the division under my command, which you ought to maintain entire, so as to frustrate with it the attempts of the enemies of public order and tranquillity. You agreed with Senor Errazuriz, and consented that the artillerymen should remain as they were, incorporated in the Maipu; and agreed also with the same person that the battalion of Carampangui should remain in garrison in Santiago, while one of the three battalions actually cantoned out of the province, should be given to me, in order that it might march with me to Concepcion; this agreement you did not think fit to carry into execution.

"Knowing that you unjustly complained that the army of the south maintained itself in hostile array in the encampment of Ochagavia, that I retained with me the twenty-four pounders I had brought from Valparaiso, to demolish the trenches, which was done in virtue of the treaty of peace, and being equally aware that you attributed to me the desertion from the corps in the division of General Lastra, I visited you personally on distinct occasions, and begged of several persons that they would do the same, so as to remove the suspicions and want of confidence with which you had been inspired, by some evil-minded individuals, who, it appears, are carrying out their plan of introducing discord. The result of these explanations was, that you sent for me to your house, in order that, in presence of five of the most influential inhabitants, we should enter into explanations, and take the necessary measures to secure the public tranquillity, and my return to Concepcion. Then did we make mutual protestations of friendship, and of a sincere union; then did you enthusiastically express yourself in favour of the cause I have defended, and which I shall never abandon; then, not only did you approve of my remaining in command of the army of the south, not only

Q

did you assure me that you in my case, would never leave it; you then said that you were perfectly satisfied and tranquil; and then, lastly, you yourself proposed, and it was agreed upon that the battalions No. 1 and Maipu, should form one only, and should remain in this capital under the command of the sergeant major, Don J. A. Vidaurre (forming the garrison with the regiment of horse cazadores,) that the battalion Pudeto should remain in Curimon, that the squadron of Hussars, and the Concepcion battalion should go to the Canton of Maule; that the battalion Carampangui, and the horse grenadiers should accompany me to Chillan to cover the frontier: that you would issue a proclamation pardoning the deserters of Chacabuco, Pudeto, and Concepcion, and leaving them at liberty to incorporate themselves in the corps they pleased. The day after this agreement was made, in presence of the before-mentioned individuals, you retracted; from motives of which I am ignorant, and all remained in the state in which it was, until information arrived that the city of Concepcion had been surprised by a hundred country people, which Felix Antonio Novoa had got together, made me return to see you, to concert the means to be sent to that province, and the force with which I should pass the Maule: we did then agree that I should take with me the battalion Maipu, commanded by Major Vadaurre, two companies of the Carampangui, that of its sergeant major Anguila, and the regiment of the horse grenadiers; and that you would shortly treat about sending a force of infantry and cavalry to the canton of Maule. I am also assured that you failed in this agreement; and new measures, new dispositions entered into by you, which have for their object to isolate me, and take from me the command of the army of the south, daily comes to my knowledge, for which act you have no faculty or authority whatever. I know, with certainty, that you insist on attributing to me designs of placing General O'Higgins at the head of the republic, against the wish of the country; and this appears to be nothing else than seeking pretexts with which to ruin me, now that there is no motive or proof to convict me.

"The man who labours for the liberty of the nation; he who has given repeated proofs of his disinterestedness and respect for public opinion, cannot think of stifling it by obliging the republic to receive a mandatory, whom it resists. To deliver myself up to you as I have done, as on the 14th and 16th of December last, was not the best means, señor general, to place in the government Don Bernardo O'Higgins. Even children look with contempt upon the imputation through which unjust suspicions are wished to be infused. What proof? What indication even is there to attribute to me such a design? It would be easier and more likely if I could bring myself to it, to brave the execration and hatred of the public, treading under foot the will of the people, that I should do it in order to place myself in command, and not in order to place in it another. Undeceive yourself, as all have done: for me there is no General O'Higgins, nor other feeling, but the law, the liberty of the people, and public opinion, which I respect, and which I never will oppose. The day that I swerve from these sentiments, let the indignation of my countrymen, and all the ills that can affect man, fall upon me.

"If my honest intention—if my disinterested services to the country—if my true impartiality and disinterestedness have gained for me the esteem of my fellow-citizens, I shall always feel honoured to merit it through these means; and, well supported by just public opinion, any persecution will be an honour to me. No one can be persuaded, that the friendship I have professed for General O'Higgins is sufficient cause for condemning myself to an eternal obscurity.

" One letter is not sufficient to detail all the occurrences with which my moderation has been exercised and proved; but you know them, and the public is not ignorant of them. We cannot remain longer in this state, and it is now necessary that you decide frankly; and make known to me your pretensions and designs, even as I do to you.

" I beg of you to examine minutely, and impartially, the powers which the treaty of peace has given to you, the only powers that can be brought into action; and I pray of you, for the good of the country, that you will give to the articles of that treaty their true meaning and tenor. Lastly, that you examine and see, whether if it lies within the limit of your attributes, to make essential variations in the corps which were given up to you by treaty—such as changing the chiefs, more particularly when the general government is upon the eve of installation, in which resides exclusively such acts.

" We never can, without a good understanding proceed harmoniously; and never were these explanations more necessary than now.

" The treaty of peace has been broken in Concepcion, here likèwise, and in other parts; but until now I have considered it prudent to dissimulate to these violations, for the love of peace: it is in your hands to prevent a continuance of disorders; and if you have not ceased to be the same general who drew your sword to make the country's rights respected, and who has known likewise how to respect its wishes, I cannot doubt but that you will lend yourself to the prevention of the ills that threaten us.

" If you doubt my good faith, if you even still suspect the rectitude of my intentions, I shall offer to my country the last sacrifice, to put on one side entirely all my wrongs, so that guarantees of tranquillity may be arrived at; and if this be not sufficient, it will not be difficult to know on whom will fall the responsibility, and the misery that will come upon the country, owing to your want of confidence. Frankness, I repeat, is necessary to arrive at,—what we most desire.—Speak then to me, and dispose of yours, &c.

(Signed) "JOAQUIN PRIETO."

No. 2.

Santiago, January 18, 1830.

" To Señor Don Joaquin Prieto,

" My esteemed friend; I have received yours of this date, which you have been pleased to send me, with yours of yesterday, relating to the demanding of explanations upon certain events, which can only be imputed to you, inasmuch as you disregarded the orders I have issued as general-in-chief of the whole army of the republic. In accepting this command, contrary to my character, I have only considered the critical situation in which the country found itself, and as citizen and general of it, it was my duty to employ all the means within my reach to the end of restoring to it order and tranquillity.

" You accuse me, that I take measures that appear to be dictated by a want of confidence; and to this I must reply to you, that as general-in-chief of the army, I am invested, with power, as well by my situation as according to the stipulations of the treaty of peace, to dispose of the army as I deem necessary; thus it is, that if I had resolved upon sending some troops to Concepcion, it was under the idea that no revolution had taken place there, which you are not ignorant

of; but convinced, that had you gone there with troops,
you would do nought else than commence a war, in my
opinion, interminable by these means; I resolved to suspend the march of them for the present.

" You talk to me of having been invited, before you
moved from Chillan, to a close alliance and friendship; but
I cannot do less than satisfy you, that on my part there was
no indication to justify such a step; notwithstanding, I
know not the ignoble feeling of resentment, and even if this
hypothesis were admitted, I have sufficient fortitude to stifle
it, when the object is to unite with my fellow-citizens, in
co-operating to sustain their rights.

" When I repaired to the encampment, in which you were
the day after the treaty of peace was sealed, with the propositions upon which you take your stand, I went only
with the object to explain any doubt you might have with
respect to various articles of it; but neither I, nor the other
impartial citizens, have given any other interpretation than
that expressed in the tenor of them. The army neither
could, nor ought to interfere in anything relating to the
provincial and local authorities, and was confined to the
general of the country; because, otherwise, the army
would have been made the instruments of a party—conduct
which would have degraded it to the utmost abasement.

" The third article leaves no doubt, that by it the generals
of both divisions had ceased to hold their respective commands, and General Lastra, on his part has complied most
religiously; and when I remonstrated at the commencement
with you, you satisfied me with the pretext that you had
not the baggage to appear in the capital.

" If I permitted you to continue at the head of the division, believing it then convenient, it has been through.

tolerance; but the recent events in the province of Concepcion, and other circumstances, oblige me not to replace
you in the command, as I had thought to do. This power
the treaties give me, and the character of general-in-chief,
with which I am invested. You, contrary to what is provided in them, say, in order to retain it, that it was conferred on you by the legitimate government. It is certain
that the legitimate government named you provisionally,
and until General Borgoño's health should be restored, in
which case your command should cease. I do not avail
myself of these grounds to convince you of the error in
which you are, but I am impelled by the duty of seeing
the treaties duly executed.¹

" When you endeavour to exculpate yourself from the
suspicions that many citizens have, (that you exert yourself
for the return of General O'Higgins), I must allow the
powerful reflections which you allege ; but, am also certain
that your conduct has been sufficiently tortuous, since you
openly disobey the commands, which, as general-in-chief, I
dictated; and I am even aware that you gave a counter
order to the authorites of Coquimbo, that they should reject
Colonel Tupper, whom I had destined to that point, believing
that his services would be advantageous.

" With respect to the collocation of Colonel Puga, can
you be ignorant that the general-in-chief of an army has
the power, in such circumstances to replace and suspend
the chiefs in it? But it is his duty to give account of it to
the general government. The said Colonel Puga was unjustly deprived of the command, and for that reason I had
him replaced in it; he is recognised by the army, and the
same body of Cazadores consider him in command.

" Lastly, S'or General, the army and the nation recognize my authority as general-in-chief of the forces of the republic; under this supposition, I dispose of them as I think convenient, satisfying in this manner the public confidence. I alone have to answer to the nation for the charge I exercise; and you and other individuals of the army only have to execute what may be commanded for the public service, by the supreme chief whom it recognizes.

" If perchance you have any doubt relative to the cessation of the command of the division in conformity with the treaty, you can call upon the plenipotentiaries who acted in it, and you will be convinced with their exposition of the same, of what I assure you; moreover, your own uncle, Don Augustin Vial, assured frankly the rest of the citizens who composed the deputation to treat, that he would answer, that you would comply most religiously with the tenor of article three with the greatest pleasure.

" If, after what is stated, you should dare not to listen to the imperious voice of your duty, from this moment I shall hold you responsible to the nation for the evils that may arise from your disobedience, as a subaltern general. Whoever may address to you other language, desires to precipitate you into an abyss of evils, which you may lament when no remedy is left you.

" On the 16th of last December, the commission ceased, which you say the country conferred on you, in this case you fulfilled its wishes, and to day the cause that you endeavour to give currency to is very different. Do not be deceived, and listen to the exposition which your attached friend lays before you.

(Signed)   " RAMON FREYRE."

" Santiago, January 18, 1830.

" Captaincy-General of the Army,

" Until now have I tolerated your permanency in the command of the division of the south against the tenor of the treaties of peace, because I believed it convenient; but those motives having ceased, and the present circumstances demanding your retirement; you are exonerated, from this date, from the charge which was confided to you, conforming in this particular with the tenor of article three of said treaty.

" With this object in view, I repeat to you my distinguished consideration, &c.

     (Signed)   " RAMON FREYRE.

" To the Señor General of the Division, Don Joaquin Prieto."

     •   " Santiago, January 18, 1830.

" The Junta has received the honourable communication from the Senor General of the Army of the South, and it is with extreme sorrow the Junta perceives the disagreement it endeavoured to impede by all prudential means; and feels extremely that this incident, caused doubtless by the enemies of the public good, obliges it to take this measure of separating the army, whilst the Junta has not been able to organize the civic troops, owing to difficulties which it has not been possible to remove.

" Under these circumstances the Junta hopes that the Señor General, in retiring from the capital, will not leave the province, for in it he may obtain security for his army, and protect the liberty of the country, threatened again with new troubles.

" These are the sentiments of the junta, in whose name the president who subscribes himself has the honour to thank the general for his patriotism and disinterestedness, offering him, at the same time, all the considerations of its great respect.

(Signed)   "Jose Tomas Ovalle, President.
"Juan Francisco Meneses, Secretary.

"To the General-in-chief of the Army of the South, January 19, 1830."

General Freyre sent for the horses of the Hussars; but they were delivered up to General Prieto; then the Hussars were marched from their quarters to the artillery barracks. However, General Prieto, during the night, took possession of the hill of Santa Lucia, which commanded the whole, got up some cannon, and, surrounding the barracks, obliged them to capitulate. Next day the junta appointed General Prieto to be the general-in-chief of the army. General Freyre left the capital during the night, for Quillota, to join the battalions Nos. 1, 7, and 8. General Prieto sent for me, and strove to induce me to join him, but I excused myself on account of being aid to General Borgofio, and stated that it would be impossible for me to serve in an army, even if I had been unattached, when such an excitement had been fomented against foreigners (los estrangeros.) He said that I belonged to the army of the south, of which he was now the general, and that I had been included in the late promotion; that he was my friend, and expected me to join him. I informed him that I had been ordered by the government to remain with General Borgofio, and that I did not wish to obtain a

grade by seconding a revolutionary movement, and added,
that if he was my friend, he would not oblige me to take
part against General Freyre, who was also a friend of
mine; but in case he would allow me, I would retire to
an hacienda, and remain neuter until the unfortunate
rupture would be at an end.

The general's brother, Don Manuel Prieto, Don
Joaquin Echaveria, Don Gaspar Marin, Col. Arriagada,
Major O'Carrol, and others, who were present, strove to
induce me to join the general; and as a stimulus, Don
Manuel Prieto told me they were striving to get their
injured friend, General O'Higgins, back to Chile. I replied, that unless the general could return to his native
country without any disturbance, I would never wish to
see him in Santiago, for I well knew the parties who had
caused the late revolution, and who had deceived them;
on this, an old friend of mine, Don Gaspar Marin, replied rather hastily, and in an angry manner, that I was
mistaken; I replied that General O'Higgin's name had
been made use of on more than one occasion, and that it
had afterwards been prostituted to serve other purposes.
Don Manuel Prieto strove to contradict me, and persuade me they were certainly toiling for O'Higgins; on
which I said he was only fagging for a roll of tobacco
(alluding to the estanco) as big as himself, for he was
very corpulent; one of the factors of the estanco of
tobacco, Don Juan Badiola, who was present, left the
room; and soon after Major Arteaga, one of the aid-de-
camp's, called me out, and the general chided me for having
spoken so freely; after which he inquired on whose estate
I wished to reside; I replied, that of Don Juan Francisco
Larrayn, at Aculeu; on this, and after a little considera-

tion, he gave his leave. Next day, when on the point of setting out for the estate of my friend, I was arrested, and conducted to the governador-local, Don Angel Ortuzar, who informed me that the junta had ordered him to do so, on account of having received information that I was about joining General Freyre; on which I referred him to General Prieto, and soon afterwards I was permitted to leave for Aculeu. I was also stopped at the bridge of Maipu by a party stationed there; but on explaining matters, was allowed to proceed. I had not been many days in the country, before I was sent for again by the general, and, on my presenting myself, he demanded why I had not acknowledged the government. I was surprised at this question, and stated that I had received no intimation to that effect; he said, that the chief of the staff, had by his orders, sent me an official note; and on my informing the general I had not received any but the one that had called me in, he sent for Major Santivanes, who informed the general that he had sent the note to General Borgoños; on this General Prieto exonerated me from any neglect, and bade me, as a friend, send in a suitable answer. On visiting General Borgoño, I received the following note :—

"No. 183.

" Commandancia-General de Armas,

" Santiago, February 17th, 1830.

" La Ex'ma Junta Gubernativa has thought proper to issue on the 12th of this month the following decree.

" ' The National Congress of Plenipotentiaries, that have been happily installed on this ever-glorious day for Chile, having ordered this junta to demand that all the civil, military, and ecclesiastical authorities that exist in this province, do immediately acknowledge and give due obedience to the supreme national authority they are invested with.' I transmit this supreme disposition to you, for your compliance, hoping to receive the

testimony of your acknowledgment, as required, in order that I may report
upon it.   " Dios guarde a V. M. A.
                                        " De order del S'r. Jl. del Exto.
                                                " J. J. SANTIVANES.
" Al Sargt. Mor de Exto., Don Thos. Sutcliffe."

To which, after due deliberation, I sent the following
answer.
                                        " Santiago, March 2d, 1830.
" I have not answered your note, No. 183, until to-day, on account of
having been on leave at Aculeu, and its not being delivered until my recall
to the capital. Having maturely considered its contents, and in answer,
have only to state, that I have no other will, than that of giving due obedience to the orders of my chief, and the supreme national authority. I
embrace this opportunity of offering you the consideration of my esteem.

                                        " THOMAS SUTCLIFFE.
" S'or Commandante General de Armas y Sargt. Mor de Exto.
" Don. J. J. SANTIVANES."

I delivered this to the chief of the staff, who on reading its contents, seemed satisfied. Next day, Lieutenant-
Colonel O. Carrol, aid-de-camp to General Prieto, called
upon me, and strove to induce me to join the general ;
I informed him, that until I should receive an order from
government, I could not leave General Borgoño ; for
which he said, that I would not have to serve him long ; for
both he, and a considerable number of chiefs, and officers,
who had refused to recognize the junta, would soon be
" dado de baja," cashiered ; he argued much, and told
me that the general expected me to join him ; for if I did
not, I would not receive my promotion as lieutenant-
colonel, (he had been promoted.) I replied I did not want
any grade that would be acquired by joining in their
domestic quarrels.

I was afterwards appointed by government to be
adjutant to Colonel Luna, chief of the staff, resident in

the capital; and on taking leave of my general, he gave me the following certificate.

" DON JOSE MANUEL BORGOÑO, GENERAL-IN-CHIEF OF THE ARMY OF THE SOUTH, AND MINISTER OF STATE IN THE WAR DEPARTMENTS.

" I certify that Major Don Thomas Sutcliff has served as my aid-de-camp from the month of October, 1826, until March 1830, having, during this period performed different important services, and in all manifested the greatest zeal, integrity, and honour.

" JOSE MANUEL BORGONO."*

" Santiago, March 15th, 1830."

I was promoted to the grade I held when I first joined the Chilian service, (lieutenant-colonel of cavalry,) for all the chiefs and officers who were true to government were rewarded with a grade. The troops marched from Quillota to Valparaiso, and after having provided some warlike stores, General Freyre engaged vessels to transport them to Concepcion and Coquimbo. His excellency, Don Francisco Ramon Vicuña, with his ministers, had already left Valparaiso for Coquimbo, in the brig of war, Aquilles; but on their arrival, the partizans of General Prieto prevailed, and the Aquilles was given up to them, and the president and ministers were made prisoners.

The plenipotentiaries of the provinces were assembled, and elected Don Francisco Ruiz Tagle, and Don Thomas Ovalle, to be president and vice-president of the republic, who superseded the junta. The president was brother-in-law to my friend, Don J. Francisco Larrayn, and a gentleman with whom I had been on friendly terms, as well as nearly all his family connections, ever since my arrival in Chile; so, on my visiting him, he proposed

* The certificate of General Don Manuel Borgoño was published in my manifesto previous to my leaving Chile.

making me his aid-de-camp, stating it was better for him
to have my personal services, than those of a stranger;
but I begged to be excused, and informed him what had
occurred with General Prieto. On this, at the request of
his brother-in-law, he appointed me chief instructor of the
militia.

"Calera, March 27th, 1830.

" My esteemed Friend,

" I have experienced the greatest pleasure in hearing you have been
appointed Chief Instructor of Militia.

" I have written to the Inspector-general, and to Francisco,* in order
that you might be appointed to this corps.

" I wish you every happiness, and beg you will command your friend,
and S. S. Q. B. S. M.

"JOSE NICOLAS LARRAYN Y ROJOS."

" Al Tente. Col. del Exto., Don Thomas Sutcliffe."

His excellency having attached me to this corps, bade
me take up my quarters on his hacienda, La Calera.
This was too good a post to refuse; for now I had one
that would keep me free from civil broils.

General Prieto marched to the south, for General
Freyre had left Coquimbo; he afterwards disembarked at
the mouth of the Maule, and narrowly escaped drowning.
His secretary, El S'or Fernandez, perished by the boat,
in which he and the general left the vessel, in being
upset on the bar. One of the transports, the Oliphant,
Captain Kennedy, with troops on board, was totally
wrecked on the coast of the province of San Fernando;
but the soldiers, passengers, and crew, saved their lives.

All the promotions of the late administration were
cancelled, and the generals, chiefs, and officers, as well as
several of the civil departments that had not acknowledged the new government, or had accompanied General
Freyre, were cashiered, "dado de baja;" among whom

* His excellency the president of the republic.

was my friend and patron, General Borgoño, who had
only just left the capital for the province of Coquimbo,
on account of the ill state of his health, and the annoyance
he received from the party he was opposed to. This was
a masterly piece of intrigue of the Spanish faction, who
had by their manœuvres got hold of the administration;
and five individuals who had taken the lead in all the
late disturbances, were either in the ministry, or with the
army—viz. Don Diego Portales, Don Pedro Vrriola, Don
Joaquin Tocarnal, Don Francisco Meneses; and Don
Vitorino Garrido, a Spaniard, although he held no ostensible authority, was the principal director.

When General Freyre left Valparaiso for Coquimbo,
he sent Colonel Biel and a division, to act in the province of Concepcion; these were pursued by the Aquilles, .
(this vessel proved to be a valuable acquisition to the
malcontents,) and she anchored at the entrance of the
bay of Talcahuano, in order to blockade the port, and
intercept any vessels that might arrive with troops.
However, she only captured one vessel.

Colonel Tupper, who had accompanied the division,
and had been left in command of Talcahuano, felt annoyed
at the appearance of the Aquilles; and, although he well
knew that soldiers would make bad boarders, and worse
boatmen, he formed the desperate plan of seizing her
during the night; and his enterprise was materially
furthered by the captain and crew of an English whaler
offering her boats and their assistance.

With this unexpected and highly essential aid, the
colonel was induced to make the attempt on the night of
the 17th of February, and accordingly set out with six
boats well armed : by some mismanagement they could

not fall in with the brig, and at daybreak pulled into the
port of Tome, where they lay concealed until night;
when, having added more boats and volunteers to their
party, they ventured again; but unfortunately only three
boats—the captain of the whaler's, Colonel Tupper's, and
Captain Wynter's got alongside; the rest had lagged
behind: as the crew of the Aquilles were on the alert,
the boarders were repulsed, with the loss of seven men
killed, and twenty-three wounded, amongst whom were
the captain of the whaler, Colonel Tupper, and Captain
Wynter; the first escaped, the last remained on board,
but Colonel Tupper was knocked overboard; however,
he swam to a boat, and strove in vain to urge the men
to return to the attack.   On the first boat's return to
Talcahuana, it was reported that he was killed; but his
arrival soon dispelled the gloom that had been excited,
and the gallant colonel was rapturously received by his
friends.

Nothing gave me greater disgust than the proceedings
of a few of the Spanish faction in Santiago on the arrival
of the report of Colonel Tupper's death; for a gang, with
a band of music, headed by Los S. S. Meneses, Garfias,
Fierros, with a mob at their heels, made their appearance at the house of his excellency the president,
Don Francisco Ruiz Tagle, crying out, " Muero Los
Franceses y Yngleses, y viva la religion." I was present
when one of the trio cried out, "Albricios Señor Presidente, el Perro Tupper es muerto," (I wish you joy
Señor President, for that dog Tupper is killed.)

His excellency did not express his approval of their
exultation over a fallen enemy; and his respectable
mother, Doña Rosaria Portales, was so affected that she
fainted; however the godos kept up their saturnalia

R

until daylight next morning; but before mid-day they had the bitter mortification to learn, that all their doings had been to no other purpose than that of throwing an eternal stigma upon them, and others of their fraternity, who in Valparaiso went to serenade the colonel's lady with music, on the news of her husband's death!!

Colonel Tupper was only slightly wounded in the arm, and in a few days he marched with Colonel Biel to invest the town of Chillan, which was garrisoned with about 400 of General Prieto's troops. Colonel Tupper led on an attack on the night of 9th of March, and carried the outer works, but on finding it impossible to enter the town, he retreated, after having suffered a severe loss. Colonel Biel soon after received orders to march and join General Freyre at Longomilla, near the river Maule, for General Prieto, who had augmented his forces, had, with a complete train of artillery, marched towards Talca. General Freyre, who, although inferior in number, and without horses to mount the whole of his cavalry, or manage his artillery, crossed the Maule to meet his opponent; and on the 15th of April he entered the city of Talca, where his division was received by its patriotic inhabitants with the greatest enthusiasm, and who jointly with the principal chiefs, strove to induce the general to remain in Talca, where he could not be attacked without great loss to the assailants, until they could procure horses for the cavalry and artillery; and as there is no forage to be obtained in the neighbourhood, his rival could not provide for his horses, nor molest him there.

General Prieto made his appearance on the 16th, and offered battle, which was not accepted; and judging that his rival had determined on keeping his important posi-

tion, he, through the aid of a wily Spaniard, who had
taken a conspicuous part in the late revolution, succeeded
in deceiving General Freyre, by two Colonels and others
sending him word that they were still his friends, and
would join him with their troops as soon as the division
should be placed in a position favourable to their design.
No sooner had the deluded and infatuated general received this intelligence, than he felt fully persuaded that
his popularity amongst the chiefs, officers, and soldiers of
his rival's army, (many of which owed their grades to
him), was such that nothing now was wanting but that
the troops should face each other, and then an end would
be put to the civil war without bloodshed.   Under this
supposition, and contrary to the advice of his friends, he
unwarily quitted his strong position, on the morning of the
17th, and marched against his opponent with only 1,700
men and four field-pieces drawn by oxen.   General
Prieto had 2,200 men, of whom one-third were cavalry,
besides twelve field-pieces well served.   No sooner had
General Freyre abandoned the envied position, than
his opponent threw his light troops between those of
General Freyre and the city of Talca ; and, on gaining
this point, he commenced the action, which continued
four hours.   General Freyre, finding he had been egregi-
ously deceived by his quondam friends,* and seeing his
cavalry put to route, ordered the infantry to retreat across
the river Lircai ; however, finding this impossible, he left
them, and followed the cavalry, who had commenced
their retreat.   Colonels Rondissoni, Tupper, Castillo, and
Amunategui, who commanded the gallant remnant,
withstood the attacks of the whole of General Prieto's
force with the greatest valour and obstinacy, until

* Vidaurre and Villagran.

R 2

they were completely broken and routed, after having
left about 600 men dead on the field, amongst whom were
the chief of the staff, Colonel Elizalde, and seventeen
chiefs and officers. Never had party-feeling been carried
on to such a pitch as in this unfortunate battle, and where
patriots were actually cutting each others throats at the
instigation of their common enemy, and who had induced
the victors to give no quarter to the foreigners (estrangeros); and, although I regret to record it, I feel it my
duty to publish the following facts, related to me by
Colonel Amunategui, brother-in-law to General Borgoño,
who commanded the artillery :—" No sooner had we been
completely routed, than I strove to escape with Tupper,
but we were overtaken by Captain Garcia, of Colonel
Baquedano's regiment, who gave us in charge of a corporal ; he then galloped off, I suppose, for orders, during
which interval Tupper strove to induce the corporal
to conduct him to Talca, and made him a liberal offer,
but in vain, for Garcia soon returned, accompanied with
Indians and others, who fell upon us.* I received a severe

* A private letter written by a gentleman in Chile, the chargé d'affaires
of the United States of America, and which was never intended to meet
the eye of the family, as it was addressed to a British officer commanding
a ship on the South American station, also a perfect stranger, thus speaks
of their unfortunate relative :—
" The heroism displayed by Tupper surpassed the prowess of any individual that I ever heard of in battle; but, poor fellow! he was horribly
dealt with, after getting away with another officer. A party of cavalry and
Indians was sent in pursuit, and they boast that poor Tupper was cut to
pieces. They seemed to be more in terror of him, on account of his personal bravery and popularity, than of all the others. Guernsey has cause
to be proud of so great a hero—a hero he truly was, for nature made him
one." An English gentleman, holding a high consular appointment in that
country, also wrote :—" I trust you will believe that any member of the
family of Colonel Tupper, who may require such services as I am at liberty
to offer, will be always esteemed by one, who for many years has looked
upon his gallant and honourable conduct as reflecting lustre upon the English name in these new and distant states."

wound in the neck, but was saved by Garcia; poor Tupper was run through by a lance, and sabred to death.

Thus perished, at the early age of twenty-nine, one who, if he did not fall in the service of his own country, at least did honour to that country in a foreign clime. From his earliest youth he gave indications of that fearless and daring spirit which marked his after-life; and when he left Europe, he was generally thought to bear a striking resemblance to his late uncle, Major-General Brock, at the same age. This similarity extended in some degree even to their deaths, as the Indians of either continent were employed as auxiliaries in the actions in which they fell, and both were killed in the months that gave them birth. It was observed of Colonel Tupper by no mean judge, in the early part of his career: "C'est un officier à toute épreuve, qui réunit à sa brillant valeur des connaissances très-distinguées." His tall, manly, and strikingly handsome person, his almost Herculean strength, the elegance of his manners, and his impetuous valour in battle, gave the impression rather of a royal knight of chivalry, than of a republican soldier.* The influence and popularity which in a few short years he acquired in his adopted country, by his own unaided exertions, and under the many disadvantages of being a stranger in a strange land, best prove that his talents were of the first order, and that he was no common character. The attachment of his men to him was constant and unbounded, for he not only possessed that bravery which, with the brave, is the surest passport to affection, but that kindness of heart which ever wins a way to the human breast. The union of so many excellent qualities, joined to his previous services to Chile, ought at least to have procured him quarter; but unfortunately in civil wars, they who aim at arbitrary power seldom spare any one who may successfully oppose their despotic views, and both gratitude and humanity would fain throw a veil over his last moments. He deserved far better than to have fallen by the order of a band of assassins, whose cause and conduct were in every way worthy of so foul a deed. The opinion of his friends, however, will correct the errors of fortune, which denied him a better field for the exercise of his endowments. He is dead, but his memory lives, and though his mangled corse now lies far from the tombs of his forefathers—

"Unknell'd, uncoffin'd, and unknown;"

yet it is some melancholy consolation to his deeply afflicted family to reflect, that he is not lamented by them only, and that his false, perjured, bloodthirsty murderers, cannot deprive their unhappy victim of his fair name. But, as a French traveller wrote of him—" N'est-il pas déplorable que de tels hommes en soient réduits à se consacrer à une cause étrangére?"

* In height he was about six feet two inches, and his figure was a perfect model of strength and symmetry. His countenance was benign and "pleine de franchise,"—his complexion florid,—and he had a profusion of beautiful dark chesnut hair.

Captain Bell,* a post captain in the Chilian navy, who was an aid-de-camp of General Freyre, was overtaken, and also put to death in cool blood.† General Freyre, Colonel Biel, Colonel Rondisoni, Major Latham, and others who were eagerly sought after, luckily escaped their bloodthirsty pursuers. This sanguinary contest decided the fate of the liberal party. Although my employment in the capital had freed me from sharing the risks and toils of my less fortunate comrades, who had either been butchered or cashiered, for having acted as men of honour ought to have done, by sacrificing their lives or fortunes in defence of the legitimate government, I felt grateful to a kind Providence that I had been exonerated from having to take an active part during the conflicts of

Colonel Tupper married at Santiago, in 1826, Maria Isidora de Zegers, a native of Madrid, and grand-daughter of Manuel de Zegers, Count de Waserberg, in Flanders. He left two infant daughters, and his young widow, from whom his death was kept concealed for some time, gave birth a few weeks after to a son, who, it is to be hoped, will resemble his father in every thing but his misfortunes. The British and a few of the foreign merchants in Chile, most liberally united to present the unhappy widow with some solid proof of the estimation in which they held the worth and gallantry of her unfortunate husband, and being joined by a small number of the natives, the amount raised was about seven thousand dollars, several of the English contributing five hundred dollars each. An act of such unusual generosity should not go unrecorded, as, while it redounds so much to the credit of those engaged in it, it speaks volumes in favour of the deceased.‡

* Captain Bell was one of the founders of the Chilian navy, and had rendered many important services to his adopted country. He left a widow and children to deplore his loss, and, fortunately for them, they were supported by their worthy relative, El S'or Canonigo Meneses.

† The bodies of these victims were sought by a worthy patriot, a clergyman, but he could only find that of Colonel Tupper; it was horribly mutilated; he gave it a silent and private sepulchre, from which it was afterwards exhumed, and the ashes are now deposited by his widow in the public cemetery of Santiago, but she was obliged to erase the words, " Patria Infelice Fidelis," from the marble slab that covers the monument she erected to his memory ! !

‡ Memoir of Colonel Tupper, by Ferdinand Tupper, Esq.

Ochagavia, and Lircai; and the following letter and
certificate from their excellencies, the late presidents of
the republic, will shew that I did my duty to my adopted
country :—

"Tango, August 8th, 1838.
" S. D. Thomas Sutcliffe.

" My dear Sir,—I find no difficulty in acceding to your indication,
and in assuring you that your military conduct during the short time you
were under my orders, was good; and that you never merited the least
censure.

" It is also true, that during the different epochs that I have exercised
civil and magisterial duties, including that of the supreme command of the
republic, I have never heard of any action of yours, either as a soldier or
citizen, that might tarnish the good opinion you have acquired amongst our
countrymen, for your honourable conduct and fulfilment of the duties
with which you have been encharged.

" Please to accept the sentiments of esteem and friendship of your
'atento servidor.'
" F. A. PINTO."

" Lieutenant-Colonel Don Thomas Sutcliffe has solicited a certificate
from the Subscriber relative to his military conduct and services.

" Confining myself to the epoch in which I was president of the republic
of Chile, I cannot do less than declare that he has acted with honour in all
the duties in which he has been employed. I have had him near to my
person, and have always observed in him an adhesion and interest in the
great work of our independence and emancipation; and for the end that
may suit him, I subscribe this, giving him thanks for the services he has
lent to the cause of our liberty.*
" FRANCISCO RAMON VICUNNA."
" Santiago de Chile, April 13th, 1838."

The remnant of the routed troops who capitulated
to General Aldunate, at Cus-Cus, near to Illapel, was
united by Colonel Biel; but they were cancelled by
government. Colonel Biel, and Colonel Rendissoni, with
Monsieur Chapius, (a literary adventurer,) escaped on
board of neutral vessels in Valparaiso: and General
Freyre, who had taken refuge near to Santiago, was

* Both of these affidavits have been published in Chile.

treacherously delivered up to his enemies, thrown into
prison; and afterwards, with others, exiled to Peru.
Shortly after his arrival there, he published a pamphlet
in justification of his conduct during the revolution of
1829 and 1830; from which I will make the following
extract.

"It does not enter into my plan to justify the movements which preceded the battle of Lircai. The dispro-
portion between the contending forces was excessive.
Neither tactics nor prodigies of valour could avail against
this immense disadvantage. The liberals were routed.
Would that I could throw a veil not only over a conquest which proves neither courage nor talent in the
conqueror, but also over the horrid cruelties which succeeded the battle. The most furious savages, the most
unprincipled bandits, would have been ashamed to execute the orders which the rebel army received from
General Prieto, and yet which were executed with
mournful fidelity. Tupper — illustrous shade of the
bravest of soldiers, of the most estimable of men! shade
of a hero to whom Greece and Rome would have erected
statues!—your dreadful assassination will be avenged. If
there be no visible punishment for your murderer,
Divine vengeance will overtake him. It will demand
an account of that infamous sentence pronounced against
all strangers,* by a man who at the time was the pupil
and the tool of a vagabond stranger,† indebted for his
elevation and his bread to the generosity of Chile."

> *   ———— " They never fail who die
> In a great cause : the block may soak their gore ;
> Their heads may sodden in the sun, their limbs
> Be strung to city gates and castle walls—
> But still their spirit walks abroad ! !"   BYRON.
>
> † Garrido, a Spaniard.

A relative of Colonel Tupper has favoured me with the following extract, published in Guernsey, 1835, which will help to elucidate the causes of the late civil commotion, as well as to give a brief sketch of the services he had rendered to his adopted country.

"William De Vic Tupper, whose life we are about to narrate, was born in Guernsey on the 28th of April, 1800, and was so named from his paternal uncle, who fell in a duel, in Guernsey, with an officer in the army. He was the fifth of ten sons, and one of thirteen children. His father was a younger son of a much respected jurat or magistrate of the Royal Court, who died in 1802, leaving five children.* Having received an excellent education in England, partly under a private tutor in Warwickshire, De Vic, the name by which he was always designated, was sent, on the restoration of the Bourbons, in 1814, to a college at Paris, in which he continued until the arrival of Napoleon from Elba, being then gratified by a glimpse of that extraordinary man. When he landed in France, although he had barely completed his fourteenth year, his stature was so tall and athletic as to give him the appearance of a young giant; and on being asked his age at the police office, that it might be inserted in his passport, his reply was received with a smile of astonishment and incredulity, which afforded much subsequent amusement to his elder fellow-travellers. At the age of sixteen his strength and activity were so great, that few men could have stood up against him with any chance of success. On his return to Guernsey, every

---

* Two sons,—Daniel married Catherine. daughter of John Tupper, Esq., jurat; and John married Elizabeth, daughter of John Brock, Esq.,—and three daughters, Emilia, wife of Sir P. De Havilland, bailiff; Elizabeth, wife of W. Le Marchant, Esq ; and Margaret, wife of L Carey, Esq.

interest the family possessed was anxiously exerted to indulge his wish of entering the British army, but owing to the great reductions made after the peace of 1815, he was unable to obtain a commission, even by purchase. Those relatives, who could best have forwarded his views, had been slain in the public service, and in that day few claims were admitted, unless supported by strong parliamentary influence. He attended the levee of the commander-in-chief, who promised to take his memorial into early consideration; but his royal highness had first to satisfy the cravings of an insatiable oligarchy, whose iniquitous misrule has at length succumbed to the desperation of a long-injured people. This was a cruel disappointment to one, whom nature ever intended for a military life, and it ultimately drove him to a distant land, to shed that blood, and to yield that breath, which he in vain sought to devote to his native country.* Happy for him and for his friends had it been otherwise, as it will quickly be seen that he was endowed with qualities, which must have rendered him conspicuous in any service, but which, in a civil strife, only hastened his destruction. Thus disappointed, he spent two or three years in Catalonia, of which province a relative† was British consul, and 'the young Englishman' received the public thanks of the municipality of Barcelona, for having boldly

---

* How different is the success of members of the same family in the same pursuit! His first cousin, William Le Mesurier Tupper, entered the army in the 23d Royal Welsh Fusileers, in September, 1823, and in August, 1826, was a captain in that distinguished regiment.

† The late P. Carey Tupper, Esq., who enjoyed a pension of £600 sterling a year for his services in Spain during Napoleon's invasion, and for which he declined the offer of an English baronetcy and a Spanish barony. During a long residence in that country he formed a very valuable collection of paintings and cartoons, part of which were sent to England. A younger brother was British consul at Caraccas, and subsequently at Riga.

exposed his life to extinguish a conflagration which
threatened to destroy a whole barrier of the city. Here
his vanity was constantly excited by exclamations in the
streets on the manly beauty of his person. The profession
of arms continuing his ruling passion, he embarked at
Guernsey late in 1821 for Rio de Janeiro, whence he
proceeded to Buenos Ayres, and thence overland to
Chile. His family was averse to his joining the patriot
cause, as it was then termed, and he arrived at Santiago
a mere soldier of fortune,—without, we believe, a single
letter of introduction to those in authority. But his appearance and manners, and a perfect knowledge of three
languages, English, French, and Spanish, all of which he
spoke fluently, soon procured him friends. The Italian,
in a less degree, was also another of his acquirements.
The garrison of Valdivia having revolted, Colonel Beauchef, who had served in Europe, and who led, with Major
Miller, the troops in the successful attack of that fortress
by Lord Cochrane, was sent from the capital to endeavour
to bring the mutineers to submission, and he requested
that young Tupper might accompany him. They landed
there alone, and, with great personal risk, succeeded in
securing the ringleaders, who had ordered their men to
fire on them as they approached in a boat; but Colonel
Beauchef having previously commanded them and obtained their regard, the men fortunately refused to proceed to extremities with their old commander. Young
Tupper is also said to have excited their astonishment by
the manner in which he seized on one of the ringleaders,
a very athletic and powerful man, and led him captive to
the boat. For this service, and for his conduct in a campaign against the fierce Araucanians, whom the Spaniards
had never been able to subjugate, he was made in Janu-

ary, 1823, over the heads of all the lieutenants, captain of
the grenadier company of battalion No. 8, commanded
by the same gallant Frenchman, Colonel Beauchef. This
company consisted of upwards of one hundred exceedingly
fine men, and accompanying the battalion shortly after in
an expedition to Arica, it excited the surprise of the comparatively diminutive Peruvians, and to which its captain
appears not a little to have contributed. This expedition
was soon recalled from Peru to proceed under the director, General Ramon Freyre, against the island of Chiloe,
so long and so bravely defended by the Spanish governor,
Quintanilla. On the return voyage from Arica to Coquimbo, the vessel, which conveyed the grenadiers of
No. 8, was short of both provisions and water, and of the
latter only a wine glass full was at last served out in
twenty-four hours to each individual. Although the heat
was intense, and two of the grenadiers died, the company,
when drawn up to receive the scanty draught, invariably
refused to touch it until their captain had tasted of each
glass ; and one dying soldier would confess himself to no
one but his captain, so strong a hold had he already gained
on the affections of those he commanded.

"We have already said that an attempt was about to
be made to wrest the island of Chiloe from the dominion
of the Spaniards. In pursuance of this object, battalion
No. 8 was embarked at Coquimbo in January, 1824, and
landed on the small island of Quiriquina, in the bay of
Talcahuano, where it remained until the preparations
were completed. The troops were formed into three divisions, and Captain Tupper was named second in command
of the third, but the nomination giving great umbrage to
several majors and lieutenant-colonels who had been
passed over, this arrangement was annulled, and battalion

No. 8 was directed to take the advance. The expedition reached Chiloe on the 24th of March, and the next day battalion No. 8 gained possession of the fort of Chacao, which offered but a slight resistance. On the 31st, a detachment consisting of two battalions, Nos. 7 and 8, and the grenadier company of No. 1, disembarked at Delcague, and at noon on the 1st of April commenced its march, through a very woody and broken country, towards the town of San Carlos. Two companies of grenadiers, under Captain Tupper, formed the vanguard of this detachment. A strong Spanish force awaited them in ambush at Mocopulli, which is an immense bog surrounded by underwood, having a masked gun on an adjacent eminence. The grenadiers and No. 8 marched through the mouth of the defile perfectly unconscious of their danger, and when within a few paces of the enemy so murderous a fire was opened upon them that they were thrown into the utmost confusion. The enemy was invisible, and in a short time two hundred of the patriots had fallen, while No. 7 halted in the rear and refused to advance. Captain Tupper is represented as having behaved here with the most devoted heroism, charging twice into the thickets with the few grenadiers who would follow him to so perilous a service. In the second charge three men only accompanied him, one of whom was killed and another received a bayonet wound in the face, while Captain Tupper was himself slightly wounded in the left side by a bullet,—another perforated his cap,—and a Spanish sergeant made a blow at him with a fixed bayonet, which he struck down with his sabre, and it went through his leg. The bushes, however, favoured their escape, and, after being nearly surrounded, they rejoined the battalion, which had retreated a short distance. Colonel Beauchef,

as a 'dernier ressort,' now boldly resolved on attacking
the enemy in close column. Animated by their gallant
commander, the men formed, although they were previously in complete disorder, and No. 7 had retreated,
and carried the position at the point of the bayonet, pursuing the royalists for about half a mile. But the field
was dearly purchased, the detachment engaged, of scarcely
five hundred men, having three hundred and twenty killed
and wounded, including thirteen out of eighteen officers,
and seventy-one out of one hundred and thirty-six grenadiers composing the vanguard. The division having thus
suffered so severely, and the nature of the country being so
favourable to its defenders, Colonel Beauchef returned
next day to the ships; and the lateness of the season,
added to the intelligence of the arrival in the Pacific,
from Spain, of the Asia, 64 guns, and Achilles brig, of 20
guns, compelled the squadron to sail for Chile. The
latter vessel is the same which Colonel Tupper attempted,
in 1830, to carry by boarding. He was rewarded with a
brevet majority for his conduct in this disastrous affair,
and he wrote nearly two years afterwards, in allusion to
some remarks relative to the Chile troops, as follow :—
' The observations in F——'s letters, respecting our troops,
are not at all just; the Chile soldiers are as fine a class of
men as I have ever seen, extremely brave, and very capable of fatigue, indeed to a degree of which your English
soldiers have no idea. Moreover, they are very robust,
and so contrary to what F—— supposes, we have not a
single black in the regiment. The discipline is tolerable
now, and the clothing is superior to any I have seen in
Spain. I perhaps speak passionately, as I dote on all my
brave fellows, particularly on my old company of grena-

diers, with the fondness of a brother; the feelings of
absolute adoration with which they regard me, and of
which so many have given me such melancholy proofs,
are surely sufficient to draw my heart towards them. I
wish you could see my gallant servant as he now stands
before me,—his dark and sparkling eye intently fixed
on my countenance, his sun-burnt visage, his black
mustachoes, and his athletic figure, altogether forming as
fine a soldier as can well be seen.'

" Early in the year 1825, Major Tupper expressed an
anxious wish to obtain an appointment in one of the
British mining associations, which at that period were
established in Chile, and, as his letter on the subject
contains other information, we extract the following particulars :—

"'Santiago, 25th of May, 1825.—Military services
are here no longer required, and foreign officers are
therefore looked upon as a burden, which, sooner or
later, must be shaken off. A feeling of envy attends us,
which renders our situation extremely galling to every
man of honour; and some of my companions in arms are
indeed to be pitied, who, having lost their limbs in the
service, are totally dependent upon the generosity of this
ungrateful republic. As to myself, I cannot so much
complain, as I suffer little or no inconvenience now from
the bayonet wound I received in the last action, my leg
only swelling occasionally in cold weather.

" ' Nor is it easy to steer a safe course in a country so
disposed to anarchy: a congress has been established in
three different periods, and has always terminated its
sessions in tumult and disorder. There is no stability in
affairs, and the director, Freyre, is totally destitute of
political courage; he dare not be absolute, and the mass

of the people is much too ignorant to admit of other government than the iron hand of a despot.'

"In October, 1825, the director, Freyre, was deposed by an asistocratical faction, and the conduct of Major Tupper, (now effective of No. 8,) on the occasion, will be best explained in other extracts from his letters, dated at Santiago in 1826, and addressed to his family.

"'February 18.—The director has wished frequently to make me his aid-de-camp, and I have as often declined the situation. In a country like this, distracted by party, and still subject to all the disorders of the revolution, the stout heart and the stalwart arm are of more effect when they are backed by a few good soldiers. About a month before our departure for Chiloe, the director was deposed by the efforts of a party supported by two regiments,—he was obliged to leave the city in the morning; at two in the afternoon Colonel Sanchez was elected in his place; in the night I formed a counter revolution in my own corps, brought over No. 7, and, in spite of the other two regiments, replaced Freyre in his situation before ten o'clock the next morning.'

"The Morning Chronicle in January, 1826, concluded an account of this political commotion in the following words :—

"While the conduct of an English officer, Major Tupper, is mentioned in terms of high commendation for the firmness and steadiness with which he prevented the troops from being drawn aside from their duty, we are, on the other hand, very sorry to perceive the manner in which French influence has been exerted on this and other occasions in Chile."

The decisive battle of Ayacucho having, with the solitary expectation of the fortress of Callao, effected the

liberation of the whole continent of Spanish America, it
was resolved to renew the attempt to drive the Spaniards
from the islands of Chiloe, which form the natural keys of
the Pacific when approached from Cape Horn. Another
expedition in consequence, commanded again by the
director in person, set sail from Valparaiso, in November,
1825, and, after touching at Valdivia, reached Chiloe in
January, when barely two thousand men were disembarked. Major Tupper commanded the grenadier companies of Nos. 6 and 8, forming part of the advanced
division, and was left by its commander, Colonel Aldunate,
chiefly to his own direction. The enemy, in force
considerably above three thousand men, including four
hundred cavalry, occupied a strong entrenched position,
his right flank resting upon the sea, his left guarded by
impenetrable woods, his front palisaded and strengthened
by a deep and muddy rivulet, which offered but two
passes, one near the wood defended by three hundred
men, the other on the beach. On the 14th Colonel
Aldunate, with six flank companies, took the breach, while
Major Tupper with his two companies, carried the pass near
the wood in a few minutes, with little loss, by jumping
over the palisade, when he escaped almost miraculously, as
before his men could join him he was exposed to a tremendous discharge of musketry, which covered him with
mud, and shot away one of his epaulettes. The royalists
having been driven also from a second position, their
cavalry attempted a charge, but were completely routed
by the grenadier company of No. 8. The enemy now
retreated to his last and strongest position on the heights
of Bella Vista on the road to Castro, the principal town
of the island, and was attacked unsuccessfully three different times by five flank companies. Colonel Aldunate

s

then called Major Tupper, and pointing to the royalists, said,—"The glory is reserved for you—dislodge the enemy immediately." This was a most desperate service, as the road, or rather path, was so narrow as to admit of only three or four men abreast; but taking a flag in his left hand, Major Tupper ordered his grenadiers to follow him without firing a shot. By running quickly he reached the crest of the heights with the loss of only six men killed behind him, his escape appearing so astonishing to the survivors that they were convinced he wore a charm. Here he encountered a Spanish officer, named Lopez, commanding we believe the rear-guard, who resolutely maintained his ground; a personal combat ensued, and the Spaniard was killed by a sabre cut, which nearly clove his head in two. There was unhappily no alternative, as the gallant Lopez would neither surrender nor give way. In the mean time fourteen or fifteen of the Spaniards having fallen by the bayonet, the remainder fled, and were vigorously pursued for about a league on the road to Castro, when orders were brought to the grenadiers to halt. In this pursuit a colonel and about fifty men were made prisoners. The action lasted altogether nearly four hours, and on the whole the enemy, whose troops consisted partly of militia, showed but little conduct or courage, having indeed been routed by the eight companies, which were the only troops seriously engaged on the side of the patriots, whose entire loss did not exceed one hundred and seventy-five men in killed and wounded. A gallant North American, Lieutenant Oxley of the navy, was killed in an attack on two gun-boats, the stronger of which was taken. Major Tupper, having volunteered, assisted at its capture, although, as a Chileno officer of his regiment, from whom we derive the information,

writes, " it was not necessary that he should, as an officer
of the army, seek to fight by sea, particularly when he
was not ordered." Major Tupper mentioned, that throughout the action " Colonel Aldunate had distinguished himself much, and that General Borgoño had given great
proofs of ability." The surrender of the island was the
immediate consequence of these successes, and Major
Tupper was rewarded with a brevet lieutenant-colonelcy,
although much more was promised him when the impression, which his behaviour left, was fresh in the mind of
the director. But a foreign officer in any country must
naturally expect that his gallantry and devotion will be
viewed by many a native with a jealous eye, and indeed
too often treated with frigid indifference when his services
are no longer required.

"The chief part of the expedition having returned to
Chile, and Colonel Aldunate being appointed governor
of the islands, No. 4 was left in garrison; but in May
following that battalion revolted in favour of O'Higgins,
and the governor arrived at Valparaiso for assistance,
having been made prisoner by the insurgents, and compelled to embark. Lieutenant-Colonel Tupper volunteered
to accompany him back, and they proceeded with less
than three hundred men to Chiloe. On the 12th of July
the Resolution transport, in which was Lieutenant-Colonel
Tupper with the troops, Colonel Aldunate being in the
Achilles brig of war, was obliged to bring up to the eastward of the island of San Sebastian, the tide running out so strong that she could not stem it. They
attempted to reach the Achilles, anchored on the opposite
coast, with the flood, but the ebb making again before
they could do so, they were driven so fast on the island

s 2

of San Sebastian that they had scarcely time to drop an anchor, which brought them up with a very dangerous reef on their lee quarter. Here they remained for several hours in imminent danger of losing both the ship and their lives, when they fortunately drove past the reef in consequence of the anchor breaking. On their arrival near the small island of Lacao on the 13th, at sunset, Lieutenant-Colonel Tupper was ordered to attack the fort of Chacao with one hundred men, and he left the ship at midnight with his favourite company of grenadiers of No. 8 and a few soldiers of No. 1, landing in the cove of Remolinos, where he surprised a neighbouring battery, making prisoners the few artillerymen who garrisoned it. From them he learnt that in the battery of San Gallan, which occupied a strong position on the road from Lacao to Chacao, there were two officers and fifty men of the insurgents, and instantly directing himself towards it by a road almost impassable, as it was very boggy, and intersected by fallen trees, he reached the battery at five o'clock A.M. Advancing alone with the guide, he perceived that no sentry was guarding the land-side, ' and throwing himself on the enemy with intrepidity, he managed to take them prisoners—not one, except an officer, escaping. In the attainment of this object, no more than twenty soldiers could keep up with their commander, owing to the narrowness of the road, and also because it was necessary that those in advance should push forward, so as to arrive before daylight. On our part there was no loss whatever, and on that of the enemy only four wounded. This undertaking being completed, Lieutenant-Colonel Tupper marched towards the port of Chacao, and took the battery there, which was abandoned

by the enemy.   On receiving intelligence of these operations we made sail at eleven o'clock A.M., and at five in
the afternoon anchored in the said port.'*

"Colonel Aldunate having landed with the remainder
of the troops, the insurgents were reduced to submission
without further difficulty, as the natives in great numbers
presented themselves, and offered to act against them.
Indeed the greatest danger apprehended throughout was
from the season, the gales of wind on that coast being
very violent during the winter."

> ' In horrid climes, where Chiloe's tempests sweep,
> Tumultuous murmurs o'er the troubled deep.'

"A newspaper, published in English at Buenos Ayres,
observed in reference to the departure of this small expedition, which left Valparaiso in the Achilles and Resolution on the 25th June :†

"'Colonel Aldunate is an officer of honour, and if he has
been surprised once, he will, for this reason, know how
to take better precautions hereafter.   Besides, he is accompanied by Major Tupper, whose character is well
known, and whose valour cannot be better estimated than
in the words of our correspondent:—'Four hundred brave
soldiers, and Tupper at their head, are sufficient to annihilate all the royalists there may be in Chiloe.'"

"The above extract reached England in October, 1826,
and about the same time the bailiff,‡ or chief magistrate
of Guernsey, received the following letter from a British

* Extract translated from Colonel Aldunate's despatch. Of the despatches, in which we know that honourable mention was made of Colonel
Tupper's name, this only has accidentally reached us.

† On this day his brother, Lieutenant Tupper, mortally wounded, was in
the last agonies of death on board H. M. S. Sybille, at Malta.

‡ Daniel De Lisle Brock, Esq., succeeded the late Sir Peter De Havilland as bailiff, in 1821.

officer* of high rank and reputation, who had previously been lieutenant-governor of the island :—

"'Though I always like to converse with you, ... yet I do not know that I should have sat down to write to you exactly at this time, but that I have had a long conversation with Mr. Miller, who is brother to a celebrated general of that name in the Peruvian army, and who has himself lately arrived from Santiago.

"'He there knew your nephew, young Tupper, and his account is so creditable to that fine fellow, so honourable to our country, and must be so gratifying to his highly respectable family, that I cannot defer communicating it to you. He says that in point of appearance he is the handsomest man he has ever seen in either hemisphere ; that he is esteemed one of their best soldiers, extremely active and habile ; and stands so well with all parties, that no change in the local politics of the country could be in any way disadvantageous to him ; and he adds, that he is perfectly idolized by the troops he commands, particularly those who have served with him in action ; and to crown all, he says, with a partiality very justifiable, especially to so distinguished a brother, that when they speak of young Tupper they call him another General Miller. This, at all events, in coming from my friend, is the acmè of panegyric, for the brother is really a first-rate character. I could not resist telling you all this upon the testimony of a cool, sensible, and unprejudiced observer. Pray remember me to Savery and my other friends, and believe me, &c.'

"Lieutenant-Colonel Tupper, on his return from Chiloe to Santiago, in August, 1826, learnt that he had become lieutenant-colonel effective, in consideration of his services

* The late General Sir John Doyle, Bart., G.C.B., &c.

in the recent reduction of that island. In December he joined at Talca the army of the south, under General Borgoño, whose object was to destroy a horde of bandits composed chiefly of Indians, and of nearly a thousand strong, who ravaged the province of Concepcion in summer, retiring on the approach of winter to the eastern side of the Cordillera.* Their incursions had been of late so frequent and destructive, that it was absolutely necessary to put them down. Three divisions, to act on different points, were accordingly formed, and Lieutenant-Colonel Tupper was appointed to command a squadron of dragoons, with which he passed the Cordillera, parallel with the town of Chillan, in pursuit of the bandits, and went to the eastward as far as the river Nanken, in the province of Mendoza. Pincheira contrived, however, to elude all pursuit, and before the end of the campaign Lieutenant-Colonel Tupper was sent by General Borgoño on a mission to the capital, where he arrived in April, 1827, and on the first of May following was appointed first aid-de-camp to the supreme government, an office of trust and respectability. At this time General Pinto, a statesman of liberal principles and enlightened views, although perhaps wanting in political firmness, was elected president in the place of General Freyre. Much was expected from the administration of the new president, and it was hoped that he would be powerful enough to remove many existing abuses, but those interested in their continuance proved in the end the stronger party. General Pinto, having been employed in a diplomatic capacity in England, was a warm admirer of every thing English,

* They were commanded by Pincheira, the son of a European by an Indian mother, who held the rank of colonel in the Spanish service, and committed his depredations under the Spanish standard.

and his chief aid-de-camp ever found in him a sincere and
steadfast friend. He wrote on June 27th :—

    " ' I consider my commission in this service as secure
as an employment under any South American government can well be. My pay is that of a lieutenant-colonel
of cavalry, with one hundred and fifty dollars per month,
and my situation is at present ' Edecan Mayor,' or aid-
de-camp in chief to the president of the republic, General
Pinto, a very clever man, who has resided in England
for some time. This situation I shall probably hold for
some years if I continue in the service."

    " And on August 4, 1827 :—

    " 'The president mentioned to me some time back, that
should the present governor of Chiloe resign, as was expected, he would send me there. My pay would then be
four thousand dollars per annum, and there are other
advantages.'

    " In October, 1827, a midshipman of H. M. S. Doris
unfortunately killed a Chileno sergeant, who had attacked
him with his bayonet during some disturbance in the
theatre at Valparaiso. It appears that this young officer
was stabbed twice by the sergeant, who was intoxicated,
when in his own defence he drew out a pocket pistol and
shot him dead. Sir John' Sinclair, who commanded the
frigate, gave up the midshipman to the authorities on
shore, the inhabitants of the town declaring that they
would have vengeance either of him or of some other
British officer ; and the president of Chile ordered a court
martial, which was composed partly of foreign officers
in the service of the republic. At the solicitation of the
British consul-general, Lieutenant-Colonel Tupper undertook the defence, and it is said conducted it with so much
ability that the result was an acquittal, although it was

generally expected that the prisoner would have been
found guilty of murder, such was the irritation of the
public mind against him, and in that case the consequence
might have been fatal.

· " Lieut.-Colonel Tupper again wrote on April 5, 1828,
as follows :—

" ' Our congress met on the 25th of February; it is
very badly composed, and will not, I fear, do much good.
The provinces begin to be greatly divided, thanks to the
system of federalism.   I think the whole of South America is in a dreadful state of anarchy and confusion,—so
much ignorance and so little morality.   I believe it is
impossible that the different states can constitute themselves for many an age ; and what Moore says of another
country applies particularly to them :—' And there is certainly a close approximation to savage life, not only in
the liberty which they enjoy, but in the violence of party
spirit, and of private animosity which results from it.'

" While acting as aid-de-camp, Lieut.-Colonel Tupper
was engaged in the suppression of two or three dangerous revolts, incited by the party to which we have
just alluded, and whose private interests had suffered,
when, in 1823, many exclusive privileges were abolished.
Their first object was to supplant General Pinto in his
high office, so as to accomplish their insidious designs
under the cloak of legal authority.   We subjoin extracts
from two letters, which the subject of this memoir wrote
to a brother at this period.

" ' Santiago, August 17th, 1828.—My long silence has
been owing to a trip which I made last month to San
Fernando, (forty leagues south of Santiago,) to suppress
a mutiny among the forces quartered there.   General
Borgoño, having been ordered to take command of the

troops destined to put down the mutineers, requested the president to allow me to accompany him, which was acceded to. We left this place on the 4th of July, with two hundred infantry, and were subsequently joined by about four hundred militia cavalry. On arriving near San Fernando we found that the mutineers, battalion No. 6, about three hundred in number, had taken up a strong position to the north of the town. Not judging it prudent to attack them, we passed on to San Fernando; the general sent me before him, with two weak companies of infantry, to take possession of the place; on arriving in the Plaza Mayor I was charged by a body of dragoons, two hundred strong, who, having declared for the mutineers, had just arrived from Curico, about twelve leagues south of San Fernando. After a little skirmishing I succeeded in driving them out of the town, having lost on our part two men killed and five wounded, which casualties arose from the fire of a detachment of No. 6, which had possessed itself of a church steeple. The general soon after joined us. Immediately after this affair the dragoons reunited out of the town, and joined battalion No. 6. Both corps marched to Santiago, seizing all the horses on the road, and were so expeditious as to put it altogether out of our power to overtake them. They were met near Santiago by one hundred cuirassiers and four hundred militia infantry. After exchanging a few shots, the government party took to their heels, and ran into Santiago. About sixty of the militia were cut down by the dragoons, and the mutinous troops marched in the evening to the artillery barracks. We arrived next day close to the capital, and they, finding our force so near, the people enraged against them, and altogether opposed to the change of government which they had in view,

accepted a general pardon, and submitted to the constituted authorities. And thus ended the business, being,
I dare say, only the harbinger of the civil wars which are
about to break out over all South America. It was
reported in Santiago that I had been killed in the affair
of San Fernando; I hope the report will not, by any
channel, have reached you. Since these things came to
pass, the congress has sanctioned a constitution, which
many think is likely to allay our political effervescence,
while others imagine it will prove another apple of discord; for my part, I am of opinion that the elements of
political organization are, throughout South America,
inefficient to the establishment of good government, and,
perhaps fortunately for these states, that despotism, which
is the child of anarchy, will ere long crush in its iron
grasp as well the seeds of discord as the tree of liberty.

> ' E'en now
> While yet upon Columbia's rising brow
> The showy smile of young presumption plays,
> Her bloom is poison'd and her heart decays.
> Even now in dawn of life her sickly breath
> Burns with the taint of empires near their death,
> And like the nymphs of her own withering clime
> She's old in youth, she's blasted in her prime !'
>
> MOORE.

" 'August 18.—I have been compelled to melt the
seal of this letter to inform you that a very dangerous
conspiracy was discovered last night, of which the object
was, as usual, to drive the president from his situation.
It is ascertained that the intention of the conspirators
was to murder the president, General Borgoño, myself,
and about ten others, among them Viel, a French officer.
Part of the battalion No. 6, and the dragoons, had already
entered into the conspiracy. The principal persons ac-

cused have absconded, and we have only been able to
seize three of the subordinate agents.'

"'September 15.—I think I mentioned in my last
letter that a conspiracy had been discovered, the object of
which was to effect an entire change in the government;
it was intended to seize upon the president, and upon
several of those who surround him, putting them to death,
if the least resistance were offered. We had, however,
timely notice of the affair, and were enabled to suppress
the mutiny entirely in one battalion. An order having
been sent at the same time to arrest some officers of
dragoons; the whole regiment rose and marched to the
province of Concepcion, where, being met by a superior
force, they were obliged to lay down their arms. On the
18th of this month, the civil authorities and military will
swear to the maintenance of the constitution. There are
two houses of representation elected every two years;
foreigners can occupy every situation excepting that of
president and minister of state. On the whole I think
the constitution is not a bad one, but the popular elections
are too frequent.'

" On March 10, 1829, he again wrote to his brother as
follows :—

"' I procured Miller's memoirs yesterday, and turned
over to the taking of Chiloe in 1826; the author had
much better have said nothing about it. He states our
force at four thousand men, while the real number embarked at Valparaiso was this :—

' Artillery	59
Battalion No. 1	459
„ 4	583
„ 6	550
„ 7	371
„ 8	378
Dismounted Cavalry	142
	2542

" ' Of this reduced number not quite two thousand men were disembarked at Chiloe, as upwards of one hundred men were left sick at Valdivia, and more than four hundred remained on board the ships. The Chilotes had considerably upwards of three thousand men, of whom four hundred were cavalry. Major ——, so far from distinguishing himself, would, I think, have been tried in the English service for cowardice. He commanded the first column of grenadiers, and I the second; notwithstanding, my column led the van during the whole action, he bringing up the rear at a considerable distance, and certainly not being under fire during the four hours the affair lasted. Besides, he did what I think no brave man would do; he took off his epaulettes when the first shot was fired, and gave them to his servant in presence of both columns of grenadiers.'

" In reply to some questions from his brother, relative to a narrative by Doctor Leighton, an English surgeon, of an expedition in the Indian territory in 1822, published in Miers' travels in Chile; he wrote from Santiago in October, 1829 :—

" ' About a month previously to the expedition which Leighton narrates, Colonel Beauchef sent me with thirty men to endeavour to surprise Palacios in his dwelling, situated in the Indian territory, about forty or fifty leagues to the northward of Valdivia. The intended surprise was planned upon the information of a deserter of ours, who had resided some time with Palacios ; he offered to guide me, and averred that the dwelling of the bandit could be reached in one night. We set out accordingly, and after a most fatiguing night's march arrived by daybreak only on the borders of the territory of the Indians of Tolten. If you have a good map you will see this

river laid down. These were friendly to us, and they
assured me that I could not reach the dwelling of Palacios
in less than three days' very hard march. I at once perceived that Beauchef had been grossly deceived, and that
I had no chance of success in the object of my expedition,
I was, however, too young in my enthusiasm to be so easily
turned back. I continued, I may say, merely for the fun
of the thing, and to have a little insight into the customs
of the Indians, who are rather numerous about there. I
was regaled by some caciques, and I skirmished with
others; I even made love to the dryades of the land, with
whom, however, I was not successful. I got a terrible
box on the ear from one sylvan beauty, which almost
felled me to the earth. On the third day I was nearly
surprised by Palacios himself, at the head of two or three
hundred Indians. However, I was not surprised, and
I took up so good a position, and showed such a countenance, that, as Palacios himself afterwards confessed to
me, he and his Indians thought the attack would be too
difficult. I retreated,—he dodged me until I reached
Tolten, and then left me. The Indians of Tolten, although
friendly, did not accompany me, as they considered I was
going to certain destruction. Palacios was much dreaded
by them; he was a native of Valdivia, had been a sergeant in the Spanish army, and spoke the Indian language perfectly. He was subsequently betrayed into the
hands of the patriots and shot in Valdivia, where he had
just arrived when our first expedition to Chiloe touched
in that port. I spoke to him for more than an hour.'

"On the retirement of Colonel Beauchef in June, 1829,
Lieutenant-Colonel Tupper unfortunately for himself, as
it necessarily embroiled him in the approaching commotion, accepted the command of his old battalion, No. 8,

and on the following month he was made full colonel. A
few weeks before hostilities commenced between the rival
parties, Colonel Tupper with the same prophetic spirit
which is visible in a preceding letter, and with a presenti-
ment which was too soon to be realized, thus wrote to a
member of his family in Guernsey :—

"'I naturally cannot consider my life of long duration;
I am too immediately acted upon by every revolution in
this country not to be prepared for death, and to be perfectly resigned to it when the day shall arrive; even in
my time how many foreign officers have not perished by
climate and by the sword. I shall have lived long enough
if I leave my children a subsistence and a name un-
blemished.   My late elevation in rank is an earnest of
my rising reputation, and I have perhaps reason to hope
that when I fall, my rank and the circumstances of my
death will place an obligation on Chile towards my family,
which she may be willing to acknowledge.'

"Spain has indeed much to answer for, not only to her
late South American colonies, but to general civilization
and humanity, for three centuries of the grossest misrule
that ever disgraced any age or country. Her dominion
on that continent, having been from the first pregnant
with avarice and cruelty, is perhaps the foulest blot on
the moral history of the world. But she has not escaped
the punishment of her political offences, and the hand of
retributive justice is surely visible in her present state of
degradation.   Were it otherwise, an 'unholy' alliance of
despots dared not have decreed that the will of her king
should be superior to the voice of her people, and that
the obstinacy of one man should bring desolation over a
whole country. Too proud to acknowledge his weakness,
and too vicious to yield where submission would be a

virtue, the wretched Ferdinand has prolonged the contest with independence abroad and freedom at home,
until his character has become a by-word among nations.
Proud and once mighty Spain is indeed fallen—her coasts
unprotected, her commerce destroyed, her power a nullity,
her name almost a term of reproach, she presents a sad
spectacle of the evils arising from a long course of absolute government! And if such be the lamentable position of the mother country, can it be a matter of surprise
that the acquisition of independence found her colonies
totally unprepared to appreciate the blessings of rational
freedom? They had been so long and so studiously de-
based, that he, who expected that a native master-spirit
would at once appear among each of them to suppress
the constant struggles for power, and to allay the prolific
elements of anarchy and confusion, the natural consequences of that debasement, must have been little acquainted with the workings of the human mind. The
effects of so cruel a system of policy could only be mitigated or removed by years of probation and suffering.
In Chile the Spaniards, on their final expulsion, left an
intolerant priesthood and a selfish oligarchy,—the one
anxious to preserve its sway, the other to continue in
possession of several royal monopolies, which were of
course inconsistent with the general welfare and republican
feelings of equity. The predominance of both, now united
there for mutual support, must disappear before the increasing knowledge of the people; the impious league of
church and state, for interested purposes, cannot long
exist with genuine liberty, as to question the tenets of
the one will be to draw down the vengeance of the other,
will be to stigmatize constitutional resistance as infidelity,
and religious information as political disobedience.

In June, 1829, General Pinto was re-elected president of the republic for five years, but unfortunately he declined the office, and this unexpected refusal not only compromised his best friends, but was the main cause of all the bloodshed which followed. In the subsequent crisis General Freyre's conduct was inconsistent and vacillating; and General Prieto,under the guise of obtaining the recall and return to power of the exiled Director, O'Higgins, whose aid-de-camp he had formerly been, having marched his troops from Concepcion towards the capital, a coalition of the disaffected there was formed to support him, and through his means to seize on the reins of government. The mob, ever fond of change, was induced, by large bribes, and the hope of plunder, to act under this coalition, which, if at first weak in numbers, was very formidable in resources. General Freyre attempted to assume the command of the garrison of Santiago, but the field officers of the different corps refused to obey his orders, and resolved to acknowledge only the existing authorities. Thus foiled, he introduced himself into the barracks of No. 8, during the absence of the colonel, and ordering the battalion under arms, he endeavoured, in an insidious harangue, to gain over the soldiers to his own purposes, well knowing their defection, as composing the finest battalion in the service, would prove fatal to the constitutional cause. Colonel Tupper, being quickly informed of the attempt, mounted his horse and galloped furiously to the barracks. He rushed in, and the difficulty of his situation will be easily conceived— a foreigner opposed singly to a native of the highest present military and late civil rank, and beloved also by the soldiery,—but the result will best prove the attachment of his men towards him. Addressing them in Spanish, he

T

spoke briefly to this effect :—"Soldiers! the captain-general
has led you to victory—your colonel has also led you to
victory: whom do you obey,—your colonel or General
Freyre?" The whole battalion instantaneously responded
as one man,—" We obey our colonel—Viva el Coronel
Tupper!" and General Freyre and his suite, among whom
was Admiral Blanco, were happy to escape unhurt, the
soldiers having, we believe, levelled their muskets at them.
On their way to the barracks they were followed by a large
mob, who attempted to force the gates, but on hearing
Colonel Tupper order the guard to prime and load, the
people well knowing his resolute character, dispersed in a
moment. This attempt was the more dangerous, as battalion No. 1, was quartered in the same barracks, and would
have immediately followed the secession of No. 8. Freyre,
on his return home, was taunted by his wife with the baseness and inconsistency of his conduct on this occasion.
Her family belonged to the constitutional party, and this
beautiful young woman told her husband that the soldiers
had acted like men of honour, and in her indignation she
threw a plate on a marble table, whence it glanced off and
shattered a large and valuable mirror into pieces. She was
probably the cause of his returning to that party which he
should never have forsaken. It may be added here that
Colonel Tupper, during his short command, had been enabled, from his personal influence with the president to do
much for the welfare of his battalion, which, having been
repeatedly distinguished in battle, was proud and jealous
of its reputation; and the officers, who were principally
very young men of the first families in the country, adhered
to their colonel to the last with inviolable fidelity. He had
established a school in the regiment, and whenever the pay
of the men was in arrear, he borrowed money on his own

responsibility from his friends, and discharged the claims of his soldiers.

" Amid the distrust and confusion which prevailed during this eventful period in Santiago, General Prieto arrived by easy marches in the neighbourhood, and encamped his army on some heights within a league of the city. General Lastra, having served chiefly in the navy, was appointed, as he was a native Chileno, first, and Colonel Viel second in command of the constitutional troops, and daily skirmishes preceded the decisive action of December 14th. Subjoined in a transcript of the last unfinished letter which Colonel Tupper addressed to his brother, and which not only best explains the origin of the contest, the objects of the different leaders, and the part which he took in this trying moment, but affords a general specimen of his style of correspondence without the most distant idea of publication. It should, however, be remembered, that the letter was written in the hurry and confusion attendant on his approaching departure for Concepcion, for which port he sailed with his battalion on the 28th of January.

" ' Valparaiso, January 26, 1830.—I have not the slightest idea when I addressed you last, or indeed what chapter in my history I then concluded ; it is nevertheless certain that the eventful period, which has since intervened, has been so chequered with incident, so replete with tumult and strife, that had I the pen of Cæsar I could almost imitate his commentaries, if indeed any string of occurrences in this wretched country could merit such a book with such a name.

" ' I am afraid that poor Chile has forfeited for ever the reputation of comparative tranquillity and organized government, which hitherto had been the boast of those interested in her welfare. The scenes we have lately wit-

nessed, and the illiberal and even furious hatred evinced
throughout the country against all foreigners, have perfectly
astonished even those who were least friendly to the character of these people, and least sanguine in their prognostics of future prosperity.

" 'I really sit down in absolute despair of being able to
make you understand the cause and course of late events,
or to write such a narrative as will not confuse you, and of
which the tediousness will not disgust you; it is indeed a
hard task, and I would rather make bricks for the Egyp-
tians;—but I know that you will expect some account from
me,—let me therefore cross the Rubicon at once. I would
give you Cæsar's language in his own words if I recollected
them, but much riding has long jostled classic lore out
of me.

" 'You know that the elections closed about six months
ago: they were gained by a party called the ' Liberales,'
in contra-distinction to the ' Peleucones,' who are the aris-
tocrats of the country and shun all innovations, and to the
Estanqueros, who are the vampires of the state, a party
whose object is to raise itself to opulence by exclusive
commercial privileges, inconsistent with the general prosperity. The O'Higginists form another party, the object
of which is to bring back O'Higgins and absolute government.

" 'I have said that the ' Liberales' gained the elections;
General Pinto, their chief, was elected president for five
years by the electoral colleges, (not by congress,) the constitution stating that any individual, having more than one
half of the votes of the electoral colleges, becomes president of course,—otherwise the election is left to congress.
The vice-president is elected by congress, who, next to the
president, unite most votes from the electoral colleges, or,

as the ' Liberales' have it, from among all those who have votes at all. Now Pinto had more than half the votes of the colleges, and was therefore recognized president. The election of vice-president became the attribute of congress, and this was amost interesting point, as by this time General Pinto had positively declined the acceptance of the presidency.

" 'The constitution enacts, that the vice-president is to be elected by congress from among those having the immediate majority of votes,—' Mayoria immediata.' Those opposed to the ' Liberales' construe the meaning to be that the vice-president is to be elected from the two having most votes from the colleges, while on the other hand the ' Liberales' contend that the vice-president may be elected indiscriminately from all those who have votes. In consequence congress, composed almost exclusively of ' Liberales,' elected as vice-president the individual third on the list of candidates, that is, leaving out the two with more votes. This individual, however, resigned also, and the functions of government then devolved on the president of the upper house, who issued a convocation ordering a new election of presidents by the electoral colleges.

" 'General Prieto, an old friend of O'Higgins, had been named, previous to the elections, general of the army of the south, (situated on the Indian frontier,) and there is now no doubt that from the day of his nomination he intended to subvert the government, and to render the O'Higgins party once more paramount in Chile. Even very shortly after his nomination, reports were received in Santiago that his conduct was extremely suspicious, and that his intentions were secretly hostile.

" 'On learning General Pinto's election to the presidency, he declared himself, and issued a proclamation in which he asserted his refusal to obey the established authorities, avowing as his motive the necessity of liberating the people from the rule of an illegal congress. When the news of Prieto's revolt reached Santiago, the president of the upper house, Don Francisco Ramon Vicuña, was exercising the functions of government from causes already detailed. He had the more reason to be alarmed at his situation that both the Estanqueros and Pelucones declared for Prieto, and coalesced to destroy with one effort the government and the liberal party, by which it was supported.

" 'There is little doubt that matters would have still gone well had General Freyre acted with his accustomed integrity, but this weak man was completely led by two or three of the ' Estanqueros,' and, though the natural enemy of Prieto, he positively refused to support Vicuña,—on the contrary, leaning considerably to the other side.

" 'I was at this time quartered with my corps in Santiago, and I considered it my duty to support the government and congress, because I think that the case is extremely rare in which a military man can with honour do otherwise, and because I was satisfied that the matter in question was not one in which the interference of the military was at all called for; the greatest grievance urged by the rebels being confined to the allegation that the letter of the law had not been adhered to in the election of vice-president. I knew moreover that all parties, whatever their avowed object might be, only sought the furtherance of their private views; that they all wished to be in place, and to plunder the country at discretion; and above all, I considered that no free government or orderly state could exist an hour if the military were once allowed to throw the sword into the scale, and decide points of legislation by the force of arms, as is now too generally the case in South

America. Fortunately the chiefs, who were in garrison in the capital, were much of this opinion. We determined to give Prieto battle in support of legitimate authority, and the several corps therefore left Santiago. The enemy was encamped about a league from the city, on ground higher than ours, though not otherwise favourable to him, as many ditches and walls (with the exception of the position itself low) rendered ineffectual his immense superiority in cavalry. He showed us his front, his right resting on a farm-house called Eyzaquirre, much strengthened by walls and ditches, and his left on another called Ochagavia, scarcely less capable of defence. A large body of cavalry was stationed on the right of Eyzaguirre. We marched in parallel columns; the battalions in close columns of companies, Pudeta* forming the left of the line. Each flank was protected by two pieces of artillery,—a howitzer in the centre ; our cavalry, about one hundred and eighty strong, was advanced considerably before our left flank.

" 'The battle began by a charge which the enemy's cavalry, posted at Eyzaguirre, made upon our cavalry, which, being much weaker, fled instantly. The enemy's cavalry pursued ours so vigorously, that the greater part passed our column within fifty paces; the rear companies faced about and opened fire, which soon obliged them to retire.

" 'Our column had already halted on coming within range, and a very smart cannonade opened on both sides ; the enemy's guns were extremely well served, but did little execution notwithstanding, as, owing to the chance

---

* His regiment, No. 8, so called from a place in Chiloe, where the two flank companies of the battalion distinguished themselves in the battle of Bella Vista. The two other battalions in the action were No. 1 or Chacabuco, and No. 7, or Concepcion.

of the ricochet, every ball went directly over the column it was intended for, and one went through my flag.

" ' We had halted in front of Ochagavia, at the distance of little more than half a mile from the house. Our three light companies were ordered to move to the right and to attack the left of Ochagavia; I was ordered to lead the attack in front; we expected to have much to do, but were mistaken, as the enemy abandoned the house after skirmishing a little, and we occupied it immediately.

" ' We now held possession of the position which had originally covered the enemy's left flank, having experienced a very trifling loss; however, our light companies, supported by the grenadiers, commenced a sharp firing in the direction of Eyzaguirre, and No. 1, or Chacabuco, was ordered to support them, Pudeto and Concepcion bringing up what now might be termed the reserve. This was twice charged by the enemy's cavalry, which had formed behind Ochagavia's house, but these charges were rendered ineffectual by the steadiness of both battalions and by the nature of the ground, which was not favourable to cavalry. The enemy behaved well, and evidently suffered much from these charges, as well from musketry as from grape shot, and made off quite discomfited.

" ' In the meanwhile the light companies and grenadiers, vanquishing all opposition, beat the enemy's infantry out of Eyzaguirre's house in a very short time, and occupied the second position, making many prisoners, among whom the Choco Silva with his host. My major, Varela,* even took all the knapsacks of No. 3; and he has assured me on his word of honour, that Anguita, the major of that battalion, sent an officer to him to beg that he would cease firing, and that they would lay down their arms. This was

* Slain also at Lircai on the 17th of April, 1830.

complied with, and all the soldiers who had not dispersed were disarmed and made prisoners. The firing had of course then become very slack, and in fact the battle was considered to be over by those who occupied Eyzaguirre's house.

" 'Immediately on repulsing the cavalry, the battalions of Concepcion and Pudeto marched towards Eyzaguirre's house. On arriving near it, the firing having now almost ceased, I saw General Prieto ride up a little to the left of my column to Colonel Rondisoni, and, as I then understood, gave himself up a prisoner of war. I soon after received an order to cease further aggression, and to recall the skirmishers, which I immediately complied with.

" ' A small part of the enemy's infantry, about two hundred and fifty men, which still held together, was situated some ten paces on the other side of a wall close to us ; the soldiers were resting on their arms, and appeared, to all intents and purposes, to have yielded themselves prisoners of war. We formed our corps in line along the wall, and I asked General Lastra's permission to disarm these troops, but he would not consent, saying it was useless to humiliate the enemy further.'

" Here the letter thus abruptly terminates without even a signature, owing to the writer having sailed so soon after from Valparaiso, and been doubtless busily employed in the intermediate time in consulting with General Freyre, and in superintending the preparations for the conveyance of his battalion. This sudden termination is the more to be regretted, as the writer was evidently about to narrate ; what, however, is too well authenticated to admit of the slightest doubt ; the perfidious conduct of General Prieto, who, when he found that the battle was lost, rode up to Colonel Rondisoni, and endeavoured to obtain by stratagem what he could not by force of arms. Taking the colonel by the hand, he declared that the contest was over, and that he was anxious to avoid the further effusion of blood. With these professions he was permitted to pass on unguarded to the rear, where Colonel Viel appears to have been deceived by similar declarations, as he not only ordered that the swords of the officers, who had. surrendered, should be returned to them, but allowed Prieto to proceed to the farm-house of Ochagavia, accompanied by part of one of his battalions, which had also surrendered, but had not been disarmed! From Ochagavia, Prieto sent officers to Lastra and Viel, with assurances of his anxiety to terminate at once the strife which was desolating the country, and with entreaties that they would come to him to hold a conference for that purpose. They went, and, by this second unaccountable step, suspicions of something worse than incapacity or indifference to the constitutional cause are doubly excited. On their arrival, Prieto told them that they were his prisoners, and pretended that not he, but they, had sought the cessation of the combat. He next sent for the remaining constitutional chiefs, under the pretext that their presence was requisite to assist in the conference; but Colonel Tupper, 'this chief, whose eulogium our pen is too feeble to compose worthily,—this bold chief, whose memory will live in the hearts of all true Chilenos, even after his brilliant course is run,—this chief, we say,'* after consulting his companions, returned for answer, that unless Lastra and Viel were released in a few minutes, Prieto would be attacked, and himself and his followers be put to the sword. Prieto now became alarmed and released his dupes, but not until the feeble Lastra had been compelled to sign a treaty, which he agreed to sus-

---

* Extract translated from a printed " Aviso al Publico."

pend all offensive operations for the present, alleging afterwards that he did so to regain his liberty. In confirmation of
this account, gleaned from public documents, the truth of
which might otherwise be questioned, it may be as well
to add the following extract from a private letter, dated
Santiago, 14th of December, 1880, and written by one
Englishman to another, both perfect strangers to Colonel
Tupper's family :—

" 'This being agreed to, Lastra and Viel went over, but
they were no sooner arrived than Prieto said, 'Deliver
your swords,—you are my prisoners.' They were greatly
enraged at so felonious an action. Prieto requested Lastra
to sign a document to the effect that Tupper should surrender with his battalion; but, be this true or not, certain
it is that Prieto sent to Tupper, stating that his presence
was necessary, as Lastra and Viel could not come to any
decision without him. Tupper replied that he would not
go over, and insisted on Lastra and Viel immediately
returning to their stations. After waiting a short time, and
no appearance of these officers, he sent to Prieto to say that,
if they were not released in five minutes, he would immediately attack, and show no quarter either to him (Prieto)
or to any other who might fall into his hands. This had
the desired effect; the officers were given up, but Prieto
implored that the war should cease, and that a treaty
should be entered into.

Notwithstanding that a convention, obtained under such
circumstances, was anything but binding on General Lastra,
whose first act should have been to punish him by whom
he had been so grossly deceived, an armistice of forty-
eight hours took place, during which General Freyre was
appointed, by mutual consent, to the command of both
armies, Prieto and his troops being most imprudently,

if not most treacherously, admitted into the capital, although his infantry had, or might have been made prisoners, his artillery captured, and his cavalry completely discomfited.

This action was fought on the morning of the 14th of December; the numbers on each side were, we believe, about two thousand men; and fully two hundred men appear to have fallen, the greater part of whom belonged to Prieto's army. Colonel Tupper is represented to have behaved on this day with more than usual gallantry, although his letter is so barren as to his own conduct; but he had the bitter mortification of seeing the success, to which he had mainly contributed, rendered perfectly unavailing by this ridiculous treaty. During the battle about one hundred and fifty of Prieto's mounted followers penetrated into the city, either in search of plunder or in the hope of causing a diversion; and after sacking the French consulate, for which outrage a compensation of thirty thousand dollars was exacted by a French squadron in 1831, and committing other depredations, they proceeded to the house of Colonel Tupper with the view, it would seem, of murdering his wife, who was far advanced in pregnancy. Not finding her at home, and understanding that she had taken refuge at the bishop's residence, they galloped thither, and, breaking open the portal, declared that they were come to kill "la muger del Ingles Tupper." The bishop approached them in his robes, with a large crucifix in his hands, and the demons fled almost as soon as they saw him. On hearing their cries, a deep swoon happily came to the relief of their intended victim; but the previous anguish of this unhappy young woman, then in her twenty-third year, may be more easily conceived than described. She had heard, during the morning, every

shot fired by the contending armies, and did not yet know
the fate of her husband ! The day after the action, Colonel
Tupper waited in plain clothes on General Freyre, and resigned the command of his regiment, determined to serve
no longer under such leaders and in such a cause; but
unfortunately he was prevailed upon by his old commander
to accept the appointment of commandant of arms, or
military governor of the town and province of Coquimbo,
a very desirable part of the country, and a situation of
emolument, as well as, at that time, of great responsibility.
To a young officer, with an increasing family and limited
means, the offer was too tempting to be refused, although
he never entertained a favourable opinion of General
Freyre's abilities, giving him credit only for good intentions.
He was at Valparaiso, preparing to embark for Coquimbo,
when Freyre arrived in the former town, Prieto having, as
Colonel Tupper had all along foreseen and apprehended,
attempted to take him prisoner, and compelled him to seek
security in flight from the capital. In this manner Prieto
obtained possession of a fine park of field artillery, and incorporated the constitutional cavalry with his own. Among
other charges of duplicity, General Freyre accused Prieto,
in a letter of January 18th, which was published, of having
excited the authorities of Coquimbo not to receive Colonel
Tupper, whom he had destined for that command in the
conviction that he was best fitted for it. Colonel Tupper,
now bound in honour not to abandon Freyre in his difficulties, very reluctantly resumed the command of his battalion, and proceeded with it to Concepcion, which province
was in favour of the liberal party. The three battalions of
infantry, which had fought against Prieto on the 14th of
December, followed the fortunes of Freyre; each, previously to their departure from Valparaiso, issued a manifesto

to the citizens, and we translate that of Pudeto, or No. 8, which was by far the most poignant and uncompromising, and although written in an inflated tone of defiance, the language was well suited to the Spanish character of those to whom it was addressed.

"The battalion of Pudeto, ever faithful to its oaths, swears to maintain the constitution.—Fellow citizens, confide in its honour which has never been violated. Enemies of order tremble: you well know Pudeto.

"His Excellency, Captain-General Freyre leads us to victory. His name electrifies the hearts of the brave, and guarantees the pacific citizen in his employments.

"The infamous Prieto will be for ever intimidated; this soldier without honour, who, deriding in repeated instances the most sacred engagements, aspires to despotism by the most unjust means.

"Valparaiso, 27th January, 1830."

Prieto doubtless never forgave this fearless, but perhaps imprudent, mention of his treachery, and probably the commandant of the battalion was from that moment marked out as the object of his sanguinary vengeance.

Brief Extracts relative to the late Colonel Tupper.

" Few situations can be more distressing than those of foreign officers, who, having entered the service of the new republics, in order to combat the foreign enemy, have in the end found themselves involved in the domestic disputes of their adopted country, and at times either from principle, old attachments, or other strong causes, have been in a manner obliged to take active service with one or other of the parties.

" These observations have been elicited from us on reading a letter from Chile, which, although dated in December last, throws some light upon the situation in which the late Colonel Tupper was placed; an officer who, in the war for the independence of Chile, was one of its most distinguished heroes, and had gathered ' golden opinions from all sorts of people, and yet he fell a victim to civil dissensions."—*British Packet, Buenos Ayres, July* 17, 1830.

A letter from Valparaiso, of the 29th April says : " In a battle near the Maule, on the 17th of this month, eight hundred men fell. Freyre is defeated, and three foreign officers, (among whom is unhappily Tupper), were killed."—*English Chronicle, August* 24, 1830.

Conclusion of a letter, dated Santiago, May 14, relative to the affairs of Chile: " Freyre, with seventeen hundred, and Prieto with two thousand two hundred men, met again at Cancharayada, when the former was beaten; sixteen officers and six hundred rank and file were killed. Amongst them were Tupper, Captain Bell, of the navy, and, it is believed, Rondizoni. Freyre and Viel escaped with three hundred cavalry, and have made their way past Santiago, towards Coquimbo. Troops have been sent against them. Prieto remains at Talca. We do not know what has occurred at Concepcion.

" Tupper was an extraordinary fine young man of twenty-nine. His death is sincerely lamented by all parties."—*Times, London, September* 3, 1830.

His Excellency Don Francisco Ruiz Tagle not being willing to allow himself to be dictated to, by the leaders of the Spanish faction, offended them; and finding it impossible to govern under such circumstances, renounced the command; and Don Thomas Ovalle was, on the 21st of March, elected in his place. Don Francisco Tagle retired to the Calera; and on the 16th of April I was deprived of the rank of lieutenant-colonel, and placed on one-third of my pay as Sart. Mor.

" Commandacia General de Armos,
" Santiago, April 17, 1830.

" The minister of war has on the 16th of this month issued the following decree.

" ' His excellency has thought it convenient to suspend the commission that has been given to *El Sargt. Mor*, Don Thomas Sutcliffe, as Instructor of Militia, and place this chief on the half-pay list until farther orders.'

" Which I communicate to you for your information, and corresponding results.

" God guard you, M* A*
" JUAN DE LUNA."

I waited on his excellency the president, who was entirely ignorant of what had occurred; however, he referred me to Don Diego Portales, who had been appointed minister of war; he stated that he had deprived me of the employment I held, on account of my being a

" pipiblo," (one of the liberal party,) and for not having accompanied General Prieto.

Although I was included in the general promotion that took place during the civil commotion, I never applied for my commission afterwards, although I had the decree of the former government, on account of the new administration having cancelled all the promotions made by Don Francisco Ramon Vicuña, and General Don Ramon Freyre, and the repugnance I had to receive the one offered to me by General Prieto. Being now reduced to the paltry sum of forty dollars per month, in place of one hundred and fifty, which would have been my pay as lieutenant-colonel of cavalry; and having no expectations of active employment from government, I was obliged to economise, so I sold all my horses but one, dismissed my servants, gave up my apartments, left off smoking cigars, and by making arrangements with an hotel keeper, I found I could make ends meet, so as to reside in the capital; but the outcry which was got up against all foreigners, made it disagreeable for me to remain in Santiago, so I accepted the invitation of Don Juan Francisco Larrayn, and obtained leave from government to accompany him and his family to their estates, which was one of the most charming spots in Chile. Aculen is nearly thirteen leagues from the capital; there is a beautiful lake adjacent, which is about eight miles in circumference; also two small islands in it, which at times are almost covered with nests from the innumerable quantity of aquatic birds that resort to it; there is also a good supply of excellent perch, and pere-reys, (kingfish;) and being a lover of field sports, I enjoyed myself in shooting, hawking, and fishing during the day, and the evenings with the amiable and accomplished family of my host, enjoying "otium cum dignitate," on half-pay: one morning we were alarmed by the sudden appearance of the family and father of the governor of Rancagua, who informed us that they had fled from their homes on account of Pincheyra having made his appearance in the neighbouring valleys. On this I ordered my horse, and taking my servant, and one or two "Huassos," who had been soldiers, I set off for Rancagua, and on my way called at "La Compania." My friend, Don Juan de dios Correa, had sent off a party to the Cordillero; and after refreshing my horses, I continued my route to Rancagua, which I found in the greatest confusion; I called upon the governor, El Señor Quadra, and informed him that his family were safe in Valdivia, and that I had arrived to render any assistance he should require; he thanked me for my offer: I immediately took an account of the arms, &c., and after having put myself in possession of what had occurred, and what measures had been adopted, I wrote to the Commandante Gral. of the army, who immediately sent an officer with arms; however, Pincheyra, retired after having plundered a few that resided near to the Cordillero.

I had the satisfaction of receiving the following official note and certificate from the chief of the staff.

" Commandancia General de Armas.

" Santiago, January 9, 1831.

" The perusal of yours of the 6th, in which you announce your having marched to the city of Rancagua, to assist the governor, on account of the approach of the bandits, who have menaced that department, has been so satisfactory, that I feel obliged to express to you my full assurance, on account of your having displayed the noble sentiments that characterize you, to the benefit of the public security, thus acting like a good and honourable officer. The danger having now ceased, there is no further necessity for you to incommode yourself, unless such occurrences should be repeated ; in that case you may offer yourself again to that government, in order that you may be employed with utility, whilst you remain where you are actually residing on leave of absence, which I state to you for your satisfaction, and in answer to your note. God guard you Mᵃ Aᵃ.

" JUAN DE LUNA."

"Juan de Luna, Commandante Jeneral de Armas, e Inspector Jeneral Interino del Ejercito, &c. &c.

"Certify, that El Sargt. Mor de Caba. Don Thomas Sutcliffe has served as adjutant of this staff, from the beginning of March, 1830, when I took the command; that afterwards he was commissioned to instruct the cavalry of Tango, from which he was retired and placed on half-pay until this date. That his behaviour during all this epoch has not merited the slightest censure. He has always been punctual when called upon for duty, and observed the best conduct; and for the ends that may suit him, I give the present in the city of Santiago, April 28, 1831.*

"JUAN DE LUNA."

I experienced still farther satisfaction, when the governor of Rancagua, Don Manuel Ortuzar, got me the appointment of military commandant of the department, which for particular reasons that were stated to him, I declined accepting. On the 21st of March, 1831, his excellency the president of the republic, Don Thomas Ovalle, departed this life after a short illness, at the age of forty-three; he was generally respected, and his loss regretted: he was succeeded by El Señor Don Fernando Errazuriz, as provisional president, who governed until the 18th of Sept.; and then General Don Joaquin Prieto, who was elected president of the republic, took the command. As he had to govern five years, and on account of the cool reception which I experienced from his excellency, I requested and obtained leave to reside in the country all the time I should be on half-pay, so as to be exonerated from having to attend processions, and other duties imposed upon the officers residing in the capital; so I returned to Aculeu, and was determined to remain quiet until the period of his government should end; in fact, I had little choice, for he had as minister of state in the war department, Don Pedro Urriola, the hero of the disturbances, that occasioned so much bloodshed in 1827 and 1828; besides which, almost

* Published in my manifesto.

all the other offices in government had been filled up by pseudo-patriots, who were well known to be the sworn enemies of liberal governments, as well as others who had been the promoters of all the disorders that had afflicted Chile ever since 1822, in order that they might creep into profitable employments, to restore, as they have said, religion, in the name of liberty and justice.

CHAP. VIII.

AMONGST the promotions that followed the consolidation of the new government, was that of General Don Manuel Bulnes, who received the command of the army of the south, when his uncle, the president Don Joaquin Prieto, was called to the supreme government. General Bulnes commenced by adopting active measures against the horde of bandits, who having taken advantage of the civil broils of 1828-9 and 1830, had, with the assistance of their allies, not only been enabled to re-organize their " royal army," and act again on the offensive, but had the audacity to lay the rich haciendas of the departments of San Fernando and Rancagua under contribution, and even plunder the mines, and defenceless town of San Jose, situate on the banks of the Maipu, a few leagues distant from Santiago, the capital of Chile, and thus strike terror to its inhabitants. However, the general had the satisfaction of putting an end to this cruel and destructive warfare on the 11th of March, 1832. As I have already, in the former part of this work, mentioned many particulars respecting Pincheyra, I will now give a brief account of the final extermination of this horde of merciless bandits, by translating a few documents and an extract from the work of El Reverendo Padre Fr. Jose Javier Guzman, which was published in Chile, by the director of the ministerial press, and under the patronage of the supreme government:—

MEMORABLE ACCOUNT OF THE GENERAL DESTRUCTION OF
THE HORDE OF THE BANDIT PINCHEYRA.*

"One of the actions that have given glory to the arms
of the Patria, is the triumph that has been obtained under
the command of the valiant General Don Manuel Bulnes,
on the 14th of January, 1832, against the daring bandit,
Paul Pincheyra, and his associates. In order that this
proposition may be truly understood, I will give some
previous notice of the character of this cruel and fearful enemy of the Patria by referring to several of his
forays, and conclude by giving an account of our glorious
victory.

"Paul Pincheyra, a native of the department of San
Carlos, and a man who followed no occupation or trade,
nor was he ever willing to be a soldier, turned robber, and
in company with his brothers, and others of the same class,
committed many depredations in the haciendas of the
eastern part of the provinces of the bishopric of Concepcion. This courageous leader was cunning, impudent,
daring, enterprising, tyrannical, and ferocious; he followed
no other system than that of robbing, plundering, and
marauding. The fame his name had acquired, made many
reprobates join him daily, principally deserters, and others
who followed dishonest practices. In this manner these
monsters collected almost insensibly such a force, that in a
short time they were well enabled to assault the haciendas
and towns, and caused great uneasiness to the government
of the state. This horde left their impenetrable asiles
many times during the year, and spread terror and devastation amongst the unprotected towns; they were also aided
and assisted by the Indians, who were interested in the
plunder of the haciendas, and the numerous captives that

* Guzman, book 2, page 692—702.

they took with them from the towns and villages. I will now relate some of the daring enterprises of Pincheyra:— About the end of November, 1825, the Spaniard, Zinozain, with twenty-five followers, joined the bandits. These marauders had taken refuge amongst the Indians, in order that they might, under the pretext of serving the cause of the King of Spain, commit depredations and incommode the patriots, although they were in quiet possession of the government. After having made some arrangements with Pincheyra, they on the 1st of December marched against the province of Chillan with more than 200 soldiers, and 600 auxiliary Indians. On the general's receiving information of this daring movement of the enemy, he ordered the brave Commandant Don Manuel Jordan to meet them with a squadron of cavalry, and other detachments, who were on the 25th of December, 1825, unfortunately defeated in the hacienda of Longabi, and on account of the superior force of the enemy, all were slain, except one ensign and six soldiers of this valiant band, who escaped to carry the dreadful intelligence of the fate of their unfortunate commander and comrades, to the headquarters at Chillan. Pincheyra and his colleagues were elated, and profiting by this unequal victory, not only was supplied with arms,* but augmented his horde daily with the deserters and robbers who flocked to him in numbers, so that he soon became so strong as not to content himself with pilfering the haciendas that were contiguous to the Cordillera, but advanced so far as to visit Niquen, and the neighbourhood of Cauquenes; and what seems most incredible, his daring courage made him venture to march within the Cordillera de los Andes, to plunder the defenceless town of San Jose,† distant only ten or twelve leagues

* By the Spanish faction.   † Since the disturbances of 1829 and 1830.

from this capital, having traversed above one hundred and
fifty leagues of the almost impassable range of the Cordilleras to perpetrate this robbery.

" Pincheyra had formed with his numerous followers a
kind of citadel or intrenchment, which was constructed in
an almost impenetrable valley, from which he sallied forth
to make his assaults upon the towns, and bring female
captives to form his seraglio. All this foretold the ruin,
destruction, and even the predomination of the country, if
an opportune stop were not put to their proceedings,
before this insolent and daring band would become more
numerous.

" In this alarming and distressed state of tribulation and
dread, was the republic, when our president, Prieto, took
the reins of government, for he no sooner received them,
than he made known to General Bulnes his well-formed
plans, and the steps he had taken and already adopted to
vanquish Pincheyra, and exterminate the strong force he
was daily accumulating : he gave him secret orders how to
take Pincheyra by surprise, and route him in his intrench-
ments, which were considered inexpugnable. The brave
General Bulnes desired this moment as eagerly as the
president, and did not demur an instant in putting the well-
concerted plans that his excellency had communicated to
him, into execution."

I here take the liberty of interrupting El Reverendo
Padre Guzman, who has entirely thrown into oblivion, at
least in this work, the memorable occurrences which took
place since the affair of Longabi, 1825, until 1829, when
their excellencies, General Don Ramon Freyre, General
Don Manuel Blanco, Encalada, El Señor Don Augustin
Eyzaguirre, and lastly, General Pinto, whilst presidents of
the republic, did their utmost, and I will prove by the official

documents I now cite, that General Don Jose Manuel
Borgoño nearly put an end to this horrible warfare in 1827;
therefore the motto of "Palmam qui meruit ferat," ought
not to be effaced from the shield it had honoured.

Out of the respect I owe to a general, whose aid-de-camp
I had the honour of being, from 1826 to 1830, and the
meritorious chiefs and officers that accompanied him in the
arduous campaigns of 1827 and 1828, against the horde of
bandits, and who so nobly sustained the reputation they had
gained by their honour and bravery; I will attempt to
assist my worthy friend, El Padre Guzman, for I am sure
that he must have forgotten the decided interest his meritorious and patriotic relative, Don Augustin Eyzaguirre,
took, to effect the extermination of those marauders; and
that one of his first acts as president of the republic was,
to call upon the "magnanimidad y civismo" of his fellow-
citizens, by a proclamation he issued on the 25th of September, 1826, of which I will translate an extract.

"CHILENOS,

"I am aware of the losses you have sustained during the
sixteen years' struggle, but I am speaking with Chilians
that have undertaken the most imminent sacrifices, not only
for their liberty, but also for their honour and glory.

"Remember that your virtuous magnanimity made you
the rulers of the Pacific, with a squadron, that, subjugating
the Spanish forces, fixed the basis of the liberty of the
south; recollect your immense aid and voluntary exertions
to send the liberating army to Peruchilenos; remember
the battle of Maipu, and measure my confidence by your
civism.

"To-day I do not treat of the glory, but of the preservation of the fortunes of Chile, and the lives of its
citizens. I speak to you who know how impetuous, obsti-

nate, and terrible is the war of the barbarians, who without doubt will attack us the moment the season will permit them; and if we do not anticipate, and prepare resources and troops to chastise them, we shall either fall victims; or a desolating war will be prolonged. I am in want of assistance, and, out of respect to your property, I can only depend on your spontaneous oblation, to which you are invited: succour me now, and by the end of the year I hope that, with the new organization of the treasury, I shall be enabled to redeem the branches that are now in pawn, and then our natural resources will be sufficient to cover the wants of the state. . . . .

"EYZAGUIRRE."

His next step was to appoint General Don Jose Manuel Borgoño to the command of the army of the south, and place the provinces of Colchagua, Maule, and Concepcion under martial law, during his military operation. The official reports of that general, at the close of the campaign of 1827, will show how far his patriotic exertions were crowned with success. I also refer to the following official statement:—

                                        "May 5th, 1827.

   "Ministry of War,

   "The evils and disasters that a prolonged and destructive war has occasioned in the meritorious provinces of Concepcion, having ceased, with almost the total extermination of the horde of bandits that have to this period afflicted it whilst favoured by the Indians of the frontier, who were through the medium of fallacy and intrigue brought by their instigators to pervert the tranquillity of the districts in which they have exercised their acts of cruelty; and the staff of the army being at present of no object, not only on account of this reason, but as well as the corps that belonged to it being stationed in different cantonments for the winter. 1 have decreed:—

"1st. The staff of the army of operations is dissolved.

"2nd. The chiefs and officers that formed it will pass and continue their services in the post they occupied when appointed to this commission.

"3rd. The general-in-chief will continue with the command of the expressed army, and retain the same faculties that were conferred when put in charge of this important commission, which he has executed with so much decision.

4th. The minister of war is charged with the execution of this decree, of which account will be taken—circulate it to all concerned, and order it to be printed.*

"FREYRE.

"OBEJERO."

CONTINUATION OF EL REVORENDO PADRE GUZMAN'S NARRATIVE.—"Gen. Bulnes gave the command of a corps of cavalry of about two hundred men of the horse grenadiers to Colonel Don Bernardo Letelier; and two hundred and sixty-four from the battalion Carampangue to Lieut.-Colonel Don Estanislao Angiuita; also two hundred from the battalion Valdivia, which were given to Captain Don Juan Barbosa; and to the second in command of the division, Colonel Don Jose Antonio Vidaurre, he gave two hundred and forty of the battalion Maipu, and thirty of the militia to Don Ramon Pardo, and eighty Pehuenche Indians to Brevet Captain Don Domingo Salvo.

"This division marched on the 10th of January, 1832, and halted at the foot of the mountain during the 11th,

* Official documents printed by order of government.

and there captured one of the chiefs of Pincheyra, Berra, with two soldiers; they continued their march, and the expeditions halted in the Vinilla, from whence Ensign Lavendero advanced with thirty grenadiers, conducted by Commandante Rojas, Captains Gatica and Suniga, Ensign Vallejos, and six more that had abandoned Pincheyra.

" This party was so fortunate as to take Pablo Pincheyra in the place called Roble Guacho, whilst in the house of Vallejos, with two of his servants, and one that had belonged to the regiment of cazadores, a Caballo; these, and three more that had fled to the thickets of Magin, fell that day into the hands of Rojos, and were immediately shot.

" The division destined to attack the principal force of Pincheyra had to struggle with almost insuperable difficulties, that the elevated and rugged range of Cordilleras presented; but the ardour and resolution of the soldiers triumphed over all the embarrassments that were opposed to them, and in less than three days, after incredible fatigues and exertions, they traversed the distance of eighty leagues.

" On the 14th, after a march of fourteen leagues, they arrived near to the encampment of Jose Antonio Pincheyra, and took seven out of nine that guarded the pass of El Estretcho de las Lagunas, the other two escaped.

" When the division arrived within two leagues of the enemy, they formed in three columns, and continued their march in this manner until they arrived at Las Lagunas de Epulanquen, where the bandits were stationed.

" The general's orders were executed with so much precision and celerity, that, notwithstanding the enemy had intelligence of the expedition, the effect of the

simultaneous movement of the columns was, that of the
most complete surprise; and after taking advantage of
the panic, and to impede the possibility of their flight to
the territory of the Indians, various detachments were
sent to take possession of the passes. The result of this
movement was, that, after a short resistance, in which
many of the bandits and their allies the Indians fell,
the rest surrendered, with the exception of Pincheyra
and fifty-two more, who, favoured by darkness and good
horses, escaped by scaling a mountain hitherto thought
impassable.

" The greatest mass of Indians fled at the commencement of the onset, and were stopped by a party of cavalry
that had gained the pass; they then turned upon their
pursuers, who completely routed them, and left the ground,
for the space of three leagues, strewed with dead bodies.
The famous caciques, Niculman, Coleto, and Triqueman,
fell in this action; these were the principal allies of Pincheyra, and furious instigators of the ravages committed
by the race of Pehuenches. ›

" Few of this confederated band escaped being killed
or taken prisoners, and their families fell into the hands
of the conqueror.

" The general, by the intrepidity and good conduct of
the troops, not only managed to defeat the enemy, but
happily exterminated that formidable horde, and by
adopting such precise manœuvres, he obtained a complete victory with little loss on his part.

" The general, in the official despatch sent to government from the field of battle, spoke in the highest terms
of the brilliant conduct of his chiefs and officers, and
recommended the meritorious co-operation of Rojos,
Zuniga, Gatica, Zapata, Yañes, and Vallejos, who, de-

fending the cause of the king,* joined Pincheyra; but being horror, struck with the ferocity of that horde of bandits, had ceded to the insinuations of General Prieto, before he gave up the command of the army of the south.

"General Bulnes did not consider he had fulfilled the object of his expedition, on account of the escape of Pincheyra; and in order to consummate the victory, sent fifty horse-soldiers, who were accompanied by Rojos, and thirty of the late followers of Pincheyra; but after eleven days of fruitless pursuit, in which they were, on account of scarcity, obliged to live on horse-flesh, returned to the encampment without having effected their object."

I here conclude Padre Guzman's narrative, and will give a translation of General Bulnes' official account to government respecting the final surrender of Pincheyra.

"OFFICIAL DOCUMENT.

"Head-quarters, Chillan, March 12th, 1832.

"Señor Minister,

"The triumph that was obtained by the forces under my command on the 14th of January last against the "Caudillo," denominated Colonel Don Antonio Pincheyra, ought to be consummated by the capture of his person, on account of the importance of his name; for the miserable remnant that escaped, scarcely merited our attention to follow them. To this end I detached parties of about

* These individuals had never served in the Spanish army, but had, to my knowledge, been the inseparable companions of Pincheyra, (and as bloodthirsty and rapacious as any of their gang) ever since I had commenced to serve against these marauders, in 1826, as aid-de-camp to the commander-in-chief.

one hundred men under the command of Don Antonio
Zuniga and Adjutant Aguilera, composed of cavalry and
friendly Indians, who by forced marches managed to find
them between the rivers Latue and Salado, situated at
the distance of one day's march; they halted with the
design to fall upon them by surprise at daybreak the following day; but Pincheyra having discovered the track
of two of the spies that were sent to reconnoitre, fled with
fourteen men just in time to evade the attack, in which
the individuals whose names are included surrendered.

" The party took every advantage of their success, and
considered they had penned Pincheyra up in the Cordillera; but he was then on the banks of the Malalue,
and requested an interview with ensign Don Pedro
Lavanderos—which was granted; he there declared that
his formal resistance to deliver himself up to Zuniga, was
on account of the pardon that had been offered to him by
the supreme government, which he hoped to obtain, and
in that case he would only surrender himself to me—
permitting him to present himself accompanied by
Lavandero: which being agreed to, he came with the fourteen men that formed the remainder of his routed forces,
to which may be added the Indians who invaded Talca
Regue, to steal cattle, amongst whom was found Pedro
Fuentes, well known for his crimes, and he was immediately shot.

" I can well assure V. S. that only four men, conducted
by one Vicente Pereira, who had separated from the
fugitive Pincheyra previous to the attack of Latue, and
who took the direction of the Pampas, now form the re-
liques of this gigantesque banditti, whose terrible fame
has disappeared jointly with its existence, leaving the
republic to lament no more their destructive warfare.

I have the satisfaction to announce this to V. S., to the end that you may inform S. E., and recommend to his consideration the conduct and laudable privations with which Zuniga and the others I have mentioned have contributed to the success of this enterprise.

"Dios Gue a V. S.

" MANUEL BULNES."

Pincheyra maintained above 2,000 souls in his encampment of Latue ; the spoils that fell into the hands of the general were considerable, for the enemy was well provided with warlike stores, and had immense droves of horned cattle.

About 200 were killed, and more than 700 made prisoners ; upwards of 1,000 women were released, and restored to their relatives and homes.

Zuniga and his honourable companions were rewarded with commissions in the army; a corps was formed of the followers of El Señor Colonel Don Antonio Pincheyra, denominated Carbineers of the Frontier ; and his Excellency, the President of the Republic, gave this fallen and faithful ally of the Spanish faction, an asylum on his own estate. Thus ended the war that had nearly annihilated the ill-fated provinces of the south, and kept Chile in constant agitation ; and which had been fomented and encouraged by many who now had acquired a share in the administration, and aggrandized themselves at the cost of so much bloodshed.

The following document will show that the wily " godos" had completely outwitted their credulous allies, the " O'Higginistas,"—who had materially aided and assisted them against the liberal party.

Some months had elapsed since General Prieto had

been invested with the supreme command, and nothing
had been done with respect to the restoration of General
O'Higgins to his rank, and native country. Many of
the too credulous " O'Higginistas," finding they had been
duped, began, when it was too late, to repent having lent
their energies to the common enemy ; and one of their
leaders who had a seat in the legislature, tired of waiting
to see his coadjutors put their promises into practice, presented the following propositions to congress :—

" The deputy who subscribes, has the honour of
submitting a few reflections to the consideration of the
representatives here assembled, and by which they are
called upon to support an eminent act of national
justice, long since reclaimed as an indemnification due
to a public man for his great services and elevated
virtues.

. " I speak, Señores, of the restitution of that distinguished citizen, Don Bernardo O'Higgins, to his rank of
captain-general.

" It is unnecessary for the justification of this chamber,
to refresh your memory by detailing the important services
our illustrious countryman has rendered the republic,
and for which it is deeply indebted to him, for his name
is united with the most memorable events of our political
revolution, and identified with the most glorious recollections of our emancipation."

Yet this victim of the vicissitudes that are inseparable
from a prolonged revolution, and the animosities that are
fomented by domestic dissensions, has been residing for
nine years in a foreign country, and suffering the reverses
of fortune with heroic resignation.

" The whole republic knows the necessity of redeeming

the national honour, and of fulfilling this duty in a manner so as to merit the public gratitude, for which the deputy that subscribes submits the following articles for the examination and deliberation of this chamber :—

" 1st. Demand the executive power to show the motives that caused Captain-General Don Bernardo O'Higgins to be cashiered.

" 2nd. That a report be immediately given relative to the conduct and adhesion that citizen has shown towards this country, ever since his name had been erased from the military list.

" 3rd. When obtained, a commission must be named from out of this chamber, to report on the following project of a law.

" Articulo unico :—To satisfy the national honour, according to the public wish, and as an indemnification due to great services, we restore citizen Don Bernardo O'Higgins to his rank as captain-general, from which he was illegally deprived. Communicate this to the executive power.

" Santiago, July 13, 1832."

Don Gaspar Marin supported his views in an able and eloquent speech, which, with the motion, was received and responded to by a general acclamation, for the " godos," who were present, found it impolitic to offer the slightest opposition ; but they observed, that as the president, General Prieto, " was known to be an old friend of General O'Higgins, and to whom he was indebted for his elevation in the army," he could, without the necessity of the projected law, make use of his own prerogative, and render to General O'Higgins the justice that was demanded.

x

These arguments induced Don Gaspar Marin to leave the affair in the hands of his friend, General Prieto. The "godos" had no sooner gained this point than they caused a report to be circulated, in which it was stated that the president, on seeing it was the desire of the nation that General O'Higgins should be reinstated in the rank he had been so unjustly deprived of, had not only performed that act of justice, but had written to him, and inclosed a passport, with an invitation for him to return to his native country. This farce was carried on still further, for the minister of state sent for a stanch friend of General O'Higgins, who was about to leave for Peru, and entrusted him with a packet, sealed with the seal of office, and directed—" To his Excellency Señor Captain-General of the Chilian army, Don Bernardo O'Higgins, (this contained a blank enclosure). By this dexterous manœuvre the "godos" gained time, which was all they desired, for they knew well that before the trick could be discovered, they could invent another that might retard the voyage of a man they dreaded, and whose presence in Chile was so much desired by the true patriots.

I shall now take a retrospective view of the leading events that occurred in Peru since my escape from Callao, in which may be seen a brief narrative of the noble deeds of Bolivar, O'Higgins, Sucre, and Guize,—how the final consolidation of the independence of Peru had been thwarted by the Spanish faction,—and how the treatment of those two champions of liberty, Bolivar and Sucre, in Peru, equalled that of O'Higgins and Freyre, in Chile.

After the affair of Callao, General Bolivar concentrated his forces at Pativilca, and sent to Colombia for all the troops that could be spared; for his situation became daily more critical, as the Spaniards, whose partisans had put the fortresses and Lima into their hands, were gaining ground rapidly. Nothing gave the Limanians greater disgust than that of seeing the ex-president, Torre Tagle, his minister of state, Berindoaga, the governor of the department, Echaveria, and others, (who had remained concealed in Lima until the Spanish forces under Generals Monet and Rodil entered), receive the enemy with embraces, and other demonstrations of joy. It was now that those " traitors to the patriotic cause" were seen in their true colours, and to whom may easily be traced all the disturbances and party feuds that had given such severe checks to the progress of liberty. Torre Tagle and his associates were daily seen dining and carousing with the Spanish chiefs; and the former issued a kind of proclamation to the Peruvians, in which General Bolivar was depicted as a tyrant; and he counselled the Peruvians to remain faithful to the Spaniards, who were their legitimate rulers; however, this public display of his duplicity brought upon him the execration of his countrymen; and he was obliged to take refuge with some of his colleagues in the castle of Callao, where they subsequently suffered the most horrid fate.

It may now be seen how their intrigues had protracted the advance of the patriot cause; and which of the two, Rivaguera or Torre Tagle, were the traitors: and whether the former did not render an important service to Peru, although the loser, by not only appreciating the services of the Colombian auxiliaries, but by inviting General Bolivar to come also with 5,000 or 6,000 more troops, if possible, and take the command of the whole of the Peruvian forces; and had not that magnanimous and indefatigable patriot responded to the summons, what would have been the fate of Peru, under the auspices of

x 2

Torre Tagle, Echaveria, Berindoaga, and their worthy partisans?

No sooner had news arrived at Pisco of the affair of Callao, than Admiral Guize, who commanded the Peruvian navy, sailed for Callao, and his gallant conduct there is fully explained in the following letter:—

"Protector, off San Lorenzo, 27th of February, 1824.

"DEAR SIR,

"The government of Lima despatched expresses to the admiral at Pisco, and according to arrangements he anchored near to this island, and immediately sent a flag of truce to the Mulato general, and received an answer, that the forts were in the hands of the Spaniards, and that he could not listen to the proposals of surrender and forgiveness, which the admiral promised.

"The admiral weighed immediately, to attack the forts and shipping in this single frigate; and, notwithstanding the unequal forces, for three purposes: 1st. To try the disposition and capacity of his men, who were mostly landsmen and recruits, and unaccustomed to the imposing appearance of those formidable batteries. 2nd. To give an opportunity to the revolted, to rise against the Spaniards; and the 3rd. To contradict in an indisputable manner, the malicious reports spread by the Spaniards, and other enemies of South American Independence, that the crews of the frigate and the squadron, had listened to the various proposals made to surrender on the most advantageous terms to the enemy.

"We went into action at three o'clock P. M., (the flag of truce having arrived at half-past one,) and kept them in play till twenty minutes past four: having fulfilled the object for which the attack was made, we hauled off and anchored in our former berth, with the loss of only one man killed, and several shots in our hull, but not to injure us; the admiral now resolved on the destruction of the Venganza, which we heard was fitting out for sea; and in effecting this, Captain Addison of this ship, (Spry having resigned,) in four boats and fifty men, all volunteers, effected as brilliant a piece of service as has ever been performed with such inadequate means, since the commencement of the war; perhaps, it stands unrivalled, for under the fire of the batteries he boarded, cut adrift, and burnt the Venganza and Santa Cruz, and returned without the loss of one man.

"The result of this gallant enterprise was four ships, a brig, and schooner, burnt, and fourteen vessels of various classes cut out, whose names are as follow:—Ships of war, Venganza, frigate, 50 guns; corvette, Santa Rosa, 20 guns; merchantmen ships burnt, Ocean, O'Higgins, President; Ships cut out, Canton, Huron, Americana, China, Tomas, Providence; brigs, Ontario, Herald, Mercedes, Ariel, Chile, and a Genoese brig, name unknown; schooners, Betsy, Caroline, and one burnt, name unknown: as I write to you in the greatest haste, you will excuse further particulars at present, as the Shakspeare (whose captain was buried in this island) will sail to-day for Valparaiso. The forts are saluting, whilst I write to you, no doubt for the arrival of the Spaniards; and we are preparing for another attack to-night, the result of which I hope to transmit to you. Wishing you health, happiness, &c. I beg to remain yours sincerely.   " HENRY FREEMAN."*

" Admiral Guize was killed at Guayquil, and the frigate Protector burnt there by accident."

The last act of the Peruvian congress was a patriotic and laudable one, for General Bolivar was invested with the dictatorship of Peru.

The Colombian army was concentrated at Huaras, and afterwards marched to Pasco, where General Bolivar having fixed his head-quarters, organized and augmented his army.

General O'Higgins, wishing to participate in the glories about to be acquired in Peru, addressed General Bolivar on the subject; from whom he received the following answer.

" Huaras, June 14th, 1824.

" MY DEAR GENERAL,

" The receipt of your esteemed letter has given me much pleasure, and I answer it by my secretary, Heres, who repeated the idea that I had of your desire of being in the field of battle on the day that we decide the fate of Peru.

" I have already indicated to you my desire to see you in the liberating army:—a brave general like you—feared by the enemy, and well known to our chiefs and officers, cannot do less than give a greater estimation to our army.

" For my part I offer you a command, which, if it does not correspond to your merit and rank, will at least be sufficient to honour any chief who wishes to distinguish himself in the field of glory, for a division of Colombians under your orders will be confident of victory.

" So, my dear general and friend, I urge you to accept my invitation, if your physical and moral state can permit such a sacrifice; if your health is good, it will not be a great one, unless your evil star punishes you for having been generous and constant.

" My dear general, accept the sentiments and distinguished consideration of your friend, &c.   " BOLIVAR."†

* Captain Freeman was killed in attempting to board the brig of war Arequipeña.   †_This letter was published in Chile, Nov. 7. 1832.

General O'Higgins responded, by joining the army; in which he was incorporated, and acknowledged as "Gran Mariscal" of Peru.

General Bolivar reviewed his army at Pasco on the 2nd of August, 1824, which was about 9,000 strong; and on the 6th he defeated the Spaniards at Junin, without a shot having been fired on either side, for the battle was decided by the cavalry, whose arms were the lance and sabre, and only lasted three-quarters of an hour. The loss of the patriots did not exceed fifty killed, and one hundred wounded; the Spaniards lost about three hundred and sixty killed, about one hundred prisoners, and a number of wounded, who, as well as those of the patriots, died on account of the intense cold they experienced.

Whilst General O'Higgins was at the head-quarters at Huamanga, General Bolivar gave him a Colombian paper, and after referring to the calumnies that had been circulated all over America, in the Chilian papers, said as follows :—" I am intimate with the author of this article which speaks so honourably of you, so that, had I not been personally acquainted with you previous to my having perused it, I should have become a great admirer of you, for I know no one in whose penetration, judgment, and impartiality I could place more confidence, than El Señor Rivas, who is a man of such strict honour and integrity, that nothing could induce him to insert any article, favourable or unfavourable, that was not in strict accordance to the dictates of his conscience."

El Señor Rivas had resided in the capital of Chile during the years 1818, 1819, and 1820, therefore he had a favourable occasion of forming an exact opinion of the character of General O'Higgins, and he had no sooner perused the calumnies that had been remitted to him in

Chile, than he published an article in a paper he had the honour of forwarding to General Bolivar, and from which the following is an extract.

" The virtuous General O'Higgins does not merit that his countrymen call him arbitrary, whilst he is suffering in adversity, after the important services he has rendered to them.

" He who conquered in Chacabuco and Maipu, and gave a constitution to the Chilian people at a time he had been proclaimed dictator by the voice of the people, is a creditor to their respect, gratitude, and even admiration—

" He who organized the treasury, created the national army, established the press, and even protected the writers who impugned government—

" He who founded schools on the Lancasterian system, conceived the idea of liberating Peru, and has given credit to Chile, by the wisdom and circumspection with which he carried on his administration—merits at least the esteem, and consideration of the Chilians."*

· General Bolivar, after having given the command of the army to General Sucre, returned to Lima ; and the Spanish generals, wishing to profit by the absence of a chief, whose name alone spread terror and dismay amongst their followers, concentrated their forces, which amounted to about 13,000 men, and 24 pieces of artillery. In November, the viceroy, General La Serna, calculating on an easy conquest, marched against General Sucre, but was totally defeated by the patriots at Ayacucho on the 9th of December, the Spaniards leaving 15 generals, 16 colonels, 68 lieutenant-colonels, 484 officers, and 3,200 soldiers, prisoners of war ; while the rest were killed, wounded,

* El Venezolano.

or dispersed. This victory, and the death of General
Olañeta, who was subsequently killed in Tumusla, (Upper
Peru,) with the surrender of Callao, crowned the efforts
of the patriots; but General Bolivar, after having suffered many disappointments and vexations through the
intrigues of the common enemy and their partisans, who
not only had spread the flame of discord amongst the
patriots of Chile and Peru, but had also managed to
create civil disturbances in Colombia; therefore, after
having been elected president for life of Peru, General
Sucre also of the state of Upper Peru, (called Bolivia, in
honour of the liberator,) and his constitution adopted by
both states; than he embarked for Colombia on the 3rd
of September, 1826. General Santa Cruz was left as
president of the council of government, and General
Lara remained with the Colombian troops in Peru. No
sooner had General Bolivar left Peru, than the enemies
of order corrupted a Colombian colonel, Bustamente,
who arrested Gen. Lara, and other chiefs, and sent them
to Guayaquil. General Santa Cruz, notwithstanding
his ministers had resigned their offices, remained at the
head of affairs; and the rest of the Colombians were got
rid of in March, 1827, and the constitution of Bolivia
abolished, by a congress, which, in June, 1827, elected
General La Mar, a native of Guayaquil, and who had
been governor of Callao during the Spanish government,
to be president of Peru.*

* One of the first acts of the government of La Mar was that of
augmenting his army to 12,000 men, waging war with Colombia, and
then sending troops to revolutionize Bolivia; thus to overturn every plan
that had been put into practice to free Peru, and South America, from
the influence of Spain; and they were about to make concessions by
opening the ports of Peru to the vessels of that nation, and for which they
were justly criticized by that patriot Vidaurre, who in one of his writings
says : — " I wish for security, justice, and good laws, but you only want to
open our ports to the fleets of our enemy."

The inhabitants of Bolivia were also induced to act as their neighbours had done, (i. e. get rid of the foreigners,) and the malcontents were assisted by troops that were commanded by General Gamarra,* who attacked their liberators, the Colombians; and General Sucre, after having been badly wounded, and finding it impossible to maintain his authority, came to terms, and evacuated Bolivia in a manner that corresponded to his honour and patriotism; thus Peru in 1826, and Bolivia in 1828, only changed masters, under whose auspices they had to experience the fruits of that anarchy and disorder which subsequently occurred.†

* Now (1841) president of Peru.

† The details of the battles of Junin, Ayacucho, and the occurrences up to the final expulsion of General Sucre, may be found in the " Memoirs of General Miller," book 2.

PREVIOUS to the destruction of the forces of Pincheyra, and shortly after his visit to the province of Santiago, I had requested active employment on the frontier, which was not acceded to—but in May, 1832, I was appointed to the civil and military command of the departments of Donigue and El Parral, which were in an unsettled state. This was both a good and honourable charge; but as I was intimate with many of the malcontents, who were of the liberal party, I felt awkwardly situated; I therefore requested his excellency, the president of the republic, to exonerate me from the civil appointment, for, being a foreigner, I was not the most proper person to fulfil the magisterial duties during such a crisis, nor did I wish to interfere in the political disturbances, except when obliged in the performance of my military duties. His excellency would hear no excuses, I therefore thought it proper to inform him that I was personally acquainted with several of the liberals, and intimate with El Señor Gutierres, who was a bitter enemy of the government. The president seemed displeased at my naming the latter individual; and after calling him everything but a gentleman, he stated that I had no desire to be employed, and upbraided me for being a "Pipiollo."*

* One of the liberal party, or patriots.

However, I had no sooner left the audience-chamber, than I made out a memorial, in which I requested to be employed in the army on the frontier, and added the certificate and official note I had received from the commandante-general of the army, and sent it in to the war-office; but as I received no answer during a fortnight, returned to Aculeu, satisfied that government could dispense with my services. In July I received the following decree, signed by his excellency, the president of the republic, and his minister of war, Don Pedro Urriola :—

" War Department.

" June 7th, 1832.

" As there is not at present any appointment where the supplicant can be employed in an active manner, he will be attended to when an occasion offers.

" Rubric of S. E.

" Urriola."

General Don Jose Ygnacio Zenteno, who had charge of the war-office, forwarded me the memorial with the following letter :—

" Santiago, June 28th, 1832.

" Señor Don Thomas Sutcliffe.

" Muy Señor Mio,

" I enclose to you the decree of the supreme government, whose delay has impeded me from answering your esteemed of the 31st of last month. The want of a proper appointment for you is at present an obstacle to give you active employment; but the decree of the supreme government, united to your good and meritorious services, recommends you so highly, that your desires will soon be satisfied; and to forward them, I will esteem it an honour to use the utmost influence of

" Your Aff'mo. S. S. Q. B. S. M.

" Jose Y. Zenteno."

As I now had leisure, I was resolved to profit by the occasion, and visit my friends who were residing near the sea-coast. Descending, therefore, the Maipu as far as the hacienda of Huachun, I visited Doña Mercedes Guzman de Toro, who was residing at Las Juntas with her family. The two haciendas are divided, and managed by her sons, Don Bernardo, Domingo, Alonzo, and Nicasio. These young gentlemen, although they have been educated in Europe, reside on their estates, and dedicate themselves to a country life; they have their cattle in good order, having increased their artificial pastures by irrigation, and raise extensive crops of wheat and hemp; they are industrious, and it is rare to see young gentlemen content themselves in attending to the drudgeries of a farmer's life; their domains are extensive, and they take a lead in the modern improvements which have of late been introduced into Chile. This family was favourable to the late government, and the husbands of Doña Louisa and Doña Juana Toro were great sufferers, the first being an exile in Europe, and the latter, whose brother was the last president of the liberal government, had met with severe pecuniary losses.* I visited the neighbouring estates of Las Esmeraldas and San Diego, belonging to S.S. Lecaros and Barros, and the port of San Antonio, which is now open for the export trade; there are but a few decent houses, although it is a favourite bathing-place. Some of the neighbouring gentlemen have begun to erect substantial granaries; and they have laid out ground for a new town, which, in a few years, may be a very flourishing place. The anchorage is pretty good, the bay is well sheltered from the northward, but entirely open to the west and southwest, so that there is almost always a deal of surf, which makes it difficult to load or unload the boats. Quan-

---

* Since I visited Huachun, the family have obtained leave for the colonel to return to Chile, on condition that he remains quiet; and he now resides with his lady on the estate.

tities of fine fish are sent from this to the capital and
neighbouring towns. The river Maipu enters the sea
about one and half leagues from the port, but is not
navigable. The estates of Santo Domingo, belonging to
Don Fernando Luco and Don Francisco Zerda, are on
the south bank of the Maipu, and extend along the coast.
There are several lagoons, from which a quantity of salt
is collected annually. Both of these gentlemen cultivate
large quantities of wheat. Don Fernando Luco has built
a fine and commodious house, and generally resides there
with his lady, in a manner, as we at home say, "quite
comfortable." On my return I visited Melipilla, the
capital of the department, which is a neat and middle-
sized town, its population is about thirty thousand three
hundred souls. This is one of the most fertile districts
in the province of Santiago. I also visited Doña Zabiera
Carrera, at San Miguel; she was accompanied by her
daughter, Doña Domitilla, and sons, Don Santos and
Don Pedro Valdes; the latter is a lieutenant in the U.S.
navy, on furlough. This lady may be classed amongst the
heroines of South America; having played a conspicuous
part; she has consequently suffered much from the perse-
cutions of her enemies, and the untimely end of her
unfortunate brothers, Don Jose Miguel, Don Juan Jose,
and Don Luis Carrera. Her faithful friend El Doctor
Tollo resided with her; and as he condoled with her in
her troubles, and accompanied her on her emigrations;
he may some day publish her history.

The following is an extract from the the Dumfries
Magazine of 1825.

" The three Carreras, who acted so conspicuous a
part in the first revolution of Chile, have ceased to be
spoken of since their escape to Buenos Ayres, along with

O'Higgins and others, from the vengeance of the successful Ossorio. General Carrera, on returning early in 1817, from his visit to the United States, with a few American officers, and a small supply of arms, was astonished to find his two brothers at Buenos Ayres upon their parole of honour, and also to learn that they had not been permitted to join the army of Independence in Chile. He himself shortly afterwards became an object of suspicion, and was seized, and sent prisoner on board a brig belonging to the government. Alarmed at this proceeding, his brother, Don Louis, fled from the city upon the 19th of July, and was followed by Don Juan Jose upon the 8th of the ensuing month; their intention being to effect their escape into Chile. But being pursued, and taken near Mendoza on the 17th, they were thrown into prison, and afterwards brought to trial by Monteagudo. On the morning of the 8th of April, 1819, they were sentenced to be shot; at three o'clock of the afternoon, the unfortunate brothers were informed of the fate which awaited them; and at six o'clock on the same evening the sentence was carried into execution. Meanwhile their brother, Don Jose Miguel, had eluded either the justice or the vengeance of Puyerredon, by escaping from the brig in which he had been confined at Buenos Ayres, and flying for refuge to Monte Video."

I have extracted the following from a work, entitled " Five Years' Residence in Buenos Ayres, by an Englishman."—The execution of his two brothers, Don Louis and Juan Jose, in Mendoza, and other political affairs, had made him vow eternal enmity to the government of Buenos Ayres; particularly to San Martin, whom he much disliked. In his vengeance, he had raised the Indians to assist him. This act lost him many friends.

He was betrayed into the hands of his enemies, in the
city of Mendoza, and immediately put to death ; which it
is almost needless to observe, he underwent with courage,
and was buried, it is said, in the same grave with the
brothers he so dearly loved.

" Carrera was in the prime of life, tall, and elegantly
formed; his desperation and courage rank him as one of
Lord Byron's heroes, though not exactly, ' with one
virtue linked to a thousand crimes.'

" His widow, who was a fine woman, and infant family,
I afterwards saw at Buenos Ayres. One of the latter, a
little girl not five years of age, was imprudently asked,
in my presence, what had become of her father? ' Murdered by the Mendoceans,' she quickly replied."

During the government of General Pinto in 1828,
their remains were translated to the capital of Chile,
when I witnessed the honourable manner in which they
were laid in state in La Compania; their obsequies and
interment were attended by the public authorities and
principal inhabitants of Santiago. The faithful friend of
the family, El Doctor Don Louis B. Tollo, pronounced a
short but pathetic funeral oration to their memory.

Doña Zabiera occupied herself in her garden, which
is handsomely laid out in the English style, and in
attending and assisting the poor in her neighbourhood.
The kind treatment visitors generally receive in San
Miguel, leaves a lasting impression on such as have
experienced the polite attention of this worthy lady and
her amiable family. I next visited La Calera, in the
department De la Victoria. This estate belongs to the
late president of the republic, Don Francisco Ruis Tagle,
where I was stationed during his government. It is
extensive, well laid out and cultivated ; a deal of hemp is

grown, and there is also a quantity of cordage manufactured. The houses are substantial and commodious, as is
also the church. The gardens and pleasure-grounds are
tastefully laid out; and there is an artificial lake, with
water-works attached. I have visited this estate frequently, and enjoyed the hospitality of Don Francisco
and his amiable lady Doña Rosaria Larrayn. This
hacienda formerly belonged to the Jesuits, and some of
their rules and ceremonies are still observed by its proprietor, who generally gives two or more " corridos de
exercicios" annually.

These are held yearly on many of the large haciendas,
which have a series of chambers, almost contiguous to
their chapel, in order that those who attend may be com-
fortably lodged, called Casa de Exercicios; and some
have been endowed by the former proprietors, with a
yearly stipend for this purpose. When there is to be a
meeting, notice is generally given, and a number of tickets
are issued to the men or women on the estate, according
to those who take the lead, for each has nine days of
penitential praying; and the sermons of the most celebrated preachers that can be procured, must be heard,
before they can be shrived; and then they consider themselves as beginning the world again. Although they are
provided with plenty of good and substantial food, their
nine days' residence is no sinecure, for they are not
allowed to converse with each other, and generally have
a handkerchief tied on their heads, that nearly covers
their eyes. They are early and late at their prayers and
distributions; and, for the seven first nights they have to
flagellate themselves, with a discipline, with which they
are provided, or a strop, during the period a priest
sings the penitential prayer. I frequently have heard

them at this work, and wondered how they could stand
such a self-flogging, but one animates the other. Their
poor backs get sorely lacerated, and the walls show that
they have been unmerciful, even to themselves; others
mortify themselves by wearing a belt of bristles or pointed
wires, called " cilicios " It is the interest of the landed
proprietors to have these exercicios, for they keep their
" inquilinos" in order; many a restoration of stolen property and remuneration follows, as well as marriages.
The friars and other priests are well paid and fed, and
are extremely fond of following up the rules of San
Ygnatio Loyola. There are several houses of this kind in
the capital, other towns and haciendas, where the poor of
both classes are admitted gratis. On some estates where
there is no house of exercicios, they have missions, that are
attended only during the morning and evening service,
and nearly the same ceremonies, especially that of flagel-
lation, are performed. On leaving La Calera, I rode
over to Serro Negro, the estate of General Don Jose
Manuel Borgoño; he and his family had retired from
the capital ever since the pseudo-patriots had deprived
him of his rank and pay. General Don Francisco
Antonio Pinto was his neighbour; he also had been
cashiered, but both managed to live respected, and bring
up their families, by imitating Cincinnatus; and turning
their attention to agricultural pursuits. I next visited
the hacienda of El S'or Xara; here is a fine garden, and
his lady, Doña Transita, has bestowed extraordinary pains
in adorning and keeping it in order; she is of the
Carrera family, and the hospitality of Santa Rita is proverbial in the province. On my return to Angostura,
the family of Don Juan Francisco Larrayrr were preparing to leave for the capital, and I accepted the invitation

Y

of a neighbouring gentleman, Don Justo Salinas, who had been suddenly bereft of his lady, Doña Ana Maria Cotapos, who had been alarmed during the period that Pincheyra was in the neighbourhood, with a report of fire arms; she received a fall that occasioned her death. Don Justo was left with seven children; (the lady's first husband was the unfortunate General Carrera, of whom mention has been made.) As I had a favourable opportunity of seeing the mode of the Haciendadoes managing their estates, I will now give a description of the Rodeos, Matanzas, Trillas, Vendimias, and other field sports of Chile.

The haciendas in Chile, especially those of Mayorazgos* extend over a large tract of country, especially if situated near the Cordilleras; the rest are from 8,000 to 12,000 quadras (a square of four acres), all under this size are called " hijuelas, estancias, and chacaras.

The rich proprietors reside with their families in Santiago, or the capital of the province where their estates

---

* The mode in which property was distributed in the Spanish colonies, and the regulations established with respect to the transmission of it, whether by descent or by sale, were extremely unfavourable to population. In order to promote a rapid increase of people in any new settlement, property in land ought to be divided into small shares, and the alienation of it should be rendered extremely easy. But the rapaciousness of the Spanish conquerors of the new world paid no regard to this fundamental maxim of policy; and, as they possessed power which enabled them to gratify the utmost extravagance of their wishes, many seized districts of great extent, and held them as *encomiendas*. By degrees they obtained the privilege of converting a part of these into *Mayorasgos*, a species of fief, introduced into the Spanish system of feudal jurisprudence, which can neither be divided nor alienated. (*During the administration of General Pinto, the congress wisely abolished the mayorasgos; and the administration of the government that got into power by the revolution of 1829 and 1830, re-established them again.*) Thus a great portion of landed property, under this rigid form of entail, is withheld from circulation, and descends from father to son unimproved, and of little value either to the proprietor or to the community.—*Robertson's History of America.*

lie, and only visit them at stated periods, accompanied
with their families and a few friends, to make their so-
journ more agreeable. It is highly amusing to a stranger
to be of their hospitable party, for in the country the
Chilians are seen in their true native character, and as
they divest themselves of all etiquette, are free and con-
vivial.

On the largest estates there are but few persons that
receive a salary; yet the proprietors consider themselves
fortunate if they have from two to three hundred "inquilinos." These may be called serfs, although they are
at liberty to change their domicile at pleasure; but so
long as they reside on the estate they have to perform
sundry services, and assist at all the rodeos and trillas,
without any other emolument than their rations, the
privilege of a cottage, with a small plot of land, and leave
to rear a few animals. However the "huassos" seem
well satisfied with their condition, and bring up large
families, which by the bye, is no burden to the cottagers
in Chile. The men are generally employed as labourers,
and earn one and a half to two reals per day (nine-pence
to a shilling), besides their rations; however, the money
generally remains on the estate, for the owner has a
"bodegon," (store), where he disposes of no small proportion of his meat, grain, wine, and spirits, as well as
other articles, to his "inquilinos a rodeo." The mayor-
domo" summons the "capatazes," and "vaqueros," who
warn the serfs to repair to the place appointed, on horseback, with their dogs. The "battu" begins at day-break,
each individual takes his station, and when ready, a
general shout commences the operation; this, and the
barking of the dogs, arouse the animals from their lair,
which, when thus alarmed, generally flock together, and

Y 2

are easily driven from their pastures, (which often covers
several miles of woody and mountainous land, without
leaving many behind) into the " rodeos." This is a series
of staked enclosures. The accompanying plan exhibits the
design of one that was on the Hacienda de la Compania,
belonging to my friend, Don Juan de Dios Correa de
Saa :—

DESCRIPTION:

No. 1.   The principal pen, where the whole of the cattle are shut in when
         driven from the Potreros.
    2.   For such as are selected, to cool in, whilst the rest are let out to
         their pastures.
    3.   For the animals that are to be sold or slaughtered.
    4.   For the horses.
    5.   Passage from the pens to No. 3.
    6.   For the small droves, separated in No. 2.
    7.   For the calves.
    8.   Entrances.

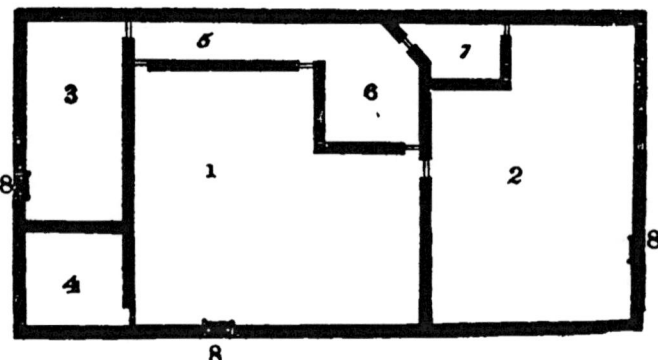

Length three hundred varas, two hundred and seventy-six yards.

It is during a rodeo that the Chilian Huassos are seen
to advantage, whilst they are scouring the woods, and
riding at full gallop up and down the steep hills, and
almost impervious thickets of thorn, "algaroba," and
patches of cardoon, where a stranger could scarcely find

a passage, or be able to ride without incurring the danger of breaking his neck, or being sorely lacerated. I have often seen them throw their lasso at full speed, and entangle and secure the wildest animal in situations that have surprised me; and still more so, to see them bring a strayed one back to the herd in perfect safety. The lasso is a strip of green hide of considerable length, and made pliable, some are plaited, at one end there is a running noose, the other is fastened to the girth of the saddle; few Chilians travel without their lasso, in the use of which they are uncommonly expert; in fact they ought to be so, for when children their amusement is the ensnaring of cats, dogs, and even poultry, with their lassito. The lasso has often been used in warfare, and many a Spaniard has been dragged from the ranks, or gun, dismounted by the intrepid huassos. In the southern provinces a missile is used, called "bolas," that are made from three stones, or round pieces of iron or lead, enclosed in a piece of leather; these weigh from six to eight ounces each, and are attached to thongs of about three feet in length, which, when, knotted together, complete the bolas. The person who uses this missile takes the bolas by the knot, and gallops after the animal, or ostrich, he may be in pursuit of, and when he arrives at a convenient distance he lets two of the balls slip through, and retains the other in his hand, and begins twirling them round his head, and casts them from him, as a stone would be propelled from a sling. An expert huntsman, or what is called a good "boleador," can almost ensure his aim at the distance of one hundred paces. The bolas generally entangle the legs of the animal, and causes it to fall, or otherwise impede its flight; then the huasso is enabled to secure it with his lasso; the bolas is also used in

warfare both by the Chilian cavalry and the Indians, and
is a fearful missile. The huassos have a peculiar way
of riding, and generally depend on their enormous spurs,
and stirrups to keep their seats. The principal rodeos
are in September, (spring); the rest are held in order to
change pastures, unite the cattle, or to count, castrate,
and mark the calves. "Apartando" is the separation
and selecting of the cattle. This is an amusement of
which my friends Don Justo Salinas, Don Jose Rafael
Larrain, and others whom I visited, were very fond,
and showed their dexterity, not only in horsemanship, but
in the precision and celerity with which the animals were
separated, according to their age and condition, and sent
to their different pastures. When they castrate, and
mark the calves, they are taken out of the pen by tens,
their fore and hind feet are secured with lassos, and when
tight, the animal is thrown down on its side; the points
of their horns are cut off, and then they are branded and
castrated. The animals when set at liberty, are so enraged,
that they run about bellowing with pain, and attack such
as are near them, to the no small diversion of the by-
standers. The animals that are to be sold, or slaughtered,
are put into good pastures of alfalfa (lucerne). The
matanzas (time of killing), commences after Christmas,
and the number of cattle that are to be slaughtered is
regulated according to the size and quality of the pastures;
a certain portion is always kept as stock, the rest must
be either sold or slaughtered. The animals when killed
are dragged into the shed, a man takes charge of two,
and with the assistance of a boy, skins and cuts them up
in such a manner, that the meat, fat, and bones are
separated with the greatest precision and dexterity; the
meat is cut up into shreds, a little salt is sprinkled over it

and it is then hung up to dry; next day it is laid on the ground which has been covered with brushwood, and when perfectly dry, is packed up into parcels called "lios," generally weighing about two hundred and fifty pounds. These are secured by strips of green hide. The bones and fat are tried and rendered, and the result poured into the paunches of the dead animals that are preserved for this purpose, and when filled, are called "panzas de graza;" the suet is cut up into bits, pounded into a consistence, and packed up in hides, each package weighing about two hundred and fifty pounds, half a mule load; the heads, kidneys, and offal, except the livers, which are dried for the dogs, are the perquisites of the butchers. I have often passed hours in the ramadas, witnessing their mode of cutting up an animal, and admired the nicety with which the peon separated or disjointed each piece, previous to cutting the meat into shreds, and calling each by its proper name, as in anatomy. The proprietors regale their friends during the "matanzas," with huacha-lomos, matahambres, and estomagillos; these are favourite roasts, which they seem to relish best when cooked by a peon, and eat in the ramada; they are generally served up with potatoe sauce, called "pevre," hot bread, and "chacoli," (country wine). I often made a hearty breakfast, and considered it no bad fare for "a half-pay officer, who had been obliged to rusticate." The greatest regard is paid to cleanliness, for "charke," (dried beef) is the common food of the Chilians, and it is sold at the rate of 2d. or 3d. per pound; it is eaten either roasted, boiled, or concocted into the national messes of "charke can, and valdiviano." The hides and horns are bought by the agents of foreign merchants for exportation, and have a sure sale, but the charke, fat, and suet are retailed on the estate, or sent to an agent to dispose of in the capital or Valparaiso. One of my friends with whom I often enjoyed a few weeks' hospitality, Don Valentin Valdivieso, is famed for his " cecina" (dried beef,) which is made up in small and assorted packages; and, as the cleanliness of his " ramada" is proverbial, he has a sure and rapid sale for his produce.

TRILLAS.—The harvest follows the matanzas. Don Juan de Dios Correa de Saa, whom I used to accompany for several weeks during the spring and harvest, had the greatest crops of wheat of any haciendado in Chile, he generally had above one thousand fanegas (a fanega is one hundred and fifty pounds), sown on his own account; which, at a fair average, yield fifty for one in the department of Rancagua; and in the southern provinces, from sixty to one hundred: yet there are many drawbacks, such as smut and other diseases, as well as heavy rains and hail. Several kinds of wheat are cultivated in Chile—Trigo Blanco, (white), and Candial, (brown), are the most general: the first is most esteemed, but more liable to casualities, the last is hardy and sure; barley is also cultivated, but I never saw either oats or rye. Indian and Guinea corn serve as their substitute, and may be called the poor peon's friend; for the former may be considered as an article of food soon after the ear is formed, these are called Chocolos; next is the Chilian staff of life, (frigoles). Kidneybeans are the almost constant food of the Chilian labourers, and are to be found at the conventual, as well as at the tables of the richest inhabitants who deign to eat their " porotos," (one of the numerous names of the bean). Common peas, beans, and galvances are grown, but in small quantities.

At the harvest the wheat is cut about a foot from the

ground, and carted into a circular enclosure, called an
"area," which varies in size according to the quantity;
it is surrounded by stakes interwoven with brushwood;
which is piled up in the centre, and, when considered
full, a part is spread on the ground, then a number of
mares are driven into the "area," several mounted men
follow them, and keep driving them round, and changing
them, until the whole is trod into atoms. The wheat is
then separated from the straw and chaff by being thrown
up into the wind, which carries the lighter particles to a
distance; when there is not sufficient wind, the wheat,
straw, &c., is thrown into a heap, called a "parva," and I
have known the rain to commence before sufficient wind
could be had to winnow it; and, it often occurs that the
wheat is either lost or damaged: this mode of winnowing
wastes a great deal of grain,* for I never saw any straw
used, but what had still a quantity of wheat amongst it;
when the winnowing is concluded, the wheat is transported
to the granaries, and the straw generally remains in the
field, if distant from the capital, and is either used as
fodder for the cattle during winter, or in the manfacture
of adobes, or mud walls.

VENDIMIAS.—The vintage is conducted in Chile as in
all other wine-countries, except that, in order to preserve
the liquor, a quantity is boiled until it becomes a sirrup,
"arrope," which, when mixed with the rest, is called
"cosido:" wine "mosto" is only made in the southern; cosido, chicha, and chacoli, is made in all the
northern districts. Almost every hacienda has one or
more vineyards; the farmers also have them in their

* My friend, Alexander Caldcleugh, Esq., has got me to send him a
thrashing and winnowing machine, which may suggest some change in the
present mode of thrashing.

estancios and chacaras; and in the year 1834, it was estimated that there were about 25,000,000 vines in culti-vation;* and these are valued at two shillings each (half a dollar.) The wines and brandy are very cheap; for an "arroba" of about thirty-two bottles seldom sells for more than three or four shillings; and the chacoli, and chicha, are still cheaper; the same quantity of spirits may be had for twenty-five or thirty shillings; good wines, not inferior to European, might be made, but these do not suit the tastes or pockets of the Chilians; so the proprietors only make a little for their own use. I have tasted excellent white wine on the estate of Don Justo Salinas, from the chacara of General Don Francisco Lastra, at Opaquinda, and red wine at Cucha-Cucha; that from the hacienda of Gen. Don Ramon Freyre, may be compared to marcella, sherry, and port; and Alexander Caldcleugh, Esq. has taken wine from Copiapo, and the estate of Don Justo Salinas, to England, which has been pronounced fit for the best tables in Europe; still there is no encourage-ment for the proprietors to make such wines, as nothing but chicha, chacoli, sancochada, mosto, chivata, and la yegua tordilla, can please the taste of the Chilian huassos, or common consumers.

The estate of Don Justo Salinas is delightfully situated at the foot of the mountains of Angostura; there are only about nine hundred quadras of level land that can be irrigated, and this is in the highest state of cultivation; his fields are laid out in the European style, and the

* "On account of the distance of Peru and Chile from Spain, and the difficulty of carrying commodities of such bulk as wine and oil across the isthmus of Panama: the Spaniards in those provinces have been permitted to plant vines and olives; but they are strictly prohibited from exporting wine or oil to any of the provinces on the Pacific ocean which are in such a situation as to receive them from Spain."—Recop. lib. i. tit. xvii. i. 15 —18.

roads are beautifully shaded with poplars and willows; his houses are well built and spacious, and his gardens tastefully laid out; the whole being watered from the river of Angostura, which, in summer appears to be only a brook; but during the rainy season it shows itself a broad and rapid stream, that often does much damage to the estates in the neighbourhood; its waters, during the dry season, are as clear as crystal. This has now become a fashionable resort in the summer, for I persuaded my friend, Don Justo Salinas, to build an inn or posada, where parties might find every convenience; and bathing sheds were also erected over the stream for their accommodation; and previous to my leaving Chile, I had the satisfaction of hearing my friend say, it had been a profitable undertaking. The streams about Angostura abound with excellent fish; there are also quantities of water-fowl; and, as I was fond of field-sports, I found plenty of occupation; my friend, Don Justo, and his chaplain, often accompanied me on a fishing excursion, and the latter found it such a source of amusement, that he generally passed all his leisure on the banks of the river. One night, the chaplain, who was a Franciscan friar, caught a large fish, and was elated with his success. Don Justo had been less fortunate, and, unseen by either the friar or myself, managed to hook the fish, and slip it into the water; he then said he had a bite, and, on his giving a sudden jerk, broke his rod; however, he jumped into the stream and landed his fish, which was still alive, and, to keep up the trick, said, as he was wet, he would take it home, and left us. I was highly amused with the chaplain; for he considered that Don Justo had exchanged fishes, and taken the one he had caught, which was the largest with him; but, on examining the fish, I found that he had left part of the line and hook which was fastened outside of the fish's mouth; which let me into the secret, and made me enjoy the joke.

I often accompanied other friends on fishing excursions; and a neighbouring gentleman, Don Eulogio Vidal, who was married to La Señora Doña Josefa Dumont, Countess de la Conquista, with whom I often resided, enjoyed all manner of field-sports; his lady was the mother of the wife of Don Juan de Dios Correa, and was the richest heiress in Chile.

Most of the rivers in Chile abound with fish, such as peje-reyes, king-fish; cauque, another species · truchas, river perch; bagre, loach; anguillas, eels; tollo, dog-fish; lisa, mullet; robalo, a species of pike, and craw-fish. Peje-reyes and cauques are fine fish; the first are like sparlings, and grow to the size of a herring; the back, sides, and belly are covered with silver scales, with a dark golden streak on the back; they are delicious food, and are to be got likewise in the mountain streams amongst the Cordilleras, as well as in the sea; they are caught in abundance in the bays and sea-ports; they take the bait greedily. The largest are to be found in the lake of Aculeu, where I have caught many, by trolling with an artificial fish, or a grub, called "guzano de trevol;" grasshoppers and worms are good ground-bait. The cauque is of the same species, but larger, and rises to the fly; they afford excellent sport, but are not so good to eat as the peje-reye. The trucha is a fine and well-flavoured fish; it abounds in all the southern rivers; it is similar to the river perch. I have caught many above sixteen inches in length. They afford excellent sport, and take a worm bait, or the eye of a fish, and are trolled for by an artificial crab made of partridge feathers. As they are very strong good tackle is requisite. They bite best about sun-set and sun-rise, but may be caught at all hours. The bagre is a delicious fish, not unlike the loach, but much larger, for I have caught them above five or six pounds weight; it has no scales; its back and sides are of a dark brown, its belly white; it has a sharp spine on its back, not unlike the cat-fish, and barbs on each side of its mouth. They are caught from sun-set to sun-rise, with a worm or fish-bait. Bagre fishing is profitable, but not amusing; they often annoyed me when trolling for other fish, by breaking my tackle.

Eels are only plentiful to the southward of the Bio Bio, where they are caught in buckets or fish-pots; they are more like snakes than the European eels; they are pretty good food, but not esteemed by the Chilians.

The tollo is a species of dog-fish; I have caught them in the Maipu, Mapocho, Payne, and Angostura; they are good eating, and easily caught by trolling, or with a worm-bait; they have a sharp spine on the back, and are caught at the mouth of the rivers; at sea they are of a large size; their skin is used by cabinet-makers to polish their wood with.

Two kinds of mullet are caught at the mouths of the rivers or lakes that admit the sea; they are from twelve to sixteen inches in length, and afford excellent sport, for they rise to the fly; they are strong and vigorous, and delicious food. The smallest species is reckoned the best.

The robalo is a sea and river fish. I call it the pike, for its habits are nearly the same, and it is caught either by trolling or with ground-bait. They are generally from two to three feet in length; the flesh is white and delicious, and they afford excellent sport. There are several other kinds of fish, but of little note, the correct names of which I am unacquainted with.

Crayfish and small crabs are to be met with in all the rivers; the first are excellent, and caught in weirs that the natives throw across the streams, and from which they derive more profit than from angling; I almost always caught as many fish as I could conveniently carry, in a few hours; and often whilst at Chillan, the head-quarters of the army, I used to amuse myself by angling. I was often so successful, that General Borgoño, and the staff-officers, used to jeer me by stating, that I must have purchased the fish. One morning, however, they followed me,—I had only been about an hour and a half at the river, and had caught more than thirty fine truchas and cauques, when my servant informed me of their approach; I had just time to secrete all but a few. The general and those that accompanied him expressed their surprise to find me there; and on observing me catch several, the General, Colonel Biel, Colonel Beauchef, Lieut.-Colonel Tupper, and one or two more, seemed eager to have rods, so I gave two which I had to spare to the General and Colonel Beauchef: although the day was wet and uncomfortable, they remained until dinner time, and enjoyed the sport, for they caught several; the colonel proved the best fisherman, for he produced more than I had in sight; but when I displayed those which I had hidden, they were all fully convinced that I had not purchased the fish. They afterwards provided themselves with tackle, and often accompanied me on fishing excursions, or went by themselves to profit by the amusement.

There are many species of foxes in Chile, which are either hunted by the natives for their skins, or on account of the damage done to their poultry or lambs; the culpeu is nearly as large as a harrier, and is easily taken. Foreigners in the neighbourhood of the capital often purchase foxes, and turn them out in a large enclosure, which affords some amusement to the natives, who often assemble to see the "gringos" congregate at the farm of a Yorkshireman who was fond of this sport, and who encouraged these "soi-disant" hunters, until he, as well as many of them, was obliged to desist on account of the many falls and bruises they had received. There is also an animal called "biscacha," which may be compared to a rabbit, though different in size and shape; they burrow in the earth, and may be found about sun-set at the mouth of their holes. What the Chilians call "liebre," (hare,) is like a diminutive species of deer; they are good eating, and found in the southern provinces; there is also a very large species called "guamul;" this animal is one of the supporters of the Chilian arms: Molina has described it as partaking of the horse and deer; but the skins of this animal that I have seen, were not different from those of deer. An animal called chinchilli, is much in repute on account of its skin, and numbers are trapped annually, as well as two species of castors; "quipo," and "guillin;" the first abounds in the northern provinces, and the latter are caught in the lakes and rivers; the sea-otter also, with the seal, is caught on the coast, but mostly to the southward of Concepcion.

As I have visited my friends in the neighbourhood of Aconcagua, and Putaendo, and amused myself in hunting the guanacoe; I shall give a brief account of the field-sports of Chile.

During the winter, and just after a heavy fall of snow, which generally covers the Cordilleras to their base, numbers of guanacoes descend to the low country; and

as there are particular spots where it is easy to drive the
animals into natural enclosures, many are caught and
killed ; the Chilians display great dexterity on these
occasions, and the young gentlemen turn out in a fanciful manner, with long untanned boots, or gaiters, that
cover their thighs; they are often made of the skin of the
puma, or seal, and have an infinite number of buttons,
and thongs, the first are generally of silver ; these
and their enormous and showy spurs, whose rowels prevent their heels from touching the ground,—their lasso,
and bolas, large knife, and a profusion of sheep-skins,
are their accoutrements; and, when mounted on a fiery
steed, with their neat jackets, poncho thrown over their
left shoulder, straw hat, and segar; they are what the
Chilians call a " lacho, " exquisite."

The flesh of the guanacoe is pretty good, but it is
mostly hunted for its skin and wool ; the latter is, as
well as that of the vicuña, another species, manufactured
into hats ; I have also attended the puma hunts, which
are more fatiguing than profitable ; however, it is the
interest of the haciendadoes to destroy the " leones," and
a smaller species called the " guinas," a species of wild
cat ; and huntsmen are retained, who with their dogs
follow, and often destroy the puma.

I once, shortly after my arrival in Chile, went to the
Hacienda of Cauquenes, belonging to the late Marques
de la Casa Larrayn, for the purpose of seeing a puma
hunt; the party was led by a Vaquero, and a huntsman,
with several dogs of a small size, who soon scented out
the track, and we followed for the space of two leagues
amongst the Cordilleras, where they stopped, and we
discovered part of a dead calf, that was covered over
with branches and leaves, which I was informed had been

CHILLIAN'S HUNTING THE GUANACOE.

Fisher, Son & Co. London & Paris

done by the puma. We were some time before we found out the track the animals had taken, and at last one was discovered in a " quillai," (soap-tree.) The Vaquero ordered the dogs to be secured, and then a man got up the tree with a cane and a lasso, to secure the puma; but he became faint-hearted, and dropped both of them to the ground : he was so situated as almost to impede another from climbing up, so I took aim with my double-barrelled rifle, and let the puma have the contents as near as possible under the fore-shoulder ; but, it remained stationary, and soon afterwards the poncho of the poor fellow was covered with blood. The Huassos were alarmed, and afraid I had wounded him ; and whilst they were making such allusions, both fell from the tree. The puma was killed by my shot, and the Huasso almost dead with fright. One of the dogs that had got loose fastened upon him, which soon brought him to his senses, to be sorely roasted and annoyed by his companions. The animal was about the size of a large Newfoundland dog ; it was soon skinned, and the fat, of which there was no great quantity, was preserved for some medicinal use.

I have often seen puma hunts, but none so amusing as the one at Cauquenes ; however, I soon got tired of such adventures, for it is too harassing to have to traverse many leagues of a mountainous country, and often to remain a night or two away from home in quest of these animals; however, the huntsmen and dogs seem to enjoy their sport, and they get well rewarded for all that are destroyed. Molina has given the following description of this animal:—

" The pagi (felis puma), called by the Mexicans Mitzli, and in Peru, puma, the name by which it is best known

z

to naturalists, has by the Spaniards been denominated the lion, which it resembles in its shape and roaring, but is wholly destitute of a mane. The hair on the upper part of its body is of a greyish ash-colour, marked with yellow spots, and is longer than that of the tiger, particularly on the buttocks, but that on the belly is of a dusky white. Its length, from the nose to the root of the tail, is about five feet, and its height from the bottom of the foot to the shoulder twenty-six and a half inches. It has a round head, shaped much like that of a cat; the ears are short and pointed; the eyes large with yellow irides and brown pupils. Its nose is broad and flat, the muzzle short, the upper lip entire and furnished with whiskers, the mouth deep, and the tongue large and rough. In each jaw it has four incisors, four sharp-pointed canine teeth, and sixteen grinders. Its breast is broad, the paws have each five toes armed with very strong nails, and its tail is upwards of two feet in length, like that of a tiger.

"The female is rather less than the male, and is of a paler colour, like the African lioness; she has two dugs, and brings forth but two at a time.

" Such is the lion of Chile; it may, perhaps, in other parts of America, offer some shades of discrimination, as I have been informed that those of Peru have a longer and more pointed muzzle. The pagi inhabits the thickest forests, and the most inaccessible mountains, from whence it makes incursions into the plains, to attack domestic animals, particularly horses, whose flesh it prefers to that of any other. The mode in which it seizes its prey, resembles a cat; it approaches it by drawing itself upon its belly, glides softly through the shrubs and bushes, conceals itself in the ditches, or, if it shows itself, assumes

a mild and fawning appearance, and watching the favourable opportunity of seizing the animal which it has marked
for its victim, at one leap fastens itself upon its back, lays
hold of it with its left paw and teeth in such a manner as
to render its escape impossible, while with the right paw
it tears it to pieces in a few minutes; it then sucks the
blood, devours the flesh of the breast, and carries the
carcass into the nearest wood, where it conceals it with
leaves and boughs of trees, in order to eat it at its leisure.
As it is a common practice for the husbandman to fasten
two of their horses together in the fields, wherever the
pagi finds them in this situation, it kills one and drags
it away, compelling the other to follow by striking it from
time to time with its paw, and in this manner almost
always succeeds in getting possession of both.   Its
favourite haunts are the streams to which animals usually
repair to drink, where it conceals itself upon a tree, and,
scarcely ever fails of seizing one of them.   The horses,
however, have an instinctive dread of these places, and,
even when pressed by thirst, approach them with great
precaution, carefully examining upon every side, to discover if there is danger; at other times one of the boldest
goes forward, and, on finding the place secure, gives
notice to his companions by neighing in a sprightly
manner.

" The cows defend themselves well against the pagi ;
for, as soon as he appears, they range themselves in a
circle around their calves, with their horns turned towards
their assailant, await his attack in that position, and not
unfrequently destroy him.

" Notwithstanding his ferocity, the pagi never ventures
to attack a man, although he is continually hunted and
persecuted by the latter.

z 2

"He is hunted with dogs trained for the purpose, and, when hard pressed by them, either leaps upon a tree, seeks an asylum upon a rock, or, placing himself against the trunk of some large tree, defends himself in a furious manner, killing many of his enemies, until the hunter, watching his opportunity, slips a noose around his neck. As soon as the animal finds himself taken in this manner, he roars terribly, and sheds a torrent of tears. The skin serves for various uses ; good leather for boots or shoes is manufactured from it, and the fat is considered as specific in the sciatica."*

Hunting of wild horses, (lobos): There are but few of these animals in Chile, at least on the north of the Bio Bio, for I have only seen them on the Isla de la Laxa. The Indians come over to hunt them, principally for food, or their skins. Yet, on the eastern side of the Cordilleras, there are numerous herds. Those who hunt wild cattle are provided with lacs, or bolas, which I have already described. The horseman follows the wild animal, and, whilst at full speed, whirls the bolas round his head, and, often at the distance of one hundred paces, succeeds in entangling the feet of the one he has pursued, and thus impedes its flight ; he then secures it with his lasso. The Gauchos of Uraguai hunt wild horses in the following manner :—

"Caza de los Baguales."—It is necessary in order to hunt wild horses, to have at least thirty men well mounted, under the orders or direction of their leader or employer. Their first care is, to observe the route which the animals generally take when pursued, then they form what is called a "manguera," which is nothing more than an immense pen, "rodeo," already described. From the principal

* Natural History of Chile, by Molina.

entrance they form two lines, composed of stakes, that are
about four or five feet distant from each other, and secured
by cross-poles, to keep the animals from breaking through
or leaping over them; these two lines are sometimes about
a league in length, and form an angle; the extreme points
can scarcely be visible from one to the other, and affords a
space capable of receiving from four to five thousand horses.
When this preliminary arrangement is concluded, they begin by training about fifteen mares, or horses, to set off at
full gallop from the entrance of the "manga," and not stop
until they arrive in the large "rodeo." These are called
"guides;" and if stopped in their career, the hunt will be
frustrated, and all the labour entirely lost.

On the evening of the day which has been appointed for
the hunt, the "baguales" are driven to that part of the
plain which is opposite the "manga," and at daybreak the
leader of the hunt reconnoitres the animals; after which,
he stations his men at the distance of two hundred
paces from each other, and separates the trained guides
into two equal divisions; one opposite the entrance of the
"manga," and the other in the centre; and then eight or
ten horsemen are sent to unite the "baguales," taking care
to make a large circuit, so as not to be seen too soon, which
might endanger the result of the hunt, which commences
as soon as they succeed in getting the animals between
them and the manga; they then gallop towards them,
making the air resound with their shouts, and agitating it
with large flags of red cloth. Their charges are made, as
well as can be executed, in a straight line, and with great
velocity. As soon as the "baguales" pass by the men that
have been previously stationed by the leader, these unite
with the first, and charge with them; the men stationed
with the trained guides, hearing the approach of the herd

of wild horses, when at a league's distance; and as they near the men, give the appointed signal, and retire behind the stakes. The baguales, on observing the guides, gallop on before, redouble their speed to join them; then the men follow up, excite the ardour of their horses, redouble their shouts, and by agitating their red flags, they augment the terror of the frightened animals, so as to impede them from seeing the snare, and by this means are driven into the rodeo. The huntsmen follow immediately after, and form up before the entrance, while ten or twelve close it up with strong poles. This ends the hunt.

Two days afterwards, those animals, which have not tasted food or water, are slaughtered.

Hunting of baguales, when successful, is lucrative. The formation of a rodeo capable of containing from four to five thousand, costs about nine hundred dollars; the hide of a horse when sold, brings to the proprietor about one and a half to two dollars, without the mane or tail, which is also an article of consideration.*

The ostrich, " avestrucho," is only to be met with on the plains of the eastern Cordilleras and Pampas; they are caught with bolas, and afford good sport; their flesh is not eaten, but their eggs are reputed good; they are generally hunted for their plumes, which are coarser and inferior to those of the African or Asiatic ostrich; the natives make them into parasols, or dusters, " plumeros."

The condors are often caught and killed in the following manner:—

The Huassos make a pen of sticks and bushes of about seventy yards in length, and place a dead animal in it, which soon attracts the condors, for although none may be within sight, such is their acute sense of smelling, that

* El Araucano, No. 305.   August 25, 1837.

numbers are soon seen to soar above the carrion, and alight
and commence their attack, and soon glut themselves in
such a manner as to almost impede their taking the wing.
The men, who have been secreted behind the bushes,
being armed with clubs, rush out upon them, and soon
destroy many; for the confined space of the pen that has
various crossings prevents the escape of the condors; and
the sportsmen repay themselves for their trouble, and for
a severe contusion, perhaps, from the wing or beak of their
aerial opponent, with the feathers of the wings, for which
they have a sure and ready market. Molina gives the following description of the mode of catching the condor.

" The husbandmen make use of every stratagem, to
destroy so dangerous a bird. For this purpose they sometimes envelope them in the skin of an ox newly slain, and
place themselves on their backs upon the ground : the
condor, deceived by the appearance, approaches the supposed dead animal, to devour it, when the person within,
whose hands are protected by strong gloves, dexterously
seizes the legs of the bird, and holds it until his companions,
concealed hard by, run up to his assistance, and despatch
it with clubs.

" The condors feed either upon carcasses, or upon
animals which they kill themselves, and thus supply the
place of wolves, which are unknown in Chile.

" They frequently attack flocks of sheep or goats, and
even calves, when they are separated from the cows. In
the latter case there are always several of them together,
who fly upon the calf with their wings extended, dig out its
eyes, and in a few moments tear it to pieces."

The bird is in Chile called " manque," and is unquestionably the largest that has the power of supporting itself
in the air. Linnæus makes its wings, when extended, six-

teen feet from one extremity to the other; but the largest that I have seen was but fourteen feet and some inches. The body is much larger than that of the royal eagle, and is entirely covered with black feathers, excepting the back, which is white. The neck is encircled with a white fringe, composed of projecting feathers, about an inch in length. The head is covered with short and thin hairs; the irides of the eyes are of a reddish brown, and the pupils black. The beak is four inches long, very large and crooked, black at its base, and white towards the point. The greater quills of the wings are usually two feet nine inches long, and one-third of an inch in diameter. The thigh is ten inches and two-thirds in length, but the leg does not exceed six inches; the foot is furnished with four strong toes; the hindmost of which is about two inches long, with but one joint, and a black nail an inch in length; the middle toe has three joints, it is nearly six inches long, and is terminated by a crooked whitish nail of two inches; the other toes are a little shorter, and are armed with strong and crooked talons. The tail is entire, but small in proportion to the size of the bird.

"The female is less than the male, and of a brownish colour; she has no fringe about the neck, but a small tuft upon the hinder part of it. She builds her nest upon the most steep and inaccessible cliffs, and lays two white eggs larger than those of the turkey."*

The "torcas," ring-dove, affords a profitable amusement to the poor iuhabitants of Chile, who, during certain periods, kill numbers in the following manner.

These birds, when they leave their roosting-places, generally the head of a valley or ravine, fly in immense flocks, and within a few feet from the ground, and do not diverge

---

* The condor forms one of the supporters to the Chilian arms.

until they descend to the plains, or are alarmed; so the
natives generally erect a series of blinds of the branches of
trees, or squat themselves behind the cactus or stunted
myrtles, and await the successive flights that generally
descend for the space of half an hour about sunrise, when,
with a forked stick, crossed with a thong, they often succeed in killing several birds with a single blow, and, if the
sportsman be adroit, he seldom returns with less than a
dozen.

I have often accompanied Don Justo Salinas, and other
friends, whilst at Angostura, and as we stationed ourselves
with our fowling-pieces in the rear of the whole, we, without
interrupting their sport, made havock amongst the birds,
and brought down numbers at each shot.   The ring-doves
are good food, and many of the natives derive no small
emolument from these as well as from thrushes ; they kill
perroquets nearly in the same manner.   Parrots in Chile
are also an article of food, and when unfledged are considered a delicacy.   During the winter of 1834, whilst
residing on the Hacienda de la Compania, I was surprised
one morning, after a smart frost, to see the Huassos
arriving with numbers of parrots which they had found
benumbed on the trees, so that by shaking the branches
they fell to the ground; on inquiry, my friend Don Juan
de Dios Correa, informed me he had often heard of parrots
being caught in such a manner.

Hawking in Chile is confined to the chase of the partridge, and is a pleasant and profitable sport ; the Chilians
are fond of it, and display a deal of tact and dexterity in
the training of the falcon, and in hawking.

There are no game-laws here, but it is requisite to
ask leave of the owners of the property, on account of the

cattle being disturbed by the guns, and the danger of setting fire to the fields during the dry season; the trouble of asking leave is often repaid by a kind invitation to lodge there for the night; and a guide is generally sent to point out where game is abundant.

CHAP. X.

On the 14th of September, 1830, it was decreed that all the monasteries should be re-established in Chile, and their revenues and property, that had been alienated by the former governments, restored to them, and every encouragement given to repopulate their vacant cloisters.

On the 11th of January, 1832, the convent of missionaries of Chillan was reorganized, and subsequently Los R.R. Padres Gonzales and Zenon were commissioned to fetch friars from Italy and Spain, to illustrate the Chilians.

Don David Barrey, in his "Noticias Secretas de America," book 2nd, page 509, says as follows:—

"During several years' residence in Cadiz I had an excellent opportunity of informing myself how the apostolic companies assembled, and left that port, which was the one selected by government to provide a passage for all who were sent to preach the ' Evangelio,' in the Indies.

" Almost every year missionary commissaries of various communities arrived from America, in order to take reinforcements to their convents; these soon visited the interior of Spain, and began to enlist their 'religious recruits:' circumstances permit me to use such a profane expression for the turbulent, who were persecuted by their superiors; others, who would not subject themselves to the rules of the cloister, and who had become the scandal of the province; and others, who, being informed of the happy life of the friars in South America, as well as their numerous advantages, became desirous of making a change, flocked around the commissary of the mission, and prepared to leave their native country.

" When the number was completed, they were taken to Cadiz, where the governor compelled the owners of vessels to transport the friars to their destined port. But although government paid their passage, the captains, sooner than take them on board, have often been known to retard their voyage for months, rather than be troubled with such passengers. And the friars generally wished to go in the vessels of such as had manifested their repugnance to receive them, so that the governor had frequently to send a party of soldiers with the friars, to oblige the captains to receive them, or to force the missionaries to embark in another vessel."

With such missionaries, the South Americans will return to that happy and religious state they formerly enjoyed under the pious, moral, and austere guidance of those holy friars, whose sainted deeds are immortalized by those eminent writers, Los SS. Don Jorge Juan y Don Antonio de Ulloa: see "Noticias Secretas de America," pages 347, 382, 490, 492—499, 500, 503, 507, 511, 518, 520, 523—535.

An invitation and funds were sent to the Bishop of Santiago, who, ever since he was exiled from Chile, in 1826, had been a pensioner of the court of Spain, at Madrid, for his decided loyalty to Ferdinand the Seventh.*

On the 27th of June, 1823, the minister of state read a message from his excellency, the president of the republic of Chile, to the senate, in which he called upon them to sanction the following law:—" That all the Spanish

* This prelate died on the eve of his return to Chile, and now there are three bishoprics in the republic.

vessels should be treated as neutrals, and such as might enter the ports of Chile from Spain, or any other foreign port, should be subject to the same rules, and pay the same duties for the merchandise they imported, &c. as the vessels of any other nation that had not obtained greater privileges by treaties." The minister also stated to the senate, that government had, on the 6th of last September, requested the legislature to make a law, in order to abolish the discretional and arbitrary power that had been conferred by the legislature on the 5th of May, 1821, relative to the sequestrated estates of the partisans of Spain; and, as this was the second time it had been urged, he desired the senate to attend to it in preference to any other business. This was attended to, and all the confiscated property that had been publicly sold by the former administrations, was subsequently restored to the parties that reclaimed it, without any other remuneration to the purchasers for improvements, than the acknowledgment of such sums as had been paid into the public treasury, and this to be considered as part of the consolidated debt of the republic. But the project of opening the ports of the republic to the commerce of Spain caused great excitement, both in the senate, and amongst others, who although they had been deluded so as to have made a common cause against the administration of 1828, 1829, and 1830, would not prostitute their opinion any longer, nor tolerate the inordinate presumption of the Spanish faction.* Govern-

* Five out of seven of the committee, who were appointed to report upon the project, Los S. S. Don Fernando Errasuria, Don Jose Vicente Izquierdo, Don Jose Antonio Huici, Don Juan Augustin Alcalde, and Don Mariano de Egaña's opinions, were, "That the president of the republic might, if he thought it convenient, enter into negotiations of peace with the king of Spain, should that monarch acknowledge our independence, and, on the congress approving the articles of his message of the 26th of July last, as the stipulations that might take place in the said treaty."

ment, aware of the fermentation of the Chilians, and the
energetic speeches of several of the senators, who in stre-
nuous language declaimed against the project, and unreason-
able request of government, and, in the most pathetic style
depicted the excessive cruelties of the Spaniards, who had
moistened every part of the territory of the republic with
the blood of the patriots; and who still breathed nothing
but hatred, blood, and vengeance against the Americans;
and appealing to their auditors, questioned them, whether,
in case the ports of Chile should be opened to the commerce of Spain, " would not that nation propose new and
exorbitant pretensions, as a recompense of the acknowledgment they might accede to?" Therefore the minister
of state had the mortification of having to make his appearance before the senate on the 25th of July, and say
that " Although government is perfectly persuaded of the
utility of the proposed law, in the message of the 26th of
June; he, in consideration of a superior order, would withdraw it, 'en voz,' and in the name of the president of the
republic." The president of the senate told the minister,
" That as the motion was in its second discussion, it could
not be delivered to him without the consent of the senate;"
but on being put to the vote, it was unanimously returned;
and on the secretary delivering it to the minister, he took
his departure. A paper edited by some of the Spanish
faction, " El Constitucional," expressed in the most indig-
nant terms their reproval of this act of patriotism, and said
that, " The president of the republic, his ministers, the
members of the council of state, with the exception of one,
various senators, many of the deputies of congress, and an
infinite number of citizens, were in favour of the project of
opening the ports of Chile to Spanish vessels. The editors
of that paper are well known in Chile; and if their state-

ment be true, the following verses from the press of that worthy patriot, Don Jose Miguel Infante, published at that period, may serve to show the decadence of illustration in Chile:—

A DIOS LIBERTAD BUEN VIAGE, Y VOLVERAS? YO TE ESPERO.

Oh! que mal que conocias
El caracter de este pueblo !
Aquellos arcos triunfales,
Los vivas y juramentos
De Independencia o muerte
De no sufrir ni un momento
Las cadenas....inosente !
Eran solo pasatiempo.
A Dios libertad, etc.

Los *maturangos*, por mas
Que los llamen majaderos,
Son los hombres que ban mostrado
Atucia y entendimiento :
Al verte se acurrucaron,
En las conchas se metieron,
Y ahora salen triunfantes
Erguidos y peri-puesto
A Dios libertad, etc.

Ya se cierran las escuelas,
Ya se abren los conventos ;
Frailes de todos matices
Ya preludian el Te-Deum
Ya la Santa inquisicion
Prepara los quemaderos
Para tantos herejotes,
Y tantos libritos nuevos.
A Dios libertad, etc.

Ya vuelven las distinciones
De nobles y de plebeyos :
Desgraciado del que exija
Su salario a un caballero !
Que lo lleven a la carcel,
Que lo metan en un cepo,
Y si chista, que se pudra
Y pague su atrevimiento.
A Dios libertad, etc.

O! pueblo docil y amable!
O mansisimos corderos!
Ya empuño vuestro pastor
El gran cayado de hierro :
Ya no andareis estraviados
Ya tendries quien os equilme,
Por falta de buen gobierno;
Quien os lleve al matadero.
A Dios libertad, etc.

No, libertad, no te alejes;
No abandones este suelo
Que broto bajo tus plantas
Nuevas flores, frutos nuevos:
Verdad es que no te quieren
Ciertos *beatos* y opulentos;
Pero si te aman los *Chilenos,*
Pero te adoran los *patriotas.*
A Dios libertad, buen viaje
Y volveras? Yo te espero.

CHAP. XI.

As I have given but a succinct description of the provinces which I visited during my military vocations, I will now, with what I have been enabled to add from subsequent observations, proceed to submit an historical account of what is now termed the republic of Chile, with its political division into provinces, departments, sub-departments, and districts.

In 1826 the legislature of Chile divided the republic into the following provinces:—Coquimbo, Aconcagua, Santiago, Colchagua, Maule, Concepcion, Valdivia, and Chiloe, but subsequently a new province, Talca, has been created from a department of that of Colchagua.

The jurisdiction of the state extends from the desert of Atacama in lat. 24° N. to 45° S., and from the Cordilleras de Los Andes to the Pacific ocean with its adjacent islands, and those of Juan Fernandez.

Chile has since 1826 been governed by a president, who is elected for five years, and may be re-elected to serve five years longer;* he is assisted by a council of state, and the legislature is composed of senators and deputies. Each province is governed by an intendant, who has the aid of governors of departments, and subaltern magistrates.

* His Excellency General Don Joaquin Prieto, has been re-elected in 1836.

2 A

COQUIMBO.

This province extends from the confines of Bolivia to the river Chuapa, and is divided into eight departments—Copiapo, Freirina, Vallenar, Elqui, Ovalle, Combarbala, Illapel, and La Serena. Its principal rivers are Copiapo, Huasco, Serena, Barrasa, and Chuapa. It has three ports—Huasco, Copiapo, and Coquimbo; sixty-two districts; 1,549 haciendas and farms; and in 1834 a population of 99,841 souls. Its capital is the city of La Serena, founded in 1542, by General Valdivia, and rebuilt in the year 1554, by Don Francisco de Aguirre.

It seldom rains in this province, especially to the northward of the capital, and the temperature is mild and salubrious. As I have already given a description of the city, port, and productions of the province, I will conclude with an account of the newly discovered mines in the northern departments, and a few official statements. The silver mines lately discovered in the mountains of Copiapo, may compete with those of Potosi in Peru, and Guanajato in Mexico.

"In May, 1832, the rich veins of silver of Chanarcillo, Pajonal, and Bandurias, were discovered, from which ore was procured that yielded from one to three thousand marks, a cajon.*

"In the mines of Volados and Peraltas, lumps of pure silver have been found, one of which has been calculated to weigh from thirty-five to forty quintals, (a quintal is 100 lbs.), and it is presumed that in less than two months the owners of the mine will clear half a million of dollars. I have to state that this is not supposed to be the best mine, for there are two or three that are calculated to be still richer—such is the progress of our national wealth.

* A mark is eight ounces, and a cajon of ore is about fifteen mule loads.

In other times, no sooner would such a treasure have been discovered, than a vessel would have been despatched to receive it on board, to have had the honour and glory of carrying the lump of silver, in order to present it to the monarch of Spain.

" This mine is of a considerable extent, and the vein of metal so rich, that the proprietors, who were poor men, have become gamblers, and have staked as much as one hundred doubloons on a card. In order to ostentate their immense wealth, they generally sit at the mouth of their mine on a lump of pure silver, about a yard in height, and of the same width."*

The silver mines of Chile, under the Spanish government, did not produce more than 23,500 marks; but in 1834 they yielded 164,953 marks, seven times more than in the former period; and those of copper, which gave only 25,000 quintals annually, have tripled their products, which, on adding the value of the gold that is coined, and the copper ore that is exported, the wealth of the mining districts can scarcely be calculated. However, the above and following statements will give a pretty fair estimate :—

GOLD, SILVER, AND COPPER, EXPORTED IN THE YEAR 1834, FROM CHILE, AND COINED.

	Marks.	Oz.	Value.
Gold exported from Valparaiso	11	7	
Gold coined in the Mint . .	3840	2	Dollars.
Total	3852	1	. . 525,291 6

SILVER.

		Marks.	Oz.
Exported from	Valparaiso	67,793	0
Ditto	Coquimbo	83,979	5′
Ditto	Huasco	3,879	4
Ditto	Copiapo	3,878	0
Coined in the Mint	. . . . .	5,405	0
	Total . . .	164,935	1
	Value . . .	1,484,416	1

* Guzman's History of Chile, book i. pp. 73, 74.

2 A 2

COPPER.

		Quintals.	Pounds.	Value.
Exported from	Valparaiso . .	17,771	37	
Ditto	Coquimbo . .	33,360	58	
Ditto	Huasco . . .	23,434	71	
Ditto	Copiapo . .	2,698	36	
				Dollars.
	Total . .	77,265	2	1,081,710 2¼

COPPER ORE.

		Quintals.	Pounds.	Value.
Exported from	Valparaiso . .	6,389	32	
Ditto	Coquimbo . .	9,499	0	
Ditto	Huasco . . .	20,961	92	
	Total . .	36,850	24	66,791
	Total value . . .			3,158,149 1¼

This is the treasury report for 1834, but in 1838 I was credibly informed that the amount had greatly increased, on account of the prosperity of the mines of Copiapo. Also, near to Chillan, in the province of Concepcion, a valuable gold-washing had been found. Although the vigilance of the coast-guard has diminished the clandestine exportation of the precious metals, still the small bulk of them offers such facility for smugglers, that no inconsiderable part of the mining products leaves the country without having paid the duties. Notwithstanding the cargoes of ore that are shipped off to Europe, the exportation of copper has been augmented; and, in order that the reader may form a just estimate of the progressive wealth of the mining districts, I will insert a treasury statement of the years 1831 and 1832:—

" La Serena, August 14th, 1832.

Silver.	Marks.	Copper.	Quintals. lbs.
" Exported from Coquimbo	58,907		61,892 0
" Sent to Santiago .	12,000	sent to Valparaiso	16,000 0
Total .	70,907		67,892 0

" Jose Novoa."

Although I was personally acquainted with the treasurer and collector of customs, Los SS. Almenavar, and Cordovez, I could never obtain a true statement, but I have been credibly informed that the whole amount at the custom-house, &c., did not exceed 103,000 dollars in the year 1824.

TRIBUNAL DE CUENTAS.

" The treasuries of the province and custom-houses of La Serena Huasco, and Copiapo, produced, during the years 1831 and 1832, 141,335 2¼ and 154,537 3¼ dollars.

-    " RAFAEL CORREA DE SAA."

The industry of the mining districts places more than 3,000,000 dollars in circulation annually, and their supplies are imported from Aconcagua, Santiago, Colchagua, Talca, Maule, Concepcion, and Chiloe. The following Treasury statement will show the imports of provisions from the southern provinces, by sea :—

" La Serena, July 30th, 1832.

CUSTOM-HOUSE AND TREASURY OF COQUIMBO.

Wheat	32,297	Fanegas, (150lbs).
Meal	2,809	do.
Flour	26,397	do.
Beans	6,549	do.
Walnuts	470	do.
Potatoes	550	do.
Galvanzes	93	do.
Aniseed	70	do.
Charqui (dried beef)	4,684	Quintals.
Tallow	2,462	do.
Cheese	508	do.
Butter	69	do.
Almonds	49	do.
Fat Jars	7,442	
Hams	1,066	

" JOSE NOVOA."

The prices of provisions in the year 1834, in Coquimbo, were as follows:—

Charqui . . . . . from 6 to 7½ per quintal.
Wheat . . . . . . from 3½ to 5 per fanega.
Beans . . . . . (Frijoles) 5 to 6 do.

which are considerably dearer than in the other provinces.

Wheat varies every year, according to the crops; still, the average is from 6 to 24 reals* a fanega, in the southern, and from 24 to 40 reals in the northern districts. There is a great deal of manœuvring and speculation in grain. Corn laws have been established, in order to protect the landed proprietor, viz.—When the Chilian flour does not exceed the value of four dollars the quintal, flour that is imported pays two dollars per quintal, or as follows:—

Price in Chile.	Duty on Foreign Flour.
4 dollars per quintal . . .	2 dollars per quintal.
4 to 5 do.	1 to 4
5 to 6 do. . . .	1
6 to 7 do.	4
7 upwards	Free from duty.

All the wheat and flour that is imported into Chile, can only be allowed to enter the port of Valparaiso.

Molina states that "Copiapo and Coquimbo, although near the sea, and as rich in minerals as the others, have never suffered from earthquakes; and while the other parts of the country have been violently shaken, these have not experienced the least shock, or been but slightly agitated."

However, since my residence in Chile, several severe shocks of earthquakes have been felt in this province, and particularly that of the 23rd of April, 1833, which nearly destroyed the town of Huasco, and many houses, &c. in the department.

* A dollar is eight reals.

ACONCAGUA.

This province extends from that of Coquimbo to the Cuestas de Chacabuco and La Dormida, and the rivers of Limache and Con Con; it is divided into six departments, San Felippe, Andes, Putaendo, Quillota, La Ligua, and Petorca, and subdivided into fifty-eight districts, in which are 1,380 haciendas and farms, with a population of 137,039 souls; there are three ports, Papudo, Conchali, and Quintero, and the principal rivers are Quillota, Putaendo, La Ligua, Longotoma, Quilimari, Conchali, and Chuapa, and its capital is the city of San Felipe, founded in 1740, by Don Jose Manso y Velasques. The principal pass to Mendoza is in this province, and although there are eight " boquetes," or passes in the cordilleras of Chile, this is the most frequented, for there are generally guides and muleteers in waiting at each side, to accompany and conduct travellers, and " casuchas," (hovels), constructed of brick and stone, have been erected by a former president of Chile, Don Ambrosio O'Higgins, an Irishman, where, at certain distances, shelter from tempests or snow-storms may be procured. Many dread the passage of the cordilleras, but I have known several, amongst whom were females, who have crossed them in the winter, without having experienced many difficulties; and, during my residence in Chile, few casualties occurred which had been attended with the loss of life.

This province is very fertile, and produces abundance of cattle, wheat, fruits, hemp, (the best in South America), wines, and spirits, and has many excellent gold, silver, copper, and other mines.

SANTIAGO.

This province extends from that of Aconcagua to the river Cachapaul, and is divided into six departments,

Santiago, Victoria, Rancagua, Melipilla, Casa Blanca, and
Valparaiso; these are subdivided into sixty districts, in
which are 1,788 haciendas and farms, and have a population of 253,887 souls; there are five rivers, Lampa,
Colina, Mapocho, Maipu, Cachapaul; and two seaports,
Valparaiso and San Antonio. The city of Santiago is
the capital of the republic, and was founded in 1541 by
General Valdivia; it is well built, but its churches and
public edifices are of so many different orders of archi-
tecture, that I find it a difficult undertaking to describe
them; they are generally built of burnt brick, or stone;
and some of them have withstood many earthquakes, especially those of 1647, 1657, 1822, and 1835. A procession
is held annually, in order to commemorate the earthquake
of the 13th of May, 1647, which nearly destroyed the
city. The president of the republic, and all the ecclesiastical, civil, and military bodies, with a numerous concourse of citizens, attend it; and the image of our Saviour,
"El Señor de Agonia," is carried about the city in great
pomp. This image was saved during the earthquake, and
received no other damage than that of the crown of thorns
having slipped over the head, and got tight round the
neck. El Reverendo Padre Ovalle says, in his fourth
volume of his History of Chile, that this miraculous image
"suffered no other injury than that of the crown of thorns
having got over the head, and on account of the impossibility to replace the crown there again, it has ever since
remained round the neck;" and El Illmo. Señor Don
F. Gaspar de Villarroel, bishop of Santiago, says, "that this
image of our Saviour is the work of El Padre Figeroa,
who, being neither a carver nor a joiner, made it by a
miracle."

The city of Santiago would, if it was properly regulated

PRINCIPAL SQUARE & STATE HOUSE . SANTIAGO DE CHILE.

Fisher, Son & Cº. London & Paris

by its municipal body, be one of the cleanest and most
salubrious cities in South America. It is laid out in
squares of 138 yards in front, and divided by streets of
about 11 yards in width; all are paved, and the principal
ones flagged on each side; those that run from the east to
west have canals, which are constructed to irrigate the
town, and carry off the filth.

Since my arrival in Chile, a great many improvements
have been made in the capital, and a spirit of innovation
has commenced in the mode of building, for in lieu of the
low-built houses, built of " adobes," (bricks dried in the
sun,) that took up the sixth or eighth of a square, there
are now substantial houses built of brick and stone, that
only occupy one-half of the ground, and are of two or
three stories in height. Don Ambrosio Aldunate has built
an edifice, occupying one side of the principal square,
that is four stories high; the lower range is occupied by
the stores of the most respectable tradesmen; but the
upper stories are all empty, and will, perhaps, have to
remain untenanted on account of the dread of earthquakes;
there are also a series of neat wooden shops under the
portico, which give it the appearance of a bazaar. The
state-house or palace is a long irregular building, divided
into three departments, one of which is the residence of the
president of the republic; the treasury and public offices;
municipal hall, and prison: on another side is the cathedral, and the residence of the bishop; the other is of
private dwellings and shops. In the centre of the square
is a fountain, in which is a beautiful marble monument
made in Italy, allegorical of the independence of Chile,
from which pure water gushes to supply the city.

There are two promenades; that of winter is on or along
the Tajamar, which is a series of strong parapets, that

are built of brick and stone, about eighteen feet from their
foundation, six in thickness, and well supported by buttresses; this was projected and partly built by Don Ambrosio O'Higgins, Conde de Ballenar, when he was president of Chile, and now extends along the margin of the
Mapocho, about 4,260 yards from the bridge, in order to
protect the city from the river, which, although in the dry
season it appears to be nothing but a petty stream, has often
during the rains been so swollen and rapid as to threaten
Santiago and La Chimba with destruction. I have often
heard strangers express their surprise at seeing the superb
bridge, and wonder at the Chilians having commenced such
an expensive undertaking as the building of it and the
Tajamar must have been; and the Chilians themselves
have often said,

"O vender puente, o comprar rio;"
"Either sell the bridge, or buy a river;"

in order to ridicule Los SS. O'Higgins and Zanartu,
who projected these useful, and now properly appreciated
undertakings; for had it not been for the parapets during
the year 1827, Santiago would have been washed away.

The walk on the Tajamar is incommodious, although a
favourite one; close to the city there is a short alameda,
with a few seats, and a fountain, with several willow and
poplar trees; and near to the east end is a race-ground,
where on a feast-day numbers of Chinganas are congregated.
The races in Chile are of a short distance, and from one to
two or three quadras; the horses are not saddled; they
are rode only with a sheep-skin, or cloth, and by boys who
are well trained; the horses start at full speed. The
Chilians are very fond of such sport, and there are often
races of consideration; these are run on the Lomas, a plain
about one and a half or two leagues from the capital, on

the Valparaiso road; on these occasions it is well worth the
while of a stranger to attend, for both high and low almost
vacate the capital; and there is a great display of equipages,
from that of his excellency the president, to the primitive
bullock-cart, or as our countrymen say, " Noah's arks." An
Englishman, and from Yorkshire too, Don Thomas Ap-
pelby, was fond of racing, and had one of the best breed of
horses in Chile; I saw him sell one of his mares to a commodore of the American navy for 100 dollars, an enormous
price in Chile, for the common brood-mares are only worth
from six reales to a dollar in the southern provinces. The
following advertisement copied from a Chilian paper, will
show the value of his horses.

" To complete the number required to effect the above-mentioned raffle,
only a few are wanting. Any person being desirous of a share, is referred
to the English hotel in Santiago, or to the house of D. Basilio Benegas,
called Sto. Domingo, who at the same time begs leave to impress upon the
minds of every true sportsman, that this beautiful animal is brother to the
renowned chesnut horse bought by Messrs. Sewell and Patrickson for 29
ounces, and sent to Lima; the day after the sale was made, Mr. Thomas
Roskell arrived from Lima with instructions to give 55 ounces (doubloons
of £3. 12s.) for the horse.—Mr. Richard George from the same place, who
came shortly after, would have given 1,000 dollars, and two gentlemen from
the house of Mr. Jno. Begg, were authorised to go even to the immense
sum of 2,000 dollars. This wonderful animal was the theme and admiration of every foreigner as well as the natives, for his beauty and superior
qualities, in speed, wind, and bottom. He may be justly termed the Chile
Eclipse,—he never was beat by any horse either in Chile or Peru. The
mares, sisters to the said horses, have been sold for 100 dollars and upwards.
The present horse in point of colour is by far superior, being a beautiful
jet-black fine soft hair, with only one small white speck on one hind foot.—
I have no doubt but that his racing qualities would be fully equal to the
others, were he trained for the turf.—20 ounces (doubloons of £3. 12s.)
have been offered for him by Mr. Hemmenway of Valparaiso, and 18 by
Mr. Robert Macfarlane of the same place, for the purpose of sending him
to England.

" The only motive that induces the owner to dispose of him, is in consequence of the breed now being increased.—*Mercurio de Valparaiso*.

The chinganas are held either in houses, " ramadas,"
sheds made of the boughs of trees, or in carts, that are

latticed over, and covered with gaudy trappings, and flags ;
each has two or more musicians and singers; these are
well dressed and decorated, and no small quantity of paint
is bestowed on some of their faces; their instruments are
the harp, guitar, and ravel; and as the carts and ramadas
are generally close to each other, their music, if so it may
be called, is to a stranger the most discordant noise that
can be heard; for let the reader figure to himself, about
twenty or more persons in an area of about thirty yards,
singing, or bawling as loud as their lungs will allow them, to
the tunes of the above-named instruments, as well as others
who are drumming with their hands on the bottom of the
harp, whilst the " samba queka," or other favourite step, is
danced; these are the amusements of the lower classes;
but still many even of the most respectable enjoy a " baile
de golpe," and the chingana of " Las Señoras Petorquinas,"
who were the stars of their profession, was well patron-
ized, for they drew an immense concourse on their commencement, and reaped no small emolument from their
agility.

The Alameda de la Canada is one of the handsomest in
Chile, or of any I have seen in South America. General
Don Bernardo O'Higgins commenced it in 1821, and the
following governments have continued it. It is about 970
yards in length, and may be of advantage to the proprietors
and inhabitants of the west end of the city, if the succeeding governments will take the hint, and carry the alameda
to the river, then the entrance to the city would be greatly
improved; and not only accessible to every street, but it
would increase the value of all the property in that neighbourhood.

This promenade is divided into three walks, and on
each side is a road for carriages; there are three canals

or asequias, two of which are handsomely constructed,
and lined with bricks ; there are six rows of beautiful
and shady poplars, that protect such as frequent the
walk during the day from the sun ; the middle walk is
furnished with stone seats, and at the bottom is a fountain, placed in an octagon. During the summer evenings,
and especially on a feast-day, it is a pleasure to visit this
promenade, for it is then crowded with the beauty and
fashion of the capital, who leave their equipage in the outer
street, and take a few turns, to enjoy the cool breeze, and
animate and enliven the scene.

Santiago is governed by a municipal body, and divided
into eight departments, each has an inspector, and subalterns ; there are three hospitals, a house of correction, and
depôt for the convicts, who are employed as scavengers.
The porters and water-carriers have a tax imposed upon
them, which is to assemble once or twice a month with
clubs and lassos ; they are divided into several gangs,
have a district assigned to them, and then commence at an
early hour to catch and kill every dog they meet with, in
order to free the city from them, except such as have col-
lars, or are with their owners ; a cart brings up their rear,
into which the carcasses are thrown, and no small emolument is derived from the skins ; however, this cruel spectacle might be obviated, by imposing a small tax upon
those who keep more than one dog, and a fine when found
at large, and recognized without a collar having the owner's
name and number on it.

The police of Santiago is composed of a mounted corps
of four commissaries, two adjutants, five sergeants, seven
corporals, one trumpeter, and sixty-seven men, whose duty
it is to keep order during the day ; and the night-watch is

under the control of a person appointed by government, and consists of thirty-seven on foot, and sixteen mounted : the whole are supported by a rate levied on each householder.

There are several market-places; the principal, La Recoba, is a building that occupies a "quadra," having shops on each side, and encloses a space that is divided into departments for the sale of meat, flour, fruit, vegetables, &c.; it is kept tolerably clean, and well worth the while of a stranger to visit it on a morning; but he must not expect to meet any ladies or respectable persons making purchases, for all the marketing in Chile is performed by the servants, who are tenacious of this privilege, and at times insult such foreigners as dare to introduce the custom of their own country, by being their own purveyors; for, it is a matter of notoriety, that almost every servant has his own interest at heart, and no few "llapas," douceurs, are given to the "caseres," customers.

Shopping is almost always performed by the respectable class in the evenings, and it is surprising to see their judgment of colours. A few foreigners keep retail-shops, and these are principally Frenchmen.

Few foreign merchants reside in Santiago, for ever since the custom-house has been built in Valparaiso, the principals reside there; but there are a number of tradesmen and mechanics; the last, if steady, get constant work, and I have known several, such as tailors, shoe-makers, coach-makers, cabinet-makers, &c. realize a handsome competency in a few years.

The neighbourhood of Santiago, and the valley of Mapocho, is laid out in villas and "chacaras," which are in the highest state of cultivation, and in which nearly all European fruits are grown; but their principal produce are the vine, and a species of lucerne, (alfalfa;) the latter supplies the capital with excellent forage.

The plain of Maipu, which was an uncultivated desert, and infested with robbers, has since my arrival in Chile been transformed into a multitude of good farms; and two canals have been added (to irrigate these hitherto unprofitable lands) by a joint-stock company formed in the capital; and in Coquimbo another has been established: thus by the perseverance of its spirited members, immense plains of barren lands have been brought into cultivation; since the year 1822, landed and almost every other property has increased considerably in value.

What would have been the situation of Chile had she enjoyed peace and quiet, instead of the many years of disorder and revolutions that have followed her emancipation from Spain! but now as the fertile provinces of the south are freed from that marauding banditti who so long infested them, no calculation can be made of the increasing wealth of the republic.

Foreigners are allowed to carry on mercantile affairs, deal as retailers, or follow their profession or trade, in any part of Chile ; their persons and property are respected, and protected by law, for they have the same recourse to it as the natives. Neither themselves nor their vessels can be pressed, nor detained for the public service; and in order to make their situation still more congenial to them, consuls are allowed to reside in the seaports ; all foreigners, whether resident or not, may make their wills in any part of the republic, only subjecting themselves to the same formalities and laws as the natives, without any reference to the difference of religion of the testator or heir ; they can also dispose of their property, that may be out of the

dominion of the republic, just as they may find convenient,
but must adhere to the laws with respect to what is in
Chile, with the following exceptions:—"They are not subject to the Chilian laws, that determine the legitimate portion of their descendants or ascendants, only with respect
to such as are domiciled in Chile, or who have become
citizens of the republic; they are not subject to any kind
of ' manda forzosa,' tax.

"The succession of such as die intestate, and leave property in the territory of the republic, will be ordered
according to the laws of their respective countries, but the
lawful heirs must prove them, and their family rights; but
if such heirs are established in Chile, or become citizens,
they will be subject to the laws of the country.

"Such as leave widows, 'chilenas,' cannot deprive them
of their right, although entitled to testate according to the
laws of their own country.

"The consuls may represent the rights of the heirs,
without necessity of a power of attorney; but it will be
necessary, in order to receive the property.

"If a foreigner dies without an executor or heir, the
consul must be notified, who, as soon as he hears of the
death, must take an account of the property; and should
there be no consul of the nation he belonged to, an account
of his death must be advertised in the newspapers; and a
magistrate will take an inventory, and see the property
deposited, (of such as die in Chile,) with the assistance and
intervention of the minister, or consul of the nation he
belonged to; and should there be no diplomatic agent, the
defender of absentees will act in their place.

"If the period of two years should expire after due
notice had been given to the consul, or published in the
papers, before any heir or empowered agent should pre-

vent himself to claim the property, it will be sold by auction, and the amount must be deposited in the public treasury, where it will remain for two years longer; and if not claimed within that period, it will be adjudged to the State. Such property as cannot be kept without loss, or extraordinary expenses, must be sold, with a judicial authority, on showing in a legal manner the necessity, or utility of such a sale.

" Those who hold the property in deposit are subject to all the obligations and responsibility; they have the power and faculties of administrators, and enjoy the emoluments that are allowed by the laws to the ' curators,' of the property of absent persons.

" A foreigner may, if he wishes, become a naturalized citizen of the republic, by proving that he professes some art or trade, or that he has property either in land or commerce, and that he has resided ten years in the territory of the republic; but if he has married a Chilian, three years will be sufficient ; if a foreigner, and has a family, six years. The municipal body of the town he resides in will, without any cost of stamp, &c. give him the necessary document, and then the senate will declare whether or no he will be competent; and the president of the republic order his ' carta de naturaleza' to be made out."

In conclusion: Foreigners are nowhere received with more urbanity, or treated in a more hospitable manner, than in Chile; for, nearly all I have known have, after a few years' residence, become so much attached to the country, as to leave it with regret when called away; and several who had visited Europe with their families have, as soon as they had concluded their business, returned with pleasure. This bespeaks the Chilian character.

The climate of this part of Chile is the finest in South

America, and well merits all the praises its historians
have published. The summer, which is during December,
January, and February, is not so hot as in other countries
under the same latitude; and, although the heat of the
day may at times be oppressive, the evenings and nights
are delightfully cool and refreshing; and the natives, who
generally take their "siesta" during the day, make
amends by enjoying themselves until a late hour at night,
in visiting, or other recreations, under the canopy of a
blue and cloudless sky; still the inhabitants of Valparaiso,
and other parts of the coast, enjoy a milder climate, and
are less subject to the mutations experienced near to the
Cordilleras. The winter, which is in the months of June,
July, and August, is not, as some have reported, "so very
chilly;" for, during my residence, I only on one occasion,
and that was in the month of August, 1832, saw snow
fall on the plains, and this was considered a great
novelty. There is sometimes a little frost which freezes
the water during the night, but it almost always disap-
pears before mid-day, except to the southward of the
Maule.

Still, the want of a comfortable fire-side, in lieu of the
Spanish chafing-dishes, "braseros," makes an Englishman feel the nights, during the rainy season, uncomfortable; and many have, not without great difficulty,
obtained permission to erect fire-places in the houses they
had rented; but now several of the modern buildings
have one or more fire-places, in which wood or charcoal
is burnt. It never rains on the north frontier of Chile,
except in the Cordilleras, and twice or thrice during some
winters in Copiapo; four or five times in Huasco and
Coquimbo; and more frequently in the departments of
Combarbala and Illapel.

The following observations may serve for the provinces of Aconcagua, Santiago, and Colchagua; but it may be well to remark, that the winter of 1832 was considered a severe one. I have copied them from Mier's Travels in Chile, and the Mercury of Valparaiso.*

Barometrical Observations made between Valparaiso and Mendoza, at several Stations on the High Road over the Cordillera de los Andes, in the Months of October and November, 1819.

Height of Bar.in inches.	Degree of Thermom.		Stations.	Calculated heights above level of sea in feet.	Mean estimated height.
	Attached.	Detached.			
30.002	59	57	Valparaiso in a house	30	—
28.683	68	57	Summit Cuesta of Valparaiso	1260	1269
29.023	62	60	Post-house Peñuelas.........	941	941
29.185	57	56	Casa Blanca	745	745
28.972	52	51	Vinilla.................	893	} 917
26.892	42	39	Ditto	942	
27.991	51	45	Summit Cuesta de Zapata .	1850	1850
28.855	62	61	Curicavi	1560	1560
27.4	75	62	Summit Cuesta de Prado...	2543	2543
28.184	72	65	Post-house Prado	1773	1773
28.235	55	56	Santiago de Chile..........	1665	} 1691
28.188	62	65	Ditto	1727	
27.876	62	53	Post-house Chacabuco	2020	2139
27.318	70	56	Summit Cuesta de Chacabuco	2632	2996
27.473	58	56	Villa Nueva, Santa Rosa ...	2422	—
26.898	70	67	Primera Quebrada......	3050	—

These were taken by Don Felippe del Castillo Alba,† in Santiago, by an English barometer, whose "termino medio" is 28 $\frac{20}{100}$, and in a room situated on the north side of his house, in which the barometrical height has been corrected, and was of a regular temperature.

"Santiago de Chile, 1832.

"*January.*—A slight shock of an earthquake was felt on the 18th, at five minutes past 2 P. M., and heavy thunder and lightning in the Cordilleras on the 31st, from 7 to 9 P. M.—Barometer's height 28 degrees 27½ minutes on

---

* Barometrical Observations.

† This gentleman has a chronometer and other nautical instruments, that are said to have belonged to H. M. ship Bounty, Captain Bligh; I have seen the first at the store of Mr. Smith, watchmaker, of Santiago de Chile, it was as large as a saucer, and in a silver case.

the 4th, lowest 28. 10. on the 28th, 29th, 30th, and 31st.—Maximum of Farenheit's thermometer 79. on the 28th, 29th, 30th, and 31st in the afternoon.

" *February.*—Minimum 71. on the 1st of Feb. 29., we had a slight shock on the 2nd, at 8 A. M., and thunder and lightning on the 1st, from 6 to 8 P.M. —Bar. 28. 30. on the 22nd, lowest 28. 10. on the 2nd and 3rd. — Max. ther. 82. on the 3rd, 80. and 81. on the 2nd, 6th, and 7th.—Min. 73. on the 18th.

" *March.*—Smart showers on the 14th and 27th.—Bar. 28. 35. on the 28th, lowest 23. 10. on the 14th and 21st.—Max. 68. on the 27th and 28th.

" *April*—A slight shock on the 17th, at 37 minutes past 1 P. M., and rain on the 12th, 28th, 29th, and 30.—Bar. 28. 35. on the 13th, 19th, and 23rd, lowest 28. 15. on the 1st, 6th, and 7th.—Max. ther. 72. on the 6th.—Min. 64. from the 25th to 30th.

" *May.*—A slight shock on the 9th, between 3 and 4 A. M.; rain on the 9th, 19th, and 31st.—Bar. 28. 33. on the 20th, lowest 28. 10. on the 8th. —Max. ther. 64. on the 8th.—Min. 56. on the 30th and 31st.

" *June.*—Rain on the 2nd, 5th, 6th, 14th, 24th, 28th, and 29th, with a slight frost on the 24th.—Bar. 28. 40. on the 14th, lowest 28. 11. on the 19th.—Max. ther. 58. on the 2nd and 19th.—Min. 53. on the 26th.

" *July.*—Rain the 14th, 22nd, 23rd, and 26th.—Bar. 28. 40. on the 14th, lowest 28. 10. on the 5th.—Max. ther. 53. on the 31st.—Min. 52. on the 3rd and 26th.

" *August.*—Rain on the 7th, 12th, 13th, 20th, 25th, 26th, 27th, and 30th, during the commencement slight, but latterly very heavy; on the 11th a severe hail-storm, but of short duration ; and on the 12th it snowed from 5 in the afternoon until half past 6, and the depth of the snow on the ground, and tiles of the houses was from 5 to 6 inches, which remained for 48 hours.—Bar. 28. 55. on the 31st ; lowest 28. 10. on the 3rd, 4th, and 7th.—Max. ther. 69. on the 6th.— Min. ther. 52. on the 17th and 18th.

" *September.*—Rain on the 6th with thunder, 7th, 9th, 10th, 11th, 12th, 19th, 22nd, 25th, and with hail on the 26th.—Bar. 28. 50. on the 12th; lowest 28. 05. on the 19th.—Max. ther. 61. on the 23rd.—Min. ther. 53. on the 13th.

" *October.*—Rain on the 1st, heavy and as usual on the 2nd, 6th, 30th, and 31st.—Bar. 28. 40. on the 2nd, 3rd, and 4th ; lowest 28. 05. on the 5th.—Max. ther. 64. on the 31st.—Min. 57. on the 3rd and 4th.

" *November.*—A smart shock on the 7th at 11 A.M., and on the 19th a severe one at $6\frac{3}{4}$ A.M., but no damage was done. Rain on the 3rd and 5th with some showers with thunder on the 6th.—Bar. 28. 30. on the 5th, 9th, 13th, 14th, 20th, 21st; lowest 28. 05. on the 29th. — Max. ther. 7. 5. on the 30th. — Min. ther. 62 on the 8th and 9th.

" *December.*—Cloudy with strong winds and meteors, particularly on the 20th, the 7th, 9th, 11th, 12th, 13th, 14th, and 16th.—Bar. 28. 35. on the 15th; lowest 28. 05. on the 20th, 21st, and 29th.—Max. ther. 75. on the 29th —Min. 70. on the 7th, 9th, 11th, 12th, 13th, 14th, and 16th."

In the province of Talca, Maule, and Concepcion, the rains are still more frequent, and heavier. I have known it to rain for fifteen days without ceasing, except at short intervals, during the year 1827, in Chillan. To the south-ward of the Bio Bio, and in the Archipelago of Chiloe, I was informed that it rains at least two-thirds of the year.

The snow generally commences, in the Cordilleras, in March, and continues falling until November. Hail-storms are unfrequent, and seldom do much damage.

Thunder is often heard, and lightning is seen amongst the Cordilleras ; but I have never known of its falling, or doing any damage, in the low countries. " Celages," or meteors, frequently appear, and are said to announce earthquakes ; but I have often seen them, and felt no severe shocks for many years afterwards. The winds are generally from the south-west, and blow very strong, especially when the sun is to the south of the equator ; but although it blows a gale during the day, it generally ceases, or falls calm about sun-set. The high winds during the summer, and the clouds of dust and sand they raise, are almost intolerable, especially to travellers, who prefer the night, and particularly so when they have moonlight to pursue their journey.

The north winds only blow hard when the sun is to the northward, and almost always during the winter months bring snow or rain ; there are seldom strong winds from the eastward or westward, except during the evenings or night ; those during the summer are agree-able, and often entice the Chilians to enjoy a promenade under an unclouded sky, and who, when they have moon-light, often remain in their public walks till morning.

Mr. Miers justly says, " Whatever advantages Chile may present in the excellence of its climate, and the pro-

ductiveness of so much of its soil as can be irrigated, they
are more than counterbalanced by the earthquakes, to
which the whole country is continually subject; for of all
our terrestrial phenomena, none can equal the frightful
sensations of the violent agitations of the grounds beneath
us, attended, as they are, by the loud hollow rumbling
noise which accompanies them, and by the cracking sound
of the materials of which the houses are constructed.
Nothing can be more lamentable or awful than witnessing large houses, nay, whole towns, in a short space of
time levelled to the ground, crushing perhaps in the
falling ruins their miserable inhabitants: nothing can
approach the consternation of the people, who, on the
first alarm, rush into the open air with the greatest terror
depicted on their countenances, calling for mercy and
salvation.   Even the brute creation participates instinct-
ively in the general panic; the animals, affrighted, run
in all directions, sending forth mournful cries, as if conscious of the danger that awaits them.

"Upon the first symptoms of an earthquake, all the
natives rush out of their houses, fall upon their knees,
beat their breasts violently, and cry aloud, " Misericordia!
misericordia!" (mercy! mercy!)   For three years I was
mortified at their pusillanimity, and was frequently reprimanded for never stirring out of the house upon the
occurrence of pretty smart shocks; but having been a
witness of, and a sufferer by, the great earthquake of 1822,
I confess that my courage failed me, and I was afterwards
no less forward than others in flying out of doors on the
slightest annunciation of an earthquake.   The natives
distinguish the shocks into two classes: the slighter ones
are said to be " temblores," and those strong enough to
produce fissures in the ground, or to overthrow or damage

buildings, are called "terremotos." The temblores are
of very frequent occurrence; their intervals are irregular;
they happen at all hours of the day or night, and in every
month in the year; sometimes, though rarely, at the
distance of two months; at other times at the interval of
every few days; while at others many frequently happen
in one day. Sometimes there is an indication of their
approach by a previous rumbling noise, like that of a
very heavy artillery waggon rolling quickly over a stone
pavement at a distance: at other times, the shocks happen
instantaneously, without any noise; and sometimes the
noise alone is heard without the slightest sensation of
motion. I have noticed the occurrence of strong and
frequent shocks in May or June, after the first falls of
snow in the Cordillera; or in October or November, after
a storm in the Andes. These observations, however, must
not be taken as a rule, as they may have been mere
accidental results: we cannot, indeed, reasonably expect
to meet with any exterior prognostic of these phenomena,
since they proceed from internal and subterraneous operations, the causes of which we can only conjecture.
Captain Hall's observation is correct, when he says, that
the susceptibility of persons to the approach of earthquakes increases by a continued residence in the country;
arising probably from the apprehension and a more constant anticipation of their occurrence, as well as from the
observation of the greater uncertainty of their extent,
their force, and duration. After the great earthquake of
1822, I never retired to rest without making preparations,
in anticipation of their possible occurrence, by opening
all the doors of the house, and clearing away chairs and
tables, that we might not fall over them in running into
the open air in the dark. Even in the soundest repose,

I have generally found myself upon my legs, in the act of retreating from my room, without being sensible of any motion or the first indication of the rumbling noise preceding a shock, and have even reached the open air before I was awake, or before the shock itself has followed the noise. A person who has become alive to the feeling can acutely distinguish a slight shock, when another newly arrived, and a stranger to the sensation, will notice no motion whatever.

"The great earthquake before alluded to happened during my residence at Concon, at the mouth of the Quillota, or Concon river. At half-past ten o'clock on the night of Tuesday, the 19th of November, 1822, as my family were retiring, the first oscillation was felt. It was very sudden and violent; we were all alarmed, and paused for an instant, when the falling of the glasses from the sideboard, the cracking of the timbers of the roof, and the rattling of the falling tiles, caused us to rush out of the house. The earth was violently convulsed, heaving up and down in a manner hardly conceivable, and as little capable of being accurately described, as our feelings. The timbers of a large corridor were breaking in all directions, and flying off in fragments, while the air was filled with dust from the falling roof. The situation of our two children instantaneously occurred to us. I rushed into the falling building, snatched one boy from one of the front rooms, and, carrying him in my arms, ran to the back of the house, where the other boy was in bed; my sensation in this painful situation cannot be imagined. I ran with my two boys to their mother and their aunt; and by the time I joined them, the great shock was ended; it continued about two minutes. After a lapse of about three minutes, the agitation returned violently, and con-

tinued for about a minute, when several of the strong
pillars of the corridor were shivered. During this time
there was a loud rumbling noise, like the distant echo of
thunder in a mountainous country. The heaving of the
ground seemed not only to consist of horizontal oscillations, but also of violent uplifting concussions, as if repeated explosions were exerting their force upon the roof
of a hollow cavern under our feet, threatening to burst
open the ground, or blow us all into the air. Our sensations were truly horrible. There was nothing remarkable
in the appearance or state of the atmosphere ; the moon
and stars shone with their usual resplendence. Anxious
to ascertain the state of my mills, which were on the edge
of the river, about fifty yards from the house, I proceeded
towards the spot, and was met by my English workmen,
who told me the building had been thrown down, that
the walls on both sides had been precipitated into the
mill-stream, and the roof had fallen in. While making
a survey of the damage, another violent shock warned
me of my danger : the mill at the time of the first shock
was in action ; the miller, a young man recently arrived
from England, on hearing the first noise of the earthquake, concluded that a nail, by some accident, had got between the mill-stones : he therefore shut down the sluice-
gate, and raised the running-stone. At this moment the
walls of the outer room fell, and caused him precipitately to
quit the building. During three quarters of an hour we
experienced continual and severe shocks, the intervals
between which seldom exceeded five minutes, every time
shaking down portions of the buildings. Our Creole
servants walked about the inclosure almost in a state of
despair, thumping their breasts, and repeating their Ave
Marias. Another of my English workmen, who lived in

a cottage close by, soon joined us; part of his house had been thrown down. The major-domo of the neighbouring estate, sent by his master, came to learn our fate, when we heard that his house, as well as the chapel, had also been levelled to the ground. In the course of the night, a friend came from his residence at Quintero, a few miles to the northward, to ascertain what had befallen us—his own house, like ours, had been shaken to pieces; he informed us that the ground over which he had passed was much altered, and torn in many places in wide rents. The sand-hills had been thrown into the Quintero lake, and the ford at the usual place across it was greatly swelled so that the water rose above his saddle. This appears to have been caused by an influx of salt-water into the lake, during the great rise of the sea which accompanied the first and most violent shock. At Quintero great part of the house was destroyed, and the family, consisting of my wife's sister, her husband, child, and servants, had escaped without much serious injury; though, in the endeavour to make her escape, a large book-case fell, knocked her down with her infant in her arms, and fell upon them. She was happily extricated from this perilous situation by her husband, with only a few bruises. We lighted a fire in the middle of our inclosure, and seated ourselves around it till the morning dawned, when I was better able to ascertain the damage that had been done. The house was not so much ruined as I expected; the outer walls were rent in several places, and the partition walls thrown down. I had recently put on a new roof of good carpentry, one hundred and twenty feet long and fifty wide; and this was secured by the corridor, and strong iron ties running through the walls at proper intervals, and but for this we should probably have been all buried in the ruins of the building."

I shall now introduce an account of the great earthquake experienced in Chile on the 20th of February, 1835, written by Alexander Caldcleugh, Esq., F.R.S. F.G.S. F.L.S., with which I have been favoured by the Royal Society:—

"The phenomena attending this great disturbance of the surface of the earth have been so varied, and the extent of its effects so considerable, that I should almost deviate from my duty, if I did not endeavour to draw up and transmit to the Royal Society some account of a convulsion which has laid in ruins three provinces, and caused incalculable damage to the southern part of this country. I am the more inclined to take this step, from a happy concurrence of circumstances having drawn several scientific observers to Concepcion shortly after the catastrophe, who have obligingly confided their notes to me. I trust therefore the Royal Society will not consider that I am about to trespass upon its time.

"An idea, in some degree fanciful, prevailed for some time after the conquest of these countries by the Spaniards, that these convulsions of the earth's crust occurred at intervals of a century; afterwards it was supposed that about fifty years was the term which usually elapsed between great shocks; but, since the commencement of this century, the repeated catastrophes which have occurred, especially in the years 1812 in Caraccas, 1818 in Copiapo, 1822 in the province of Santiago, 1827 in Bogota, 1828 in Lima, 1829 in Santiago, and 1832 in Huasco, have prepared the minds of the inhabitants to expect at all times these frightful oscillations of the earth, which, although they cause little sensation at first, after some time affect the nerves in a manner not easy to account for, by ordinary causes. That they happen at all times and in all states of the atmosphere seems clearly decided. The finest weather, and the most variable, equally prevail at the moment; but many are the fancied signs by which the coming earthquakes are predicted, and in the faith of which the inhabitants confide, as they think their experience bears them out. While some place great confidence in rats running violently over the ceilings of the room, others prepare for a shock when they observe the stars twinkling more than usual, and all fears are removed when much lightning coruscates in the Cordillera. As far as my own observations go, little reliance can be placed on the two former prognostics; something more certain seems to be due to the latter. A few hours previous to the earthquake which I am about to describe, immense flocks of sea-birds proceeded from the coast towards the Cordillera, a circumstance which occurred prior to the great shock of 1822; and it is affirmed, by too many respectable persons not to be entitled to some degree of credit, that on the morning of the convulsion all the dogs disappeared from Talcahuana.

" The summer in Chile had been rather colder than in preceding years. The mean of the thermometer in Santiago (two thousand feet above the level of the sea) for the months of January and February was 72° of Fahr. The mean of the barometer for the same period was 28·25, which is about one-tenth of an inch below its usual height.

"From the 1st of February the barometer was unusually low in Santiago; and on the 14th, six days prior to the earthquake, the barometer at half-past six A.M. stood at 28·1, the thermometer at the same time being 73°. A slight oscillation, which lasted twenty seconds, was felt on this day; on the 20th the barometer marked 28·17, and the thermometer rose to 76°: the weather fine. In Concepcion,

in the night of the 17th to 18th the barometer fell four-
tenths of an inch, but gradually recovered itself, and indicated nothing extraordinary on the morning of the 20th.
In Valdivia, according to the observations most obligingly
communicated to me by Captain Fitzroy, of the Beagle
surveying ship, the barometer stood on the 16th of February at 29·92, and continued to rise gradually until the
end of the month, with an increased temperature. From
my own observations, deduced from many oscillations, I
have remarked that the barometer usually falls shortly before any considerable shock, and then returns to its ordinary
mean. On the 26th of September, 1829, a very severe
earthquake was experienced in this city, which did much
damage to most buildings; the front of the house I then
inhabited fell down; and it is worthy of remark, that the
instant after every shock a burst of rain fell, which soon
moderated, until a fresh tremor caused it to re-commence.

" The igneous vents of the whole range of the Cordillera may be said to have been in remarkable activity
both preceding and at the moment of the late convulsion.
From the flat-topped volcano of Yanteles, in front of
Chiloe, to the lofty range of the Andes in Central America,
all the information which has been obtained gives details
of violent eruptions. On the 20th of January the volcano
of Osorno, north-east of Chiloe, burst forth with inconceivable fury; and the lava was seen at night rushing
out of the crater and rolling down the side of the mountain, elevated 3,900 feet above the level of the sea. The
reflection of the flame reached double that height, and is
described to me by Mr. P. G. King, of the Beagle, as
presenting the most magnificent object he had ever beheld. From the plains of Talca, eighty leagues to the
south of the capital, two volcanos were observed in activity

a few days after the 20th of February. They are both
situate near the lake of Mondaca, twenty-five leagues
eastward in the Cordillera; and another new rent was
observed on the estate called Cerro Colorado, on the right
bank of the river Maule, and near its source. The volcano
of Peteroa, and another near it, whence a stream of
asphaltum flows, and those of Maipu and Aconcagua
have been for some months in a state of activity.

"In the month of January the volcano of Coseguina
in Central America became exceedingly active, and ejected
a body of lava which covered a circumference of eight
leagues three yards and a half deep, burying all the farm-
houses, sugar-works, and cattle: the ashes continued
falling for five days, and reached upwards of three hundred leagues from the centre of desolation and ruin.

"It was at half-past eleven o'clock on the morning of
the 20th that the earthquake commenced, with an atmosphere as serene and beautiful as the elements beneath
were convulsed and threatening. The first oscillation,
gentle, and attended with little noise, was but the pre-
cursor of the two succeeding undulations, which were
extremely violent; the duration from the first to the last
vibration was about two minutes and a half, and the direction appeared to be from south-west to north-east.
The sensation occasioned by the undulatory movements,
seemed to me to be similar to that which would be produced by standing on a plank, the ends of which rose and
fell two feet from the ground. The small streams of
water which ran down the streets were checked, and
thrown over the edges of their channels. In Talca,
eighty leagues to the south, the effects were still more
violent: the oscillation commenced without being accompanied by that rumbling noise which usually is the fore-

runner of these awful phenomena. In Concepcion, where the great violence of the earthquake was felt, it was the second undulation which caused the havoc in the buildings; and previous to that and the many succeeding shocks, a violent report was heard, proceeding from the southward, as from a volcano in that direction. All the houses in the port of Talcahuano, which were situate on the low lands beneath the hills, were laid prostrate; and about half an hour after the vibration, when the inhabitants were returning to their houses from the heights and open spaces, it was remarked that the sea had retired so much beyond its usual limits, that all the rocks and shoals in the bay were visible. It flowed again, and again retired, leaving the ships dry which were at anchor in the harbour. Then an enormous wave was seen slowly approaching the devoted town, from the direction of the Boca Chica. For ten minutes it rolled majestically on, giving time to the inhabitants to run to the heights, whence they saw the whole place swallowed up by this immense breaker.

" In this moment of terror, men saw the roller with little accordance as to size; some compared it to the height of the loftiest ship, others to the height of the island of Quiriquina. It carried all before it, and rose by accurate measurement twenty-eight feet above high-water mark. A small schooner of eighty tons, nearly ready for launching, was lifted over the remains of the walls, and found lying among the ruins three hundred yards from her stocks. The reflux of this roller carried everything to the ocean. Another and a larger wave succeeded; but taking a more easterly direction, the ruins of Talcahuano escaped, but the Isla del Rey was ravaged by it. A fourth and last roller, of small dimen-

sions, advanced, but nothing was left for further devastation. While these great waves were rushing on, two
eruptions of dense smoke were observed to issue from
the sea. One, in shape like a lofty tower, occurred in
the offing; the other took place in the small bay of San
Vicente, and after it had disappeared, a whirlpool succeeded, hollow, in shape like an inverted cone, as if the
sea were pouring into a cavity of the earth. In every
direction in this bay, as well as in Talcahuano, vast bub-
bles broke, as if an immense evolution of gas were taking
place, turning the colour of the water black, and exhaling
a fœtid sulphureous odour.

"At San Tomé, on the other side of the bay, the roller
did immense damage; and on the island of Quiriquina
the cattle dashed off the cliffs from panic. In this island
the waves injured houses forty feet above the present
level of high water, and during the three following days
the sea ebbed and flowed irregularly.

"In the bay of Concepcion, the strata of clay-slate have
been visibly elevated, from about three to four feet. This
alteration of the relative position of sea and land is clearly
distinguishable, by a rock off the landing-place, which,
previous to the shock, was nearly level with high water,
being subsequently found to be raised three feet higher;
and the buoy on the Belen Bank has now four feet less
water than formerly. A vessel lying at anchor had one
fathom less water alongside her than before the shock;
but it is very likely that she changed her position. At
the port of San Vicente, a little to the south of Talcahuano,
the land has also risen about a foot and a half; and along
the shore of the latter bay, even at high water, beds of
dead muscles were left as proofs of the upheaval of the
strata.

" To the southward of the entrance of the bay of Concepcion there is a small island called Santa Maria, about seven miles long and two wide. Capt. FitzRoy examined with great care the line of beach in the southern cove, as well as the northern part of the island ; and from the visible evidence of beds of dead shell-fish, from soundings, and from unbiassed oral testimony, it appears placed beyond the shadow of doubt, that on the latter side the elevation of the land has not been less than ten feet, in the centre of the island about nine, and in the southern cove about eight feet. This upheaving has almost destroyed the southern port of the island, for it now affords but little shelter to vessels, and the landing is bad. Everywhere around the island the soundings have been diminished a fathom and a half; and the cliffs, of the height of 150 or 200 feet, are split and rent in all directions, and huge masses precipitated below. Both Captain FitzRoy and Captain Simpson, of the Chilian navy, are of opinion that the uprising of the strata, both in this island and in Concepcion, at the time of the earthquake, was considerably greater, and that the many subsequent minor oscillations may have caused a subsidence to the level before recorded. At Subul, a little to the southeast of Santa Maria, the elevation of the strata appears to have been about six feet.

" At Nuevo Bilbao, the port of the river Maule, seventy leagues north of Concepcion, about an hour and a half after the shock, the sea flowed above the usual water-mark, and continued for half an hour in that state before a reflux took place. Fifty minutes afterwards the sea, greatly agitated, rolled on the coast and up the river with extraordinary violence, and reached a height of twelve feet above the water-mark. By this last inroad,

2 c

two schooners, anchored in the port, carried away their
cables, and were found among the bushes one hundred
and fifty yards from the beach.

" A third rush of the sea occurred half an hour afterwards, which ascended to a height of nine feet; and for
the space of forty-eight hours repeated rollers came forward, but with diminished violence. No elevation of the
coast has been discovered at this port, but on the bar at
the mouth of the river, which has always rendered the
entrance to the port both difficult and dangerous, two
feet more water has been remarked ; and in consequence
of the fall of an immense point of a mountain into the
sea, it is hoped that, owing to the new direction given to
the current, no further accumulation of sand will take
place.

" In Valparaiso the sea was observed to advance and
recede rapidly, but gently and without violence.

" It would be of little avail to distress the Society with
the details of the ruin caused in all the southern provinces
of Chile by this convulsion. To the southward of Talca
scarcely a wall has been left standing, and even to the
north of this line the damage caused to every description
of building has been most serious. Throughout the provinces of Cauquenes and Concepcion, the entire crust of
the earth has been rent and shattered in every direction.
In some places fissures of several feet in depth and width
have been discovered, intersecting the country for considerable distances. On one estate near Chillan, thirty
leagues from the coast, extensive fissures have been the
vents of muddy eruptions of salt water, which have made
large deposits of a kind of grey pulverulent tufa; and on
the same estate a great many circular pools of salt
water were discovered, and many new thermal springs

Furland lith

SUGAR MILL DRIVEN AT JUAN PERNAMBIZ, PORTO DE FEBRE, 1835.

J. & P. London & Paris

have burst forth. In many places the ground swelled like a large bubble, and then bursting, poured forth black and extraordinarily fetid water.

"The limits to which the oscillations extended were, to the north as far as Coquimbo, and to Mendoza on the eastern ridge of the great chain of the Andes. Vessels navigating the Pacific within a hundred miles of the coast experienced the shock with considerable force. The bark Glenmalia, bound to Valparaiso, when ninety-five miles from the coast, and in front of the Maule, had her course through the water suddenly checked, and her rate of sailing altered from seven knots to one, and the master conceived the vessel was dragging over a sand-bank. The sea was strongly agitated, and appeared to lift the vessel twenty feet. Such was the alarm, that the boats were nearly lowered; no soundings were met with.

"The Island of Juan Fernandez, a mass of basalt three hundred and sixty miles from the coast, experienced the earthquake, but with less violence; the sea rose to the height of the Mole in a similar manner to that of Concepcion, and then receded, leaving the bottom of Cumberland Bay dry to some distance from the shore, and in the second rush rose fifteen feet above the usual level, carrying all before it. At the same time the governor, Major Sutcliffe, observed a dense column of smoke issuing from the sea about a mile off the Point Bacalao, which lasted until two o'clock in the morning, when an immense explosion took place, which threw the water in every direction; during the rest of the night great bursts of flame rising from the same spot illumined the whole island. Captain Simpson, about a month after, sounded near the spot in every direction, and found no bottom in less than sixty-nine fathoms. It is worthy of remark, that

2 c 2

when on the 24th of May, 1751, the city of Concepcion
was destroyed by an earthquake, and by the inroad of
the sea, the rising colony of Juan Fernandez was swallowed up in a similar manner by immense rollers. The
governor, his family, and thirty-five persons, perished by
the catastrophe.*

"After the earthquake, the usual atmospheric changes
occurred. In many places the most awful hurricanes
completed the dismay of the inhabitants, and added to the
catastrophe. To these succeeded deluges of rain, a
circumstance most unusual at that period of the year.
At the hot springs of Cauquenes, where the water issues
at the temperature of 118° of Fahr., the heat was lowered
after the earthquake to 92°, a circumstance which occurred after the shock of 1822. The diminished temperature lasted but a short time.

"At the risk of being tedious, I have given a detail
to the Society of the changes effected in the earth's surface
by this violent convulsion. After examining the extensive area of its vibration, after observing the uprising of
an island and the adjacent coast, together with the erup-
tion of a submarine volcano, it is difficult to deny that the
same causes are still in operation, which ages since raised
tertiary formations to their present lofty site in the great
range of the Cordillera. Surrounded with these continued changes on the surface of the earth, it is impossible
not to respect the opinions of those philosophers who conceive that the continent of America has risen into existence
at a more modern period than that which therefore may,
with more propriety, be termed the Old World.

* The author of this journal published an account of the earthquake
that occurred on the Island of Juan Fernandez, in a separate form, which
may be hrᵈ of all booksellers.

" Owing to the early hour on the 20th that the oscillation commenced, comparatively few lives were lost, but
the frequent occurrence of these catastrophes, by causing
organic defects, may very probably explain the causes of
the short duration of human existence in these countries."*
    " Santiago de Chile, 12th June. 1835."

PROVINCE OF COLCHAGUA.

This province extends from that of Santiago to the
river Teno; it has three other rivers, Rio Claro, Tinguirica, and Chimbarongo, that unite with the Cachapaul, which takes the name of El Rapel before it enters
the sea; there are also several rivulets, the largest of
which is El Bichuquen.   In this province are three
lakes, Tagua-Tagua, Cauquenes, and Caguil ; the latter
was occasioned by an explosion of the volcano of Peteroa,
which took place on the 3rd of December, 1760, and
threw out such a quantity of lava and ashes, that it
filled the neighbouring valleys, and caused the waters of
the Tinguirica, as well as the course of another river, to rise,
the latter being impeded, for ten days, by part of a mountain
which fell, and filled its bed.   The water at length forced
a passage, overflowed all the neighbouring plains, and
formed the lake.†   Tagua-Tagua covers a large extent,
and is beautifully studded with islands, which, as well as
the shores, are covered with trees.   Numbers of swans,
flamingoes, scarlet and white spoonbills, wild geese. ducks,
and divers, frequent the lake ; besides a species of otter,
called guillins, and quipos : here is an abundance of fish,
principally truchas and pexereys.

The lake of Cauquenes is in the Cordilleras, and often
nearly dry ; it abounds in wild-fowl, and in its neigh-

* Don Alexander Caldeleugh's report.   † Molina's History.

bourhood are the famous baths of Cauquenca, visited
by invalids who have rheumatic complaints, or by
others that have required the use of mercury. During
the summer months many resort to Cauquenes for amusement, or to visit such of their friends as are invalids; here
is a square building called an inn, where accommodation
may be had at a reasonable rate; but it is advisable
for such as have to remain for any period, to provide their
own bedding and plenty of blankets, and not to depend
altogether on the innkeeper for their comforts. There
are four baths or holes, about five feet long, two of which,
El Pelhambre and Pelhambrillo, are so hot, that it is
painful to remain in them for the time prescribed for im-
mersion. When the patient is taken out of the bath, his
attendants wrap him up in blankets, and carry him to
bed; when the perspiration that ensues is excessive. All
whom I have known to have visited these baths have
declared the cure to be effectual, and many arrive from
Peru, and other parts of South America, to visit the baths
of Cauquenes and Colina.

Molina says, " that mineral waters are common in
Chile. The most celebrated are those of Peldegua and
Cauquenes. The source of the former is on the summit
of one of the exterior mountains of the Andes, to the
north of Santiago. It consists of two springs of very
different temperature, one hot, and the other cold; the
former is sixty degrees above the freezing point by
Reaumur's thermometer, the latter four degrees below it.
They are about eighty feet distant, and their waters are
united by means of canals, so as to form a tepid bath,
which is found very efficacious in many disorders. The
water of the hot spring is oily to the touch, and foams
like soap-suds; it abounds with mineral alkali, which

appears to be combined with an unctuous substance in a state of solution. It is clear, inodorous, impregnated with a very little fixed air, and its specific weight is but two degrees above that of common distilled water. Its heat is probably owing to the effervescence of a large body of pyrites in the vicinity of its source. The water of the cold spring is iron and vitriolic, and, when mixed with that of the warm, deposits Glauber's salt and a yellowish ochre."

The baths of Cauquenes are in one of the valleys of the Cordilleras, near the source of the Cachapaul. The springs are numerous, and of various qualities and temperatures. Some of them are cold, others hot; some acidulated, and impregnated in a greater or less degree with iron; while others are alkalescent or vitriolic, and several, like those of Pisa, are merely gaseous. The principal spring is very warm and sulphuric; its margin is covered with a yellow efflorescence of sulphur, and the water has a strong hepatic smell; it contains, besides, an alkali and a neutral salt. The surrounding mountains abound with every kind of mineral, and near the spring are great numbers of willows, which are covered with a species of manna, in globules of the size of grains of gunpowder.

The province of Colchagua is very fertile, and exports great quantities of grain, cattle, charke, dried fruits, and wine; there are many gold mines, some of which are worked by foreigners, especially those of Yaquil, belonging to my friends Los SS. Davidson and Nixon. Marbles of a superior quality, both of the black and variegated kinds, may be got in any quantity near to San Fernando; and yeso (calx vulcanica) is abundant in the Cordilleras of this province; this is used by the Chilians in their

process of making wines, as well as in whitewashing
their edifices and houses; the coast abounds in salt-water
lakes, and from which great quantities of salt is procured.

The original inhabitants of this province were the
Promaucians, a brave race of people, that repelled the
invasion of the Incas of Peru, who had conquered all
the northern part of Chile. The Spaniards under
Almagro found the Promaucaes too powerful for them;
but Valdivia, in 1545, by his sagacity and prudence,
induced these brave warriors to become his faithful
auxiliáries, and with their assistance he continued his
conquest into the Araucanian territory.*

The city of San Fernando is the capital of the province, it was founded in 1741 by El Conde de Superunda: it is laid out in squares; and has two convents,
besides a parish church. This city has not progressed
much since Chile has gained her independence; for it is not
only menaced by the river Tinguirica, which has done considerable damage, but it has been in contemplation to
remove the archives, and make Curico the capital of the
province. This change has caused many bickerings, and is
supposed to have created the disturbances that brought on
the revolution of 1829 and 1830; for it was here that
Los SS. Urriola and Silba corrupted the battalion
No. 6, which attacked the legal authorities in Santiago
in 1828, and finally aided in defeating the liberals at
Lircai.

The province is divided into three departments, San
Fernando, Curico, and Rengo, which are subdivided into
16 districts, containing 21 parishes, 24 public schools,

---

* The Promaucians have been celebrated by the Spanish poet, Ercilla,
see " La Araucana," Book i. pages 13 to 15.

2,562 haciendas and farms, with a population of 167,518 souls.

The following report of the province, relative to the earthquake of 1835, was drawn up by the governor-intendant.

" Intendencia of Colchagua,
                                " San Fernando, February 27, 1835.
" Señor Ministro,

" At twenty-six minutes past eleven on the morning of the 20th, this province has experienced a frightful earthquake; and the moment it had ceased, I sent circulars to the governors of the departments, requesting them to forward all the particulars, in order that I might make a circumstantial report to the supreme government, of the damage, &c.

" This city has not suffered much from the shock, and I have heard that little damage has been done in the neighbourhood; but as I cannot depend upon this information, I will inform V. S. as soon as I have received answers to my circulars.

                    " Dios Guarde, A. V. S.
                    .   " FELICIANO SILVA."

In the principal towns in this province, only the churches and public buildings suffered ; the roofs were much injured, and a few old houses fell, but no lives were lost.

PROVINCE OF TALCA.

This is the smallest province in Chile, and, until 1833, was a department of that of Colchagua, from which it is separated by the river Lontue, and extends to the river Maule; it is divided into 17 districts, which contain six parishes, 472 haciendas and farms, with a population of 60,810 inhabitants. The city of Talca is the capital of the province, and was founded in the year 1742 by

El Conde de Superunda, near to the rivers Claro and
Lircai: there are many good gold and copper mines in
this province; and amongst the former are those of
Chuchunco, and El Chivato, on the banks of the Maule;
there are also good gold-washings, and other minerals,
and beautiful marbles.   Molina says, that " a little hill
at the north-east of Talca consists almost entirely of
amethysts. Some are found enclosed in a grey quartz,
which serves them for a matrix, and others isolated
among the sand. They are more perfect both in colour
and hardness in proportion to their depth; and were
those who search for them to dig deeper, they would,
most probably, discover them in the highest state of
perfection. A short time before I left Chile, I saw some
that were of a beautiful violet, and would cut glass
repeatedly without injuring their points.

Among them were a few of as fine a water as the
diamond, and, perhaps, they may serve as precursors to
that most valuable gem. They are so abundant, that, in
some of the crevices of the rocks, those of a fine purple
may be discovered at almost every step."

There is also " a little hill which furnishes a species
or cement sand, known by the name of Talca sand, (arena
talcensis). This sand is finer than that of Puzzuoli in
Italy, and appears to be a volcanic production, as its
earthy and ferruginous parts are half calcined. The
inhabitants employ it, in their buildings, for those walls
which they intend to whiten; as of itself it forms a very
strong cement, to which the lime adheres firmly."

The city of Talca is half way between Santiago and
Concepcion, and about 270 miles from Valparaiso; yet it
has the advantage of having a navigable river, El Maule,
which receives El Rio Claro, about four leagues and a half

from it, and by which the produce may be easily transported to the port of Bilbao or Constitution. This may
in a short time be a great trading place. During the
administration of General Pinto, steps were taken to
improve it, and Captain Forster of the C. N. was sent
there for that purpose: the port, as it is, cannot be
entered by vessels that draw more than eleven feet, for
the bar is dangerous; yet with a little expense, and an
experienced person who would undertake to make a
breakwater, to connect a point of land with a reef that
forms a bank at the entrance of the Maule, so as to
prevent the river during the rainy seasons from flowing
over it; the channel would then be deepened, and vessels
of heavy burden might enter with safety. The harbour is
capable of holding many vessels; and it is well sheltered
from the prevailing winds: the only inconvenience is that
of the sudden rise of the waters, whereby vessels have
been carried out to sea, and lost: an old comrade of mine,
Major Carson, who had received a pension for his services,
had settled here, and was carrying on a good coasting-
trade; but one night his vessel, completely laden, was
taken out to sea; her crew managed to leave her before
she crossed the bar; she was a fine schooner, called the
Juanna. A Chilian man-of-war fell in with the vessel
not far from the port of Valparaiso, her commander
boarded her, and found the hatches battened down, and
in good order, her anchors out, and a dog on board;
however, although the Monteagudo was bound to Valparaiso, this naval officer, knowing that the vessel belonged
to a " Gringo," would not allow any of his crew, although
he was intreated to do so, to man her, and conduct her to
port. The English commodore ordered a vessel to go in
search of the schooner, as soon as he heard of the circum-

stance. The governor of Valparaiso, after a considerable delay, sent a vessel also; but no tidings were brought back of the schooner, and poor Carson lost his all. The foreign merchants offered to purchase him another vessel, &c.; but he was so sorely annoyed at the conduct of the commander of the Monteagudo and his partisans, the Godos, that he would not risk any capital during their administration.

Much timber is carried from this port, and as it is plentiful and cheap, several foreigners have commenced building vessels. A couple of small steamers would do well, were they to ply between this port and Valparaiso, for they could ascend the Maule, and its tributary rivers, Rio Claro and Longomilla, where produce may at all times be purchased cheaper than in any other part of Chile, and be had in great abundance. This port suffered greatly during the earthquake; as will sufficiently appear from the following account of that dreadful calamity.

"Talca, February 26, 1835.

" I had commenced this letter in the port of Constitution, and discontinued on account of the earthquake of the 20th.

" The first shock was announced with the usual warnings, so that every one had time to escape.

" The earthquake lasted about two minutes and a half, but the shocks did not exceed a minute.

" The town has been completely destroyed; the earth opened in many places, and water issued from the fissures, that alarmed us; but what filled us with consternation was a violent inundation of the sea, that took place one hour and a half after the shock, so that the

river rose about three yards, and in thirty minutes fell to
its level again.

"I was with a friend on the side of the hill observing
this extraordinary phenomenon, which, after a space of
fifty minutes, was repeated, and then the sea was agitated
as if with a tempest; the river rose to about four yards,
and the vessels broke from their anchorage, one of which
was left in a potatoe field: the flux and reflux continued
for forty-eight hours, when the sea and river returned
to their natural level.

"*El Araucano*, No. 234, March 6th, 1835."

"Intendencia de Talca.
                                        "February 22, 1835.
"Señor Ministro,

"The morning of the 20th of this month appears to
have been destined as the epoch in which Talca was to
have disappeared from the list of cities.

"At twenty minutes past eleven the earth began to
shake gently, without any rumbling noise, as has been
observed in other earthquakes. This alarmed the inhabitants, who, fearful of the results, fled from their dwellings, and a most terrible shock followed, that in less than
three minutes reduced the city to ruins.

"In a word, the earthquake has caused so many
lamentable effects, that the greatest part of the citizens
have been obliged to accommodate themselves in straw
huts, or beneath trees.

"The effects of the earthquake have been with very
little difference the same as in all the province; the particulars of which I must defer detailing until I obtain exact
information. The only consolation we have is, that the
Omnipotent Being has, amidst the tribulation with which
he has afflicted this city, been merciful, for we have only

lost twelve persons killed, and three badly hurt. Still
the conflict of the inhabitants is considerably augmented,
on account of the near approach of winter, and the
scarcity of our resources whereby we might be enabled to
construct a place to dwell in.

" Dios Guarde A. V. S.
" JOSE DOMINGO DE BUSTAMANTE."

The city of Talca was well built, and had a fine parish
church, with convents of the Franciscan, Dominican,
Augustin, Mercedari, Jesuits' college, and an hospital,
dedicated to San Juan de Dios. This was a fine building, and did credit to its munificent founder, El Conde
de Maule; there was also a fine municipal hall, and a
large building for exercicios. Talca has fifteen districts,
and was the second inland city of Chile, and its inhabitants of some of the best families, and mostly decided
patriots; still it was in its neighbourhood, Cancharayada
and Lircai, that the Spaniards and their prototypes
defeated their opponents.

PROVINCE OF MAULE.

This province extends from the river Maule to the Nuble;
it has seven other rivers, Longomilla, Putagan, Achiguena,
Longabi, Purapel, Perquilanquen, and Niken; six of these
enter the first, which is navigable to that of Niken. The
port of Constitution belongs to this province; and the
city of Cauquenes is the capital. There are five departments, Linares, Parral, San Carlos, Qurihue, and Cauquenes; these contain thirteen parishes, 2,219 haciendas
and farms, and 120,185 inhabitants. This province is rich,
for its productions of grain, wine, fruits, cattle, cheese, (the
best in South America), gold mines and lavaderos, salt and

timber, are abundant, all which may be conducted by water
to the port. The following are the official and private
accounts of the disasters occasioned by the earthquakes:—

" Intendencia del Maule.

" Señor Ministro,

" This is written on a hill close to where the city stood,
and from whence I direct it to V. S., that S. E. may be
informed that Cauquenes, as well as all the towns of the
province, have been totally destroyed by an earthquake
on the 20th of this month, at a quarter past eleven. Only
seven dead bodies have as yet been found, but it is feared
many more are interred in the ruins, which, as soon as
the movements of the earth cease, which still frequently
occur, will be sought for. This is all I can report at
present.

" Dios Guarde A. V. S., Domingo Urutia."

" Cauquenes, February 22, 1835."

" I went to El Parral, to see if ought could be saved
from my ruined granaries, and witnessed the most singular
phenomena :—first, a storm, where hailstones as large
as filberts, not only destroyed the wheat that had been
collected in heaps and covered with straw, but entirely
demolished farms, vineyards, &c. Next a furious whirlwind, that tore up and destroyed trees, huts, &c. and
carried the roofs, as well as a wine-press, into the air, and
made such a noise, that the theologians of the place 'said
it was the last trumpet.' All the women paraded about,
begging mercy, with the images of saints that had been
disinterred from the ruins. In the seventy districts of
this province there is not an edifice left standing."

This province extends from that of El Maule to the
river Imperial, and is divided into eight departments,
Concepcion, Talcahuano, Puchacay, Rere, Laja, Lautaro,
Coelemu, and Chillan; these contain 2,698 haciendas, and
118,384 inhabitants. Its principal rivers are, the Bio
Bio, Damas, Carampangue, Cauten, Tabalobo, Laja, and
Bergara; there are several other considerable streams,
and four small lakes; and the principal sea-port is Talcahuana, (open to foreigners), the rest, Colcura, Tome, and
other bays, are only visited by coasters.

Concepcion, were it not for earthquakes, inroads of
the Indians, and ravages of domestic marauders, would
now have been the wealthiest province in Chile. The
fertility of its soil, temperature of its air, abundance of
grain, fruits, wines, (the best in Chile), rich gold-mines
and lavaderos, especially those recently discovered near
Chillan, supply of fish, and, above all, its incomparable
bay and port of Talcahuana, will, notwithstanding those
fearful drawbacks, induce many to migrate, and settle
there. I visited Talcahuano and Concepcion six months
after the earthquake of 1835, and found many substantial
stores and houses erected, both in the port and city,
mostly by foreigners; others had erected flour and
saw mills, and a bay-fishery for whales has been established by some foreigners, headed by one called the

Flying Dutchman, on the Island of Quiriquina, from whence
ana bundance of excellent testaceous fish, choros and picos,
are procured, and sent to every part of Chile. Numbers
of seals and sea-otters are caught on this coast and
adjacent islands.

The city of Penco, or Concepcion, was founded by
General Valdivia, in October, 1550, and soon became the
second city in Chile, but it was abandoned and afterwards
destroyed by the Indians, by whom, under Lautaro, it
was burnt down in 1554; it was again rebuilt, and that
Indian destroyed it again, after having massacred the
garrison and inhabitants. Don Garcia de Mendoza
rebuilt the city, and, being well fortified, it withstood
repeated attacks of the Indians until the year 1603, when
it was destroyed, as well as all the cities and towns founded
in the Araucanian territory, by the great Indian warrior
Paillamachu.

It was rebuilt again and well fortified, and was the
most populous city in Chile, for the Indians had ceased to
molest it; but in 1730 it was totally destroyed by an
earthquake, attended by an inundation of the sea, which
overflowed the greatest part, and swept away everything
that it met with in its course. Notwithstanding these repeated misfortunes, the inhabitants obstinately resolved to
persevere, and built it anew in a handsome manner, but did
not enjoy it long, for in the month of May, 1751, this
devoted city was again destroyed by an earthquake, and
an influx of the sea, which entirely covered it: the inhabitants fortunately escaped, and took refuge in the
neighbouring hills, but continued for thirteen years in an
unsettled state, not being able to agree among themselves
in rebuilding it. At length they resolved to abandon
its former site, and founded a new city at the distance of

2 D

a league from the sea in a beautiful plain, called Mocha, upon the northern shore of the Bio Bio. In 1603, Concepcion was erected into a bishopric; there were six convents, San Francisco, Santo Domingo, Mercedes, San Augustin, San Juan de Dios, and Trinitarian nuns, besides a college of Jesuits. The cathedral was a fine edifice, there were many other buildings of note, and the city had become very populous, when it was again destroyed on the 20th of February, 1835. The following are the official and private accounts of that dreadful calamity :—

" Govierno Militar de Valparaiso.

" March 5th, 1835,

" Señor Minister,

" By the correspondence and passengers that have arrived on the 3rd, 4th, and to-day, the information we have received respecting the earthquake of the 20th of February, and its disasters in the province of Concepcion and Maule, has been confirmed.

" Concepcion, Talcahuano, Penco, Tome, Arauco, Colcura, Pemuco, Yumbel, Rere, Los Angeles, La Florida, Coelemu, Ranquil, Cauquenes, San Carlos, Quirigue, and other towns of these provinces, have been totally destroyed, as well as the ports of Talcahuano, Penco, Tome, and Constitucion, that were inundated by the sea, which also rose as high as the walls of Arauco, and Colcura.

" In Concepcion about fifty individuals have perished, but few are missing in Talcahuano, on account of the inhabitants having had time to escape before the town was inundated.

" Little damage has been done to the shipping, except

the national schooners, Juana, and Jertrudis, that have
been left high and dry in the port of Constitucion.
"Dios Guarde A. V. S.
"RAMON CAVAREDA."
El Araucano, No. 283.

The governor-intendente of the province of Concepcion reports:—"From Concepcion, in the midst of
its ruins at half-past six in the evening of the 20th of
February, 1835 :—

"Señor Minister,
"A tremendous earthquake has entirely destroyed this
city; not a temple, public edifice, house, or a single
room, has escaped; the ruin has been complete, and the
horror frightful; there are no hopes of Concepcion, nor
have I expressions wherewith to describe the dreadful
catastrophe. This may appear exaggerated, but it is in-
sufficient. The families are wandering about, errant and
bewildered, there is no safe retreat or shelter for them—
all, all is in ruins, our age has not witnessed such complete or universal destruction. Do me the honour to
inform S. E. of our sufferings, and state that I have not
yet heard the results.
"Dios Guarde A. V. S.
"RAMON BOSA."
El Araucano, No. 233.

A PRIVATE LETTER.
"Concepcion, February 22, 1835.

"Who could have expected, my dear R., that I should
ever be enabled to write to thee again! preserved as
I have been by a miracle from the terrible earthquake of
the 20th!

2 D 2

" I scarcely believe that I may yet be permitted the pleasure of speaking to thee! how horrible! I was dictating the last correspondence, in order to despatch the post, when about three-quarters past eleven in the morning, I felt the first impulse of the earthquake, that in a few moments reduced the city of Concepcion to be nothing but a vast and afflicting heap of ruins.

" I ran directly to the court of the " intendencia," for as the edifices began to totter and fall around me, sentiments of self preservation made me use every exertion to extricate myself, and find my way I scarcely knew how through the immense clouds of dust that arose from the ruins, and observed the horizon, for I could scarcely discern objects that were within my reach; but, how prodigious! For, during this conflict of nature a sudden gust of wind cleared the atmosphere. I saw the gateway, and rushed into the street, which to my terror had several rents: my house was in the front of me, I saw the roof fall in and bury everything.

" The necessity I had of attending to the sufferers in general, made me forget my own losses, nor can I yet learn what has been the fate of my books, documents, &c. and should it rain all will be lost.

" I traversed the ruins in every direction to procure the help of the police, for it was necessary to, attend to extinguish the fires, that almost always occur during such calamities. Concepcion has disappeared: there is not a single dwelling. I reside with the intendent in the principal square, and write this to thee at twelve o'clock at night, on my knees under a shed where several families are huddled together, for there is no other accommodation; besides which, I am badly provided with writing materials; this, and the fatigue of having been in constant bustle and apprehension ever since our troubles commenced, impede me from relating to thee all the incredible disasters I have witnessed.

" No correct account of the numbers that have perished has yet been obtained; fifty bodies have been found amongst the rubbish, two are of elderly ladies, who have left no family ; and the searchers are still busy amongst the ruins. However, the number of individuals that have been found missing are inconsiderable, amidst such devastation.

" By the next opportunity, further details will be communicated to thee by thy brother."

El Araucano, No. 238.

" Intendencia de Concepcion, March 5, 1835.
" Señor Minister,

" I herewith forward to V. S. copies of the reports given to this intendencia, by the governors of the departments, in which they announce their ruin.

" We still experience continual shocks, but none like that of the fatal day in which the fright of the second shock made the greatest part of the inhabitants fly to the neighbouring hills, where they remained for several days ; and such was the want of shelter, that they had not wherewith to defend themselves from the scorching rays of the sun, which were almost intolerable. The heights were covered with fires during the nights, that dispelled the darkness, for their light seemed to console them during their sufferings.

" Members of each family sought each other, for the instinct of self-preservation had made all escape as they could. How afflicting it was to see fathers and mothers climbing the heaps of rubbish, amidst clouds of dust that almost obscured the atmosphere, in order that they might save their children, or relatives, in the vicinity of their homes, or schools!

"These spectacles were frequent, and repeated in every direction; and the streets, which for moments were freed from the clouds of dust that arose from the fallen edifices, presented to our view numerous inhabitants, whose lamentations at times broke through the air, and deafened the subterraneous noises that occurred during the shocks that succeeded each other.

"It is impossible for me to describe every particular occurrence that took place during this terrible earthquake, or enumerate the extent of its disasters.

"In the midst of so much destruction, there has as yet been only fifty-one killed, and eight badly hurt; many have received contusions, and it is impossible to collect an exact account, until the whole of the inhabitants return to the city.

"After the first moments of terror and dismay, I turned my attention towards protecting the property, extinguishing the fires, and preparing everything necessary to extricate such as had fallen amongst the ruins. The troops of the garrison were detached to cover different parts of the city, where they still remain, and the police are patrolling day and night.

"The intendencia, public offices, and troops are accommodated in the principal square under sheds built of timber, &c. procured from the ruins; but this shelter had scarcely been erected, to screen us from the burning sun that was so severely felt during the first four days, when on the 5th we had a severe shower, and continual rain for several hours during the day and night. This came as if were to consummate the ruin that the earthquake had commenced.

" The unfortunate inhabitants were exposed to the inclemency of the rain, nor had they time to save the remains of their property that had been buried. It is therefore incalculable the losses that this accident had occasioned. But what will the extent of damage be in the province, at a time when all the crops of grain, its principal production, have been without shelter from the rain ; besides which, nearly all the roads that cross the mountains are destroyed, nor can they easily be repaired under existing circumstances.

" We were sorely afflicted with the idea that the whole of the cities of the republic had experienced the dreadful effects of the earthquake, founded on the extra-ordinary violence we had felt, and with which its first shocks reduced this city to ruins ; and the unusual move-ment of the earth, which was accompanied with a dreadful roar, that made it appear as if waves were coming from the southward, where it has originated; and what is most remarkable is, that each shock was accompanied with a noise, as if occasioned by the explosion of a volcano in that direction.

" My fears were still augmented with the daily intel-ligence of the devastation of the cities of the neighbouring provinces of El Maule, and Talca; but it is impossible for me to describe the heartfelt pleasure and universal content that we all experienced when we received the joyful intelligence that the capital, and ' other towns in the northern provinces, had escaped the dreadful calamity.

" This statement does not contain a proper or cir-cumstantial account of what has occurred, nor ought I to occupy my time any longer, whilst so many sufferers require my utmost exertions to alleviate their miseries.

"Do me the honour to explain this to S. E.

"Dios Guarde A. V. S.

"RAMON BOSA."

El Araucano, March 16.

"Govierno de Talcahuano,

"Señor Intendente,   "February 23, 1835.

"My hand trembles whilst I am describing the dreadful spectacle this town presents, and that ten days ago formed the hopes of this province, but is now nothing more than a heap of ruins, nor can we ever calculate on its re-edification.

"On the 20th instant, at twenty minutes past eleven o'clock A. M., we experienced a most tremendous earthquake, which in the space of three minutes threw down all the roofs, and the greatest part of the edifices of this town; and the almost continuous shocks which followed, augmented progressively the destruction.

"About half past twelve o'clock there appeared near the Boca-Chica, and near the coast of Tome, an immense rolling wave, which in a majestic but dreadful manner advanced, overwhelmed, and destroyed the numerous villages on the coast, overturning the rocks in its passage; and, to consummate the work of destruction, sweeping to their foundation the edifices to the eastward.

"In a few minutes the sea receded about twelve quadras, leaving the vessels in the bay dry, carrying with it the property which formed the fortunes of my townsmen, and of the inhabitants of the province; and it was as if the inhabitants of the centre, and the creek (caleta), were not to be favoured, for there came at half past one a mass of water, as smooth as a basin of milk, which bathed all that had escaped the fury of the first rollers, and destroyed their habitations. About twenty minutes after the sea retired, the vessels began to run foul of each other, and got their cables entangled in an inconceivable manner.

"About the same time was observed near the Boca Grande de la Quiriquina, (an island so called,) an immense foaming wave of a prodigious height, which passed by the island of Rocnan, overwhelming in destruction the villages, drowning at the same time the inhabitants and cattle, up to the Perales.

"The shocking effects of this terrible phenomenon are shown by all the buildings being torn from their foundations, and so mixed, that no one can find or discern his property; in the town from thirty to forty have fallen victims to this dreadful blow. 'Tan feroz como inesperado.'

"The particular accounts of what has happened from the movements of the earth and sea are so strange and numerous, that I have abstained from relating them, for fear of exaggeration. The following one is sufficient :— 'The lady of Captain Hodges, on the sea's first retiring, strove to embark with her children, but was so unfortunate as to be thrown by the rolling billow to the distance of six quadras, (above 800 yards) inland, with three of her children, in one of the fragments of the boat ; her fourth child, who had held fast to a piece, not the twentieth part of the boat, was picked up near to Lilcuen, by a boat coming to this port, nearly exhausted ; but now this fortunate little creature is recovered. Lastly, a huge mass of rock, which it is calculated must weigh

25,000 tons, fell from the mountains of the Quiriquina, on the side of Boco Grande, in the bay of Talcahuano.

"Dios Guarde A. V. S.

"MIGUEL BAYON."

El Araucano, March 16.

The governors and military commandants of the different departments wrote on the 20th and 21st, and all their reports were nearly similar to each other, for all the towns and houses· in each district had been reduced to ruins, &c., so I will only give the following extract from a letter published in El Araucano of March 16th, 1835, in which is a brief detail of what was experienced in the city of Chillan.

"The earthquake of that unfortunate day is not at all to be compared to any on record.

"The most indifferent observer would have felt as if a torrent of fluid was passing beneath him, just as if he was placed upon a plank; over the falls of La Laxa. The fluid passed as if in waves that were repeated every second, and at times with such a shock, that to me it appeared as if the globe would fall to pieces, for the foundations of the houses started from the ground. This frightful movement, and the mortal agony of those who experienced it, lasted about three minutes and a half; since then, with the interval of hours, we have had several shocks, that do not let us forget the first; but what has left us as free from worldly cares as the Franciscan friars, is the heavy rains that has fallen at intervals during six days, that will inutilize all the earthquake has buried in the ruins or left exposed."

The perusal of these and many other accounts were appalling; but still a kind Providence had preserved the northern provinces from this dreadful calamity, and

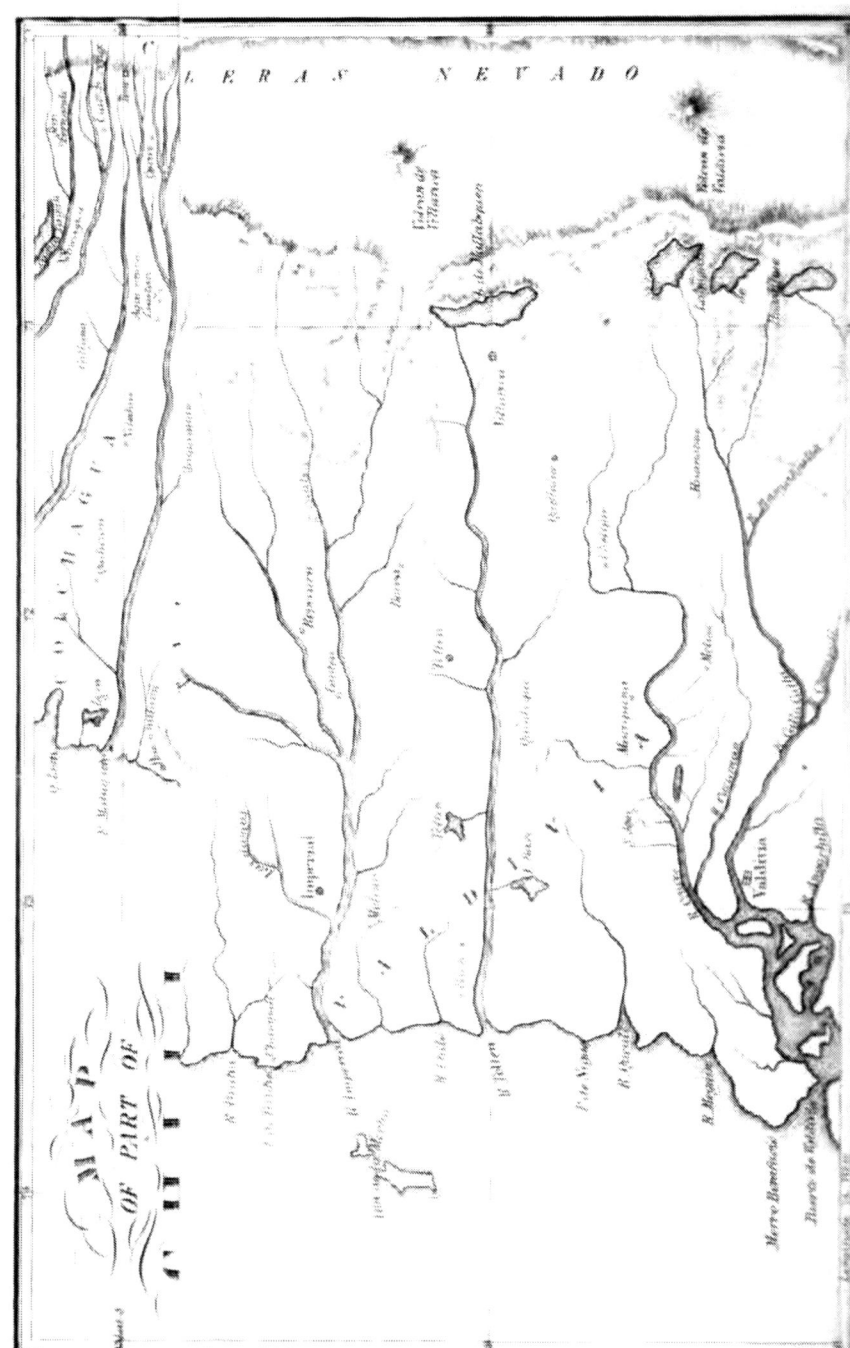

enabled government to assist and provide for the distressed inhabitants of Talca, Maule, and Concepcion. But what specially displays the wonderful dispensations of a kind Providence still further is, that although the devastation had spread over these devoted provinces, where 169 districts were almost reduced to ruins, out of a population of about 466,877, only 120 have been enumerated amongst the dead.

VALDIVIA.

This province extends from that of Concepcion to El Rio Negro; its principal rivers are—Rio Bueno, Calla Calla, Cruces, Queuli, Tolten, and El Negro; there are many other considerable streams, and six lakes—Osorno Chinchilco, Huanahue, Villarica, Raneo y Puyegue; there are several small ports, but only that of Valdivia is open to foreign vessels. The province is divided into three departments—Valdivia, Osorno, and Union; these only contain 8,860 inhabitants, for the greatest part of the territory of this, as well as that of the province of Concepcion, to the southward of the Bio Bio, is still in the possession of its rightful owners, the Araucanians

The port of Valdivia is safe and commodious. The entrance is marked by the Morros de Bonifacia and Gonzalo. The castle of Niebla stands on the north entrance, and that of Amargos on the south; there are several islands in the bay, the largest is that of Manzera, on which is a fort that commands the entrance and anchorage; near to La Niebla is the fort of Piojo; and near to that of Amargos are two batteries, called Chorocomayos, one of which covers the other; a little farther to the south is the castle of Corral: all these command the anchorage. There are some others, in all fifteen forts, which were captured, although well garrisoned, and mounted with one hundred and twenty-eight guns, by the heroic Lord Cochrane, with a single frigate. The capital of this province was founded in 1551, by General Valdivia, the conqueror of Chile. As the territory from the south of the Bio Bio has been the scene of many adventures, recorded by the poet Ercilla and La Monja Alferez, a Spanish nun, who, after having effected her escape from a convent in Biscay, entered as a soldier, and was promoted to be an ensign, in the same corps with her brother, unknown to him. I will give a brief account of the conquest of Chile, and of the prowess of the Araucanians, who are still unconquered:—

Don Diego Almagro invaded Chile from Cusco in 1535, after a fatiguing and disastrous march over the Cordilleras, where he lost many of his followers through cold, famine, and fatigue. On entering the territory of Chile, he was well received by El Inca Paulo, who met him in Copiapo; and who, to make a display of his wealth, gave Almagro a quantity of gold, supposed to be worth 1,000 ducats. Almagro was so elated with the munificence of the Inca, that he distributed it amongst his followers; and, also, forgave them a debt of 250,000 dollars he had advanced them, to equip themselves for the expedition. This show of liberality caused them to call him " the generous Almagro." However, he still was cruel: whilst on his march towards Huasco, two of his soldiers destroyed the harmony that had hitherto existed, by making extortions on the natives, who not only resisted, but put them to death. Almagro, being enraged at this, on arriving at the place where their bodies were exposed, ordered the ruler of that district,

with twenty-seven of the principal inhabitants, to be
burnt alive.

As this man was one of the conquerors of Peru, I shall
give an extract from the work of Colonel Stevenson, who
has recorded the most interesting and connected account of
the murder of the Peruvians, and their Inca, Atahualpu:—

"The Spaniards landed in Peru, at Tumbes, and after
possessing themselves, not without great opposition on
the part of the natives of that place, Pizarro began his
march towards the south. Atahualpa was at Caxamarca,
and his brother Huascar prisoner at Andamarca, about forty
leagues from Pachacamac. Atahualpa immediately sent
his brother Titu Atanchi, as his ambassador to Pizarro,
with most magnificent presents, including two golden
bracelets worn only by the Incas, to welcome the arrival
of the Viracochas, to solicit their protection, and to invite
them to visit him at Caxamarca. Huascar, at the same
time, although a prisoner, found means to send his ambassadors to Pizarro, informing him of the situation in
which he was placed by Atahualpa, and craving his
protection.

" Pizarro now found himself the arbiter of the fate of
two monarchs, both soliciting his friendship and protection, and each alleging his own right to the empire of
Peru; but Pizarro, determined that it should not belong
to either of them, and the only thing that engrossed his
attention was the safest and easiest means of possessing
himself of the treasures of both. He therefore determined to go first to Caxamarca, judging that the reigning
Inca would be in possession of the greater wealth, and
Hernando Pizarro was afterwards sent to Pachacamac.

" Francisco Pizarro pushed forward to Caxamarca,
where he arrived with a hundred and sixty soldiers. At

this time Atahualpa was at the baths, and Pizarro sent to him as his ambassadors his brother Hernando Pizarro and Hernando de Soto, and as interpreter, an Indian, named Felipe, a native of the Puna Island, in the Guayaquil river; these were accompanied by two hundred noble Indians, appointed by the Curaca of Caxamarca to attend on them; Atahualpa being informed of the approach of the two Spaniards, ordered one of his generals to form his troops, and do them the honours due to the children of the Sun. On their arrival at the palace, they were immediately presented to Atahualpa, who embraced them, and said, "Welcome, great Viracochas, to these my regions!" and having two seats covered with gold brought in, he ordered them to sit down. Atahualpa then speaking to his courtiers, said, "Behold the countenance, the figure, and the dress of our god, the same which appeared to my antecessor Inca Viracocha, and whose arrival was also predicted by my father, Huaina Capac." A species of wine was brought, and the Inca taking one of the golden goblets, the other was given to Hernando Pizarro, to whom the Inca bowed, and drank a small quantity, giving the goblet to his brother, Titu Atanchi, who drank the remainder; two more were then brought, and the Inca taking one, sent the other to Soto, to whom he bowed, and drank a little of the beverage, and gave the goblet to his other brother, Choquehuaman. Different kinds of fruit were then presented to the ambassadors, of which they partook with Atahualpa.

"Hernando de Soto rose, bowed to Atahualpa, resumed his seat, and delivered his embassy, stating, that "in this world there were two most potent princes, the one was the high Pontiff of Rome, vicar-general to, and representative of God on earth, who governed his church

and taught his divine law. The other was Charles V.
Emperor of the Romans, and King of Spain. "These two
monarchs," said Soto, "being informed of the blind idolatry
of your highness and all your subjects, have sent our
governor and Captain-general Don Francisco Pizarro, his
companions, and some priests, the ministers of God, to
teach your highness and your vassals the divine truths of
our holy religion, and to establish with your highness ever-
lasting relationship, concord, and peace."

"To this harangue, interpreted by Felipe, the Inca
answered to the following effect :—' Divine men, I am most
heartily glad that you and your companions have arrived
at these regions during the days of my life, for your
arrival has fulfilled the vaticination of my forefathers;
but my soul is sorrowful, because others must also be
now fulfilled; notwithstanding, Viracochas, I welcome
ye as the messengers of our God, and hope that the
changes prophesied by my father, Huaina Capac, and now
about to take place, will lead to the good of myself and my
people; it was on this account that neither I nor my captains have opposed your progress, as the natives of Puna
and Tumbes did, because we believe you to be the children
of our great God Viracocha, and messengers of the eternal
and all-creating Pachacamac—in obedience to our laws,
and the orders and injunctions of my father, we have received ye, and will serve and worship ye; but have pity on
me and on my people, whose affliction or death would be
more distressing to me than my own.'

"Pizarro and Soto begged leave to retire to their own
camp at Caxamarca, and Atahualpa embraced them, and
said, that he should soon follow them, to enjoy the company of the children of his God, Viracocha, the messengers
of the great Pachacamac. When the two Spaniards

had mounted their horses, presents of gold were carried to them by several noble Indians, who begged of their divinities to receive those humble marks of their respect and adoration. Pizarro and Soto then repaired to Caxamarca with their rich presents, astonished at the enormous quantities of gold which they had seen at the palace of Atahualpa.

"On the following day, Pizarro placed his cavalry, composed of sixty men, on each side of the square of Caxamarca, behind some high walls; in the centre of the square he had built a small breastwork, behind which he placed his two field-pieces, and behind these he stationed his infantry, a hundred men, and thus awaited the arrival of the Inca.

"Atahualpa made his appearance on a throne of gold, carried on the shoulders of his courtiers and favourites, with a guard of eight thousand of his soldiers in front, eight thousand on each side, and eight thousand more in the rear, besides an immense number of nobles and attendants. The troops were commanded by Ruminavi, who advanced in front, and acted as herald. Friar Vicente Valverde stepped forward a short distance in front of the Spanish infantry, holding a cross of palm-leaves in his right hand, and waited the arrival of Atahualpa, who was surprised to see a figure so different from the strangers whom he had seen the preceding day; and being informed by Felipe, the interpreter, that Valverde was the captain of words, and the guide of the supreme Pachacamac, and his messenger, Atahualpa approached, when Valverde began his most extraordinary harangue, requesting Felipe to translate it to the Inca as he proceeded to deliver it.

The priest then, in a long speech, explained to him the doctrine of the creation, the fall of Adam, the incarnation, the sufferings, and resurrection of Jesus Christ, the appointment of St. Peter as God's vicegerent on earth, the transmission of his apostolic power by succession to the popes, and the donation made to the King of Castile, by Pope Alexander, of all the regions in the New World. In consequense of all this, he required Atahualpa to embrace the Christian faith, to acknowledge the supreme jurisdiction of the pope, and to submit to the king of Castile as his lawful sovereign; promising, if he complied instantly with this requisition, that the Castilian monarch would protect his dominions, and permit him to continue in the exercise of his royal authority; but if he should impiously refuse to obey this summons, he denounced war against him in his master's name, and threatened him with the most dreadful effects of his vengeance.

"Felipe, the interpreter of this discourse, was a native of the Puna, where the Quichua language, generally spoken in Peru, was not understood; and what little he knew of it he had learnt of some Peruvians, who at different times had visited his native island. The Spanish that he spoke he had acquired during the time he had lived among the soldiers whom he served; thus it cannot be expected that he gave to Atahualpa a faithful translation of this absurd harangue, equally filled with incomprehensible matter, furious bombast, and unjust threats; indeed many mistakes are recorded, such as one God, trinity in unity, which he translated one God, and three, four Gods; that God made dust of man on the earth, which they could not possibly understand; and many other like passages were rendered equally ridiculous. The impossibility of translating the words trinity, unity, Jesus Christ, Virgin Mary, Roman Pontiff, Emperor of the Romans, &c., is quite obvious, for they could bear no translation at all, and a description of their meaning was as much above the powers of Felipe, and perhaps of Valverde himself, to explain, as the com-

2 E

prehension of Atahualpa to understand, who now for the
first time heard that such things did exist.

"When Atahualpa heard the conclusion of this rhodo-
montade fulminated by Father Valverde, he sighed, and
said, ' Ah! atay"—ah! how hard ; and after a short pause,
he addressed himself thus to Valverde : ' I should feel
happy, although every other request were denied me, if
one were but granted : procure a better interpreter, that
I may be enabled to understand what you have said ; and
that you may be better informed of what I wish to say.
I make this request, because I am certain that this
meeting ought to produce other things than what this
fellow has repeated to me.   From what I have heard, it
appears that you have come to destroy the race of the
Incas, and put to the sword all the Indians who do not
understand you.   If you are the ministers of vengeance
of Pachacamac, and come to destroy me and mine, fulfil
his orders—none of us fear death—and the vaticination of
my father brings us to meet you unarmed.

" ' Your interpreter has informed me of five great
men, whom I wish to know, God, trinity in unity, four
gods; Adam, on whom all men threw their sins; Jesus
Christ, the only man that did not assist in loading
Adam; Pope, Roman Pontiff; and Carlos Quinto, King
of all the world; but he tells me, that I am to give my
country and my people, and pay tribute to Carlos, and not
to any of the other four. I am also told, that I must abjure
my religion, and believe in Jesus Christ, who died.   If
this be true, I cannot forget the great Pachacamac, who
made our God, the sun, immortal, unless I learn who has
told you what I have heard from your interpreter.'

" This answer was translated by Felipe in short sentences, as Atahualpa spoke them; who perceiving the

ignorance of Felipe, endeavoured by this method to prevent a misconstruction of his words. On hearing the
last question, Valverde gave his breviary to Atahualpa,
and told him through Felipe, that that book informed
him of all that he wanted to know respecting the true
God. The Inca folded over the leaves, examined the
book, placed it against his ear and listened, then said, 'It
is false, it cannot and does not speak,' when he let it fall,
At this, Valverde cried out, 'To arms, Christians! these
infidel dogs have insulted the minister of your Redeemer,
the word of God is thrown under foot—revenge! revenge!'

"The soldiers immediately rushed on their unsuspecting
victims; Pizarro flew to Atahualpa, well aware that the
preservation of his life was of the utmost importance; but
upwards of twenty thousand Indians fell, before the fury of
the Spanish soldiery could be restrained, or their more than
barbarous thirst for blood was glutted. During this scene
of horror, the afflicted Atahualpa exhorted his people to
resign themselves to the will of Pachacamac, which he himself was willing to do, and not to lift up their hands against
the Viracochas; thus, he exclaimed, will the vaticination of
my forefathers be fulfilled.

"Pizarro, and a soldier called Miguel Astete, arrived at
the same moment close to the throne of Atahualpa, when
Pizarro caught hold of the robes of the Inca, and dragged
him to the ground; Astete plucked the red tassel from his
forehead, and kept it till the year 1557, when he delivered
it to the Inca Sayritupac. After the slaughter, the Spanish
soldiers proceeded to plunder, and while Pizarro was attentive to secure the Inca, part of his troops proceeded to the
baths, where Atahualpa resided, and possessed themselves
of all the gold and silver which they could find: the weight

of gold taken at the baths, and accounted for, amounted to
fifteen thousand ounces.

"Atahualpa was directly removed to a room in his own
palace at Caxamarca, and loaded with irons. Pizarro immediately sent his brother Hernando to visit Huascar in
his prison, and to endeavour to secure the treasure that he
might be possessed of; but whether the Indians belonging
to Atahualpa, who had heard of the situation of their Inca,
suspected that Pizarro intended to put Atahualpa to death,
and place Huascar on the throne; or whether Hernando
Pizarro endeavoured to deprive the guard of their prisoner,
is uncertain; but some misunderstanding having taken
place, an Indian struck Huascar with his axe, of which
wound he immediately died.

" Atahualpa having observed that the Spaniards were
more covetous of gold than of any thing which his kingdom
produced, proposed to Pizarro a ransom for himself; standing on his feet, he raised his hand, and placing it on the
wall, he said, 'To this mark will I fill this room with vessels of gold, if you will free me from these chains and from
this prison.' To this Pizarro agreed, and messengers were
sent to Quito, Cusco, and different parts of the country,
for the purpose of collecting the gold, and sending it to
Caxamarca. Some of the Spanish officers went with the
messengers of Atahualpa, and when they returned they
described the number of Indians which the country contained, and the universal obedience to the Inca, in such
terms, that they fancied a general rising would take place,
and that instead of gold, they would bring their arms and
put all the Spaniards to death; that Atahualpa had deceived
them, and was a traitor, and as such ought to be punished.
Pizarro opposed this for some time, till an accident occurred
which touched his pride, and made Atahualpa personally

odious to him. Some of the Spanish officers had written the
word "God" on the hand of the Inca, and when he shewed
it to any one, the person would point upwards; at length
he showed it to Pizarro, who could neither read nor write,
and was therefore unable to make any sign of the meaning
of the word. Atahualpa was surprised, and Pizarro was
abashed; his feelings were wounded, and he began to hate
the man who had discovered him to be more ignorant than
his inferiors. Atahualpa began to forebode his doom, and
became dejected; his own servants were not permitted to
wait on him; their places were supplied with Indians who
had attached themselves to the Spanish camp; some of
whom were unacquainted with the Quichua language, had
never been the vassals of Atahualpa, and all of whom were
inclined to insult him.

" The Indians began to arrive from different parts,
bringing with them the gold which they had been assured
would ransom their captive monarch; but that which by
them was destined to save his life, was changed by his cruel
masters into the cause of his death. From the number of
Indians who arrived daily, the Spaniards began to fear a
revolution in favour of their prisoner: they had already
received an enormous quantity of gold; Huascar was dead,
and Pizarro presumed, that by securing to himself the possession of the country, he should consequently become
master of the treasures which it contained. He therefore
determined to bring Atahualpa to trial; for which purpose
he constituted himself president of the court, and nominated
the other members.

" The libel exhibited against him consisted of various
articles; that Atahualpa, though a bastard, had dispossessed
the rightful owner of the throne, and usurped a royal
power; that he had put his brother and lawful sovereign

to death; that he was an idolater, and had not only permitted, but commanded the offering of human sacrifices; that he had a great number of concubines; that since his imprisonment he had wasted and embezzled the royal treasures, which now belonged of right to the conquerors; and that he had incited his subjects to take arms against the Spaniards.

" After this shameful libel had been read to the court by Sancho de Cuellar, Pizarro stated, that all those who should now attempt to defend the life of Atahualpa were traitors to the crown of Castile and to the Emperor, their master, and might be justly accused of opposing the increase of his kingdom and revenue; that the death of the tyrant Atahualpa would secure to Castile an empire, and to all present their lives and fortunes; that if any one opposed his death, it should be reported to his majesty, that he might reward his faithful servants, and punish those who endeavoured to deprive him of his right. After this diabolical harangue, it is almost unnecessary to say, that the unfortunate Atahualpa was sentenced to death.

" Atahualpa was immediately informed of his fate, and told, that if he were baptized, he would be put to an honourable death, such as was inflicted on noblemen in all civilized countries; but if he refused to receive this sacrament, he would be burnt to death: hearing this, he desired Friar Vicente Valverde to baptize him: the friar complied with the request, and called him Juan Atahualpa. He was then led out to the place of execution, in front of his own palace, where he was tied to a pole, and strangled; and his body received Christian burial on the spot where he was murdered, notwithstanding his last request—that he might be carried to Quito, and buried in the tomb of his forefathers.

"Pizarro attended the execution of his prisoner, afterwards wore mourning for him, and ordered his exequies to
be performed with all possible pomp. It may, perhaps, be
satisfactory to some of my readers to mention here, that
Pizarro was afterwards murdered by his own countrymen
at Lima; and Father Valverde, by the Indians of Quispi-
cancha. According to Zarate, the treasure which had been
brought for the ransom of Atahualpa, and which fell into
the hands of Pizarro, amounted to four hundred and ninety-
eight thousand ounces of fine silver, and one million five
hundred and ninety-one ounces of gold."*

The severity of Almagro caused many murmurs amongst
his followers, and from that day nothing but disasters befell
them. The Chilians were a superior race to the Peruvians,
and who not only after being exiled, defended themselves
with bravery, but they sought every opportunity to incommode or destroy the invaders; and, perhaps, would have
annihilated them all, had not the civil broils of Peru recalled them.

Almagro had penetrated Chile as far as the river Cachapaul, and found the Promaucaes a brave race of people,
and who had hitherto repelled the attacks of the Incas of
Peru. The Spaniards returned by the coast, and preferred
to encounter the arid sands of the desert of Atacama, to
the storms and snows of the Cordilleras; Almagro on his
return to Cusco demanded the government of that country,
which Pizarro refused to give; they had several encounters;
in one of which he was taken prisoner, and, in spite of his
entreaties, &c., Pizarro had him beheaded in Cusco, and
appointed Don Pedro Valdivia to conquer Chile, who with
two hundred Spaniards, some European women, and four
friars, with a numerous body of Indians, and almost every

* Stevenson.

necessary for colonizing the country, entered the province of Copiapo in 1539. He met with a warm reception, for the natives of Copiapo, Huasco, and Coquimbo gave him a deal of trouble and uneasiness, especially those of Quillota; however, he arrived at last in the valley of Mapocho.

Valdivia was an excellent orator, and animated his followers by an eloquent speech on their entering Chile; he also cajoled the principal cacique of Mapocho, Guelengala, out of his possessions, at the base of the hill Guelen, (now Santa Lucia,) where he built a fort, and founded the city of Santiago del Nuevo Estremo. Having divided it amongst his followers, they, with the help of their auxiliary Indians, soon placed themselves in security from any sudden attack from the Mapochians, who were supposed to exceed 200,000 souls; these, with their caciques, viewed the progress of the works of the intruders with a jealous eye, and formed plans to destroy them; but Valdivia penetrating their views, seized several of their caciques, and had them confined in the fort as hostages. No sooner had he marched with part of his forces to attack the Promaucians, than the Mapochians assaulted the abhorred city with fury, and set fire to many of the newly erected houses. The soldiers and inhabitants defended themselves in the fort with bravery, until Valdivia came to their assistance, and by a brisk attack routed the besiegers; during the assault, a female, Doña Ines de Zuares, cut the throats of the caciques that were in confinement. The Mapochians, notwithstanding that they had always been severe losers, repeatedly renewed their attacks, and annoyed the Spaniards so much, that some of the soldiers conspired to kill Valdivia, and return to Peru, where they might enjoy tranquillity: but their plans were discovered, and the conspirators were executed. Valdivia, then, in order to keep his followers em-

ployed, sent an expedition to the valley of Quillota, to attend
to the Indians who were employed in the gold mines and
lavaderos; for gold being at that time so abundant, it
excited the cupidity of the Spaniards, who soon founded
the town of Quillota. Having built a vessel at Con-Con,
and sent her to Peru for a reinforcement, he despatched two
officers with a party by land, and, in order to make a display of the wealth of Chile, and excite the viceroy to send
a reinforcement, he had the stirrups, bits, buckles, &c.
made of solid gold; his plans were crowned with success, for
two expeditions were soon sent, one by land, and the other
by sea; both of which arrived in Chile about the same time.
His next project was to send the admiral, Don Juan Baptista
Pastene, a Genoese, to survey the coast of Chile, who on his
return reported his successful voyage and discoveries; upon
which he was ordered to Peru for fresh succours, whence he
soon returned with a reinforcement of three hundred men.
Valdivia having now a respectable force, and the city of
Santiago well fortified, he marched against the Promaucians in 1545, and, by his sagacity and prudence, managed
to conciliate these brave Indians, and make them his confederates; after which he marched towards the coast as
far as Tilicura, where he was surprised by a large body of
Indians, and forced to retreat to Santiago. He afterwards
embarked with Pastene, and arrived in Peru just in time
to quell the civil broil that existed between the viceroy
Gasca, whom Charles V. had sent against Gonzalo Pizarro.
This important service not only made Gasca his friend,
but he sent him back to Chile with his title of governor
renewed, and an abundant supply of military stores, &c.,
besides two vessels laden with troops and adventurers, who
had been engaged in the civil broils. Valdivia on his
return to Santiago marched again to the southward, and in

October, 1550, having arrived on the banks of the Bio Bio without molestation, he founded the city of Penco, close to the bay of Talcahuano, that had already been surveyed by Pastene. The Araucanians having united with the Indians on the north of the Bio Bio, commenced a series of "ataques" on the Spaniards, in one of which their leader, El Toqui Aillabilu, and many caciques, were killed. This did not dishearten them, and another army of more than 4,000 warriors, under the toqui Lincoyan, marched against the Spaniards, who having fortified themselves in Penco, obliged the Indians to retire. Valdivia followed them, and drove them before him, until he came to the river Cauten, where he founded the city of El Imperial, which was concluded in 1552; after which he marched to the southward, and founded the city which bears his name, and gave his name to the province ; he sent his general, Don Jeronimo de Alderete, to found the city of Villarica, so called on account of the great quantity of gold that was found in its neighbourhood. Valdivia built forts at Puren, Tucapel, and Arauco, to secure the cities he had founded, and facilitate the communication with the city of Valdivia; he afterwards built the city of Angol, in a fine fertile country, and rich in gold; for lumps of gold (pepitas) were found in the lavaderos* of

* Lavaderos, (gold-washings,) are in Chile worked by the poorer class of people, who, for want of capital, are unable to work a mine; their labour is confined to excavating and collecting the earth and sand that has been deposited in the beds of rivulets, or parts that have been inundated during the rainy season ; for, in the neighbourhood of gold mines, the earth is generally more or less impregnated with large or small particles of gold; this earth is generally of a reddish colour, and a practical gold-washer can in a few minutes inform himself whether it will or not repay him for his trouble ; they always carry a poruña, (part of a cow's horn that has been cut in a manner so as to form a long bowl, that will contain more than a pint of water,) in which they mix up the earth with water, and by adding water and shaking it in a peculiar manner, all the lighter particles are soon separated, and if there is any gold, it may easily be seen at the bottom of the poruña ; others extract the gold from the earth by the same process

eight or ten marks weight; the mines of Tucapel, Villarica, El Timon, Angol, and Valdivia, were also very rich and productive; and it is said that each Indian had to give Valdivia the value of from thirty to forty ducats per week. El Inca Garcilaso says, " that Valdivia received a tribute of more than 100,000 from the Indians."

Whilst Valdivia was busied in building cities and forts, an old cacique named Colo-Colo, who had great authority, proposed to his countrymen the election of another toqui, who might fulfil the duties of such with honour and valour, and not suffer the degradation of being slaves to the Spaniards: many of the ulmenas (chiefs) met, and Lincoyan, the timid, was superseded by the brave toqui Caupolican, who soon commenced operations by taking and destroying the fort of Arauco, commanded by Don Francisco Reinoso, with eight pieces of cannon. Caupolican marched against the fort of Tucapel, which being only garrisoned by forty men, became an easy prize; the toqui did not destroy this fort, but garrisoned it with his followers, and awaited the approach of Valdivia, who with his cavaliers, and 5,000 auxiliaries, were marching against the Araucanians. The Spaniards being terrified at the sight of the dead bodies of their comrades, who had fallen in the fort, and of others that were suspended from the trees in its neighbourhood, would, had it not been for their spirited leader and officers who animated them, have returned, for they were only about two hundred Europeans. The armies soon came in sight of each other, and halted to prepare for battle. The vice-toqui, Mariantu, who commanded the right wing of the Arau-

used at the mills where the ore is pounded, and afterwards mixed with quicksilver. The best lavaderos in Chile are found in the middle range of hills that run in a line between the Cordilleras and the coast; at present, neither mines or lavaderos are allowed to be worked in the Araucanian territory, for the Indians have prohibited it under pain of death.

canians, attacked the left of the Spaniards, commanded by
General Bobadilla, who was defeated and slain, as well as
another chief whom Valdivia sent to support him. The
cacique, Tucapel, who commanded the left wing, attacked
the Spaniards and their confederates in a gallant style,
and the action soon became general, and obstinate; but the
Spaniards, whose horses, armour, and arms were so far
superior to the Indians, dealt such havoc around them,
that seeing so many killed, and getting into disorder, they
commenced to fly before the Spaniards. At this crisis a young
Araucanian of sixteen years of age, who had been brought
up by Valdivia, and served him as his page, feeling ashamed
to see his countrymen abandon the field; as if inspired,
he seized a lance, abandoned the conquerors for the
fugitives, and stigmatizing them as cowards, who were unworthy of the name of Araucanians, rallied, and managed
to reanimate them for a renewal of the attack; for
Lautaro assured them that the Spaniards had lost many of
their chiefs, that numbers were wounded, and as they were
sorely fatigued, they could make but a feeble resistance.
Turning then towards his old master with his lance,
cried aloud, "Follow me, countrymen, follow me,—victory
awaits us with open arms."* This energetic display of
courage and patriotism electrified the Araucanians, who
charged their pursuers with fury, and in their turn completely defeated, and put them to the route; almost all
the Spaniards fell on the field of battle, and only two of
the auxiliaries escaped to carry the sad tidings to Concepcion. Valdivia, seeing all was lost, attempted to escape
with his chaplain, but they were taken prisoners, and
brought before Caupolican, from whom he supplicated for
his life, and also implored the intercession of Lautaro, pro-

* Ercilla, Canto 3, page 53.

mising at the same time, that if allowed, he and all his
followers, who were in Chile, would return to Spain. The
noble and generous Caupolican was inclined to accede to
the petition of his prisoner, and assembled a council of
caciques to deliberate ; but whilst they were in discussion,
whether he should be liberated or not, Leocato, a veteran
cacique, who had great authority, felt enraged at hearing
the proposals, and before he could be prevented, with a
severe blow from his club, he levelled Valdivia at his feet,
and putting his foot upon the dead body, said, " This is the
mode to stop your altercations ; what madness would it not
have been to have acceded to the proposals of an ambitious
enemy ? who, if he had escaped, would have laughed at his
oaths, as well as at our stupidity and folly in believing
them."* In this manner, as tragical as sorrowful, did Don
Pedro Valdivia, the founder of this city, meet his fate. This
total extermination of the Spanish army, and their allies,
the Promaucians, was celebrated by the Araucanians, and
at their feast, the Toqui Caupolican taking the youthful
Lautaro by the hand, presented him to the chiefs and
warriors who were assembled, and in a masterly speech,
attributed their late victory to his valour and intrepidity,
on which he was elected lieutenant-toqui, with the faculty
of commanding an army, notwithstanding his tender age,
and his nomination was applauded by all the caciques.
Then followed a council of war; in which were various
opinions—that of the brave Tucapel was to follow the
Spaniards, not only to Santiago, but to Spain. Colo-Colo
and Caupolican's votes were, that previous to adopting the
plans of Tucapel, they had better destroy all the Spanish
forts that had been erected in the Araucanian territory; and
Lautaro was ordered to defend the frontiers whilst it could

* Ercilla, Canto 3, page 61.

be put into execution ; to effect this he fortified himself upon the heights of Marigueno, to await the Spaniards, who were expected to take revenge for the death of Valdivia. The arrival of the two Indians who had escaped from the field of battle, and their account of the extermination of the army, threw the inhabitants of Concepcion into consternation ; but the brave Villagran took charge of the government, and, placing himself at the head of the troops, exhorted them to defend what had been conquered, and to revenge the death of their countrymen. Then having made preparation, with a strong body of Spaniards and auxiliaries, he crossed the Bio Bio : here he was soon attacked by the Araucanians whilst passing a defile ; but after an action of three hours, he defeated and pursued them to the foot of Marigueno, where Lautaro had fortified himself, and who awaited the approach of the Spaniards. In vain did Villagran attempt to carry the fort, nor could he dislodge his adversaries with six pieces of artillery, which he kept playing on them from a neighbouring eminence.

Lautaro ordered the intrepid Leucotar to take the cannon with his company, and not to return without executing his order. The warrior no sooner heard the commands of Lautaro, than he attacked the artillery with resolution, and brought the six guns in triumph to his chief, who charged the Spaniards with such desperate fury, that they retreated in great disorder, and Villagran, who was wounded and unhorsed, would have been a victim, had not thirteen of his soldiers, who performed prodigies of valour, rescued him from the Indians, and remounted him again. The Araucanians did not lose 1,000 men, while their enemies lost 3,000, who were left dead on the field. Villagran, with the fugitives, returned to Concepcion, where he found the inhabitants overwhelmed with sorrow and dismay, and, on the approach of Lautaro, they embarked their women, children, and aged parents in two vessels that fortunately were in port, and abandoned the city, that they might march with the troops to Santiago.

Lautaro, finding Concepcion abandoned, set fire to the city, and having reduced it and all its riches to ashes, he returned to celebrate his triumph, and receive further orders from Caupolican. But Villagran returned with a reinforcement, and rebuilt the city, which was again destroyed by Lautaro, who, proud of his victories, was determined to march against Santiago.

This warrior left the camp of Caupolican with only seven hundred warriors, and without meeting any opposition he crossed the Maule, and then commenced operations against the abhorred Promaucians, fortifying himself on an advantageous position on the banks of Rio Claro. There he was attacked by Don Pedro Villagran, cousin to the general, who was an invalid. Lautaro, having been attacked repeatedly, at last defeated the Spaniards, who retreated to Santiago. General Villagra having recovered from his illness, left the capital with 196 Spaniards, and 1,000 Indians; and by marching near to the coast, with great precaution, he took Lautaro by surprise, who at the first attack was transfixed by an arrow from the bow of a Promaucian, and he fell dead in the arms of his followers, who, sooner than yield to their enemies, defended themselves to the last extremity, and shared the fate of their young and intrepid leader. (Ercilla records the death of Lautaro in Part 1st, Canto 14.) This victory was celebrated in Santiago, and the Spaniards could but applaud the valour and military prowess of Lautaro, whom they called the Chilian Hanibal. In 1577, the viceroy of Peru sent his son Don Garcia Hurtado de Mendoza, with ten ships and a numerous reinforcement of cavalry, who disembarked at Penco, and began to treat with the Araucanians; but during the armistice he built a fort on the Serro Pinto, and had it well served with artillery. The toqui Caupolican was no sooner informed of this act, than he crossed the Bio Bio, attacked the fort, and would have carried it, had not a reinforcement of 2,000 Indians, and a squadron of cavalry arrived from the city of El Imperial, to assist Mendoza, who defeated the Araucanians after hotly a disputed battle.

Amongst the prisoners was the brave Galvarino; and his conqueror vented his rage upon his captive, by ordering his hands to be chopped off, and then setting him at liberty. On his joining his countrymen, they were so much inflamed against the Spaniards, that they swore eternal vengeance; and such was their excitement, that the women took up arms, and embodied themselves as soldiers. Caupolican attacked the Spaniards, and after an obstinate battle, in which he had at one time the advantage, he was beaten; he lost twelve caciques, amongst whom was the crippled and furious Galvarino; these were hung upon trees near to the field of battle, in order to strike terror amongst the Araucanians. General Mendoza then marched to Tucapel, and founded a city, where Valdivia had been defeated, and called it Cañete, (his family name;) after having fortified it, and left a good garrison, he marched to El Imperial, where he was received with acclamations of joy by its inhabitants. The general sent a convoy with provisions and warlike stores to the new city; but the Araucanians attacked and routed them at Callincupil: the soldiers escaped to the fort of Cañete, where their arrival was of the greatest benefit, for Caupolican, notwithstanding his last defeat, marched against it, and assaulted it; the attempt lasted five hours, and finding it impossible to take it by storm, he had recourse to stratagem, and disguised one of his officers, in whom he had great confidence, whose name was Pran; he entered the city as a deserter, and passed and repassed without any notice being taken; and after having informed himself of the strength and locality of the fort, he communicated his observations to Caupolican, who decided on attacking the city at the hour of siesta. Pran had made a confidant of an Indian named Andresillo, who served the Spaniards, and who offered to assist him by opening the gate on the day appointed; but the fellow deceived him, and gave information to the Spaniards, who occupied themselves on the eve of the attack, in making preparations to receive the Indians. Next day, Caupolican was posted in ambush with 3,000 warriors, and, on Andresillo making the signal, the Araucanians approached the fort with caution and silence, and began to introduce themselves in great order, when all at once the gates were closed upon them, and a tremendous fire opened on all that were approaching, that caused great destruction, few being able to escape; for the cavalry, who were ready, pursued them in every direction. All who entered the fort were put to death, and three of the principal caciques were fastened to cannon, and their bodies blown to pieces by their savage conquerors. The body of Caupolican was sought for in vain ; he had fled with ten followers, and secreted himself in a deep ravine, where he was betrayed into the hands of his enemies; his wife, Palla, seeing him surrender without resistance, after having exhorted him to die, or gain his liberty, became furious, and, throwing her infant at him, cried out, " Coward, take thy child, for I will retain nothing that has belonged to thee."* Reynosa ordered Caupolican to be impaled, and

* Ercilla, Canto 33, page 338.

2 F

shot at with arrows; on which the toqui, without any change in his countenance, said as follows:—" With my death thou wilt reap no other fruit than that of inflaming the hatred my countrymen have against thy nation; they are far from being dismayed by the loss of an unfortunate chief; from my ashes many Caupolicans will arise, perhaps more fortunate than I have been; but if you will spare my life, I can, with the great authority I possess over my countrymen, be useful to the interests of your sovereign, and contribute, with my influence, towards the propagation of your creed, by ordering the Araucanians to embrace the faith of Jesus Christ. If you spurn my offers, and deny my request, nothing can be gained; and if you will not spare my life, I only request you will send me to your king; and if he considers it just that I must die for having defended my own country, I shall then end my days in Spain, without creating fresh disturbances in this country." Nothing could soften the heart of the cruel and inflexible Reynosa, and Caupolican finding he was to become a sacrifice, embraced the Christian faith. No sooner had he received the sacrament of baptism, than he was conducted to the scaffold, which had been erected for the purpose; where, observing the pointed stake and executioner, who was a negro, he became so much enraged, that with a kick he hurled him to the ground, saying in a loud voice, " Is there not a sword, nor a hand more worthy of executing a man of my character? this is not an act of justice, it is one of vengeance, by men who have neither honour nor education."

Reynoso ordered the victim to be seized, and he was impaled, where he expired pierced with arrows, A. D. 1558.

The poet Ercilla has recorded this infamous act of cruelty in the Araucana, Part 3, Canto 34.

The Spaniards had little rest after the tragical death of Caupolican; for the Araucanians, after a war of forty-four years, succeeded in destroying the cities and towns that had been built by their enemies, and freeing their territory from the Spaniards, who were never after able to conquer it. The city of Valdivia was twice besieged, ineffectually, by the toqui Caupolican; but it was not so fortunate in resisting the talents and activity of the celebrated Paillamachu, who, in the year 1599, surprised it at night with 4,000 men, and put the garrison to the sword, burnt the city, and carried off an immense booty, consisting of the effects of the inhabitants, and, it is said, a million in gold; he also made many captives, and, imitating the Spaniards, he quartered all that bore arms, and hung those bloody trophies upon trees; the women and girls were distributed amongst the conquerors, whilst the boys were adopted, and these, with their descendants, became the fiercest enemies of the Spaniards. The brave Paillamachu destroyed the cities of Concepcion, Chillan, Angol, Lumaco, Puren, Colla, Arauco, Cañete, Villa Rica, Imperial, and Osorno, and, after having revenged the wrongs of his countrymen, and freed the Araucanian territory of the Spaniards, he died in the year 1603.

The Dutch took possession of Valdivia in the year 1640, but were obliged to abandon it after having held it for three months.

The Spaniards returned, and, notwithstanding their having erected forts in Valdivia, Osorno, Arauco, and other places on the frontier, the Araucanians never allowed them to remain at ease; nor has that valiant race of Americans yet been conquered, although considered as the inhabitants of the republic of Chile. The president of Chile, Don Ambrosio O'Higgins, did a deal towards reconciling the

Indians, and restoring harmony and confidence, for which the government of Spain rewarded him with the title of Marquis of Osorno. I have been informed that on account of his amiability, &c. the Indians called him "Patiru Paddi Huinca," (Father Paddy* European.)

PROVINCE OF CHILOE.

This is the most southern of the republic, for it extends from that of Valdivia to Cape Horn, and has innumerable rivers, and many ports; but as the archipelago of Chiloe is only inhabited by the Chilians, little is yet known of the territory occupied by the native Indians. Chiloe is divided into ten departments, San Carlos, Carelmapu, Chacao, Calbuco, Dalcahue, Quenac, Quinchao, Castro, Lemuy, and Chouchi; these contain four parishes, 1,149 haciendas and farms, and a population of 43,832 souls; its capital is the city of San Carlos. As I have never visited this province, I must refer my readers to the work of Captain Fitzroy. There still remain the islands of Juan Fernandez, a description of which will be given in a separate work, entitled "Providence Displayed," &c.

* He was a native of Ballina in Ireland.

CHAP. XIII.

GOVERNMENT OF JUAN FERNANDES—EXPEDITION OF GENERAL FREYRE, HIS CAP-
TURE AND EXILE—SEIZURE OF PERUVIAN VESSELS OF WAR—WAR WITH THE
CONFEDERATION—REVOLUTION OF QUILLOTA, ETC.

In 1834, I was ordered to supersede the governor of Juan
Fernandez, who had been committing various excesses and
acts of cruelty there. I gained the ill-will of personages
in power for having exposed various dishonest acts of
Lieutenant-Colonel Lattapiat, their protégé. In 1835,
the Chilian patriots who had been exiled to Peru, formed
the plan of returning to, and revolutionizing Chile, in order
to depose the Spanish faction, called "Faroleros," who
had almost got possession of the reins of government; and
as the elections for the president of the republic were at
hand, they might materially assist the opposition, denominated "Liberales," and "Filopolitas," the latter were a
few patriots, who, although they held a part in the administration, were opposed to the fanaticism and intolerance of
their colleagues in power, the "Faroleros," and, it was said,
to the re-election of General Prieto. In the month of
June an attempt was made to get hold of the Chilian brig
of war Aquilles, whilst at anchor in the port of Callao.
Shortly after this was made known in Chile, the most wily
of the "Faroleros" conceived the plan of withdrawing the
garrison, and depopulating the islands of Juan Fernandez.
This was opposed by the "Filopolitas," who kept the

" Faroleros" in check. But the latter, fearing that General
Freyre or his friends might attempt to seduce the garrison,
who with the convicts might serve them materially, conceived the plan of revolutionizing the island, and attaching
the blame of withdrawing the troops, &c. to the cruelty
and misconduct of the governor. I have already detailed
the particulars of the disasters I experienced on the island,
during the dreadful earthquake that desolated the southern
provinces of Chile, and subsequently, through the intrigues
of a set of villians, who revolutionized the island, in a small
work entitled " The Earthquake of Juan Fernandez as it
occurred in the year 1835,* and from which I will extract

* " Many of our readers may recollect the accounts which appeared a
few years ago, relative to the total destruction, by an earthquake, of the
island of Juan Fernandez, in the month of February, 1835; as well as to
the appearance of a new group of islands in the neighbourhood, the products of volcanic influence.

" These accounts seemed altogether so well authenticated, that we ourselves never for a moment doubted their truth, especially as geographers
have laid open to our view so many proofs of the *creative*, as well as of
the *destructive* and *mutative* powers of volcanic energy. It seems, however
that these reports were not true : and for the sake of science generally,
and of geognostical accuracy especially, bearing as it does so much on the
safety of navigation, we rejoice that we have a true and well-authenticated
account laid before us.

" Our neighbour, Mr. Sutcliffe, who has held a high rank in the Chilian
army, was at the time of the earthquake governor of the island of Juan
Fernandez, (then occupied by the republic as a criminal colony,) and his
narrative of the events occurring about that time are plain and satisfactory.

" The pamphlet before us, however, contains not only a graphic description of the earthquake, but likewise of the insurrection of the *prisoners* in
the island ; the public documents relative to which must for ever silence
any aspersions which the press of that day, and especially the *Nautical
Magazine*, for June, 1837, must have cast upon the character or prudence
of the brave and talented ex-governor.

" The work is illustrated by several well-executed lithographic views
and charts."—*Stockport Advertiser.*

" An insurrection, at the bottom of which was a friar ! (verifying the
Spanish proverb, which says, there never was mischief without a friar for
the counsellor), took place at Juan Fernandez, in which the second in command deposed the governor, who was subsequently put on his trial at

a few documents which I received in September, 1835, on
the day of my expulsion by the mutineers, in order that the
editor of the following handsome encomium on the conduct
of the governors of the Island of Juan Fernandes, may see
that his assertion ought to have been made previous to my
administration of that colony; and that I had little to
expect from the abettors of such as had not only manifested their eagerness to depopulate the islands, but who
have notoriously protected and rewarded the very persons
who were the promoters and actors of all the disgraceful
scenes that had taken place on Juan Fernandez.* It
was the minister of war, Don J. Zavier de Bustamante,

Chile, and declared to have fulfilled the duties of his office with good faith
and efficiency. Those who plotted and executed the affair, were also tried,
and, as might be expected from Spanish justice towards Spaniards, where
an Englishman was an accuser, escaped comparatively unharmed, instead of
forfeiting their lives for their conduct. Now all these particulars were
entirely unknown to our correspondent, Captain Masters, and we have done
our duty in adding them; a course which, we hope, will serve to remove
impressions considered highly injurious to the character of Mr. Sutcliffe.
For our own part, however, we are unable to see any such tendency in
Captain Masters' account; we can fully appreciate the difficult situation
of Mr. Sutcliffe, in dealing with such persons he had under his orders, and
we trust that he may find the government just and generous enough to
compensate him for his losses. He may then with truth say, ' *Los pueblos
no estan siempre ingratos.*'

" The views and plans which accompany the work, representing the bay
during the earthquake, are useful and interesting."—*Nautical Magazine*,
No. 2, February, 1840.

* The chaplain, Padre Lopez, was not tried, *as ordained,* by a general
court-martial, but he went through the farce of a "*consejo*," where *Major
Toledo*, one of my judges, and who had taken a decided interest against me,
was the *president,* and where neither myself nor my witnesses, Joseph
Duncan, Rojos, &c., were cited to appear against him; and on Saldes re-
tracting his former declarations, wherein he, as well as Ensign Riquelme,
had accused the *padre* of being their adviser, &c. &c., he was found innocent and set at liberty, and claimed an *indemnification* from me to the
amount 500 dollars for his losses.

Saldes, in place of being transported, *as a convict,* to Juan Fernandez for
ten years, according to his sentence, (to expiate his crimes on the spot he

who informed me that several members of the government wished to break up the establishment, and the following extract of the ministerial "Gazette El Araucano" will show that his information was well founded:—

"INTERIOR.

"We know that Government intends to remove the establishment (el presidio) of Juan Fernandez to the continent of the republic. The convicts will have to be occupied in the public works, where they are so much wanted, and for which there are actually a competent number of carts nearly ready, and made of iron, in order to transport them to and fro.

"We have considered this measure under different aspects, all of the greatest importance, and find it the most opportunate and regulated to the public, to the particular, and to the moral good that by every means ought to be introduced and preserved in this country.

"Our readers are aware of the immense expense that the subsistence of the 'presidio' of Juan Fernandez is to the treasury, the freight of the convicts, their maintenance in that depôt, that of a competent garrison, and of the governor, under whose command is the island, have consumed always a great quantity of dollars in the year without any other benefit than that of having a number of malefactors

had committed them), was allowed to reside in Copiapo, and received a civil appointment from the governor.

Ensign Riquelme was not even *censured* for the part he took, but was, shortly after the trial, promoted to be a captain.

Lieutenant Dias, of the *Colocolo*, also escaped censure, and was promoted to be a commander in the Chilian navy.

El Señor Don Marcelo Ugalde was rewarded with a commission in the army, and received the grades of lieutenant of infantry, lieutenant of cavalry, and "adjudante mayor" of the "battalion Colchagua," in less than twelve months after the padre's trial.

separated from us for a certain period, that for the most part become more hardened in that establishment, and return amongst us to commit more depredations, and perhaps to receive the punishment of death.   *   *

" The separation of the island, the quality of its inhabitants, their want of occupation, and in many cases the bad disposition and irregular conduct of the governors, have promoted different insurrections; that, at the same time, have caused damage in the parts where the mutineers have arrived, and have obliged the government to spend extraordinary sums; and have made the punishment of being transported to that ' presidio' lose the greatest part of its importance, because the convicts have been practically shown the possibility of escaping, and laughing at the punishment they were condemned to suffer for their crimes. We therefore believe that government, in putting this into execution, has meditated seriously upon the means of preserving the important possession of the island; and which truly never could be worse taken care of than in having it occupied as a ' presidio.' "—EL ARAUCANO, 1835.

I received the following letter from a worthy friend, (one of the first personages in Chile, Don Manuel Salas, who, during the return of the Spanish government, had been exiled to Juan Fernandez, and had resided some time upon the island), which, with those of the ministers of state, serve to refute the assertions of the Faroleros :—

" Santiago, September 1st, 1835.
" Señor Don Tomas Sutcliffe, Gobernador Politico y
" Militar Juan Fernandez.
" My Estimable and Valued Friend,

" I reply with pleasure to your two letters of the 23rd of April and 18th of June, which have but recently come to hand, and almost on the same day. Although I regret their delay, I feel great pleasure at their contents. I am

filled with delight at the idea that that hell, the centre of
wretchedness, desperation, and immorality, is about to be
converted into a theatre of virtues, of which not even the
sound had yet been heard. All may be accomplished by
constancy and by rectitude of intention.

"St. Helena is at the present day a garden, formed from
an arid and solitary rock, and New South Wales is going
to become one of the most brilliant parts of the British
empire. If you pause to consider what humanity may be
indebted to you, and those who enjoy the benefits, always
increasing, of which you may be the immortal author, you
will hold firm your benignant resolutions and thoughts, to
which consecrate your zeal, your talents, and your time.
Friend, great works are meritorious only in proportion to
the difficulties by which contrasted, and the smallness of
the means of carrying them into effect. You find yourself
in this case; but do not be disheartened, nor easily believe
in such stumbling-blocks as you indicate to me; the solicitation of Don Marcelo Ugalde ought not for one moment
to cause you anxiety, as it is a matter which has not invited
the slightest attention. I have inquired about it to the
very bottom, and have availed myself of the opportunity to
learn the good opinion which the president and the three
ministers entertain of you, and in which I shall endeavour to continue them as far as my influence extends.

"The Island Floriana, which, but a few years since, was
nothing but a sandy soil, inhabited by turtle, is now a place
where whalers touch, who leave there large sums, utensils,
and even people.

"Juan Fernandez offers much greater advantages to a
beneficent and active genius. The clays and soils of
various colours brought to my memory the minerals of
Golconda and Brazil. Nature is systematic; their geogra-

phical position places them in a like situation, and renders probable the same effects and equal productions. It would appear madness to those who do not wish to think, but not to those who know that this has been the beginning of all discoveries. For the furtherance of such investigations, you have fortunately three or more men with you ingenious and clever, and some with an idea of arts, who may be made useful if applied and directed with sagacity and vigilance. Some of your predecessors reaped advantages from such colleagues; extracting anchors and things which had been lost on the anchoring ground; improving the fisheries, and of curing (salting); besides other expedients of which we are ignorant. One occurs to me which might be of great importance; such is the making of bricks, of which immense quantities are brought from England and the United States, and for which you have all the elements in abundance; these are, the firewood, the clays, and, above all, the idle hands.

" Friend,—The celebrated Buren, by having taught in Holland the manner of fishing and curing the herring, has provided occupation for more than two hundred thousand persons; and Don Luis Louison, by the establishment of the manner of preparing pescado (fish corned, and dried in the sun), in Valparaiso, furnished to that poor place the entry of more than seventy thousand dollars. What a benefit! How enviable a memory! What examples!

" To prevent this suffering the delay or going out of the direct course, as happened with your favours, I avail myself of the kindness of the ministers, under cover to whom you may send me your commands.

" I enclose the annexed from our mutual friend Campino, to whom you may send your letters through the same channel.

"If you find, among the fish on your coast, one called 'berrugate,' or 'tollo,' which has on the middle of the ridge of the back a bone, which is discovered to view, to it is attributed the virtue of curing the tooth-ache. This, however, is not the most beneficial and important: but its bones, of whose admirable effects I have been a witness and an agent, administering the weight of an ounce dissolved in wine, broth, or water, are successful in stopping hæmorrhage, or the effusion of blood, infallibly, whether from the mouth or any other way. Whilst I was in that quarter I used much diligence, but did not succeed in obtaining this admirable specific, which may perhaps be now obtained. You might thus have the satisfaction to alleviate many, and of obliging one who is well aware of its importance.

"I heartily wish you much health, constancy, and patience; and reckon upon the good offices which may be in the power of, your sincere friend and servant,

"MANUEL DE SALAS."

(Seal of Office.)

"Santiago, September 1, 1895.

"Minister of the Interior,

"I have given an account to the president of your official note of last June, No. 250, in which you give a detailed relation of the state in which the establishment is at present, as also of the works you have commenced; and his excellency feels satisfied with your diligence as a public functionary, and philanthropic views as a promoter of industry, by which means the condition of those unfortunate persons there detained may become alleviated. God preserve you.

"JOAQUIN TOCORNAL."

(Minister of War's Letter.)
"Santiago, September 6, 1835.
" My Laborious Friend,

"Being always in a hurry, I cannot extend my letter
to manifest my satisfaction at your industry and advance-
ment of your insula : this will be the best attestation of
the conduct of its worthy governor, who has so much
honoured my fortunate election.   Continue, and do not
fear your detractors.   The actions are what speak per-
petually, and not the unjust detractor of the moment.
By this vessel you will receive all that has been required,
and shortly I will send your commission of Lieutenant-
Colonel, that the earthquake of February robbed you of.
Now you will receive a good remittance, and amongst
them " birds that will be troublesome," persons of family,
on whom you must keep your eyes.   I have no more
time : continue in good health, and command your affectionate friend that kisses your hand,*

"JOSÈ ZAVIER DE BUSTAMANTE,"

Previous to my return to the capital, my friend, the
minister of state in the war department, Don Jose Zavier
de Bustamante had retired from office, for the Faroleros
had disgusted him, on account of the interest he had displayed towards the restoration of the generals, chiefs, and
officers, that had been cashiered in 1830, many of whom
were suffering the greatest privations and misery.   Don
Diego Portales took charge of the war department ; and
shortly afterwards that indefatigable minister of finance,
Don Ramon Rengifo, resigned also (he had incurred the
censure of the ' Faroleros,' who were ever clamorous to
obtain pensions and other acts of commiseration for the
unfortunate and faithful adherents of their beloved

· * These documents have been published in Chile.

Ferdinand,* besides the payment of what had been taken
from the partisans of Spain during the war of independence, in preference to all others.) He was succeeded
by Don Joaquin Tocornal, who had vacated the home
and foreign departments; which were annexed to those
of war and marine; and now, as all the partisans of the
' Filopolitas' had been expelled, the ' Faroleros' had every
thing their own way, and they re-elected the president of
the republic for five years longer.

About the latter end of July, 1836, government was
informed that General Freyre had sailed from Callao
with three vessels of war, one of which, the Monteagudo,
mounted fifty guns, and their rendezvous was to be the
Islands of Juan Fernandez. A vessel was sent to Chiloe
to warn the authorities, and another went to bring the
garrison and settlers from Juan Fernandez. The expedition proved a failure, for the Monteagudo was seized by
a part of her crew, and brought into Valparaiso; from
whence, after having received a detachment of troops,
&c., she was sent to Chiloe, where, by a stratagem, they
succeeded in entrapping General Freyre and his companions. All were brought to Valparaiso, where they
were tried; and now, as there was no danger to be apprehended, they were sent, under custody of a detachment
of infantry, to the island of Juan Fernandez, where they
underwent many privations; after which, Gen. Freyre,
and several others, were shipped off to New South Wales.

---

* " El Antiguo contador," Don Manuel Fernandes, with several others,
received pensions, for they had been found fit subjects for the commiseration of a benignant and just government, who allowed the first, the trifling
sum of 1000 dollars per annum, and 600 to his wife and daughters for life,
should they survive him, for the services he had rendered to the Spanish
government, previous to the battle of Chacabuco; and at a period when
many of those unfortunate patriots, who had been (" dado de Baja,")
cashiered, were either starving, or reduced to the greatest misery!!

The rest were finally released by a Peruvian squadron, under General Moran, who set them at liberty, and disarmed the troops who capitulated.

After Garrido and Angulo had consummated their midnight seizure of the Peruvian vessels of war that were in Callao, the Chilian government declared war against the confederation; the army and squadron were re-organized, and Lieutenant-General Don Manuel Blanco Encalada took the command. I had the honour of being appointed his aid-de-camp. A revolution broke out in Quillota, where many lives were lost; and the minister of state, Don Diego Portales, with his secretary, were assassinated. General Blanco defeated his opponents; their chief colonel, Vidaurre, and several others,* were taken, tried, and executed on the 4th of July, a day venerated by all patriots; but, as those who governed Chile at that period were the enemies of such, it seemed as if that day was chosen on purpose, by the sapient Faroleros.

* The unfortunate Vidaurre, and his officers, received the punishment of death from the very same individuals who had corrupted them in the years 1828-9 and 1830. I have a copy of a document he wrote previous to his death, in which he stated that he had made the attempt to rid Chile from a faction who sought its ruin, and to subjugate his countrymen, &c. I had the task of defending nine of the officers, two of whom were shot, one was a Swede, Captain Forelius, who, in happier times, had enjoyed the particular favour of his monarch, (Bernadotte, of Sweden), and who left a widow and child to bewail his fate.

CHAP. XIV.

On the 15th of September, the expedition entitled "El Ejercito Restaurador del Peru," left Valparaiso under the command of Lieutenant-General Don Manuel Blanco Encalada, under whom I had the honour of serving as first aid-de-camp. The force consisted of four battalions, and two corps of cavalry, with a brigade of artillery, besides the skeletons of two or three corps, and a numerous accompaniment of staff-officers, &c. that had emigrated from Peru; these were denominated "La Columna Peruana." The convoy consisted of seven vessels of war, and sixteen transports; the Peruana schooner of war, with a transport, the Napoleon, had sailed two days previous for Copiapo, under the command of Major Frijolet. The British sloop of war, Rover, accompanied us.

September 22.—We anchored in Iquique: the general went on shore with several of the staff, and found that the authorities had deserted the place; and it was said that General La Fuente's brother went with them, (this general, as well as the Generals Castilla and Postigo, accompanied the expedition.) A picket of soldiers, with a band of music, landed, in order to publish a proclamation; the vessels lay at single anchor without furling their sails, and a calm prevented our proceeding to sea

until the following day. Iquique is in lat. 20° 12. 15. S.
long. 70° 13. 0. W.   Its appearance is by no means
inviting, and the coast and surrounding country has the
appearance of a sandy desert, for not a symptom of
vegetation was to be seen; the port is an open bay, sheltered from the S. and S. S. W.; there is a reef and a
small island that shelter what may be called the harbour,
where there were two small schooners at anchor.

As I did not land, I can only describe what I saw from
the ship: there appeared to be about twenty houses; the
best had English, French, and North American flags
hoisted, to show they were inhabited by foreigners; the
rest I could see were nothing more than miserable-looking cottages or huts.   The principal trade of Iquique is
saltpetre; and the produce of the mines of Tarapaca,
about fourteen leagues inland; there is no water in this
district, nor does it ever rain, so that the inhabitants have
to supply themselves with water by boats from a river a
few leagues distant to the north. Here are the ruins of an
old fort, but the place was defenceless; I was informed
that dead bodies, when buried, do not putrify, on account
of the saline qualities of the earth.   On the 24th, about
noon, we saw the "Moro" of Arica, and when within
a short distance of the port, the convoy hove-to, and
a detachment of infantry embarked in the boats belonging to the vessels of war; the Achilles brig of war,
Captain Simpson, took them in tow, and stood in towards
the beach to the southward of the port, as if to land them;
but shortly afterwards she bore up, and, with the Libertad,
flag-ship, entered the port; there were two batteries, one
of which fired a gun, and the colours were hauled down
as they neared the beach, where they landed without any
resistance; as the authorities and garrison had left the

2 g

place; the vessels came to an anchor, and remained all
night without furling their sails: next morning, 25th,
I went on shore with a Peruvian, Colonel Lopero, and
Major Wood of the Chile staff. The city of Arica is in
lat. 18° 28. 35. S. long. 70° 16. 0. W., the bay is well
sheltered from the southward by El Morro Blanco, and
a small reef that runs out to the N. W. The town was
defended by three batteries; there is a mole where boats
may load or unload when the tide serves; and the
watering-place is close to it. The valley of Arica is
fertile, but its neighbourhood, or as far as I could see, was,
like Iquique, a sandy desert. A good trade is carried
on from Arica with the interior, and the principal depôt
and residence of foreign merchants is at Tacna, about
fifteen leagues inland, where British and other European
goods are disposed of to the natives of Upper Peru and
Bolivia; a great deal of specie, cotton, wool, Peruvian
bark, and other productions of Peru, are exported from
Arica. The city had suffered much during the late revolution of General Salaverry, and the whole had a shabby
and dilapidated appearance: as it never rains, the houses
have flat roofs, covered only with mats or wattled canes;
the streets are at right angles, and there is an alameda
with two rows of willow-trees. All the foreigners had
their respective flags hoisted to denote their dwellings,
which were upon the whole the best and most substantial;
those I conversed with seemed to be inimical to our
expedition, for it caused a stagnation in trade; and as
that was their errand to South America, they spoke
feelingly. The two batteries were demolished, the
guns rendered useless, the carriages burnt, and shot, &c.
taken on board: during the night the custom-house was
plundered, and goods to a considerable value had been

stolen, for which a strict inquiry and search was set on foot. I was surprised, as well as my friend the colonel, who accompanied me, to see some females run from their doors on our approach, which showed we were unwelcome visitors. During my stay on shore, I was informed that General Santa Cruz was more popular than had been represented in Chile, and that his troops were well officered, and under good discipline; also that the most severe decrees had been issued to oblige the inhabitants on the coast to retire into the interior, the moment they received information of our attempting to land, as well as to destroy their pastures and the animals they were unable to take with them. On account of the transports having got under weigh, I was obliged to repair on board, and on informing my fellow-passengers what I had learnt on shore, they laughed at my intelligence, as proceeding from my countrymen, who were reputed to be one and all partisans of General Santa Cruz, and, of course, enemies to the Chile-Peruvian expedition. About three P. M. signals were made to anchor again, and all communication with the shore prohibited. In the evening I was informed that two Peruvians had arrived from the interior, with favourable intelligence. Next day, 26th, it was ascertained that the soldiers who had charge of the town, had, in company with some villains, who had informed them that there was a considerable quantity of specie belonging to government, deposited in the custom-house, entered it through the roof, and plundered it of merchandise only, as no cash was to be found. The general, on learning the account of the losses sustained, made them good from the military chest, and ordered Captain Carrillo to be shot, which was accordingly done in front of the custom-house; also, the subaltern officer was cashiered, for neglect in not taking precautionary measures to prevent such scandalous proceedings. Our transports having completed their water, we sailed on the evening ; and on the 29th, about sunset, we anchored in Islay. The general landed, und appointed Colonel Lopero to be governor. We received orders to be in readiness to disembark at daybreak ; but shortly afterwards these orders were countermanded, as the general had been deceived with regard to the distance, roads, and resources, from this port to Arequipa, and issued fresh orders to proceed to Aranta and Quilca. Islay is in lat. 17° 1. 0. S. long. 72° 0. 15. W. I did not land here, but from our anchorage I counted about forty tolerable houses, besides a large building, two stories high, that was the governor's residence, and custom-house ; there were four batteries, but the guns had been taken away, or thrown over the rocks into the sea. This is the nearest port to Arequipa, and had only been made a place of debarkation of foreign goods a few years before ; it was then only occupied by fishermen ; there is no water, except from a spring, or small rivulet, upon the hills, about one and a half league distant, where there is an olive grove : the rest of the coast is, as at the last mentioned place, barren and sandy ; Arequipa is about thirty-four leagues distant, and the roads are over a range of mountains and a desert, till within two and a half leagues of the capital ; only one resting-place, El Tambo, invites the traveller to alight, where refreshments may be procured, although water has to be brought from a river more than eight leagues distant. The bay is sheltered from the S. W. by an island, and where we anchored, we had seventy fathoms of cable out. At sunrise, on the 30th, we got under weigh, and, on leaving the port, a Genoese brig arrived from Arica

with Colonel Ugarteche on board, who had been sent
with a flag of truce to General Lopez, who was with a
division of the army of the " Confederacion" in Tacna.
The Libertad, Monteagudo, and several transports that
had horses on board, came to anchor near the Caleta of
Huato. This is a creek or small cove, where some fishermen reside, who have a few miserable stone hovels; they
had no boats nor canoes, but used balsas made of inflated
seal-skins; there was a little brackish water, and the
anchorage was deep and rocky. The rest with troops,
&c. proceeded with the Achilles, and other vessels of war,
to Quilca. On anchoring near the Libertad, several
vessels got foul of one another, and the barque Carmen
ran on shore; she had the greatest part of the staff and
a corps of cavalry on board, upwards of thirty horses,
and the greatest part of the military stores of the Peruvian column, besides the horse-shoes for the whole of
the cavalry. Luckily no lives were lost, but the officers
and soldiers were bereft of the greatest part of their
arms and equipages; the horses, with the exception of
two that were bruised, got on shore in safety; few of
the stores were saved, and two launches or boats were
stove and sunk before she went to pieces. The process
of disembarking and landing the horses was tedious;
several made their escape from the beach into the interior,
and were brought back by the natives: here two or three
Peruvians visited the general, and made the most generous
offers of mules and cattle, which made every one believe
that we should be gladly received, and every aid given
us on our landing, and advance up the country.

October 1st.—The schooner Carmen arrived here with
despatches from Chile; the horses, as soon as landed,
were sent away to Quilca, and had to traverse a barren

mountainous country, for six or seven leagues, before
they could meet with water or verdure. On the 3rd,
we sailed and anchored in Quilca; next day, the 4th,
I left the barque Isabella, Captain Gaymer; this vessel
took down one hundred horses, of which we lost six or
seven; we were very much crowded on board, on account
of the between-decks being occupied as far aft as the
cabin with the horses; and two days previous to leaving,
five " jefes," one captain, five subalterns, three printers,
and seventy soldiers, belonging to the Peruvian column,
were sent on board. There was only one state-room, and
two berths in the cabin; the first was taken possession of
by myself, and the rest had to battle the watch for a place
to lie down; however, the " Vicario jeneral," chaplain of
the Peruvian army, Doctor Armas, and Colonel Lopero,
were put in possession of the two berths. The five "jefes"
arrived on board, and sailed without having brought the
rations that government had provided for them, and
would have fared ill had they embarked in any other
vessel; but Captain Gaymer, being owner of the Isabella,
and pitying the case of the poor emigrants, generously
invited them to his table, where, with his viands and my
wines, they fared tolerably well. The landing-place at
Quilca is in lat. 16° 41. 50. S. long. 72° 27. 15. W. The
cove or creek is about one hundred yards wide; the vessels
anchor out in the bay, on a bank to the south of the river.
There is generally a very heavy swell in the bay. This
was formerly the port of the department, but was abandoned for that of Islay, and not a single dwelling was
remaining; it is about three-quarters of a league from the
village, which is in a deep gulley, (quebrada,) where a
small rivulet enters the sea; its water fertilizes a few
acres on either side, which were in the highest state

of cultivation. There were some patches of excellent "alfalfa," (clover ;) in one of which, nearly consumed, I found the officers' horses that had been brought from Huata, amongst whom my bat horse was only visible; but after a search of more than two hours in the vicinity of the encampment, I at last discovered my charger stowed away behind a hut, at a considerable distance; and what hurt me most was, that his back was so sore I could not mount him; a worthy officer of the Peruvian column had possession of him, and did me the favour to mount him in Huata, and ride him during the time he had been at Quilca.

General Aldunate, and General Castillo, had marched with a battalion of infantry and a party of cavalry, previous to my arrival; as soon as I landed, I waited upon the general, and received orders to be in readiness to march in the evening. On account of the scarcity of mules, I was obliged to order my baggage to be sent on board the Libertad, as Captain George kindly offered to take charge of it for me, and with Lieutenant-Colonel Espinosa engaged an "arriero" to carry a few necessaries, which scarcely amounted to half a load, and for which we had to pay fifteen dollars, whilst the regular price for a mule-load from Quilca to Arequipa is at the dearest time only five dollars. It is a tedious walk over the hills to the village, where there is a church, and about fifty or sixty small houses, made mostly of cane and timber : Quilca has been reputed unhealthy, and is about thirty-six leagues from Arequipa.

October 5th.—The Generals Blanco and La Fuente, their aides, and several others, marched after sunset, and crossed the Cuesta Colorado and the Lomas, a mountainous range, for about four leagues : here we passed the cavalry, and a battalion of infantry; the road was heavy, and the soldiers apparently fatigued; the commandant and officers were marching on foot, as those that had horses had given them to the soldiers who appeared most fatigued; and several of the officers were seen carrying their muskets, for the soldiers were heavily laden with their knapsack, great-coat, musket, accoutrements, and six packets of cartridges each, besides three days' provisions, and their canteens with water. The general, previous to leaving Quilca, had sent for all the empty bottles from the vessels, which had been distributed to those that had not canteens to carry it in; also some of the soldiers had to carry camp-kettles, on account of the scarcity of animals. On leaving the Lomas, we entered a sandy desert covered with "medanos," which are large heaps of sand in the shape of half-moons, formed by the wind, and constantly shifting so as to deface the roads, which makes it extremely difficult for travellers to find their way, especially during the night; and we were, on account of the inexperience of our guides obliged to dismount, and halt for about three hours, during the coldest night I ever experienced. However, at daylight, (6th,) the road was discovered; at seven we descended an unpleasant zig-zag path, entered the valley of Siguas, and took up our quarters at the Hacienda of Pachagui. Here we found Gen. Aldunate, and the advanced division; he had taken two prisoners, a major and a captain; the first had been set at liberty, and the latter joined us, and acted as aide to General La Fuente. Next day, (7th,) part of the rear division arrived, and the advance marched. Our general was informed that two or three of the soldiers had expired on the road, and that several others had been left behind, on which the "arrieros" that came. with the general's baggage were sent with water, &c. to search for the stragglers, and render assistance to the Peruvian column, who were to arrive next day. During the night upwards of twenty horses had escaped from where we had a guard, several of the best were amongst them ; a party went in search, and returned next day with five or six of them, and some people that had possession of them. A reward of twenty dollars had been issued for every horse that might be carried to the enemy's head-quarters; however, on the individuals that had the horses, proving they had not left the valley of Victor previous to their finding the horses, were liberated, except a negro who had joined the Peruvian column, on account of having been formerly one of Gen. Salaverry's soldiers. In Siguas bread was brought for sale, and there was plenty of forage. On Sunday the 8th, I had the honour of hoisting and displaying the Peruvian flag for the first time since we landed ; and what surprised me was, the indifference shown by a group of Peruvians who were present* ; for as soon as I had done, I took off my cap and gave three cheers, in which I was not assisted by any one of them. The owner of this estate, Don N. Ribero, was a great partisan of General Santa Cruz, two of his sons were in his service, one in command of a corps of cavalry, and the other in charge of a college; besides which, his nephew was the sub-prefect and present governor of Arequipa ; another son was on the estate of Don Mariano Ribero ; this gentleman had been twice in Chile, and was intimate with our general, and several others that accompanied him ;

* Generals Blanco and La Fuente, Major Wood of the engineers, the general's secretary, and several of the aides, were by-standers during this operation.

he received and treated us with the greatest hospitality; this gentleman showed us the papers published in Arequipa, wherein a celebrated friar, Padre Valdivia, depicted the Chilian soldiers as a horde of savages and robbers. The "arrieros" arrived with some stragglers, and their timely assistance rescued them from certain death; however, they did not fall in with the Peruvian column, on account of their having taken a different route, by which they entered the valley of Siguas, some distance below us. The artillery, that is to say, only two guns of the six, arrived, on account of the scarcity of mules, and none could be obtained here, as they had been all carefully collected, and driven away by the agents of the government.

October 9th—We marched at four P.M., and after having ascended a cuesta, nearly as bad as the one by which we entered the valley of Siguas, we traversed a sandy desert for about nine leagues; we had a fine view of the volcano of Arequipa, which bore by compass N.E. distant about twenty-four leagues, and said to be about 14,000 feet in height. We passed a deep ravine, called Quebrada Honda; and afterwards descended a cuesta still worse than any we had hitherto passed and entered the valley of Victor, which had a fine appearance by moonlight. It is extensive, and there are many fine haciendas, principally vine and sugar-cane. We proceeded about two leagues, and halted at the hacienda of Churunga, where we found the advanced division. Next day, 10th, General Blanco sent Lieutenant-Colonel Espinosa with a flag of truce to Arequipa; at three P.M. the advanced division marched: three Peruvians joined us here; one was made governor of Victor, in place of the one that had emigrated; the other was D. N. B., an officer of militia; and the other D. N. N., who had

just arrived from Arequipa; this person seemed to give
a deal of favourable information concerning the co-operation of the Arequipeños, and urged the general to push
on with his army; he also informed us that a son of his
who had taken charge of some letters from General
Castillo, whilst at Siguas, had fallen into the hands of
the enemy, and had been carried with the correspondence
to their head-quarters.

Although this person seemed to give a deal of favourable information concerning ˈthe co-operation of the
Arequipeños, &c., I could not help observing how coolly
he took the capture and detention of his son, who, according to the custom established in such cases, had
forfeited his life. During his conference with the general,
I was surprised at hearing an individual, who was with
others listening at the door, make use of the expression
in French, " Que coullon." I immediately demanded
who he was; he informed me he was a Frenchman, and
that he had emigrated from Islay by the orders of the
governor, and that the manager of the hacienda was an
intimate friend of his, and at the same time mentioned
that N. N. was no better than he ought to be. I immediately informed the general; and on bringing the Frenchman to his presence, the other did not appear to be at
ease, and shortly afterwards he retired.* We remained

* General La Fuente, on speaking to General Blanco in the presence of
Major Wood, myself, and others, respecting resources, observed, that he
would augment the Peruvian column by one or two more battalions, after
having filled up the vacancies in those already formed.

General Blanco replied to this, stating that it was better to fill up the
Chilian battalions with what remained, than load the state with the expense of so many petty corps.   General Blanco had also a warm dispute
with El Señor Martinez about the impropriety of forcing resources by breaking open doors, &c., which conversation was continued and disputed warmly
by the general's secretary, Don Juan Ramirez, and the auditor of war, Don
Ramon Rosas.

two nights at Victor, the last without any guard,
and, on account of being distant from the advanced
and rear divisions, exposed, and at the mercy of any
enterprising person. However, the aids and their servants mounted guard, and we passed the night unmolested.

October 11th.—Part of the rear division arrived; at
noon the flag of truce returned with an answer from the
prefect of Arequipa; and the soldier that accompanied
Colonel Espinosa, made his appearance on foot, having
lost his horse, &c. In the evening we marched, ascended
the cuesta, and traversed a sandy plain for about four
leagues, and then began to ascend the mountainous range
of the Caldera, where we fagged for four or five leagues
among steep defiles and ascents, where a handful of
determined soldiers might detain and perplex an army
superior to ours. We travelled all this distance without
an escort; but on arriving at Uchumayo, we found a
detachment of infantry in charge of the bridge; this is an
important pass, where a strong position could be taken on
either bank of the river, which during certain seasons is
not fordable; it was here that General Salaverry kept
General Santa Cruz at bay, and cut one of his best
battalions in pieces, who attempted to force the pass, and
Colonel Guillarte, who led them, was taken prisoner.
We passed the night near the bridge, and next morning,
12th, the cavalry of the rear division arrived; three individuals from Arequipa came, and gave the general
flattering accounts of its inhabitants, &c., one of which
was the son of Don N. N., who gave a lame account of
his being captured with the correspondence, and how he
obtained his liberty; he also gave information respecting
the enemy's position and force, which proved to be false.

In the evening we marched, and halted for a short time at Chayapampa, half a league distant from the city, where our advanced division was stationed in a commanding position. About sunset we entered the city of Arequipa ; a few " vivas" were expended on our passing the bridge, and the public square, where the Peruvian flag was displayed above the enemy's. Whilst our advanced division was passing the Caldera, they were fired upon by the militia of Arequipa, who wounded several of our men, one of whom died shortly afterwards. On account of there being no house provided for our general, he took up his quarters with Don Felipe Pardo, at that of his friend, Don Miguel Parejas: some musicians came, to celebrate the arrival of the general; and on his being informed that there were several soldiers in disguise, he ordered me to go, and request a reinforcement to be sent into the city.

October 13th.—The general having been informed that the lady of General Cerdeña had abandoned her home, and taken refuge either in the house of a foreigner or a convent, sent me to ascertain where she was, with orders to visit her in his name, and deliver his respects to her, and request she would return to, and reside in her house ; and that by so doing she would confer a favour on him, and be as safe as if her husband was in command of the city. I received good information that she was in the house of Mr. M'Clacklin, where the English consul resided ; and on informing them, both the owner of the house and the consul expressed their surprise at my visiting them on such an errand, saying they knew not where the lady was,·but supposed she had gone to Moquegua to join the general; on which I requested, if they had an opportunity, to let her know the

purport of my visit, took my leave, and made my report
to the general. Shortly afterwards, the English, French,
and American consuls waited on the general; and on
Monsieur Le Bris offering the house of General Cerdeña
to General Blanco, I was sent with a person to see what
accommodation it afforded: the house was one of the
best in Arequipa, newly fitted up, and papered, but there
was not a single article of furniture, all had been removed
to houses of different friends of the general, to prevent their
being destroyed, &c. On inquiring whether there were
any articles of furniture to be had, I was conducted to the
house of Don Juan Marco del Pont, where I was shown
a few articles barely sufficient to fit up a bed-chamber.
I requested a list, and on obtaining it, made my report
to the general, who declined this courteous offer. General
La Fuente was elected " presidente-provisional" of the
republic of Peru, by the Arequipeños; and Don Felipe
Pardo was named " ministro-general;" General Castillo,
prefect of the department; and sundry other appointments
took place. Shortly after the new government was
organized, measures were taken to facilitate horses and
mules, to mount the remainder of the cavalry, as the
corps of Peruvian cavalry had marched on foot from
Quilca to Arequipa, and the general's escort also towards
Islay and Tambo; and as all the horse-shoes belonging
to the cavalry, as well as the saddles, &c. of the Peruvian
corps, had been lost in the Carmen, orders were given to
procure them, and other articles necessary for the campaign, with the greatest despatch; but as most of the
artisans had emigrated, they could not be provided as
soon as was desired. Every thing on our arrival in
Arequipa seemed to favour us, for the first news we received was, that a revolution had broken out in Bolivia;

and the congress had declared the republic to be separated
from the confederation, as General Santa Cruz was
very unpopular; and that Don Ventura Blanco, brother
to General Blanco, was to be president; also, that the
Argentinos had defeated General Brawn, and were advancing into Bolivia; that Cusco, Puna, Lampa, and
Chuquibamba were about to pronounce against General
Santa Cruz; and that General Lopez was to unite
the troops he had in Tacna to ours, or operate in
our favour; also that General Cerdeña, the prefect,
was unwell, and unfit to serve against us, &c. The
"arrieros" having arrived from Quilea with two more
guns, as they had been sent back to fetch them—and on
account of not having the means to transport the whole
of the brigade—the general gave orders for the two
remaining guns to be kept at Quilca, until the mules that
had been promised, or others could be procured, as the
authorities of Arequipa, had, previous to our arrival taken
particular care to collect and send away all the "arrieros"
with their mules, to their own army.

October 19th.—The general having sent Major Wood
of the Engineers, and myself, to survey the country
between Paucarpata and the city, we fixed upon the
quintas of El Palomar, which is on the road from
Arequipa to Tingo, for the right; the quinta of Don
Pio Tristan and three others, on the road that leads to
Socabaya for the centre; and the quintas of Porongoche
and Miraflores, on the road from the city to Paucarpata,
for the left. On the rear of these stations there was a
road of considerable width, which crossed the front of the
city, called Llolla Grande, where the troops might be
formed, and be in readiness to march to any given point,
for the Llolla not only crossed the roads that led from

the city to the southward, but it communicated with
the plain of Miraflores, and that of the Panteon; also,
these stations were not the distance of more than a quarter
of a mile from each other. Whilst we were occupied
in taking a plan of the country from the mirador
of a quinta near to Paucarpata, a party of militia that
the prefect had sent out from Arequipa, to guard the
road, as an advanced party, deserted, and went over to
the enemy; we were lucky they did not take us with
them, to enhance their services. The general approved of
the stations, and selected the quinta of Tristan for head-
quarters, placing the cavalry in his rear, the Batallones
Portales and Colchagua on his right, Valparaiso in front,
and the Battalon Valdivia on his left. In the evening they
left their position of Challapampa, and took up the new
one. On the 21st Commandante Garcia, with a detachment
of infantry and cavalry, marched in order to surprise the
advanced division of the enemy; but on falling in with
some militia in Savandia, he attacked them, killed one or
two, and sent in four prisoners, from which we learned
that General Cerdeña was in Apoquina, in a good
state of health; and that several of the stragglers who
were missing had been carried to the enemy's head-
quarters by their militia. The general despatched a
courier to Quilca, and almost all the officers of the army
as well as myself, embraced the opportunity of writing
by this conveyance, as the schooner Carmen was to bear
the despatches to Chile. The provisional government
published a gazette, the first numbers of which being
full of favourable accounts, were sent to Chile. As
chief aide-de-camp to the general, I kept a list of the
personages that visited him, in order to find out where
they resided, so as to be able to conduct the general

when disposed to return the visits; to my astonishment, I found that only a few were persons of respectability, and that nearly all the persons of the first class, clergy, &c., had emigrated previous to our arrival. The provisional government issued severe decrees against those who had emigrated, and "forced their tenants, under pain of imprisonment," to advance their rents in order to meet the expenses of the army. On the 23rd the general was informed by the officer of the advanced party, that a flag of truce had arrived from the enemy; the general sent me out to receive the officer and conduct him to his presence; but before we started for the city, Commandante Olavarrieta, of the staff, came out to accompany us. Whilst passing the headquarters the officer was blindfolded, and when near to the city the trumpeter and soldiers that accompanied him were detained until his return with an answer.

On the 24th another flag of truce, Colonel Landasuri, arrived from General Herrera, president of the republic of S. Peru, requesting an interview, which the general answered, and gave orders to prepare the quinta of Tristan, head-quarters of our army, for his reception; but on the general's arriving sooner than he was expected, General Aldunate accompanied him into the city, and General Blanco received him at his residence, and during his stay there was a cessation of hostilities; he passed the night with the general; and next day, the 25th, on taking leave, he was grossly insulted by a group of Arequipaños which offended General Blanco so much, that he not only reprimanded those present, but sent an aide-de-camp immediately with a letter to General Herrera, in which he stated his dissatisfaction, &c., at the scandalous proceeding. On the 28th the

2 H

general received information that the enemy intended
surprising our advanced posts, on which we marched at
eleven P.M., and took up a position on the plain of Miraflores, near to the Rancheria, remaining under arms
all night, and next morning we found the information
was totally unfounded. On the 30th Colonel Necochea
marched with a detachment of cavalry and infantry,
in order to attack the enemy's advanced position; and
in Molevalle he took one lieutenant-colonel, one lieutenant of cavalry, and a subaltern of infantry, with twenty-
four soldiers, prisoners. He pushed on to Poxi, three
leagues further; but the enemy, on his arrival there, had
escaped, on account of having received information of
his approach; the lieutenant-colonel of cavalry was sent
to Quilca with Captain Valdivieso of the Peruvian
column, who allowed Lieutenant Villeno, of the cavalry,
to escape; and the subaltern was liberated on "parole of
honour." The soldiers, as well as several others who had
deserted from the enemy, joined the Peruvian column,
and by their accounts it was expected that many others
would do the same, should an opportunity present itself.
Our horses being mostly shod, and the general's escort
having arrived with a few horses and mules from Tambo,
he reviewed our army on the 2nd of November, near to
the Panteon, about a league from Arequipa; the soldiers
made a fine appearance, and mustered about 3,000 men.
I could not avoid noting the indifference of the Arequi-
panians; for only about twenty individuals, three of whom
I knew belonged to the city, were assembled to see this
(if considered a liberating army), welcome and gallant
sight. On the day following, the 3rd, information was
given that General Santa Cruz was on his way to join
General Cerdeña, and that the latter had left Puquina for

Poxi, to receive the protector. On the 4th the general gave orders for the cavalry to take possession of the roads, to prevent intelligence being carried to the enemy of our movements, and ordered the army to be in readiness to march between nine and ten at night. He could only procure arrieros and mules sufficient to carry two of the four field-pieces; the rest he was obliged to leave in care of a corporal's guard, at head-quarters, with the rest of the articles belonging to the staff, &c. The army accordingly marched at ten. At midnight the general marched also, and sent me forward to the quinta of Tristan, in order that his escort might be in readines to join him. On his arrival I informed him that the army had marched without their provisions, on account of not being able to procure mules and arrieros to carry ten sacks of bread that had arrived just after their departure: nor could a paysano be found to drive a few head of cattle. The general ordered Captain Reyes, who commanded his escort, to remain with the greatest part of his soldiers, in order to conduct, in the best manner he could, the bread and animals. We overtook the advanced division at daylight on the 5th in Mollevalle, about four leagues distant from Arequipa. Here we could not procure provisions of any sort; and the curate of this place not only informed the general that the Argentinos had defeated the Bolivian General Brawn, but he also gave him intelligence that General Cerdeña had taken up a strong position near to Poxi. We marched, and ascended a cuesta and defile for about two leagues; and when within one of Poxi, we observed the enemy's videttes on an eminence, who retired as we advanced; and shortly afterwards we met an Indian who informed us that the enemy's troops had left Poxi. The general gave orders to halt, and, in company with General Aldunate and his aides, with a few cuirassiers set off towards Poxi, ordering Colonel Destua, who had command of a detachment of light infantry, to march after him. On entering Poxi the general was informed that the enemy had retired to the heights covering the road that led to Puquino; and that General Herrera commanded the division; also, that General Santa Cruz was expected hourly to join General Cerdeña by another road, which proved that the news given the general in Arequipa was false, and which had induced him to undertake a march into such a wilderness as that in the neighbourhood of Poxi. The generals consulted about encamping in Poxi; but on account of there being no forage in the vicinity, and the army being as it were entirely without provisions, I was sent with orders for it to countermarch, and return to Arequipa;* also that the cavalry, under the command of Colonel Necochea, should halt where they were until further orders. On account of a few cavalry making their appearance, the general sent one of his aides, Captain Murillo, and another officer, who had charge of the cuirassiers, and on advancing exchanged a few shots; but the enemy retired after having requested and obtained a parley, in which the officer in command stated, that he had orders not to molest us, &c., his name was Lieutenant Valdivia, a native of Arequipa. Previous to descending the Cuesta of Mollevalle, I met a person who had been sent by General La Fuente to make inquiries, and on my relating what had taken place, he retired; I had difficulty in procuring any one to prepare a breakfast, and found that no bread had been got ready for us,

---

* General Aldunate undertook this march in a state of ill health.

so each soldier received from the provisions that had
been brought from Arequipa, on his return in the
evening, but one small loaf of three ounces weight
during a march to Poxi and back, of about fourteen
Peruvian leagues. Two days afterwards, (7th,) we were
put into confusion by a person bringing information, that
a division of about five hundred men had arrived at
dusk in the neighbourhood of Tingo; I was sent about
eleven P. M. with the informant, and another, to head-
quarters, to inform General Aldunate of this report, who,
on questioning, sent an officer and a party to reconnoitre.
This person returned at sunrise, saying, that all was quiet
in that quarter; on which I returned, and gave information to the general, and retired. I had not been in my
quarters more than half an hour, when I was sent for, and
informed that a person had arrived, who positively stated
that the enemy were there, for he had seen them; on
which the general was enraged at the reconnoitering
parties not having done their duty, and gave orders for
the army to march directly in that quarter.—(8th,) Accordingly we went, and after having advanced upon Tingo,
found we had been deceived, and that not a soldier had
been seen in the neighbourhood : this so irritated the general, that he gave orders to break up the line in front of
the city, and directed the troops to enter, and be quartered
in Arequipa, until the enemy should make their appearance, as it was impossible to gain any true intelligence of
their movements; whilst we, on the contrary, were surrounded by spies and enemies, who gave the earliest and
truest information of our movements.

The day after our return (10th) to Arequipa, a flag of
truce arrived, and Colonel Irizarri was sent to Savandia,
two leagues distant, in order to treat with General Herrera;

an armistice was proclaimed, and commissioners from
each camp appointed to observe punctuality, &c.; but
information arrived of a Colonel Gruesso having with
a party of cavalry attacked Islay, and proceeded to the
valley of Victor, and taken all the cattle that had been
collected, besides some prisoners. This affair caused a
suspension of the armistice; and on General Herrera
retiring from Savandia, he wrote to General Blanco,
stating, that he had received information from Arequipa
that he was unsafe, and regretted the conference had
been broken up by such a disagreeable circumstance, at
the same time sending orders to Colonel Gruesso to return
the cattle, and liberate the prisoners, which order was
fully complied with. The general must have had spies
near his person, for there were only five individuals present, when one of them proposed that the general should
retaliate by taking General Herrera, and those who
accompanied him, prisoners; the general was highly
offended at such a proposal, and ordered Colonel Lopero
to march against Colonel Gruesso, and he also sent
me with a letter to Colonel Irizarri; on my arrival at
Savandia, about an hour after the conversation had taken
place, I was surprised at hearing that General Herrera
knew almost every word that had transpired. Colonel
Irizarri returned in the evening, and the commissioners
left Arequipa next day, accompanied by an officer, who
came to inform the general that Colonel Gruesso had,
according to the orders of General Herrera, given up the
prisoners and cattle that he had taken. Captain Morillo
also returned from the enemy's head-quarters, and had
left General Santa Cruz there with the Generals Cerdeña,
O'Connor, Quiros, and Villagra, with all their force, which
he calculated to amount to about four thousand men,

under pretty good discipline. General Blanco would not
agree to the proposals presented to him by Colonel
Irizarri; and finding it impossible to remove his army
for want of resources, so as to force the enemy either to
terms or blows, he proposed the singular mode of deciding the war by a partial combat, which was accepted. On
the 12th, the general immediately assembled the chiefs
of the army, to whom he read General Herrera's acceptance, authorized by General Santa Cruz, and his own
answer, in which he named eight hundred men as com-
batants, Thursday the 16th as the day, and the neighbourhood of Socabaya the appointed place. I was sent by
the general for the English, French, and American consuls, whom he named as umpires, and they accepted the
appointment; the chiefs not only acquiesced in the general's proposals, but we offered ourselves as candidates
in this chivalrous mode of warfare. But we were soon
disappointed by the receipt of another communication
on the 13th, from General O'Connor, stating that General Santa Cruz would not agree to the terms; for those
proposed were only fit to prove the physical strength
of soldiers, and not the art of " estratige," On the 14th,
the general sent an officer with an answer to General
O'Connor's letter to Poxi, and shortly afterwards he
received positive intelligence that General Santa Cruz
had marched from Poxi towards Cangallo, on which he
gave orders for the troops to be in readiness, in case of
necessity; and removed from the house of Don Miguel
Parejas to the Estado Mayor, where General Aldunate
resided, and paid five hundred dollars for the expenses
of board and lodging of himself and those that accompanied him, which proved that our landlord did not suffer
much by his guests. Next morning (15th) our enemy

was seen on the heights, near the base of the volcano,
marching toward Paucarpata, where they took up a
strong position; there was a little skirmishing on the
plain of Miraflores, between our advanced parties and
those of the enemy. At noon a flag of truce arrived with
an invitation from General Santa Cruz to General Blanco
for an interview, which was accepted; and about the
same time received information from Lieutenant-Colonel
Espinosa, who was on his retreat from Chuquibamba,
that General Vigil had arrived there, and was following
him up. On account of plausible reports being given to
the general about the inhabitants of Chuquibamba, which
induced him to send a detachment to that district, under
the command of Lieutenant-Colonel Espinosa, to receive
supplies of men and animals, &c., the general learnt the
true state of the feelings of the inhabitants; for they, in
lieu of co-operating with us, or providing any resources,
received our troops in an hostile manner, and forced them
to retreat just as General Vigil was advancing, and nearly
upon him, of which he had received no previous intelligence, nor had our general, until Lieutenant-Colonel
Espinosa sent to inform him. On General Blanco leaving
his quarters, in order to meet General Santa Cruz, he
expressed himself to the effect, that he was awkwardly
situated, having to treat when his rear was menaced; he
also sent me back with a letter of General Santa Cruz, which
guaranteed his safety, to be deposited in the hands of
General Aldunate. I overtook the general near Porongoche, where General Herrera, with several other officers
had met the general, in order to accompany him to their
head-quarters. We entered the village of Paucarpata,
and found it crowded with paysanos, mostly inhabitants
of Arequipa and its neighbourhood, who followed us into

the " patio" of the curate's house, where General Santa
Cruz had taken up his quarters. On General Santa Cruz
making his appearance, in order to receive General Blanco,
the paysanos began to cry out, " Viva el Protector;" but
they were silenced, and ordered to leave the premises.
General Blanco had taken off his cap, in order to return
his thanks, in case a scene had taken place similar to the
one in Arequipa ; but he was spared that mortification.
The generals met, embraced, and retired into a private
room, where they remained some time alone; I met
several old acquaintances, and we passed the time agreeably during their interview; after which, a celebrated
personage, El Padre Valdivia, made his appearance
with another person, and he asked me several improper
questions relative to the present state of affairs, which
I silenced by analyzing this said friar's publications, which
so offended his reverence, that he ceased and retired.
We dined with General Santa Cruz, and were served at
dinner by his aides-de-camp. About 11 p. m. the general
retired, accompanied by General Herrera, and some
officers of the staff. On the 16th, after having held a
council of war, General Blanco went out to meet Generals
Herrera and Quiros, at the " Quinta" of Tristan ; we
arrived first, and shortly afterwards the generals, accompanied by Colonel Irizarri, and the secretaries who were
appointed to draw out the treaty. I was sent into Arequipa with an aide-de-camp, who was despatched to fetch
the uniforms of General Quiros, and, on arriving at his
house, his lady informed the aide that the general's trunks
had been deposited with a friend in the neighbourhood;
and on going there, we were told that they had been
placed in a convent for better security ; the aide-de-camp
sent for the trunks, and it was highly amusing to see

the pleasure evinced by the inmates of the house on the
aide's arrival, and to hear how much the nuns expressed
themselves interested in the welfare of General Santa Cruz;
for only a few days had elapsed since I had, in company
with Generals Blanco and Aldunate, and others, visited
the same convent, and then the nuns assured us that all
their prayers and wishes were in our favour, and that they
had distributed their "escapularios" amongst our soldiers,
to preserve them from harm; however, as these ladies
never meddle in politics, it is a proof of their subtleness.
I returned to the Quinta with the aide, and met the general
on my way; on dismounting, the aides of General Herrera
embraced me, and informed me that we were no more
enemies, and that Generals Santa Cruz and Blanco had
come to terms. I took my leave of the generals and the
rest, and returned to Arequipa, and went direct to the
house of Mr. Maclaclin, where the lady of General
Cerdeña had resided, with a message that the general had
requested me to deliver; but she had retired to rest,
Mr. Maclaclin, therefore, received the message, and was
glad to learn such favourable intelligence.

November 17th.—Something occurred during the early
part of the day that nearly put a stop to the negociations,
but in the evening they were concluded and confirmed;
and the moment it was made known, the bells of Arequipa,
and other demonstrations of its inhabitants, showed in a
positive manner to whose interests they were attached. As
soon as Generals La Fuente and Castilla knew the results
of the treaties, they left the city on the 18th; numbers of
the citizens that had emigrated returned to their families;
many of whom had not shaved their beards since they left.
I conversed with several, and, on speaking about the affair
of the day, I was confidently informed that they did not

like General Santa Cruz personally; but that he had, since he had been protector, kept Peru free from internal disturbances; and, also, that their persons and property were more safe and respected, during his administration, than during those of his predecessors. On this account they would support him against the pretensions of the various candidates that had appeared; at the same time, stated reasons, which, if true, were sufficient to justify their conduct.

On the 19th, General Santa Cruz reviewed his army, which consisted of seven battalions of infantry, two regiments of cavalry, and one brigade of artillery, about five thousand in all, on the plain of Miraflores: afterwards he entered the city of Arequipa, more like a conqueror returning amongst subjects that adored him, than the person he had been represented to us prior to our entry. My pen is inadequate to describe the particulars of this triumph, and the emulation evinced by the citizens in general to show their partiality towards him. In fact, the veil was withdrawn from my eyes, and many others expressed themselves undeceived with respect to the patriotism of the Arequipaños.

General Blanco dined with Generals Santa Cruz, Herrera, and Cerdeña, at the house of the latter, which had been fitted up for their reception in an elegant manner; there were several officers of rank at dinner; and what is most remarkable, only one Chileno (General Herrera, president of the republic, " S. Peruano,") sat at table. For General Blanco, and Commandante Roxas of the battalion Valdivia, and myself, who accompanied them, were, although in the Chilian service, reputed to be " estrangeros." Previous to the treaties, the general assembled the staff-officers and commandantes of battalions, &c., and laid before them the

exact situation in which they were placed; in fact, they
had little to learn;* for, on account of the scarcity of
resources, and the malice of the Arequipaños, who had
used every art to entice our soldiers to desert, which had
obliged the general to make a severe example, by ordering the execution of one who had been caught; also to
steal our horses, even during the period of armistice,
together with many other circumstances, tending to manifest how critically we were situated; they unanimously
agreed in considering it the most honourable way of extricating themselves from the labyrinth, in which so many
untoward circumstances had placed them; notwithstanding,
all would have preferred, had there been the least shadow
of possibility, to have decided the contest by a battle.

A COPY OF THE " ACTA" CELEBRATED IN AREQUIPA.

" The chiefs of the army, cited by order of El S'or JenL en
Jefe, to meet at his quarters this day, in order to hear him
explain to them, and lay before them, the situation in
which the army is placed, as well as that of the enemy, in
order that he may hear the opinions of the chiefs, so that
he may also be enabled to adopt the measures he may think
convenient to further the interests of Chile.

" Su Señoria stated, that up to the moment in which
the enemy had arrived within a league of the city, with a
force about double that of the Chilian army, it had not been
in his power to impede the re-union of the corps of General

---

* We had begun to feel a scarcity of funds, that were to be provided by
the provisional government, although our army had received one month's
pay in two instalments since we arrived in Arequipa, from our military
chest of " comisaria ;" I have been credibly informed that the subaltern
officers and soldiers of the Peruvian column had only received what was
allowed since 21st of October, viz. two reals per officer, and one real per
soldier, daily.

Santa Cruz, which have been brought from the north and south of the confederation; and that this was owing to the scantiness of the resources provided by the provisional government, which had been created on his arrival in this city; and that this government has not only placed the Chilian army in the impossibility of making any movements, but they have left the army many days without rations; and when they were supplied, it was seldom at a proper time: also, if these resources were of little consideration up to that period, it is now plainly to be seen, that they were entirely consumed; for during these last four days, nothing has been provided for us to ration the corps of the army, and maintain the hospital.

" That all the hopes that were held out for the co-operation of the inhabitants of Peru and Bolivia, ought to be considered as lost; for it is plain to be seen, that the inhabitants, instead of receiving the Chilian army as their supporters, have risen " en masse;" and we have the example of those of Chuquibamba, who have acted against the division of Lieutenant-Colonel Espinosa. Here, in Arequipa, we have not had a single recruit. It is to be seen that, in this manner, the Chilian army, in place of augmenting its force in proportion as the circumstances require, is not at all able to replace the vacancies it has suffered, and which now exceed two hundred men.

" That the United Provinces of Rio de la Plata have not co-operated as was expected; nor have they entertained the Bolivian division which General Brawn was enabled, after the action of Humaguaca, to send to our enemy's camp. We have now in sight, the greatest part of the troops, that ought to have been occupied on the Bolivian frontier, by the Argentinos.

" That in the situation our army is placed, we have no

other alternative, " partido," than to retire towards Uchumayo, with the hopes that the enemy, who, confident in
their superiority of numbers, may follow us, and then we
might give them battle in the plain, trusting to the
valour and enthusiasm of our troops, and the superiority
of our cavalry; but it is to be feared, that should we be
permitted to execute our retreat to Quilca, it would be
attended with difficulties, and a scarcity of provisions, on
account of a division of the enemy occupying our rear;
and if even the re-embarkation of our infantry should be
effected without any loss, our cavalry, with the horses
only, would have to go by land; and after a march of
fifteen or twenty days, it may be supposed they would
arrive in a very bad state, and that we should be obliged
to regulate our navigation according to their rate of
marching; and as for what we have seen in this city, we
ought to draw the same consequences, that we shall find
on the coast where we should touch at, the same difficulties
as in Islay and Quilca, without being able to commence
our operations against Lima, on account of the superior
forces that protect that city.

" All the accounts that have hitherto been given us,
respecting the forces of the protector have been false, as
well as the hopes that had been held out to us, of the co-
operation of the inhabitants, supply of resources, aug-
mentation of the army, &c.

" Believing the enterprise that we have undertaken
to be superior to our exertions, it appears that there
remains no other alternative, than that of making an
honourable and advantageous peace, or fight against
double our forces, in the confidence, that if we were not
conquered, the honour of the Chilian armies will remain
unsullied.

"That the sacred interests of Chile, deposited in the army, counsels us to act in this manner, bearing also in consideration many other causes that are too plainly seen by Los SS. chiefs; and what makes us see how painful it would be for Chile, and the army, the result of their sacrifices and bloodshed, even should fortune crown us with a triumph. Los SS. chiefs having found the judgment that Su Señoria, the general-in-chief had formed of the situation in which the Chilian army is placed, is exact; and all make the most solemn protest, to sacrifice themselves in the service of the republic, although they should have to do it without the least hope of obtaining the triumph, only with the object of maintaining the honour of the Chilian arms. But they know that the interest of the republic, its honour, its tranquillity, interests, and glory, will always remain secure, when, under such critical circumstances as those in which the army is now placed, an honourable peace may be obtained in front of a powerful enemy.

(Signed)

"MANUEL BLANCO ENCALADA.　　MANUEL GARCIA.

JOSE SANTIAGO ALDUNATE.　　JUAN VIDAURRE EL LEAL.

ANTONIO JOSE DE IRIZARRI.　　MARIANO ROJAS.

EUGENIO NECOCHEA.　　JOSE YNOJOSA.

LORENZO LUNA.　　CARLOS OLAVARRIETA."

Arequipa, 16th November, 1837.

TREATIES OF PAUCARPATA.

"En el Nombre de Dios, &c. &c.

"Art. 1st. Perpetual peace and friendship will be established between the confederation of Peru, Bolivia, and the republic of Chile; each government will bury their respective complaints in oblivion, and in future

abstain from all " reclamaciones" respecting what may
have occurred in the course of the misunderstandings
that have occasioned the war.

" 2nd. The government of the confederation repeats
the solemn declaration so often made, that they have
never authorized any offensive act against the independence and tranquillity of the republic of Chile, and in
its turn, that government must declare that it never
intended to seize the vessels of the confederation, and
make prizes of them, but only to keep them in deposit, in
order that they may be restored, as they offer to do,
according to the stipulations of this treaty.

" 3rd. The Chilian government compromises itself to
restore the following vessels to that of the confederation.
The bark Santa Cruz, brig Arequipeño, and schooner
Peruviana; these vessels will be given up to a commissioner of the protectoral government, eight days after the
treaties are signed.

" 4th. Six days after the treaty is ratified by S. E. the
protector, the Chilian army will retire to the port of
Quilca, where its transports are, to embark for Chile; and
the Chilian government will forward the ratification of
the treaties to the port of Arica, within fifty days from
this date.

" 5th. The governments of the confederation and of
Chile, compromise themselves to celebrate special treaties
relative to their mutual mercantile interests, which will
be reciprocally considered from the date on which this
treaty is ratified by Chile, as those of the most favoured
nation.

" 6th. The protectorate government offers to celebrate
a treaty of peace with the Argentine provinces, as soon
as they wish, and that of Chile must bind itself to inter-

pose its best endeavours, in order that the said object
may be gained upon the basis on which the two governments agree to.

" 7th. The two contracting parties will adopt as the
basis of their mutual relations, the principle of not inter-
meddling in their domestic affairs ; and they consent to
bind themselves, that no plans of conspiration, nor
" ataques," against the existing government, and the
institutions of each other, shall be allowed in their
respective territories.

" 8th. Both contracting parties oblige themselves
never to take up arms one against the other, without
having understood, or given all the explanations that
may be sufficient as a reciprocal satisfaction, and without
having previously used all possible means of conciliation,
or agreement, and without having explained these motives
to the government who is guarantee.

" 9th. The protectoral government acknowledge in
favour of the republic of Chile, the million and half of
dollars, or such a sum as has been delivered to the minister
plenipotentiary of Peru, Don Jose Larrea y Loredo, from
what was received from the loan that had been contracted in London, by the Chilian government, and has
entered into obligations to satisfy it, in the same terms
and periods in which the republic of Chile pays the
referred capital of the loan.

" 10th. The interests that have accumulated on this
capital, and owing to the bondholders, will be paid by
the government of the confederation, in the terms, and
convenient periods, in order that the Chilian government
may pay the bondholders, with the solid interest, oppor-
tunely.

" 11th. The corresponding part of the interest of the
2 i

capital mentioned in the 9th article, that has been already
paid by the Chilian government to the bondholders, or
the dividends that have been paid up to this date, and
that ought to have been paid by the Peruvian government, according to the agreement made between the
minister-plenipotentiaries of the republic of Chile and
Peru, will be paid by the government of the confederation, in three instalments. The first instalment, six
months from the ratification of these treaties, by the
Chilian government; the second, six months afterwards;
and the third, at the same period.

" 12th. The government of the confederation offers
to take no notice of the political conduct of any individuals of the territory that has been occupied by
the Chilian army; and considers the Peruvians that
have accompanied that army, as if they had not come
with it.

" 13th. The fulfilment of this treaty will be placed
under the guarantee of his Britannic Majesty, whose
aquiescence will be solicited by both contracting governments.

" In faith of which, this treaty is signed in the town of
Paucarpata, on the 16th of November, 1837, and refrended
by the secretaries of the legations,—Manuel Blanco
Encalada, Ramon Herrera, Anselmo Quiros, Antonio
Jose Irizarri, Doctor Juan Gualverto Valdivia, S.L.P.B.,
Juan Henrique Ramirez, S.L.C.

" Andres Santa Cruz, Gran Ciudadano Restaurador,
Capitan-General y President de Bolivia, Supremo Protector de la Confederacion Peru, Boliviano, &c. &c.

" Having found this treaty agreeable to the instructions given by me to the plenipotentiaries named for that
purpose, I solemnly ratify it in all its parts, and charge

my secretary-general to see it observed, printed, and published. Given in the head-quarters of Paucarpata, on the 16th of November, 1837.

"ANDRES SANTA CRUZ,

"MANUEL DE LA CRUZ MENDEZ,

"Secretary-General."

CHAP. XV.

NOT only the citizens of Arequipa, but even our greatest enemies, expressed their satisfaction at the conduct of our army since they had disembarked at Quilca; not a single complaint having been preferred against any individual; so the Chilian army will long be remembered for moderation and discipline, during its short campaign in the department of Arequipa.

The troops began to retire from head-quarters on the 20th at daybreak, and on the 21st all had made their exit, except General Blanco, and a few of the staff. Colonel Irizarri and two officers remained in Arequipa in charge of the sick, and to await the ratification of the treaties of Paucarpata. General Blanco accompanied Generals Santa Cruz, Cerdeña, Herrera, and others, to a ball that was given by the citizens of Arequipa, to celebrate peace; it was well attended, and the company did not retire until daybreak. I shall now give a brief description of the city of Arequipa. It is in lat. 16° 18. 0. S. and is delightfully situated on the banks of the river Chile, almost at the base of the volcano: Arequipa is said to be the second city in Peru, and its population is estimated to be about 35,000; the plains of Arequipa,

Savandia, Characata, and Mollevallc, where water can be
procured to irrigate them, arc very fertile, for not a
" topo" (Peruvian acre,) that is susceptible of cultivation,
is neglected. Nearly all kinds of tropical and European
fruits are produced in this department; and its wheat is
esteemed superior to any in America; the bread of Arequipa can be transported in a good state to any part of
Peru, and keeps for months without becoming mouldy.
In the process of agriculture a deal of " guano" (excre-
ment of sea-fowl brought from islands near the coast of
Peru) is used; it fetches a good price. The roads are
very narrow, except upon barren land; I saw no wheeled
carriages, but those that are used to conduct the sacrament to sick persons. In the neighbourhood of Arequipa
it rains at stated periods; but at the distance of about
twenty-five leagues from the coast it never rains; but
still from the appearance of the gullies, and hill-sides,
there must have been rain formerly; and what is now
only an arid and sandy desert, may have been a more
inviting spot. The climate of Arequipa is temperate
during the day, but at night I have felt it excessively cold,
and at times there are sulphuric exhalations that occasion
a shortness of breathing, which the natives call (sorroche.)
The waters are also sure to purge new-comers. The
volcano of Arequipa resembles Mount Etna more than any
I have seen, but is not so high; it seldom emits smoke; and
the surrounding country has the appearance of Sicily.
The public edifices and bridge àre of stone, and well
built; all the buildings are vaulted, and have flat roofs,
on some of which are " miradores," from which a pleasant
view of the surrounding country may be seen. The market
of Arequipa was pretty well supplied with flesh-meat and
vegetables; and ices and other refreshments are cheap,

and of a good quality; there are many beautiful villas
in the neighbourhood of the city. The inhabitants
were very kind and hospitable, and had much of the
Chilian character, especially the ladies; they have a
taste for music, and in almost every house I saw the
piano, harp, or guitar, and their principal apartments were
well furnished, and some splendidly decorated.

The foreigners spoke highly of the character of the
females; and their strongest testimony is that of several
having married natives, and with whom they seemed to
be happy and comfortable. A good trade is carried on
with the interior and Upper Peru. There are English,
French, and North American consuls in Arequipa, who
have their establishments in Islay. The produce is
brought to the city on mules or llamas; the last is a singular beast of burden, and in my opinion none but a
Peruvian Indian would have patience to drive or accompany them.

On the 21st of November, about two P. M. General
Santa Cruz and his staff, who had accompanied General
Blanco a short distance from the city, took leave; we
halted for the night at Uchumayo, and early next morning crossed the Cuesta de la Caldera. Halted and dined
at Victor, where we were hospitably entertained by an
officer that had been commissioned by General Santa
Cruz to provide for us. At nine at night, we halted at
Siguas, where Lieutenant-Colonel Rivero was stationed,
with a detachment of Peruvian troops; he treated us
hospitably, and next evening we embarked at Quilca.
All the horses belonging to the army had been sold to
General Santa Cruz, who sent persons to receive them;
and the officers got fair prices for theirs, for many
Peruvians had followed them to make purchases. On

the 24th of November, the vessels of war and transports sailed for Valparaiso, after having received orders to make the best of their way there. I embarked with four officers on board of the brig Geumul, Captain Langmaid, and after a pleasant passage, we arrived in Valparaiso on the 15th of December.

A portion of the inhabitants, mostly " employées," took upon themselves the task of being arbiters of the public opinion, and hailed our return in a most harsh and uncouth manner. I had the mortification of being told by various individuals, that had General Blanco disembarked at the mole, he would have been received with execrations, and that many had collected missiles to have pelted him with: next day, the militia paraded the streets, and their officers gave in a memorial to the governor, in which they manifested their disapproval of the treaties of Paucarpata; and in case government would annul them, and continue the war, they offered to serve without pay or rations. Lieut.-Colonel Don Victorino Garrida was the governor of Valparaiso, and he seemed to take a decided interest in the affair. I could be more circumstantial, but I will only add, that although there had been a manifestation in the capital in favour of peace, with some modification of the treaties, they were, through the interest that had been displayed in Valparaiso, annulled.

EL PRESIDENTE DE LA REPUBLICA DE CHILE.

" Santiago, December 18, 1837.

" Considering,—

" 1st. That the treaty celebrated at Paucarpata, on the 17th of November last, between the general-in-chief of the Chilian army, Don Manuel Blanco Encalada, and

Don Antonio Jose Irizarri, plenipotentiaries of the Chilian government, and Generals Don Ramon Herrera, and Don Anselmo Quiros, plenipotentiaries of General Don Andres Santa Cruz, has not satisfied the just demands of the Chilian nation, obtained a reparation for grievances, nor, what is of more importance, relieved the adjacent countries to Peru and Bolivia from the danger in which their independence and security are menaced with.

" 2nd. That although some of the articles are favourable to Chile, still there are clauses that are doubtful, and a want of explanation that renders the whole of the stipulations inutile, as they will only give place to tedious and useless altercations that may renew the war.

"3rd. That the plenipotentiaries of the Chilian government have exceeded the limits of their instructions, which they explained to General Santa Cruz previous to the negotiation, thereby confiding in the honour and loyalty with which the Chilian government gave them that special charge (especial prevencion).

" I declare,—

" That the Chilian government disapproves the said treaty; and that hostilities will commence against the government of General Santa Cruz, and those who sustain it, as soon as notice has been given of this determination.

" This government, who ardently desires peace, and is disposed to renew the negotiations by treaty, will omit no sacrifice to obtain one that may be compatible to its independence and national honour: satisfied that such a peace is the only one that the Chilians could desire, and which the justice of their cause, constancy, the efficacious co-operations of their allies, and the resources that the favour of a Divine Providence has placed at the disposition of government, gives them a right to expect.*

" PRIETO,

" JOAQUIN TOCORNAL."

* In order that the authenticity of these documents may be preserved, I present a Spanish copy of each of them, from the ministerial gazette, *El Araucano*, No. 382, of December 22nd, 1837 :—

CHILE.—MINISTERIO DE LA GUERRA.

El Jeneral Don Manuel Blanco Encalada y Don José de Irizarri, como Plenipotenciarios del Gobierno Chileno, acordaron con el Jeneral Santa Cruz el tratado siguiente.

En el nombre de Dios todopoderoso autor y lejislador de las sociedades humanas.

Deseando los Gobiernos de la Confederacion Perù-Boliviana y de la Republica de Chile restablecer la paz y buena armonia, que desgraciadamenta se hallaban alteradas, y estrechar sus relaciones de la manera mas franca, justa y mutuamente ventajosa, han tenido a bieu nombrar para este objeto por Ministros Plenipotenciarios, por parte de S. E. el Supremo Protector de la Confederacion, a los Ilustiisimos Señores Jenerales de Division Don Ramon Herrera y Don Anselmo Quiros, y por parte de S. E. el Presidente de la Republica de Chile al Exmo. Sr. Jeneral en Jefe del ejército de Chile Don Manuel Blanco Encalada y al Sr. Coronel Don Antonio José de Irizarri ; los cuales despues de haber canjeado sus respectivos plenos poderes y haberlos encontrado en buena y debida forma, han convenido en los articulos siguientes,

1º. Habrá paz perpetua y amistad entre la Confederacion Perù-Boliviana y la Repùblica de Chile, comprometiéndose sus respectivos gobiernos a sepultar en olvido sus quejas respectivos, y abstenerse eu lo sucesivo de toda reclamacion sobre lo ocurrido en el curso de las desavenencias que han mortivado la guerra actual.

2º. El Gobierno de la Confederacion reitera la declaracion solemne que tantas veces ha hecho de no haber jamas autorizado ningun acto ofensivo a la independencia y tranquilidad de la República de Chile, y a su vez el Gobierno de esta declara que nunca fué su intencion al apoderarse de los buques de la confederacion apropiarselos en calidad de presa, sino mantenerlos en depósito para restituirlos como se ofrece a hacerlo en los términós que en este tratado se estipula.

3º. El Gobierno de Chile se compromete a devolver al de la Confederacion los buques siguientes, la barca " Santa Cruz," el bergantin, " Arequipeño" y la goleta " Peruviana." Estos buques seran entregados a los ocho dias de firmado el tratado por ambas partes a disposicion de un comisionado del Gobierno Protectoral.

4º. A los seis dias despues de ratificado esta tratado por S. E. el Protector el ejército de Chile se retirara al puerto de Quilca, donde están sus transportes,

General Blanco published an "exposition," in which he gave an account of his conduct, &c. during the campaign,

para verificar su embarque y regreso a su pais. El Gobierno de Chile enviará su ratificacion al puerto de Arica dentro de cincuenta dias contados desde esta fecha.

5°. Los Gobiernos de la confederacion y de Chile se comprometen a celebrar tratados especiales relativos a sus mútuuos intereses mercantiles, los cuales serán reciprocamente considerados desde la fecha de la ratificacion de este tratado por el Gobierno de Chile, como los de la nacion mas favorecida.

6°. El Gobierno Protectoral se ofrece a hacer un tratado de paz con el de las Provincias Arjentinas, tan luego como este lo quiera, y el de Chile queda comprometido a interponer sus buenos oficios para conseguir dicho objeto sobre las bases en que los dos Gobiernos convengan.

7°. Las dos partes contratantes adoptan como base de sus mútuas relaeiones el principio de la no intervencion en sus asuntos domésticos, y se comprometen a no consentir que en sus respectivos territorios se fragüen planes de conspiracion ni ataque contra el Gobierno existente, y las institùciones del otro.

8°. Las dos partes contratantes se obligan a no tomar jamas las armas la una contra la otra, sin haberse entendido y dado todas las explicaciones que basten a satisfacerse reciprocamente, y haber agotado antes todos los medios posibles de conciliacion y avenimiento, y sin haber expuesto estos motivos al Gobierno garante.

9°. El Gobierno Protectoral reconoce en favor de la República de Chile el millon y medio de pesos, o la cantidad que resulte haberse entregado al Ministro Plenipotenciario del Perù Don José Larrea y Loredo, procedente del empréstito contraido en Londres por el Gobierno Chileno, y se obliga a satisfacerla en los mismos terminos y plazos en que la Repùblica de Chile satisfaga el referido capital del empréstito.

10°. Los intereses devengados por este capital y debidos a los prestamistas, se ratificarán por el Gobierno de la Gonfederacion en los tèrminos y plazos convenientes para que el Gobierno de Chile pueda satisfacer oportunamente con dichos intereses a los prestamistas.

11°. La parte correspondiente a los intereses del capital mencionado en el articulo 9° ya satisfechos por el Gobierno de Chile a los prestamistas en los dividendos pagados hasta la fecha, y que ha debido satisfacer el Gobierno del Perù, segun la estipulacion hecha entre los Ministros Plenipotenciarios de las Republicas de Chile y el Perù, se pagara por el Gobierno de la Confederacion en tres plazos; el primero, de la tercera parte, a seis meses contados desde la ratificacion de este tratado por el Gobierno de Chile : el segundo a los seis meses siguientes ; y el tercero despues de igual plazo.

12°. El Gobierno de la Confederacion ofrece no hacer cargo alguno por su conducta politica a los individuos del territorio que ha ocupado el Ejército de Chile, y considerarà a los Peruanos que han venido con dicho Ejèrcito, como si no hubiesen venido.

and from which I shall insert the following article:—
" Amidst these afflicting circumstances General Santa

13°. El complimiento de este tratado se pone bajo la garantia de Su
Majestad Británica, cuya aquiescencia se solicitará por ambos Gobiernos
contratantes.

En fe de lo cual firmaron el presente tratado los supradichos Ministros
Plenipotenciarios en el pueblo de Paucarpata a diez y siete de noviembre
de mil ochocientos treinta y siete y lo refrendaron los secretarios de las
legaciones, Manuel Blanco Encalada, Ramon Herrera, Anselmo Quiros,
Antonio Jose Irizarri, Dr. Juan Gualverto Valdivia Secretario de la legacion
Perù-Boliviana, Juan Henrique Ramirez, Secretario de la legacion Chilena.

Andres Santa Cruz, Gran Ciudadano, Restaurador, Captain Jeneral y Presidente de Bolivia, Supremo Protector de la Confederacion Perú, Boliviana,
Gran Mariscal Pacificador del Peru, Jeneral de brigada en Colombia, con-
decorado con las medallas de Libertadores de Quito y de Pichincha, con
la del Libertador Simon Bolivar y con la de Cobija, |Gran Oficial de
la Lejion de honor de Francia, Fundador y Jefe Supremo de la Lejion de
honor Boliviana y de la Nacional del Perù &c. &c.

Hallándose este tratado conforme con las instrucciones dadas por mi a
los Plenipotenciarios nombrados al efecto, lo ratifico solemnemente en todas
sus partes, quedando encargado mi Secretario Jeneral de hacerlo observar,
imprimir y publicar. Dado en el cuartel jeneral de Paucarpata a dies y
siete de Noviembre de mil ochocientos treinta y siete.

ANDRES SANTA CRUZ,
MANUEL DE LA CRUZ MENDEZ.
El Secretario jeneral.

EL PRESIDENTE DE LA REPUBLICA DE CHILE.

Santiago 18 de Diciembre de 1837.

CONSIDERANDO,

1°. Que el tratado celebrado en el pueblo de Paucarpata a 17 de Noviembre
del presente año entre el Jeneral en Jefe del Ejército Chileno Don Manuel
Blanco Encalada y Don Antonio José Irizarri como plenipotenciarios del
Gobierno de Chile, |y los Jenerales Don Ramon Herrera y Don Anselmo
Quiros plenipotenciarios del Jeneral Don Andres Santa Cruz, no satisface
las justas reclamaciones de la Nacion Chilena, ni repara debidamento los
agravios que se le han inferido, ni lo que es mas, precave los males a que se
ven expuestos los pueblos vecinos al Peru y Bolivia, cuya independencia y
seguridad permanecen amenazadas.

2°. Que aun en los mismos articulos de este tratado que son favorables a
Chile, se encuentran cláusulas dudosas y faltas de explicacion, que harian
del todo inutiles las estipulaciones en su actual estado, y solo darian lugar,
como debo temerse, a que despues de dilatadas e infructuosas contestaciones
se renovase la guerra.

3°. Que los plenipotenciarios del Gobierno de Chile se han excedido en
el otorgamiento del tratado de las instrucciones que recibieron, como ellos

Cruz proposed an interview at Paucarpata. I acceded to
it, and this conference brought on others, from which
resulted the treaties that were celebrated at Paucarpata,
between Don Antonio Jose Irizarri, and myself, on the
part of the Chilian government, and Generals Herrera and
Quiros, for the confederation; but before I proceeded in
this transaction, I consulted with the chief of the staff,
General Aldunate, and the chiefs of the army, who were
assembled in a council of war, in order to deliberate upon
the propositions offered by the enemy, and who being convinced of the critical situation we were placed in, and the
sincerity of the reasons that were stated, unanimously
approved their adoption, as the best steps that could be
taken under such difficult circumstances; I remitted a
copy of this "Acta" to the minister; and if this document,
to justify my military conduct, as well as the reasons I have
already stated in support thereof, are not sufficient to give
full satisfaction to the supreme government, I am ready to
answer, in court-martial, the charges that may be preferred
against me.

mismos lo hicieron presente al jeneral Santa Cruz al entrar en la negoeia-
cion, arreglándose a los principios de honor y lealtad con que el Gobierno
Chileno les habia hecho esta especial prevencion.
    DECLARO.—Que el Gobierno de Chile desaprueba el antedicho tratado, y
ques despues de ponerse esta resolucion en noticia del Gobierno del jeneral
D. Andres Santa Cruz deben continuar las hostilidades contra el expresado
Gobierno y sus sostenedores en la misma forma que antes de su cele-
bracion.
    El Gobierno' que desea ardientemente la paz y que está dispuesto a
renovar ahora mismo las negociaciones por un tratado, no omitira sacrificios
para obtenerla con tal que ellos sean compatibles con la independencia, la
seguridad y el honor nacional, satisfecho de que una paz de esta clase es la
única que convienne o que puede desear el Pueblo Chileno, y que le dan
derecho a esperar la justicia de su causa, su constancia, la eficaz co-opera-
cion de sus aliados, y los recursos que el favor de la Divina Providencia ha
puesto a disposicion de su Gobierno.
                                            PRIETO,
                                    JOAQUIN TOCORNAL.

" I am extremely sorry that the treaties have not merited
the approbation of the supreme government; it is to it,
more than myself, to judge of the convenience or inconvenience of so grave and transcendent a matter; but I
have the most satisfactory feelings that they have been
dictated by the purest motives.

(Signed)   "MANUEL BLANCO ENCALADA."
" December 20th, 1837."

The minister of state in the war department, in answer
to the expositions of General Blanco, issued a decree,
dated 17 January, 1838, in which he stated, that as there
were serious charges relative to the military conduct of the
general-in-chief during the campaign in Peru, he was to
subject himself to a trial, and a number of scurrilous, and
anonymous attacks were made upon the general and
Colonel Irizarri, in the public papers. About the latter
end of January, General Don Manuel Bulnes, and the
governor-intendente of Concepcion, Don Antonio Alem-
parte, accompanied by Los S.S. Commandants O'Carrol
and Lattapiat, arrived from Talcahuano, and marched
directly for Santiago, and soon after there was a rumour
of a change in the ministry, but El S'or Garrido, left Commandante Vidaurre in charge, and posted off to the capital,
where it was said, he and others prevailed upon the minister
of state to keep in office, which being seconded by the
friars and others, kept in the Spanish party. The Chilian
squadron were sent with the non-acceptance of the treaties
of Paucarpata, and with orders to commence operations,
should they meet with any of the Peruvian vessels, after
having landed the correspondence in Arica.

I shall now return to General Blanco: he had become
the butt of the Spanish faction, who had the administration

wholly in their hands ; and I viewed their proceeding against the general as a generous mind ought to regard all acts of injustice, and plainly saw, that if possible he was to be made a sacrifice to party feeling.

As I had material, I had taken it upon myself to falsify some of the calumnies that had been published by such as Lattapiat, who, being aggrieved at General Blanco not allowing him to serve in the last expedition, was now determined to vent his spleen, through the medium of the press, by anonymous publications against the general. But he soon unmasked himself; for in his No. 2, " Balas a los Traydores," he filled a sheet full of comments respecting the lenity of the government and judges towards criminals, and cited a glaring act, of which he himself was the hero, who had been shielded from the hand of justice, and transcribed a part of his own official note, wherein he strove to vindicate himself, when called upon to do so by the minister of the Interior, Don Joaquin Tocornal, little dreaming that I held a copy of his answer, and the original document, wherein he received his excellency's disapprobation and displeasure for his barbarous conduct in Juan Fernandez.

So, to put a stop to the press being inundated with the productions of such a set, I published one thousand copies of the following answer to El Cura Monardes, signed by Unos Porteños, and Los Porteños del Otro Dia, directed against the foreign chiefs, and particularly to calumniate the subscriber.*

* I was obliged to give security to a printer, before he would publish my answer, in obedience to the following decree of the supreme government of the 14th of June, 1830 :—

" Considering that a well-directed press is one of the most powerful means to maintain regularity and purity in the public duties of persons who are employed in the service of the republic. Considering, also, that the

They have said—" We have got some adventurers of the
old world amongst us, who have converted themselves into
preachers, in order to prove the excellence of the treaties of
Paucarpata, and are at the same time defending the author
of such a disgraceful compact."

Answer 1st.—The first part of this accusation does not
correspond to me, for I have never entered into any discussion respecting the advantages or disadvantages of the
treaties. To the second I beg leave to state, that various
individuals came, as if on purpose, to my quarters, in Valparaiso, to read scurrilous papers, and make use of indecent
language against a chief, under whose orders I had served;
and finding it impossible to remain indifferent, whilst
listening to such fanfarrons, I informed them it was
wrong to act in such an indecorous manner, as well as
circulate productions that were degrading to the nation;

scandalous abuses which have hitherto been made use of by the press, by
converting it into an instrument of the vilest passions, whereby it is rendered incapable of exercising that beneficial influence, and serves more
to lead astray, than direct the public opinion, so that well-founded accusa-
tions, that are launched by the press against such as abuse their power to
the prejudice of the public, does not excite due attention, when issued by
an organ that is habitually depraved; so that such as are accused shield
themselves on account of the licentiousness of the press, in place of justi-
fying their conduct, and by these means the worthy servants of the state
are confounded with the prevaricators, compromise the honour of the
whole, and stain the reputation of the government—

ꞁ   We have decreed and decree,

1st. Every public person, whose conduct, in what concerns the exercise
of his duties, that should be attacked by the press, must in person, or
appoint some other person to accuse the author or editor of the paper,
before the competent tribunal, and in the term prefixed by law.

2nd. He that does not act accordingly shall be suspended immediately
from the exercise of his employment, and the judge will accuse him with
the said paper before the competent tribunal. The minister of the interior
is charged with the fulfilment of this decree: print and circulate it, that it
may be seen by all.

" OVALLE.
" PORTALES."

and addressing myself in particular to Don Manuel Lastra,
(an emigrant), who was reading the second number of
"Balas a los Traydores," I told him I was informed that
he was related to the author, who was a bad artillery-
man, for he had suffered himself to be unmasked by the
rebounding of the balls he had fired at others, especially
in the second number, wherein he had criticized the tolerance and benignity of the supreme government towards
himself, for the answer of an intriguant of the first order
was not, as he has stated, directed to a court or assembly,
but by Lattapiat himself, to the minister of the interior, in
a note of June, 1834, five months previous to my super-
seding him in Juan Fernandez. Don Manuel Lastra retired
in a rage. I have not seen him since, but have heard that
he has slandered me, and a few days afterwards I received
the first article published in "El Cura Monardes," which
I answered in "El Mercurio."

Why should there be such an interest displayed to disgust, and drive me from Chile? It surely cannot be on
account of my having stated, and with good reason too,
"that it was disconsolate for a soldier to see his chief
denigrated and insulted." No! There are other and still
stronger motives that have induced my detractors to
calumniate me. The document, (No. 2.*), which I now
publish lies dormant in the archives of the "commandancia
general de armas." This and others, which I remitted to
government, in order that I might fulfil the duties of a
public functionary, and shun indecorous compromises, are
"Los torpes servicios," that in reality have brought upon
me so many vexations and misfortunes that I have had to
suffer ever since 1835; and this intriguant, who has seen

* Relative to the criminal charges that had been suppressed.

them repeatedly published, in place of giving days of
honour and untarnished glory to Chile, has shielded himself
under the protection and toleration he has thought proper
to criticize in his "Balas a los Traydores."

My paper turned the tables against Latapiatt, and sorely
annoyed him and his colleagues. The governor's secretary,
a Spaniard, called upon me, to warn me against refuting
the public opinion;* but I informed him that it was
impossible for any person of common understanding or
probity to tolerate such proceedings.

General Bulnes was appointed commander-in-chief of
the restoring army, and orders were issued to raise recruits,
&c., and Quillota was again made the head-quarters of the
army; however, as I was not in favour with government,
or on good terms with General Bulnes, I had hopes of
being exonerated from serving whilst such was the case;
but I was soon summoned to head-quarters by the following
order from the war-office :—

"February 28th, 1838.

"El Sart. Mor de Cabaleria Don Thomas Sutcliffe,
must place himself under the orders of the commander-in-
chief of the restoring army, to be employed as the general
shall think fit.

"CAVAREDA."

By such an order, it was plain to be seen, I had no
friends in government. The minister of war who had been
the president of the Consejo de Guerra, when I was tried
and acquitted for the occurrences of Juan Fernandez, knew
well who it was that had sent the charges of Aguayo against
me from the head-quarters of the army; and I also was aware
he had been ordered to do so by . . . . I also felt

---

* The calumnies invented against General Blanco.

aggrieved at my being ordered to join the army unattached,
especially at a time when government was so prodigal, as
to bestow commissions of lieutenant-colonels, &c., on
Spaniards and other individuals who had never served a
day in the Chilian army; but it was my duty to obey
Y. Callar. Whilst making preparation to march to Quillota, I was informed that Lattapiat had been appointed chief
aide-de-camp to General Bulnes. This, and the outcry that
had been raised against me, and foreigners in general, in
a scurrilous paper, "El Cura Monardez,"* made me resolve
on requesting my retirement from the army, as well as a
remuneration for my services, before I should receive any
effective appointment, for I well saw, that, should I join
the new-modelled army, my situation would be something
similar to " Poor Black Jack," whose story was published
in " El dia yel Golpe," No. 21.

, Santiago, March 2nd, 1898.

ANECDOTE.

" El Negro Juan is well known by all the merchants and
tradesmen of this capital, for he is a licensed porter; and
if the story I am about to relate should be by any one
doubted, put the question to Jack, and he himself will
relate, better than I can, all the particulars relative to his
sickness, death, and resurrection.

" Jack was a soldier, and in order to relieve himself from
the fatigues of his military duties, pretended to be sick,
and obtained his pass to the hospital; but no sooner had
he entered the walls of San Borga, than his troubles commenced, for the surgeon, without taking consideration,
or making any preliminary inquiries, or even feeling his
pulse, ordered him to have blisters applied to his legs and

* See preface.

arms. Poor negro! the reader may consider how he must have cursed his hard fortune, in contemplating his sorrowful situation. But this was not all, his unfortunate planet had other misfortunes in store, more powerful still than the blisters, for the very next day, an assistant who was an Andalusian, with a ludicrous tone that the natives of the province are accustomed to, said to him, 'How are you, my black bird? I am now going to repay thee the favours which thou bestowedst on me and my companions on the plains of Maipu. Here, monkey, stretch out these legs and arms, in order that I may cut thy 'cordovan' and cure thee, as thou meritest. Thou complainest! take patience, for it does not hurt me! La Patria knows how to reward merit, and for this they have given thee into my hands, that I may cure and comfort thee—you understand me?' The treatment he received from this compassionate Spaniard, caused Jack to faint during the operation. After he recovered from his fit, and seeing the surgeon coming as usual to visit the hospital, he laid his pitiful complaint before him, and informed him of the conduct of his assistant. But, oh! how unfortunate—the surgeon, the assistant, the apothecary, the steward, the cook, &c. were all Spaniards, and Jack a patriotic soldier! What could be done in such a situation? Nothing more than what occurred to the poor matirized Negro, and which he put into execution, in order to leave the hell he got into. He pretended to be dead, and acted his part so well, that all concluded he had ended his days; he was taken to the charnel-house, from thence to the car, that during the night conveyed the dead to their graves. Jack knew well where to perform his resurrection; and when he found himself clear of the city, he got up, and with a loud voice called out, 'Top de caat, dou Panish bag ga bone, fa hea be a soga ob de Patia dat no di yet, but lib fa to gib dee musinga,' and jumping out of the cart, he armed himself with two stones.

"The conductor, on hearing these expressions, and seeing a ghost in such an hostile attitude, was scared, abandoned his cart, and scampered off like a deer. Jack took care to profit by the occasion, and escaped also."—LAUS DEO.

How could it be possible for me to serve unattached, when the author of all my troubles, misfortunes, and vexations, since the year 1834, held a confidential post, and under such patronage my case would have been as bad as the poor Negro's. I overcame my repugnance to join General Bulnes; but I never could submit to degrade myself by serving with such an infamous . . . . as Lattapiat. So after due consideration and advice of my friends, concerning the treatment which I had so unjustly and undeservedly received from various members of the administration, I sent in a memorial, through the medium of General Bulnes, and, fearing a denial, I wrote to the Honourable Colonel Walpole, consul-general to H.B.M. in Chile, who honoured me with his attention, and favoured me with the following answer:—

" Santiago, March 7th, 1838..

" Sir,—I have been favoured with your letter of the 5th instant, announcing the resignation of your military employments in the Chilian service; and at the same time seeking, in case the government should not receive it, and strive to oppose your wishes, the protection of the British flag.

" I am most unwilling to anticipate, on the part of this government, a refusal to so moderate a demand; throwing aside all other considerations, but that of your long and meritorious services, I should imagine that you were fully

entitled to the approbation of your request; be that soever as it may, the protection of the British flag is open
to every British subject having a just claim, and I shall in
that case have infinite satisfaction in extending it to you.

" My influence, diminutive as it must be, will always be
at your service.

"I am, Sir,

"Your most obedient humble servant,

"JOHN WALPOLE, Consul-General."

I felt myself greatly obliged to the consul-general for
his kindness; for I had much to fear from the vindictive
spirit of Lattapiat's friends and abettors, and I soon experienced their effects; for, instead of being allowed to proceed to head-quarters, where I might have had a private
interview with General Bulnes, and explain the motives
stated in the following memorial, I was ordered to present
myself before the commandante-general of the staff in
Santiago.

MEMORIAL.

Exmo Señor,

Thomas Sutcliffe, &c. states powerful motives that ought
to be buried in oblivion, having placed me in the imperious
necessity of presenting this memorial, in order that I may
be allowed to retire from the army; and if fifteen years
honourable services lent to this republic, as well as my
having been one of the founders of the freedom of South
America, in the manner stated in the accompanying documents,* should entitle me to a recompense, to enable me
to retire to my native country, as a worthy veteran of
" La Independencia."

* The documents were never returned to me, although I often demanded
them.

I hope the well-known bounty of your excellency will, in consideration thereof, and this my petition, be extended towards me, in the manner that will be most congenial to the supreme pleasure of your excellency: " Por Tanto," &c.

Exmo Señor,
THOMAS SUTCLIFFE.

I arrived on the tenth, and presented myself to the commandant-general of the staff, where I received a written order to attend the judge fiscal, and give my depositions respecting the occurrences of the late campaign. I called on the judge, who kept me from eleven o'clock in the forenoon, till seven o'clock in the evening. After he had concluded his interrogations, he inquired if I had not kept a journal, and plan of the campaign, I replied, I had always kept a journal, and if he would attach it, as part of my deposition, to the records of General Blanco's process, he might have it; but that I wished to keep the plan, to present it to the general. The judge, therefore, did as I requested.

Next day I received the following reward for my services to the republic of Chile.

" Commandancia-General de Armas.
" Santiago, March 13th, 1838.

" The minister of war, with this day's date, has issued the following decree:—

" The unseasonableness of the memorial of El Sart. Mor Don Thomas Sutcliffe, in circumstances of the nation being engaged in the present war, and on account of the army to which he had been lately attached, being about to commence operations, excludes him from whatever right he may claim, in favour of the pretensions he has made for an extraordinary compensation for his past services; but yes, 'pero si,' we dismiss him from the service.

" In consequence of which, you are hereby ordered to remit me your last commission, to be cancelled.

" God preserve you,

"DOMINGO FRUTOS.

" To El Señor Don Thomas Sutcliffe."

I was not at all either surprised or disappointed at receiving this dismissal, for I had already been informed that General Bulnes had, in his report, which was forwarded to government with my memorial, done the needful; and I was sure that my enemies would not let slip such a golden opportunity of ridding their army of a chief, who had too much delicacy and independence to suffer himself to be treated in an unjustifiable manner. I called upon the " commandante-general de armas," and informed him that my last commission had already been cancelled by the earthquake of 1835; and that since that period, I had been, to no purpose, soliciting its renewal, as well as justice against Lattapiat, Padre Lopez, Aguayo, Dias, Ugalde, and others, and to substantiate which, I gave him the following note and memorial; I also told him, that government could not have considered my services of much importance to the republic; for, although, I had been three days in the capital, and twice at the war-office, " Commandancia G'ral de Armas," not a single question had been put to me, relative to my having requested my retirement; I also inquired what was the appointment alluded to in my dismissal: he replied, that General Bulnes was to employ me as he should think convenient. I then inquired if such treatment was due to a chief, who had hitherto always been employed by government in an honourable and confidential post, and who had on every occasion given entire satisfaction. To this he made no reply, but, shrugging up his shoulders, retired.

MY ANSWER.

" Señor Commandante-General de Armas."

Santiago, March 14th, 1836.

I have the honour of acknowledging the receipt of your note, in which is transcribed the supreme resolution of his excellency; requiring at the same time my last commission, in order that it may be cancelled.

Permit me to inform you, that it is impossible for me to comply with your demand, because I lost that commission during the earthquake of the 20th of February, 1835; which my repeated solicitations for its renewal, as well as the following extract of the minister of war's letter, will certify. " By this vessel you will receive all that has been required, and shortly I will send you your commission of lieutenant-colonel, that the earthquake of February robbed you of." I herewith present for your perusal, official and other documents, in which you will see that my request to be exonerated from the service, is not, nor ought it to be qualified as 'intempestivo.' No, the reasons that have obliged me to take such steps are sufficiently powerful.

› I have striven to throw a veil over many scandalous proceedings; but now I consider myself at liberty to act otherwise, and will make use of my documents, in order to prove, that the repeated acts of injustice I have received from persons in office, &c. cannot, nor ought they, in any manner deprive me of my claim for a compensation for the honourable services I have lent to this republic, nor stain the reputation of a veteran of the independence.

I beg you will return me the documents attached to the

memorial, as well as others, which I have requested ever since June, 1836, and are attached to my defence; they are originals, and are very necessary for my present purpose.

God guard you,

THOMAS SUTCLIFFE.

MEMORIAL,

Exmo Señor,

Don Thomas Sutcliffe appears before your excellency to state—

That having received through the "Commandante G'ral de Armas" the decree, in which your excellency has ordered my dismissal from the army, and on account of my last commission having been demanded, in order to be cancelled, I think it my duty to accompany the adjoining documents, and copies of others that exist in the archives of the war-office, which I had already prepared to sustain my memorial, in case it had not been acceded to, and where your excellency will see, that the motives and reasons that have obliged me to adopt such steps, have been powerful.

After the disgraceful occurrences of Juan Fernandez, I was about to request my retirement from a service, wherein I had suffered so many acts of injustice; but was prevented, and obliged to stifle my resentments, on account of the republic being involved in difficulties with Peru. The war broke out, and from that period I have not only performed the duties of a soldier, but I have served as a seaman, * when necessity required it, which the minister of war, who was then governor of Valparaiso, can certify.

---

* In 1836, I was put in charge of the corvette Valparaiso, and afterwards of the port of Valparaiso, as harbour-master.

During the revolution of Quillota, I was sick and in bed;[*]
but, although in such a state, and at the risk of aggravating
my malady, I went and presented myself to the general-in-
chief;[†] my delicacy impeded me from having my name
enrolled, so as to be a partaker of the general promotion;[‡]
but now I think proper to mention particulars, in order to
prove that my conduct has not merited the disapprobation
of your excellency, nor a degrading separation from the
army, in which I have for more than fifteen years served
with honour. I refer to the documents that exist in the
archives of the " Commandante-General de Armas," in
which there is a sufficient proof that the S. S. ~~chiefs~~,
under whose orders I have had the honour to serve, have
been satisfied with my conduct, and from whom I have
received such honourable testimonials of their friendship
and esteem.

But, excellent señor, the order I received to serve under
General Don Manuel Bulnes, to be employed in any
manner he chose, confounded me. I had many just and
powerful motives to excuse myself, and still greater, not to
serve where Lieutenant-Colonel Lattapiat was employed.
As a soldier, it was my duty to obey without attending to

* Through my exertions to save the lives of the crew of a vessel that
was wrecked during a gale in Valparaiso.

† " Don Manuel Blanco Encalada, lieutenant-general of the armies of
Chile, and vice-admiral of the national navy.

" I certify, that El Sart. Mor Don Thomas Sutcliffe, has merited my
approbation, for his good conduct, in the fulfilment of his duty as my first
aid-de-camp, during the campaign of the restoring army in Peru.

" The services that he has rendered, on more than one occasion, make
him merit being enrolled in the number of foreigners, who have gained the
estimation of the Chilians.

" Given by me, in the city of Santiago, April 3rd, 1838.

                                    " MANUEL BLANCO ENCALADA."

‡ I had come to a determination of not accepting any promotion during
the administration of General Prieto and the Spanish faction.

circumstances: I weighed well my situation, and saw that if I disobeyed the order, it would be criminal; and, if I tendered in my resignation, it would, perhaps, give motives for my conduct to be criticized.

In this alternative, I resolved on requesting my separation in the mode I have verified; still supposing, that previous to its being granted, my motives would be inquired into. They are cited in the documents Nos. 1 and 2, which partly explain the reasons of my taking such steps, during the actual circumstances; and if they, as well as what I have already stated, merit the consideration of your excellency, I await the revocation of the degrading part of the decree of the thirteenth, and believe myself to merit an honourable retirement, to be enabled to return to my native country, as a worthy "Veterano de la Independencia."

Exmo Señor,

"Por Tanto," &c.   THOMAS SUTCLIFFE.

The commandant-general returned me my note and memorial, after he had detained them several days, stating, that he would not answer the first, nor forward the latter to government; on which I attached the note to the other document, and presented the memorial to the minister of war; on the following day, I received information that I had been reinstated to my rank, and shortly afterwards I received the following "Cedula."

THE PRESIDENT OF THE REPUBLIC OF CHILE.

"Forasmuch as 'El Sart. Mor de Caballeria Don Thomas Sutcliffe' has solicited his separation from the service, and in consideration of the impossibility he finds to continue in it; I hereby allow him to retire with the use of his uniform, and enjoyment of his rank and privileges, 'con gose de fuera, y uso de uniforme.'

" For which I have delivered this, signed with my hand, sealed with the seal of government, and countersigned by my secretary of state in the war-department, and of which an account will be taken in the respective offices.

" Given in Santiago this thirteenth day of March, in the year one thousand eight hundred and thirty-eight.

" PRIETO,

" RAMON CAVAREDA.

" Seal of Government.

" Anotada a f. 177, book No. 38 of titles and decrees, of the war-office, and 'Commandancia General de Armas,' April 11th, 1838.

" JOSE ANTONIO CASTRO.

" Entered in f. 16 of the book of titles, No. 6, in the Commissary General's office, April 11th, 1838.

" JOSE MARIA LUJAN.

" ' Commandancia General de Armas,' Santiago, April 11th, 1838.

" ' Cumplase y Anotase,'   DOMINGO FRUTOS.

" ' Anotado,'   ALVARADO."

My reinstatement proves that government, notwithstanding their strong prejudices against me, had considered my motives, for having requested my separation from the service, both powerful and just; as I had sent in copies of all my documents, in which were portrayed every act of injustice I had received since my expulsion from Juan Fernandez, which I think unnecessary to trouble my readers with, because I still have my claims in the hands of Lieutenant-General Don Manuel Blanco Encalada, and

will await their result, before I publish the whole; I am
confident, that the following sentence of the minister of
war, Don Jose Javier de Bustamante, will yet be verified.

"Trabaje v, mi amigo, que los pueblos no siempre son
ingratos; y queda la complacencia de haberse hecho util a
la humanidad."

"Toil on, my friend, for the country will not always be
ungrateful; and the complacence remains of having been
useful to humanity."*

* Published in my manifest, page 4.

CHAP. XVI.

As soon as the second expedition had sailed from Valparaiso, which was nearly double the force of that of General Blanco, his trial commenced; and although he had little to expect from some of his judges, who were known to be his personal enemies, he was acquitted in the most honourable manner; however, government ordered him to undergo the ordeal of a second trial by La Corte Marcial, (a superior court), who not only confirmed the sentence of El Consejo, but added the following honourable approval of the general's conduct to it:

TRIBUNALS.

COURT OF APPEALS.—In the criminal process instituted against Lieutenant-General Don Manuel Blanco Encalada, who has been accused by various charges respecting his military conduct as general-in-chief, of El Exercito Restaurador del Peru, that have been brought before us; the following sentences have been pronounced:—

After having heard the defence read by Lieutenant-Colonel Don Pedro Nolasco Vidal, and the instructions that had been given to the general under trial, by the supreme government, relative to the campaign of Peru, which has been presented to the court, by the " defensor," all of which having been well examined, we, the court,

have declared and declare, El Señor General Don Manuel
Blanco Encalada, absolved, according to the article 23,
Treaty 8. Title 6, "de las ordenanzas generales del
exercito."—Santiago, August 7th, 2838. Domingo Frutos,
Francisco Calderon, Isaac Thompson, Nicholas Maruli,
Jose Patricio Castro, Vicente Claro.

"Santiago, August 20th, 1838.

SENTENCE OF LA CORTE MARCIAL.

"Vistos.—1st. On consideration that it could not be
known to Lieutenant-General Don Manuel Blanco Encalada, the physical and moral obstacles he found in Arequipa,
with the army under his command; especially when the
Peruvian generals and chiefs that accompanied him, led
him to believe he would receive co-operation, abundance,
and all sorts of resources.

"2nd. As he did not enter Peru as a conqueror, he
could not procure what he stood in need of by force, for
he was obliged to regulate his conduct according to the
generous and laudable instructions given him by our
supreme government, which have been presented in court.

"3rd. That in his first official communications, he
informed his excellency, in a reserved manner, by a private
letter, respecting the difficult position in which he was
situated, and could not foresee.

"4th. That had he not acted as he has done, he would
have sacrificed his army, without any advantage (infructuosamente.)

"5th. That although his forces were inferior to those
of the enemy, and in total want of resources, and the means
of removing his army, he always provoked the enemy, who
fled, to fight him; he made them respect him, and retired
without abating his military honour.

"6th. That the accusers are not of accord; and are refuted by treble number.

"7th. That the charge of having sold the horses, on account of the impossibility of embarking them, and transporting them to Chile, has been well answered, and to our satisfaction, for if he had destroyed them, he would, by such an action, have given proof of duplicity, in what had been stipulated in the treaties.

"8th. That he has completely contradicted all the charges that have been brought against him, for which reason the judge Fiscal of the process has concluded it, by absolving him.

"9th. The military rank of Lieutenant-General Blanco, his interesting and valuable services by sea and land, ever since Chile has commenced to toil for its liberty and independence, his decided consecration to the re-establishment and consolidation of the public order we now enjoy, and the noble ambition of glory in every officer, who is jealous of his honour, are still other arguments that he could not do more than what he has done; therefore, we approve of the sentence of the general officers of page 253. Let this be published in all the provinces, according to the article 23, title 6, treaty 8, "de las ordenanzas generales del Exercito," as an indemnization of El Señor General Blanco, y se devuelve Tocornal, Mardones, Mont, Gutierres, Arriaran, Pereira, Astorga."*

---

* SENTENCIA.

Santiago 20 de agosto de 1838.

· Vistos : y considerando que no estuvieron al alcance del señor teniente jeneral don Manuel Blanco Encalada los obstáculos físicos y morales que halló en Arequipa el ejército de su mando, especialmente cuando jenerales y jefes peruanos hacian esperar con la mayor buena fe, cooperacion abundancia y toda clase de recursos.

Segundo : Que nada de esto podia procurarse a la fuerza, porque no entraba al Perú como conquistador, y tenia que arreglar su conducta a las

The general's trial ended, after all his vexatious sufferings, just as the most sanguine of his friends could have wished; and I had the unspeakable satisfaction of learning from the judge fiscal and the other members of the court, that, both my depositions and journal had been corroborated by all the chiefs of the Chilian army who had acted as witnesses, &c. : so my calumniators would learn that I had not only defended a good cause, but also sustained the glory of the Chilian army, by refuting the numerous falsehoods that had been invented to criminate its worthy chief.

jenerosas y loables instrucciones de nuestro Gobierno Supremo que se han traido al acuerdo.

Tercero: Que desde su primer parte oficial ya informó reservadamente en carta particular a S. E. el Presidente de la República sobre la dificil posicion en que se hallaba y no pudo preveerse.

Cuarto: Que a no obrar como obró en seguida habria sacrificádose infructuosamente con su ejército.

Quinto: Que aunque falto de movilidad y de recursos y con notable inferioridad de fuerzas siempre provocó al enemigo que huyó batiise, le impuso, y se retiró sin abatimiento del honor militar.

Sesto: Que los tres testigos de cargo estan varios y desmentidos por triple número.

Sétimo: Que el cargo de haber vendido los caballos en la imposibilidad de su reembarque y traida a Chile, está bien satisfecho, y si los hubiese degollado daba por ese hecho una prueba de doblez en lo estipulado.

Octavo: Que ha desvanecido completamente todos los cargos, y por esto el juez fiscal de la causa concluyó por la absolucion.

Noveno: Que el rango militar del teniente Jeneral Blanco, sus interesantes servicios en mar y tierra desde que Chile empezó a trabajar por ser libre e independiente; su decidida consagracion al restablecimiento y conservacion del órden público que gozamos, y la noble ambicion de gloria en todo militar pundonoroso, son otros tantos argumentos de que no pudo hacer mas que lo que hizo: se aprueba la sentencia del Consejo de oficiales jenerales de f. 253 vuelta: désele la publicidad en todas las provincias prevenida en el articulo 23 titulo 6°. tratado 8°. de las ordenanzas jenerales del ejército, para indemnizacion de la opinion del señor jeneral Blanco: y se devuelve.

Hai siete rùbricas de los señores — Tocornal — Mardones — Montt — Gutierrez—Arriaran—Pereira—Astorga.

CHAP. XVII.

In order to show the many advantages that have accrued to Chile since the Spanish flag has been expelled from her ports, I will give a brief description of Valparaiso, and add a few other documents that may serve to exemplify the increasing prosperity of the republic, notwithstanding the infatuated Chilians had allowed themselves to be cajoled and controled by the Spanish faction; with a few cases illustrative of the treatment the Americans had received from the monsters they had been opposed to, during their long and sanguinary war of independence.

Since Valparaiso has been declared a free port, and extensive arrangements made for the deposit of bonded goods, property to the amount of many millions of dollars has been landed for exportation; and this port, which as late as 1809, could not count more than nine vessels that visited it during twelve months, is now transformed into the principal and most extensive mart in the Pacific, and where may be seen vessels from all nations, that come to exchange their merchandise for the productions of that part of South America situated on the shores of the Pacific.

Nearly all the vessels from the eastern coast of Asia, colonies of New South Wales, islands in the Pacific, and western coast of America, touch there, and vessels may be provisioned, &c., even without coming to anchor. An enterprising foreigner has fitted up two water-tanks, wherewith vessels may be easily supplied; and Messrs. M'Farlane and Green have a provision establishment near the mole, where there is always a good stock on hand. These gentlemen are the contractors for the English, • French, and Chilian navies. Stock, vegetables, and fruit are plentiful, and sold at moderate prices in the market.

Valparaiso may be compared to Gibraltar, when a free port; for vessels under every flag visit the port, and almost every language is spoken on shore.

Valparaiso has been nearly rebuilt since the earthquake of 1822; several public edifices, such as the customhouse and new churches, adorn the city. These, as well as a number of fine dwelling-houses, stores, and other handsome buildings, reflect honour on their projectors. There are also two public cemeteries, one for the natives and all other Catholics; the other, adjoining to it, is for the Protestants, who have a place of worship, where the service of the church of England is performed. This act of toleration has been sorely criticized by the " godos," but the well-known liberality of the Chilians in general keeps them in check; and it is not uncommon to see a Catholic and Protestant funeral ascending the Quebrada de Elias at the same time, to lie as it were side by side. The Rev. Mr. Rawlinson officiated at Valparaiso, and was, I believe, the first chaplain appointed. Serro Alegre is, as Pera, entirely occupied by foreigners, who have formed a small town upon the height above Valparaiso, where a number of neat dwelling-houses and villas beautify a spot, that, had it not been for an enterprising Englishman, Mr. Bateman, and a few who followed his worthy example, would have been still barren and uninhabited. The foreign merchants have built an exchange, (Bolsa), which is commodious, and underneath there is a deposit for fire-engines, (the first introduced into Chile, for the public good), which the merchants sent for to the United States at their own cost;

2 L 2

and are as an appendage to the Bolsa. There is a fine
• drawing by Lieutenant-Colonel C. C. Wood, which represents the cutting out of the Spanish frigate Esmeralda,
by Lord Cochrane, now Earl of Dundonald, who at that
period was vice-admiral of the Chilian navy, and whose
prowess, as well as that of his gallant officers and seamen,
are still recorded by the true patriots of Chile and Peru,
as well as commemorated by the good feeling of the
merchants, who have ornamented the first public edifice
they erected, by recording this memento of the gallantry
of a few, who, although they rendered such important
services to the republic, were badly requited. The population of Valparaiso was, in 1817, averaged at 10,000; in
1823, 14,000; in 1824, according to the census taken by
government, 25,000; without enumerating the foreigners,
who are now calculated to be from 2 to 3,000.

The bay of Valparaiso is unsafe during the winter
season, for it is open to the northward, and when it blows
hard there is generally a heavy sea. There have, at times,
been severe gales here, during which several vessels have
been lost, as well as part of their crews. During the summer
months the only danger is that of being blown out to sea
during the heavy squalls, and it is requisite for the vessels
to be anchored near the beach.

The following statements will show the progressive
increase of the proceeds of the custom-house, ingress and
egress of vessels, merchandise, &c., since 1809, when the
whole amount of the duties of Chile did not exceed
267,38 dollars during that year. The import and export
duties from 1825 to 1831 were averaged at 297,350
dollars yearly, and in the years—

	DOLLARS.	R.	C.		DOLLARS.	R.	C.
1831	. 365,560	5	0	1833 .	. 761,247	5	0
1832	. 470,947	7	0	1834 .	. 860,215	3	0

In 1892 the Average was about 270 Foreign Vessels, and the following Statement will show the Increase of Trade, &c., in this flourishing port.

A REPORT OF THE NATIONAL AND FOREIGN VESSELS THAT HAVE ENTERED THE PORT OF VALPARAISO IN THE YEAR 1834.

Flag.	Merchantmen.	Whalers.	Ships of War.	Total.	Tonnage of the Merchantmen.	FOREIGN TRADE.			COASTING TRADE.			
						Merchandise imported from other countries.	Merchandise in the bonded stores.	Merchandise imported from the ports of the republic.	Merchandise imported from the ports of embarked.	Timber dis-in the bonded stores.	Merchandise in the bonded stores.	Merchandise remaining on board.
						BALES.	BALES.	BALES.	BALES.	LOGS.	BALES.	BALES.
National	184	14		148	15,595	20,244	11,245	8,999				
English	89	3	19	111	20,155	898,298	176,991	221,307	367,175	291,010	47,064	29,081
French	27	2	4	33	7,506	176,140	23,815	152,925				
North American	69	10	4	83	20,700	419,905	114,742	305,163				
Sardinian	9			9	2,793	40,962	18,551	22,411				
Hamburg	10			10	1,526	24,843	9,935	14,908				
Bremen	1			1	267	249	247	2				
Austrian	1			1	295	2,621	2,617	4				
Danish	2			2	256	7,141	3,086	4,055				
Prussian	2			2	482	2,756	1,942	814				
Belgian	1			1	209	4,778	2,415	2,963				
Brazilian	1			1	152	1,101	1,101	.....				
Hotahitian	1			1	200	1,992	1,646	346				
Buenos Ayrean	3			3	598	6,399	1,627	4,772				
Bolivian	6			6	597	2,259	1,963	296				
Mexican	6			6	863	38,412	37,856	556				
Peruvian	82			82	5,561	208,464	158,439	50,025				
Total	394	15	41	450	77,700	1,856,564	588,218	788,346	367,175	291,010	47,064	29,081

Custom-House of Valparaiso, April 30, 1835.—Fuentes.

In 1836 I was harbour-master, and then there were about forty vessels entered per month. The following is a statement of the progressive increase of the Chilian treasury during the years—

	DOLLARS.			DOLLARS.	REALES.
1825	 1,727,776	1830	. .	Revolution.	
1826	 1,699,799	1831	. .	1,517,537	7
1827	 1,797,123	1832	. .	1,652,713	6¼
1828	 1,660,527	1833	. .	2,130,185	0¼
1829	 1,798,892	1834	. .	2,370,419	2¼

The following is a statement of the army and navy of Chile in the year 1834 :—

Veteran forces	. . . . .	2773 Rank and file
Naval force	. . . . .	Brig Aquilles, 20 guns
		Schooner Colo Colo, 8 do.

Expenditure for the army and navy in the year 1834:—

	DOLLARS.	REALES.
1834	755,785	7½
Civil List	490,883	2½
Total . .	1,246,679	2

I have given a financial account, in which the reports of the minister of finance, Don Manuel Rengifo, of the years 1834 and 1835, as well as other documents of importance to all who are connected with Chile, have been published.*

* " Parties acquainted with Chile, well know that there is more a want of the will than of the power to pay the dividends, and a statement confirmatory of that opinion may be found in a work recently published on foreign loans by Mr. Sutcliffe. According to this statement, which is for six successive months during the campaign in Peru, the receipts and disbursements of the treasury of Chile were as follow :—

	Receipts.	Disbursements.
	DOLLARS.	DOLLARS.
Aug. 31, 1837 . .	234,909.0½	. . 206,517.4¼
Sept. 30, —— . .	404.479.7¾	. . 374,801.7½
Oct. 31, —— . .	197,618.5	. . 185,494.7¾
Nov. 30, —— . .	193,803.3	. . 176,779.7¾
Dec. 30, —— . .	349,546.0½	. . 317,278.7¾
Jan. 31, 1838 . .	135,553.2¾	. . 104,586.5½

Valparaiso, I have already stated, had nearly been destroyed by the earthquake of 1822; therefore I will present my readers with a graphic statement of the effects of that calamitous visitation from the pen of a gentleman who resided in the vale of Con-Con:—" On the Saturday and Sunday following the earthquake, I visited Valparaiso: on my way I found the houses at the Viña de la Mar levelled to the ground. On entering Valparaiso, I was astonished at the extent of the ruin, and dismayed at the miserable appearance of the place, as well as at the forlorn and wretched condition of the people. The houses were nearly all unroofed; many had been thrown to the ground, while the thick walls of sun-dried bricks which remained were split in all directions. The desolation was horrible; the large church of the Almendral, called La Merced, presented the most remarkable ruin. The tower, built of burnt bricks and good mortar, the walls of which, up to the belfry, were six feet thick, were shivered into large blocks, and thrown to the ground. The tower was sixty feet high. The body of the church extended from north to

" Thus, for every month during this period the receipts exceed the disbursements, and exhibit the republic in a perfect state of solvency. The object of the author of the pamphlet is to show, that it is not the fault of the Chilians in general, but of the Spanish faction called the ' Faroleros,' that the interest of the Chilian Loan has not been punctually paid. At the same time, to make out this point, it exhibits the existence of resources generally, and, while it would defend the Chilians themselves, serves to exhibit that there must have been a want of good faith somewhere."—
Times, Aug. 21st, 1840. City Intelligence.

" Board of Trade, July 3rd, 1840.
" Sir,—I am directed by the President of the Board of Trade, to return you his thanks for your Pamphlet on the subject of Foreign Loans.
" I have the honour to be, Sir,
" Your most obedient Servant,
"J. LANG."
" Thomas Sutcliffe, Esq.
" H. Labouchere."

south. The walls at both ends were thrown down, both fell towards the north; the side walls, although much damaged, remained, and supported the ridge-roof of timber. The covering of the roof was entirely shaken off, and the whole body of rafters inclined considerably towards the north; and the few roofs of the houses in Valparaiso which were not thrown down, all inclined in the same direction. On each side of the church of La Merced were a number of square buttresses of good solid brick-work, six feet square; they stood at a small distance from the walls.

"Those on the western side were all thrown down, as were all but two on the eastern side; these two were twisted from the wall in a north-easterly direction, each presenting an angle to the wall.

"This twisting to the north-east was remarked in other places. At Quintero, thirty miles to the northward of Valparaiso, the heaviest and largest pieces of furniture in the house there, were turned in the same direction.

"The whole population of Valparaiso had fled to the hills on which they were encamped. At the further and narrow extremity of the town called the Port, where the houses are built upon the solid rock, the damage was not so great as in the other parts of the town.

"The governor's house, the two castles, and the churches, being the most substantial buildings, were all shivered to pieces, the destruction being here, as in other places, in proportion to the thickness and solidity of the walls.

"It was fortunate that the earthquake did not happen two hours later, as nearly the whole population would then have been buried in the ruins; as it was, about one hundred and fifty people were killed, and many were wounded or bruised.

"No bombardment could have produced such complete

ruin as the earthquake effected. The desolate condition of the people was lamentable in the extreme, and this was dreadfully increased on the night of the 27th, when, to their surprise and astonishment, it rained heavily. If any one thing more than another could add to their wretchedness, it was this unseasonable and unexpected fall of rain.

"They who had escaped from the ruin of the town, and retired to the hills with such of their property as they could save, were some of them living in tents; the greater number were compelled to bivouac in the open air, and while depending on the continuance of the usual dry weather, the rain, which so unexpectedly fell, put them into a state of almost absolute despair. It ceased, however, towards the morning; had it continued for a longer period, not only would it have destroyed their property, but it would have produced famine and disease, the most horrible apprehensions of which filled the minds and wholly occupied the thoughts of the unfortunate and miserable people. Rain in the month of November had never been known, and its occurrences during the continuance of the earthquakes was considered by the bigoted and ignorant Chilenos, as a mark of the Divine vengeance for their own sinful lives, the conduct of the people in power, and the crime of permitting the English heretics to contaminate the country."*

Soon after the earthquake of 1835, a preacher in the city of Aconcagua, attributed all the evils that had befallen Chile to the pernicious custom of reading heretical books. "The church resounded with his diatribes against Luther, Calvin, Arius, Pelagius,Vol—tai—re, and Rou—sse—a—u. Such a sermon was never heard before, either in or out of a church; nor could the auditors give it a place in their

* Miers's Travels in Chile.

memory, with the exception of their worthy "intendente." This magistrate retained the most fanatical part, and it gave him an irreconcileable hatred against books, and from that moment, he swore upon the cross of his sword, and before the Lord of hosts, that he would not spare any books that should fall into his hands. Full of this holy purpose, he issued the most strict and precise orders, that a general batter (rodeo) should be made, in order that all those 'entes materiales pero animados bichos,' (meaning the books,) should be collected, and on a fixed day and hour taken to the principal square, and burnt. A pile was accordingly made, and from about two hundred volumes that were bound in parchment; a manufacturer of fire-works begged he might be allowed to take the covers to make rockets with; but the favour was refused, for it was wisely resolved, that their explosion should make no more noise, nor infest the air with their pestiferous contagion. The ' auto de fe,' commenced with a collection of the Ecclesiastical Observer, which was declared to be a per-nicious book, as ecclesiastics ought not to be observers. Next followed the bible of P. Scio; and it was said, that the translation of such works did more harm than good ; whereupon, the spectators could not bear the slow process of examination, and of their own accord committed the whole of the books to the flames, and saw them con-sumed."*

This barbarous affair caused a great sensation amongst people of education and patriotism, and who expressed their feelings in the following manner :—

"This article, dictated by impartial justice, compels us to represent to S. E., the president of the republic, the existence of an evil that ought to be suppressed, unless his

* El Philopolita, No. 1, August 3, 1835.

laudable exertions and endeavours towards public improvement should be to no purpose. Its most implacable enemy, the ferocious hydra of fanaticism, has again reared its horrible head, and pretends to blast the first buds of civilization. In the first number of this paper, an account was given of the 'auto de fe,' that was celebrated in the city of Aconcagua, and it was stated that about two hundred books had been burnt. Now we can safely assert, that more than five hundred were destroyed; also, that the inquisitors gloried in their holy work. If their zeal had led them to ferret out books that were decidedly against our religion, or morals, and an investigation made of them under competent authority, instead of criticizing, we should have applauded their exertions. We are also informed, that many good books were burnt;* it could not be otherwise. Who made the expurgation? When was it published? Under whose authority? If acts of this nature are intrusted to men who are ignorant, and who condemn and burn all they do not understand, adieu to civilization. In vain do our laws protect the introduction of books; in vain do we study sciences, or languages, whilst the government, like Penelope, destroys with one hand, what is wrought by the other." †

The sapientipotent, governor intendente, who performed this action, worthy of a more unenlightened age, was one of the principal actors during the civil broils, and considered by his partisans to be a man of erudition; but what could be expected whilst the Spanish faction held the administration in their hands; and which the patriots had allowed to be wrested from them by their implacable enemies, whose treachery and deceit can be traced to have

* Bibles and Testaments.
† El Philopolita, No. 3, Santiago de Chile, August 19, 1835.

caused so much blood and strife ever since 1814; when those true patriots, Generals Carrera and O'Higgins, buried their personal animosities by a fraternal embrace, instead of renewing the combat;* and, on discovering the toils that had been laid by their common enemy, they reunited their forces, and issued a manifesto, of which the following is an extract.

"Would it not have been glorious for the enemies of the American cause to have seen us involved in civil dissensions; and in which they not only pretended to be the judges, but also the arbiters of our destinies— 'Infames!' This barbarous calculation of a new and unjust attack, and the frankness with which we have communicated our sentiments, have now opened the gates of the temple of union, on whose altars we have solemnly sworn to sacrifice ourselves for the good of our country, and consign the laurels of victory to that Deity, under whose august shrine we have signed the decree that will consolidate its happy destiny, and seal our eternal reconciliation."†

Had this laudable precept been kept in view, Chile would have prospered, and much blood spared; nor would it have been at all necessary for a worthy patriot to have refreshed the memories of his countrymen in the year 1836, with the horrible detail of the cruelties of their oppressors, which I recommend to the perusal of the Porteños de Valparaiso, whose spleen has already been manifested towards foreigners.—El Rdo. P. Fr. Jose

---

* They were fighting on the plain of Maipu, when General O'Higgins received intelligence of the Spaniards having invaded Chile, and commenced hostilities, during the period of an armistice, celebrated by General Gainza with the Chilians, and witnessed by Captain Hillier, of H. M. ship Phœbe.

† Generals Carrera and O'Higgins's manifest, September 4, 1814.

Javier Guzman del orden Serafico de N. P. S. Francisco, cites the following cases.

" It is not necessary for me to refresh your memory with the numerous acts of barbarity of the Spaniards, for they are already recorded in the public papers, that may be referred to, and in which are detailed the destruction of more than ten thousand individuals, who have fallen in the wars of Chile, from 1812 to 1818. The cruelties of Osorio at Rancagua; and, lastly, the murders perpetrated by Sambruno, and Morgado, in the prisons of this capital, on the very day those ' Misantropos de la humanidad' had intended to have exterminated its inhabitants.

" Is it possible that we Americans could be happy or content with a despotic government that treated us with oppression, disdain, inequality, and tyranny ?   None but the declared enemies to justice, and our Supreme Creator, can judge favourably, palliate their numerous atrocities, or decide against the good principles that reason has demanded."

In detailing the sufferings of the northern states, it will not be necessary to relate the numerous barbarities of the Spaniards in Upper Peru, Quito, La Paz, Arequipa, and other parts, for they are too well known; I will only cite the following cases.

" There was an Indian woman who was reputed to be wealthy, and a Spanish colonel, Imas, surprised her, and demanded the gold and silver she possessed : the Indian, who in reality was poor, offered every thing she had in her dwelling, and did all she could to satisfy Imas that he had been misinformed ; but the monster doubting her statements, caused her to be hung."

Ismas always marched with the advanced guard of

General Goyeneche; and he no sooner entered a village, than he ordered the principal inhabitants to feast him and his officers, at the curate's house; and as soon as the repast was over, his soldiers seized on the utensils, which were of silver, and gave them to their colonel; and as this robbery was generally committed in his presence, the owners of the plate had no other alternative, than suffer their losses in silence. At one time, a curate was ordered to provide for, and invite one hundred persons; his parishioners knowing the rapacity of the Spaniard, refused to lend their plate; but Imas ordered the curate to invite the guests, and admit of no excuse: he gave orders to his soldiers to await the signal, which would be a toast, and then to fall upon the party, and, beginning with the curate, put them to death; this atrocious act was executed with mournful fidelity, and none but the colonel and his officers were left alive."*

This bandit was tried in Lima, by a court-martial, in June, 1816: he confessed the crimes he was accused of, and said he had acted according to orders he had received from his general, for whom he robbed, and whose example he followed; that he hung the Indian by order of the general, who sent him to take her gold and life; and, lastly, that he had done nothing more than follow the example of his chief, and brother officers, who acted as he had done. The colonel was dismissed the service; and he complained, saying, that he was only persecuted for having shared the booty with his soldiers. Such was the conduct of a royalist chief in Peru, according to his own confession.

Although these painful details still live in the recollections of the South Americans, there are too many who

* Extracted from El Despertador Americano, page 92.

cast a lingering look towards the dignities they sullied, the power they exercised so mercilessly over aborigines, mixed classes, and plebeians; and so little do the multitude of any country benefit by experience, that the South American plebeians, deceived by hypocritical leaders, are forging chains to bind themselves, and forfeiting that liberty which they acquired at such a sacrifice of human life.

I had hoped that ere this they might have seen their errors, and recalled that spirit of patriotism which party feeling rendered dormant, and from which they had unconsciously fallen into a state of apathy. It is by this want of decision that they have suffered the laurels of Chacabuco, Maipu, Valdivia, Callao, Chiloe, Junin, and Ayacucho to be ignominiously wrested from them, by a faction which has long been toiling to place South America again under the dynasty of the Bourbons!

The Madrid journals, as well as the provincial papers, of recent dates, have announced the arrival of the Chilian and Peruvian plenipotentiaries, and have expressed also, their fond expectations of seeing the long lost privileges of the Cadiz and Barcelona monopolists restored to them, since the South Americans, like the frogs in the fable, are petitioning for a king. The following extract from the Times newspaper of May 20, 1841, is a favourable omen in the cause of freedom, and is highly honourable to El Infante Don Francisco de Paula, who declines to become the tool of a despicable faction :—" Count de Parsent had written to the ' Correo Nacional' to contradict, in the most formal manner, the report of alleged negotiations pending between the infant Don Francisco de Paula and Peruvian plenipotentiaries."

EARTHQUAKES AT CARACCAS.

I shall now detail the last sufferings of the Americans in Peru, during the siege of Callao; through the hard-heartedness, tenacity, and inhumanity of General Rodil, whose ferocious heart could allow him to witness more than eight thousand individuals perish with hunger, sooner than allow them to quit Callao, in order to procure food; and such was the scarcity of aliments, that after having consumed all the rats, mice, and other animals they could get hold of, they devoured pieces of hide, leather, shoes, and even the dead bodies of their fellow-sufferers, who fell dead in the streets of Callao; children expired at the breasts of their famished mothers; and the Marques de Torre Tagle, (formerly president of Peru,) gave a dozen pieces of gold plate for a single fowl to supply the craving wants of his family, who, with himself, died of hunger !!!* .

Here follow a number of cases extracted from the memoirs of Miller, to which I shall add the following: — " On the 26th of March, 1812, at seven minutes P. M., a violent shock of an earthquake was felt over the whole Captaincy. which, in little more than a minute, laid the towns of La Guayra, Caraccas, St. Carlos, Barquisimeto, and many others, in ruins. At La Guayra, it was computed that above 1,500 persons perished. Caraccas, the capital, was almost entirely demolished; the fortifications were destroyed; the walls were thrown down, and large chasms yawned in the streets, over which the twisted walls of the houses, that had not fallen, hung forward in the most frightful manner. The destruction was also very great in other parts, and the whole country in consequence, thrown into the utmost consternation.

* El Padre Guzman.

" A curious example of the influence of superstition
upon the minds of ignorant people, was exhibited upon
this occasion. By a coincidence which, though singular,
had certainly nothing miraculous in it, this terrible catastrophe happened upon Holy Thursday, on which day,
formerly, the patriots had declared their resolution not to
acknowledge the regency of Spain, and had begun to
adopt measures for securing their independence. The
multitude conceived that their present calamity was a
judgment sent upon them for the part they had then
acted; and they began, therefore, to cry out for the
establishment of the old government. In this belief they
were fully confirmed on learning that Coro, Valencia, and
Maracaybo, which were still in the royalist persuasion,
had sustained no injury; and though an edict was published, threatening death to all who should utter such
sentiments, still the opinion gained ground, and totally
annihilated their zeal for the new cause. Caroro, a patriot
town in the Captaincy, had been taken, a few days previous to this event, by a party of royalists under the command of General D. Domingo Monteverde, a Spaniard,
and immediately after the earthquake happened, the
cities around him hastened to send in their submissions.
Thus successful, Monteverde marched against the capital
—or rather against its ruins,—where the congress, as the
only means of averting the destruction that threatened
them, had appointed Miranda dictator. But such a
measure was vain. The people were persuaded that
Heaven was on the side of the royalists; and though
Miranda proclaimed martial law, and used every exertion
to revive their drooping spirits, the troops he commanded
so rapidly left him, that he felt himself compelled to surrender, without being able to offer the smallest resistance.

2 M

Some of the patriots escaped to the United Sates; Miranda and several others were sent prisoners to Spain; and the regency and the cortes were acknowledged—at least for a time—in Venezuela. The arbitrary manner in which Monteverde exercised his authority on this occasion, was such as might have been expected. The Venezuelans had their eyes opened to a sight of their folly; they transferred the favour of Heaven to the other side, and longed again to taste the sweets of liberty."*

EXECUTIONS IN MEXICO AND COLOMBIA.

" Caraccas capitulated to General Monteverde in San Mateo on the 25th of July, 1812. The basis of this convention was, that the lives, property, and persons of every citizen should be held sacred; that no one should be prosecuted for previous opinions; in short, general oblivion and amnesty were granted. How the faith of this treaty was preserved will, perhaps, best appear in the words of a respectable English gentleman, who was an eye-witness of the scenes which he describes, and whose statement was transmitted to the Admiralty by one of the English commanders on the West India station.

" ' Monteverde caused to be arrested nearly every creole of rank throughout the country; he then had them chained in pairs, and conducted to the dungeons of La Guayra and Porto Cabello, where many of them perished by suffocation or disease.' In another part of his statement he says, ' Were I to detail all the horrid excesses committed by Boves and Rosette, on the route from the river Oronoco to the valleys of Caraccas, it would be scarcely possible to find a reader who could believe such scenes of slaughter and devastation credible. Some idea,

* Dumfries Monthly Magazine of 1825.

however, of the melancholy facts may be conceived, when I assert that these monsters, in traversing a space of more than four hundred miles, left no human being alive of any age or either sex, except such as joined their standard.'

" The commandant Bustamante, in his despatch to the viceroy, dated Zitaquaro, October 23, 1811, recommends Mariano Ochoa, a dragoon, 'who, in pursuing the insurgents, had a brother who knelt to him to beg his life, which he took with his own hands.'

" Don Ignacio Garcia Revollo in his despatch to the viceroy, dated Queretaro, November 23, 1811, recommends Serjeant Francisco Montes ' as deserving the rank of an officer, for, amongst other gallant actions, he killed one of his own nephews, who, making himself known, received for answer, that he knew no nephew amongst insurgents.'

" General Truxillo, in another despatch, boasts that he ordered his men to fire upon a flag of truce from Hidalgo, accompanied by a banner of the Holy Virgin, and adds, that he did not expect to be troubled in that sort of way again. Every person with the flag of truce was murdered.

" General Calleja informs the viceroy, that in the affair of Aculco, he had one man killed and two wounded ; but that he put to the sword 5,000 seduced Indians, and that their total loss amounted to double the number. Most of them were killed as they were kneeling for mercy.

" The same general entered Guanaxuato with fire and sword, where 14,000 old men, women, and children perished, because the insurgent army had taken up its quarters there, but by a timely retreat had escaped his fury. Calleja soon after received from the regency of Cadiz the rank of ' mariscal de campo,' and the viceroy

the cross of the order of Charles the Third, as a reward
for this distinguished service.

" Extracts that have been made from only a few of
the Gazettes published in Mexico in the years 1811 and
1812, boast of 25,344 of the ' insurgents' being killed, 3,556
made prisoners, besides 697 shot after surrendering.

" Boves condemned a patriot to suffer death. A boy
under twelve years of age threw himself at the feet of the
tyrant, and implored his father's life. Boves said, ' Yes;
upon condition that you will have an ear cut off without
changing countenance.' ' That I will readily do,' said
the boy, ' But remember,' said Boves, ' that the smallest
flinch will be the death-warrant of your father.' The ear
was then cut off with a knife. Boves watched the boy,
who bore the mangling operation with astonishing fortitude. When it was over, instead of performing his promise, Boves said, ' I can see very well that you will be a
more terrible enemy to Spain than your father has been;
therefore, you shall be shot before his eyes.' It is needless
to add, that both father and son were instantly executed.

" And yet the royalists did not always escape with
impunity. In a battle which the patriots lost near the
Apure, a Frenchman was taken prisoner amongst other
officers. The royalist commander said to him, ' So
monsieur, you are a great patriot.' ' I am,' said the
Frenchman, ' and I hate the Spaniards most cordially.'
' Mighty well,' rejoined the other; ' now you shall pay
for your hatred.' ' You shall pay first,' said the Frenchman, and, drawing his sword, laid the commander dead
at his feet. The troops around sprung upon the undaunted Frenchman; but did not despatch him until he
had slain or wounded several of his assailants.

" Under all these dreadful sufferings, the Americans

still preserved their infatuated loyalty to Ferdinand, and
the conviction that his restoration would prove the harbinger of relief; when it did occur, however, it proved
only the signal for renewed oppression and still bloodier
massacres. In reward for the violation of the most solemn
capitulations, for the boasted murder of the bearers of flags
of truce, and for the most cold-blooded and indiscriminate
slaughter, they now beheld Monteverde, Callejas, Cruz,
Truxillo, and other execrable monsters, loaded by Ferdinand with rewards, and covered with decorations.

"The Americans recollected that Charles the Fifth,
the proudest and most powerful monarch of his time,
had, in a case of similar injustice, but not of similar sacrifices on the part of his subjects, listened benignantly to
their complaints, and sent out the 'Licenciado' Gasca
with full powers to redress their grievances, which he
effected. The slightest indication of a benevolent inclination towards them would even still have preserved to
Ferdinand an empire, and to the Spanish nation brothers
and faithful allies, much richer and more powerful than
themselves. But Heaven had decreed that justice and
right should take their course, and that centuries of misrule, oppression, and cruelty, should at last, through their
own instrumentality, meet their merited punishment.

"Perhaps nothing will excite more surprise than the
circumstance that America did not find in the cortes
a few sincere, generous, and powerful advocates, nor
amongst those 'liberales,' who at the same period spoke
and wrote with equal freedom and ability upon abuses
of power nearer home. The chains of America might
indeed have been lightened and burnished by the con-
stitutionalists, but the unanimity of parties on colonial
questions forbade the South Americans to indulge

in the hope that a single link would willingly be removed.

"The imbecile Ferdinand did not even vouchsafe to
listen to their complaints, although, with the exception of
Caracas, they still persisted in their mistaken loyalty to
this heartless sovereign, for three long years after his
restoration. During this period, the feelings and conduct
of the Spanish government varied not, nor had its appetite
for carnage been satiated.

"The following is a list of individuals who suffered
death and confiscation of property (without trial, or in
violation of amnesties,) in New Grenada, in consequence
of the entrance of the Spanish troops under the command of General D. Pablo Morillo, in the year 1816,
taken from official documents transmitted to the court
of Madrid :—

CARTHAGENA.

DATES.	NAMES.	KIND OF PUNISHMENT.
Feb. 26.	D. D. Manuel Castillo	
	D. D. José Ma. Portocarrero	
	D. D. José Ma. Garcia Toledo	
	D. D. Miguel Dias Granados	
	D. D. Antonio de Ayos	Shot through the back.*
	D. Pantaleon Ribon	
	D. Martin Amador	
	D. Santiago Stuart	
	D. Manuel Auguiano, a Spaniard, and colonel of engineers.	

MOMPOX AND OCANA.

Feb.	D. Miguel Carabano	Ditto.
	D. Fernando Carabano	

SANTA FE DE BOGOTA.

May 26.	Juan Maria	
June 6.	D. Antonio Villavicencio	
16.	D. D. Ignacio Bargas	Ditto.
	D. José Ramon de Leiba, lieutenant-colonel and secretary to the viceroyalty.	
	D. José Contreras	
	D. José Maria Carbonell	Gibbeted.

* Persons are placed with their backs towards the executioners of their
sentence, with the intent of treating them with greater ignominy.

DATES.	NAMES.	KIND OF PUNISHMENT.
July 5.	Jorge Lozano	
	D. D. José Gregorio Guiterres	
	D. D. Emerigildo Benites	
	D. D. Miguel Pombo	Shot through the back.
	D. D. Fran. Xavier Garcia Hevia	
	D. D. Cristiano Valensuela	
20.	D. Antonio Baraya	
	D. Pedro Lastra	
Aug. 8.	D. D. Custodia Garcia Ribera	Shot, and placed on a gibbet.
	D. Hermogenes Cespedes	
	D. D. Tomas Antonio Peña	
	D. N. Navas	
13.	D. José Ayala	
29.	D. D. Joaquin Hoyos	
31.	D. D. Joaquin Camacho	
	D. Nicolas Rivas	
Sept. 3.	D. Liborio Megia	
	A. Andres Linares	
	D. Silvestre Hortiz	
	D. Feliz Pelgron	Shot through the back.
	D. Rafael Niño	
	D. Pasqual Andreu	
	D. D. Martin Cortes	
11.	D. Dionisio Tejada	
19.	D. José Cifuentas	
	D. Bernarbé Gonzalez	
	D. José Maria Ordoñez	
	D. José Antonio Valdez	
30.	D. D. Manuel Bernardo Alvares	
	D. D. José Maria Arrublas	
	D. Joaquin Garcia, escribano	
Oct. 5.	D. D. Manuel Rodriguez Tonce	Shot, placed on a gibbet, their heads cut off, and placed in a cage at the entrance of the city.
	D. D. Camilo Torices	
	The Count de Casa Valencia	
	D. Pedro Felipe Valencia (colonel)	
	D. D. José Maria Davila	
Oct 12.	D. Salvador Rizo	
	D. Pablo Morillo	
22.	D. Francisco Cabal	
24.	D. Francisco de Paula Aguilar	
	D. Vicente Monzalve	
30.	D. D. Francisco de Ulloa	Shot through the back.
	D. D. Miguel Montalvo	
	D. D. Francisco Caldas	
	D. Miguel Buch	
Nov. 8.	D. D. José Maria Chacon	
	Six Soldiers	
21.	D. Francisco Morales	
	Two Soldiers	
27.	D. Nicolas Nueva Ventura	

DATES.	NAMES.	KIND OF PUNISHMENT.
	D. Miguel Gomez Plata, aged 80	Shot, after being tortured three times.*
Decem.	D. Antonio Campusano D. N. Ponce A distinguished individual of Ambalema	Ditto.

ZIPAQUIRA.

Aug. 3.	D. Augustin Zapata	Shot, gibbeted, and his head cut off.
	D. Juan Figueroa D. Francisco Zarate D. José Gomez D. Luis Sanchez D. José Riano Cortes	Shot.

FACABATIVA.

Aug. 31.	D. Mariano Grillo D. Joaquin Grillo	Ditto.

MESA DE JUAN DIAS.

Oct. 7.	D. Francisco Olaya D. Andres Quijano	Ditto.

VILLA DE LEYBA.

Oct. 27.	D. Manuel José Sanchez D. Juan Bautista Gomez D. Joaquin Vinana	Shot.

TUNJA.

Sep. 20.	D. Santiago Abdon Herrera D. Antonio Palacio D. Alberto Montero D. Ignacio Palaza D. Manuel Otero	Ditto.

NEIBA.

26.	D. D. Luis Garcia D. José Dias D. Benito Salas	Ditto.

* This individual came to London in 1814, with Colonel Duran, commissioned by the province of Socorro to purchase muskets, and, on his return, he fell into the hands of the Spaniards, and was tortured, for the purpose of forcing him to declare whether the English government, or any house in London, sold him the arms which he brought with him from Europe; but nothing could be extracted from him.

DATES.	NAMES.	KIND OF PUNISHMENT.
	D. Fernando Salas	
	D. Francisco Lopez	Shot through the
	D. José Maria Lopez	back.
	D. Miguel Tello	

POPAYAN.

July 8.	D. Augustin Rosas	
	D. José España	
	D. Rafael Lataza	
10.	D. Carlos Montufar (lieutenant-colonel)	
Aug.	D. D. Miguel Angulo	
	D. Emerigildo Troyano	
	D. D. José Antonio Ardila	
	D. Pedro Monzalve	
	D. José Monzalve	
	Serjeant Basquez	
	D. José Acuña	
Aug. 22.	D. José Maria Cabal	
	D. José Maria Quijano	
	D. Mariano Matute	
	D. José Maria Guiterrez	Ditto.
29.	D. José Maria Ramirez	
Sept. 24.	D. D. Manuel Vallecilla	
Oct.	D. José Pino and D. José Navia	
	D. D. Frutos Guiterres	
	The officers Salias, Vaes, Olmedilla, and two more.	
30.	D. D. Leon Armero	
Nov. 28.	D. D. Juan Nepomuceno Niño	
	D. D. Cayetano Vasquez	
	D. Pedro Manuel Montano	
	D. José Buitrago	
Dec. 12.	D. D. Francisco Antonio Caicedo	
	D. Joaquin Villacella	
	D. José Maria Perlaza	

" Another report says, ' General Morillo entered Santa
Fe de Bogota in the month of June, 1816, and remained
there till November following. More than six hundred
persons, of those who had been in the congress and provincial governments, as well as the chiefs of the independent army, were shot, hanged, or exiled, and the
prisons remained full of others who were yet waiting their
fate. Amongst those executed were the botanists Don
J. Caldas and D. Juan Lozano, (who had been ordered
by the congress of New Grenada to publish the works of
Dr. Mutis;) D. M. Cabal, an eminent chymist; D. C

Torres, highly distinguished for his learning; D. J. G.
Guiterrez Moreno, and Don M. R. Torices, both well
known for their early devotion to the cause of their country; Don Antonio Palacio-Fajar; D. J. M. Guiterrez;
D. Miguel Pombo; D. F. A. Ulloa; and many other
learned and estimable characters. The wives of persons
executed or exiled by Morillo were themselves exiled.'
The names mentioned in this account are not included in
the preceding official list. The active agent of Ferdinand,
General Morillo, in a letter to his master, published in
the 'Diario Mercantil' of Cadiz, 6th of January, 1817,
observes, that 'his work is to be done in precisely the
same manner as the primitive conquest was established;'
and boastingly assures his majesty, 'that he has not left
alive, in the kingdom of New Grenada, a single individual
of sufficient influence or talent to conduct the revolution.'
On his return to Spain, Morillo was received into special
favour, and created Count of Carthagena.

"It was not until above one million of Spanish Americans had been victims; until almost every Spaniard,
whom, with a blind generosity, they had retained in
situations of trust, had deceived and betrayed them; until
they found no hope left, from either prince or people,
that the film fell from the eyes of the natives. They at
length discovered that the phantom which they had
hitherto worshipped was unable to protect, and unwilling
to serve them, and that they had been, under the king's
name, the victims of treachery, avarice, and cruelty.

"Upon this discovery, the spirit of enlightened patriotism walked abroad. Their duties to their children,
and to the land of their nativity, became at once apparent.
The kingdoms of a vast continent immediately, and almost
simultaneously, declared their independence; and, in the

assertion of their rights, placed their whole reliance upon the justice of their cause, and the goodness of their swords."*

ESPAÑOLES.

Copy of a Letter published in "El Dia Yel Golpe" of March 30, 1838.—No. 23.

"Valparaiso, March 25, 1838.

"To-day, a Spanish bark, called Santa Susana, has anchored in the port; it is said, she is short of water and provisions, and is on her voyage to Mexico.

"The Spanish flag is flying in our bay, and amidst the Chilian squadron. What a contrast!

"It is now two P. M., and no one has ordered the detestable flag of our enemy to be hauled down.

"The sight of it causes the greatest indignation, for it calls to our memory all those atrocities which the monsters who followed that flag so pitifully committed on the Americans.

"It is impossible for me to remain indifferent to the impulse of my heart: I am a Chilian, and love my country dearly. Nothing gives me more rage, than to observe the impudence of our former oppressors. I cannot explain the uneasiness I have experienced, when I have considered the want of respect that these 'malvados' show to our institutions.—The Susana has entered without any other flag, than that of Spain. 'Is not this like a dream?' And without having acknowledged our independence, we are shamefully insulted!"

AN ARTICLE FROM THE SAME PAPER.

"The editors of the Mercury, of Valparaiso, assure us, in their number 2787, 'That the inhabitants of that

* Miller's Memoirs.

city have experienced the sweetest sympathy, at seeing
the Spanish flag flying again, after a twenty years' war;
and that only a very few have manifested their displeasure
caused by the appearance of the Spanish vessel, Santa
Susana.

"But that such scruples only arise from their ignorance
of the motives that have embarrassed the Spanish cabinet
from issuing the royal decree of the acknowledgment of
our independence."

"It is only the editors of the 'Mercurio,' whose politics
are so well known, that could proffer such blasphemies.
Until when shall we suffer, the enemies of our liberty, of
our tranquillity and ease, to abuse our tolerance?

"The author of the article that occupies our attention
is a Spaniard. Look out, fellow-countrymen!!!—After
having used seduction and deceit, the 'Mercurio' descends, or if not, his mentor, to employ menaces: up to
this point has arrived the insolence of our enemies. 'We
only await,' he says, 'until the difficult and unhappy
political circumstances that afflict Spain, shall be ended,
that its 'relations,' with these countries will be re-established, and regulated on the basis of a perpetual peace,
and sincere reconciliation.'

"Can any true American read this daring announce-
ment without indignation? Are the bayonets those that
are going to make the acknowledgment that it is to be
hoped, on the Peninsular war's ending there. But what
acknowledgment? Reconciliation, it is said. And is this
what is prescribed to us, by those who have the arms in
their hands?"

AN EXTRACT FROM THE SAME PAPER.

"Although the Spanish vessel, which has so justly
excited the public notice, arrived in Valparaiso on the

26th of last month, the Araucano (ministerial paper) that was published four days afterwards, has not said a word relative to this singular occurrence of our history. It is reserved for a future day; for all that may be wished for cannot be obtained: 'no todo lo que se quiere se puede.' "

" Valdiviano Federal."—El Doctor Don Miguel Infanta.—Editor.

EL DIA Y EL GOLPE, APRIL 1, 1838.—No. 34.

" SE CORRE,

"That the supreme government, in accordance with the council of state, (having been consulted by the governor of Valparaiso, on account of the audacious and unexpected arrival of the Spanish bark, Santa Susana,) have decreed on the 27th of March, ' all the ports of the republic free to vessels of Spain, as a friendly nation!!' "

" Imprenta de Colo-Colo."

The preceding pages of this work will give a pretty fair idea how the Chilians have allowed the fruits of so many years of toil and danger to be wrested from them by the partisans of the monsters, whose atrocities have just been detailed, and who still strive to delude their infatuated dupes, by persuading them that the earthquakes and other calamities they have experienced, have been a judgment upon them for their not only having warred against their sovereign and his satraps, but allowed their soil to be polluted with heretical foreigners, whose commiseration and patriotism had induced them to brave every danger, and aid the South Americans to free their country from their " religious, paternal, magnanimous, and humane rulers ! ! !" whose creatures have not only usurped the government of Chile, promoted their partisans to hold the highest posts of confidence,* but they have opened her ports to the commerce of Spain.

EXTRACTS FROM EL VALDIVIANO FEDERAL, OF APRIL 1ST., 1838.—No. 128.

A SPANISH VESSEL HAS ARRIVED AT VALPARAISO.

"The Spanish flag is now flying amidst the Chilian squadron. The "Mercurio" of the 27th of March, who has given us this notice, deduces that the appearance of this vessel, after a prohibition of twenty years, has excited the sympathy that the inhabitants of this country are disposed to manifest towards the nation, to whom they owe their origin.

"What a calumnious imputation to American patriotism. The appearance of the Spanish flag in Valparaiso, shows there are traitors amongst us, who have fagged, and are incessantly fagging, in order to consummate their perfidy ; or how is it? How could a Spanish vessel have the audacity, unexemplified during the whole epoch of our revolution, to enter our ports? These enemies, in disguise, are those who have sympathized with Spain; and in order to communicate it to the inhabitants, they tell them to recollect, to whom they owe their origin. The depopulaters by fire and blood of America, supposing themselves to be the populaters of it, as if the republic had no others, but what have descended

---

* Don Victorino Garrido, (a Spaniard), one of the most active agents during the disorders of 1829, 1830, 1836-7, and 1838, now military-governor of the department and port of Valparaiso, commandante-general de marine, visitor-general of the public offices, and intendent-general of the restoring army of Peru.

Lieutenant Sessi of the Spanish army, arrived from Cadiz, in 1838, and he was soon promoted to a lieutenant-colonelcy, and put in command of the battalion Santiago. I could cite many other cases, but these are a fair ensample.

from the Spanish race. With the same reasons could
the Jews and Moors demand such sympathy from Spain,
and pretend to introduce themselves again into the territory that had been for ages the patrimony of their con-
quests; not to degrade it or destroy it, but to introduce
and propagate agriculture, commerce, and the arts, that
disappeared with their expulsion; whilst in America, all
has been the reverse. It would be difficult to calculate
to what grade of prosperity this country would have been
elevated, without that conquest of horror and blood; and
to what number would have been its population at this
period."

El Doctor Don Jose Miguel Infante.—Editor.

EL AGUIJON, SANTIAGO, MAY 15TH, 1838.—No. 1.

Extract.—" There are still writers in Chile, who, with
extraordinary daring impudence, proclaim the necessity
of re-uniting the Americans with Spain, by the most
indelible and eternal ties.* This raises the just indignation of every true patriot, who never can descend to
tolerate any acts of reconciliation, under such pernicious
aspects. The natural movements of true patriotism, that
we have fortunately preserved, notwithstanding the secret
designs and deep meditations of the enemies of independence, in order that they may captivate the hearts of
the incautious, are qualified as acts of exaltation.

" The nation, jealous of its political existence, has
repulsed the first attempt that has been made respecting
our alliance with the ancient metropolis, with character
and energy.

" Every citizen has raised his voice against a measure
that would compromise the liberty that has been gained,

---

* Previous to my leaving Chile, a Minister Plenipotentiary was appointed
for the Court of Spain.

at the cost of so much bloodshed, in order to be freed
from the talons of the Iberian lion.

"The fermentation was general; and government has
at last repented a determination that was believed to be
consonant with the wish of the nation; and was obliged
to desist, to the impulse of a popular demonstration.

"But still, El Sota Cura, (under curate), strives to
bring forward a question that has received its merited
disdain, and been consigned to oblivion; he declaims,
with an emphatic tone, and still more enthusiasm than
a Spaniard, upon the advantages that America would
derive from the free and unlimited communication with
Spain.

"If the editors of that Spanish 'Folleto' would bring
to their memories the history of three centuries of the
most sanguinary oppression and tyranny, how could they
conceive to delude us with the weak voices of identity,
language, religion, and of consanguinity. Puerile logic!
and with which they have striven in vain, to entrap the
incautious. Twenty-eight years of independence are not
sufficient to make them forget their cruel oppressors;*

---

* The Indians, after enduring the most cruel oppressions for ages, in the
hopeless apathy of despair, were roused to vengeance in 1780, and Don
José Gabriel, Condorcanqui, cacique of Tungasuca, in whom education had
awakened the dormant feelings of human nature, placed himself at the head
of his countrymen. He was a descendant of the inca Tupac Amaru, who,
in the year 1562 was most unjustly beheaded by order of the viceroy Don
Francisco de Toledo.

The cacique of Tungasuca was educated at the college of San Borja at
Cuzco, and possessed virtues which in private life render a man amiable
and respected; but he wanted those essential qualifications which are
requisite to constitute the restorer of an empire. His countenance was
noble. his manners prepossessing, his stature lofty, and frame robust; his
disposition intrepid and enterprising; but his passions were violent, and
his knowledge and views in every respect too confined to realize the grand
idea of recovering the lost happiness of his country. Instead of uniting
and making common cause with the Spanish Americans, who, born on the

and our invincible hatred towards the Spaniards cannot root out the extravagant declarations of ' El Sota Cura, no, not if all the magical power of eloquence were united. The tolerance of ' La Santa Susana' has been badly interpreted by this editor, and has stimulated his pen to defend a subject, the memory of which is an offence to the national dignity; such an act, that has raised the public censure, ought not to be considered by ' El Sota Cura,' as a guarantee to forward his plans, so as to be induced to publish an article so flattering to the hopes of the Spaniards. He ought to remember, that La Patria can never condescend to accept such measures, notwithstanding the low state of desperation that it has been reduced to by political convulsions. . . . .

" America and Spain can never be re-united again ; their political and religious ties forbid it. States that

same soil, and held perhaps in more galling fetters, were entitled to the same rights with himself, he directed his hostilities equally against them as against the Spaniards, the real tyrants of both; and he met the fate which a policy so isolated and so unjust could not but ensure.

The popularity of his cause, however, amongst his own people soon attracted to his standard a multitude of undisciplined Indians, whom he had not the talent to train in military tactics, or the means to arm. He assumed not only the name of his ancestor Tupac Amaru, which means, in the Quechua language, the highly endowed, but the attributes and the pomp of the incas.

Some partial successes attended his career. The desperate valour of his unarmed followers, in which even their females partook, seemed to counterbalance the discipline, the arms, and skill of their opponents; but in the end, Tupac Amaru was taken prisoner. The details of his execution warrant a strong presumption that civilization, which in every other country in Europe has alleviated the horrors of war, and mitigated the rage of the victor, had not reached, or at least not softened, the Spaniard in America. The punishment of Tupac Amaru was dictated by the same ruthless barbarity that had formerly condemned the young and heroic Guatemozin, the last of the emperors of Mexico, to expire upon burning coals. Tupac Amaru beheld from the scaffold the execution of his wife, of his children, and of many of his faithful followers ; after which his tongue was cut out, and wild horses, harnessed to his legs and arms, tore his limbs asunder.—— *Miller's Memoirs.*

2 N

have been constituted under a republican system never can keep pace with a nation that has been the continual tool of tyrannies, and ' curiastical' passions. Our necessities, our manners, and habits, that have been formed under the shade of liberal governments, can never be confounded with the vices of the Spaniards, and which have been acquired in the schools of the most unbridled despotism. These can never associate with Americans, who are governed by laws that are sanctioned by the common weal.

" With respect to religion, unfortunately, there are still many pre-occupations in existence, as well as defects, that are contrary to the spirit of moral evangelism, and the pernicious legacy of Spanish dominion. The ' Sota Cura' may cry out in vain against the progress of libertinism, that has been introduced by foreigners ; he, as well as the fanatics, hypocrites, and violent enemies to the progress of reason, or the acquisition of learning, have given that name to those whose frankness and generosity, have striven to illuminate America. We do not wish, as the ' Sota Cura' does, to retain the heap of abuses, and ridiculous practices of the religion of Spain; these are not compatible with the grandeur and sublimity of Christianity. No, the foreigners that this editor abhors so much, are the fathers of American enlightenment, and not the propagators of libertinism ; they have cleared the opaque horizon, that has been obscured for 300 years, they have ' illustrated' our spirits with useful knowledge, modified our hearts with salutary maxims, and, in one word, they have civilized us, and taught us to know our political condition, and our rights. We are eternally bound by gratitude to them. America will be the constant friend of the illustrious nations of the old world, and the inflexible enemy of the superstition of Spain. This sincere, just, and profound regard is deeply rooted in the soul of the Americans, and cannot be debilitated by those miserable writers who, under the mask of religion, language, and consanguinity, wish to derogate liberty.

Imprenta de Colo-Colo.

The preceding may, with those documents in the preface, explain who have given never fading glory to Chile, and the reasons why foreigners who had escaped the risks of a prolonged war, should at last be expelled as exotics and mercenary adventurers.

I will now conclude by presenting the following memorials, &c., which speak for themselves :—

No. 1.

" E'xmo Señor.

" Thomas Sutcliffe, &c. &c., appears before your excellency, and states,—That during the earthquake of the 20th of February, 1835, it was notorious to all the inhabitants of the island of Juan Fernandez, and the documents, Nos. 200, 210, and 215, remitted to the ministers of state, prove, that during that terrible and unforeseen catastrophe, I, at the risk of my life, saved all the provisions, armament, boats, &c., belonging to government ; whilst all my personal property, amounting to more than 3,000 dollars, without enumerating a number of other articles, were swept into the sea; which I present, so that your excellency may be informed of the extent of my losses, and, in consideration thereof, remunerate them, so that I may be enabled to cover my losses, and return to my native country.

" THOMAS SUTCLIFFE."

" Portanto, &c."

2 N 2

" Santiago, May 9th, 1838.

" The petitioner must prove, in the courts of justice, the action he believes himself to have against the treasury, or particular persons, for the losses stated in this memorial.—Rubric of his Excellency,

" CAVAREDA."

No. 2.

" E'xmo Señor.

" Thomas Sutcliffe, &c. &c.—In the court martial that was held at Valparaiso respecting the revolution of Juan Fernandez, no notice has been taken of- the severe losses I have sustained in the fulfilment of my duty by the disorderly conduct of the mutineers, Don Nicholas Saldes, and Chaplain Friar Juan Evangelista Lopez. During the trial of this religious man, though his principal accuser, I was not even cited ; nor the two witnesses, Joseph Duncan, and Pedro Juan Rojo, my store-keeper, who were compelled to deliver up the articles of my personal property, stated in the documents, Nos. 3 to 6, against my wish, and during the time I was a prisoner. On account of this informality, the chaplain has been set at liberty, and considered an innocent man.

" Upon my arrival on the Continent, I gave notice, in my note of the 20th of September, of the scandalous conduct of the commander of the Colocolo, Don Manuel Dias, who, forgetting his duty, rendered assistance to the chief of the mutineers, receiving me as a prisoner on board of his vessel—conducting me to the Continent, and obliging me to abandon all my personal property, although Saldes sent part of it alongside the vessel. I have made him responsible for 80 cwt. of dry fish, valued at 8 dollars per cwt. which the document No. 1, in the said note in the records of the court-martial, pages 62 and

63, prove; also 200 cwt. of sandal-wood, valued at 6 dollars
per cwt., but since sold at the low price of 3 dollars to
the captain of the American brig, Lady Wrangle, which is
also proved by his two certificates, that are archived in
pages 47 and 48, jointly with the manifest from the
custom-house at Valparaiso, which gives an account of
the 200 cwt. of sandal-wood, and other articles of my property that had been sold to Captain Paty.

" With what I have here stated, and without enumerating many articles of value, my losses amount to 2,458
dollars 5½ rials, which I present to government, in order
that your excellency may deign to take them into consideration, and lessen the losses I have sustained on
account of the disorders which have taken place upon
the island ; and on consideration that the authors of such
diabolical intrigues, as well as my detractors, have been
made a laughing-stock by the sentences of the ' consejo
de guerra y corte marcial,' where I have been vindicated
in the most satisfactory manner from all the charges that
had been invented at the head-quarters of the army in
Chillan and Juan Fernandez, and now archived in the
records of my trial, which are of the same date, and
nearly of the same tenor. ' Por tanto.' I beg and supplicate your excellency to minorate my losses, so that I
may be able to cover my credit, and return to my native
country.—Es gracia, &c. Ex'mo Senor,

                              " THOMAS SUTCLIFFE."

                    DECREE.
                              " Santiago, May 9th, 1838.
" The petitioner must prove, in the courts of justice,
the action he believes himself to have against the treasury,
or particular persons, for losses stated in this memorial.—
Rubric of his excellency,   " RAMON CAVAREDA."

No. 3.

" Ex'mo Señor.

"Thomas Sutcliffe, &c. &c.—In answer to the two decrees of the 9th of May, 1838, to my memorials, in which I have requested the supreme government to diminish the losses I have sustained in the fulfilment of my duty, during my government of the island of Juan Fernandez, I beg leave to state, that I do not intend to enter into a suit, nor commence any proceedings with the ('Fisco') treasury's tribunal, nor even against the authors of the revolution of the 1st of August, that took place in that establishment, because these do not possess wherewith to pay me; nor have the señores, judges of the trial of the principal criminals, made any remarks respecting their robberies and disorders, nor in the manner in which I ought to be indemnified. It is notorious, and in the archives of the trial there is more than sufficient proof, that the revolution had been premeditated; and that in this scandalous affair, at the risk of my life, with the help of the convicts, who voluntarily ran the risk of losing theirs, by accompanying me to the assault,* I retook the

Santiago, August 19, 1836.
* Sir,—I am ordered by the minister of war, Don Diego Portales, to answer your letter of the 16th, by remitting you the copy of one he has forwarded to the governor of Valparaiso.
     Soy S. S. S. Q. S. M. B., MANUEL CAVADA.
           [copy.]
"Cruz Sanchez, José Maria Espinosa, Irene Carrasco, Mariano Rivera, Joaquin Arrevalo, Tadeo Arriagada, Andres Oliva, Alberto Briones y José Maria Perez.
"My Dear Friend,—As these individuals are to be rewarded for their good conduct during the revolution against 'Sutcliffe,' by the council of state, it would be well for you to treat them kindly, and place them separate from the rest, and free from irons, until the resolution of the council of state is forwarded to Valparaiso.
           "Yours,   "PORTALES."
"August 19, 1836."

castle of Santa Barbara, &c. &c., that had been vilely given up by the garrison to a set of villains who had lately been transported from the Continent; and after having restored order on that island, I was deprived of the command, and suffered, whilst a prisoner, for the term of six weeks, injuries and vexations. I have been transported by the commander of the mutineers to the Continent, and obliged to abandon my personal property, to the amount of more than 4000 dollars, of which there is proof to the amount of 2458 dollars, in the archives of the court-martial. I have been judged in a 'consejo de guerra' and a 'corte marcial,' not only for the occurrences on the island, but on charges that have been invented (fraguados) and remitted from the head-quarters of the army of the south, on account of private declarations, taken from Captain Don Norberto Aguayo, that are also in the archives of the trial, and of the same date, and almost the same tenor, of those that were remitted to government with my person from Juan Fernandez, which proves that, with anticipation, they had been framing imputations on the Continent to effect

---

I experienced an inward satisfaction on receiving this mark of attention from the minister: the poor prisoners were treated accordingly, and on the 7th of September I received the following copy of their pardon :—

[COPY.]

" Commandancia Gral de Armas,
" His excellency the president deemed it necessary to issue, under date of the 3rd of this month, the following decree :—
' In consequence of the merit due to the convicts, Cruz Sanchez, José Maria Espinosa, Irene Carrasco, Mariano Rivera, Joaquin Arrevalo, Tadeo Arriagada, Andres, Oliva, Alberto Briones, and José Maria Perez, assisting the governor of Juan Fernandes to suffocate the last revolution that took place in that island, I have, in accord with the council of state, pardoned them the three-fourth parts of the time for which they were transported.'
Which I transcribe to you for your intelligence and correspondent effects.
" God preserve you, &c.,
" Sept. 6, 1836. " DOMINGO FAUTOS.
" To the Governor of Juan Fernandez."

my ruin, without having had any intelligence of the disorders which had taken place on the island. I can cite many other particulars, but I believe it is sufficient only to state, that I have been completely vindicated from all the charges that the diabolical malice of my detractors had invented to accomplish their malignant intentions.

" The decisions of the ' consejo de guerra y corte marcial' declare that I have fulfilled the duties of my charge, as governor of that island, with purity and utility. ' Con pureza y utilidad.'

" In the accounts presented to your excellency, I have clearly stated the powerful motives that have obliged me to solicit my retirement from the military service, during the present war, in the memorial in which your excellency has thought proper to allow me to retire with my permanent rank, &c.

" If this exposition merits the consideration of the supreme government, I hope that your excellency will deign to allow me, at least, what will be sufficient to cover the losses I have sustained in consequence of my expulsion from Juan Fernandez, and cover the expenses of a voyage to my native country. For which I beg and supplicate your excellency to accede to this my petition, &c. &c.

" THOMAS SUTCLIFFE."

DECREE.

" Santiago, August 7th, 1838.

" Act according to what has been resolved by the decrees of the 9th of May, of this present year, in the two memorials of the same nature that were then presented to government.

" Rubric of his excellency,

" CAVAREDA."

No. 4.

" E'xmo Señor.

" Thomas Sutcliffe, &c. &c.—When I solicited my
separation from the military service of this republic, I
was, by a decree of the 13th of last March, cashiered
and excluded from a compensation for my past services.

" Therefore, justly considering that such a determination must have been caused by an erroneous interpretation
of my memorial, or on account of my having omitted
stating what were the powerful motives that had obliged
me to request my separation—on consideration that they
were too public and notorious to be repeated, and in
order that I might be relieved from the stigma of such a
decree, and maintain my reputation unsullied, I sent in
the memorial No. 5, which I now reiterate.   Your excellency has found my motives just, and, in consideration
thereof, derogated the decree of the 13th, by restoring
me to my rank, &c.

" I protest to your excellency that I should have been
serving with the same enthusiasm and honour as up to
this period, in the restoring army, had I not felt aggrieved
with the illegal proceedings that are manifested in the
document (A).

" As well as my being ordered to serve where Lieutenant-Colonel Latapiatt was first aide-de-camp to the
general-in-chief, and who has been the author of all the
disagreeable occurrences which have taken place ever
since I had the misfortune to supersede him in Juan
Fernandez, which is clearly stated and proved by the
printed documents I here accompany, which accredit in
a proper manner the motives I have already specified;
my situation was still more painful, and my feelings were
also wounded by the insults that were published against

me and other foreigners for having sustained the honour
of the army, and the truth of its operations, during the
campaign in the department of Arequipa, No. 19. These,
E'xmo Señor, were, in my opinion, more than sufficient
reasons to oblige me to request my separation, and I hope
that your excellency will take them into your bountiful
consideration, and not allow fifteen years of honourable
service to pass unremunerated, and make my case a
notable exception, without having given sufficient motives,
so as to be excluded from the recompense and grants
bestowed on other chiefs and officers, and I refer to the
following case :—

"In the year 1829, the 'reforma,' (law of military
pensions), was promulgated, and a number of chiefs and
officers received the 'reforma,' or compensation, decreed
by the national representation for their services. As the
war of the independence had ended, I also requested
my 'reforma,' which was not acceded to, on account of
my services being required by government. In 1835,
El Capitan de Navio Don Carlos Woorster, (North
American),* solicited and obtained his separation, with a
compensation; and during the last month (September),
El Commandante Don Ambrosio Acosta, (Spaniard),
has, at his own request, received his separation with a
compensation for his services.

"In virtue of which, I beg your excellency will take
my case into consideration, and deign to decree a remuneration for my past services,

         " Es Gracia, &c., E'xmo Señor,

                 " THOMAS SUTCLIFFE.

              " Santiago, October 30th, 1838.

" Decree,—The circumstances of the petitioner having
solicited his separation, when recently employed in the

     * Formerly vice-admial of the Chilian squadron.

restoring army, which was about to commence operations, places him in a different case to that of El Captain de Navio, Don Carlos Woorster, and Lieutenant-Colonel Don Ambrosio Acosta. These chiefs, although they made the same solicitudes, in order to be recompensed for their services, it was because they knew that government did not require their services, and when they were not effectually employed.

"Rubric of his Excellency,
"CAVEREDA."

I answered this decree by the following memorial.

No. 5.

"E'xmo Señor,
"Thomas Sutcliffe, &c.

"I have manifested to your excellency in the memorials and documents that accompany them, a sufficient proof, that circumstances have placed me in a different and far more critical situation than El Captain de Navio, Don Carlos Woorster, and Lieutenant-Colonel Don Ambrosio Acosta.

"I protest to your excellency, that had I received from the bounty of government an effective employment in the army, or been attached to any corps of cavalry, I would now have been serving in ' El Exercito Restaurador.'

"The decree which I received, to place myself under a general, who had given me just and sufficient motives to excuse myself from serving under his orders, and to be employed ' as he should think fit,' wounded my feelings, but, complying with the duties of a soldier, I stifled my grievances; and through ' La Commandancia General de Armas,' I specified my obedience, and requested my general's commands; but previous to my receiving an answer, I was informed that Lieutenant-Colonel Latapiatt was his chief aide-de-camp. This confounded me, and more so when I learnt I should have to serve under him, which was impossible.

"I am extremely sorry that I did not state, in my first memorial, the motives which delicacy urged me to consign to oblivion.

"I was not aware that the general would forward it to your excellency, until I arrived at head-quarters. The order I received to march to the capital, impeded me from having an opportunity of explaining my motives to him a reserved manner.

"I was cashiered, and my commission was called in to be cancelled, on the very day on which I gave my deposition to the judge-fiscal, who was appointed to try El Señor General Blanco; this prevented me from having an audience with your excellency, and El S'or Ministro de Guerra, in order that I might have stated my case, to the end of obtaining some other employment, &c.

"If I have not felt satisfied with the decree of the thirteenth of March, it is on account of my firm belief, that my conduct has not merited the displeasure of the supreme government, for having requested my separation from the service, when the circumstances that I have already cited, have obliged me to take such steps; nor that I am in the case of losing fifteen years' services, or the recompense I solicited when I was dismissed the service— without consulting my motives, even when I had been some time in the capital previous to its being decreed— which in my humble opinion, is an evident proof, that my services were of little value, or unnecessary.

"Por Tanto."

· "I beg that your excellency will, in consideration of what I have stated, and presented in my memorials, deign to decree a compensation for my services, and which I consider myself entitled to, in order that I may return to my native country, &c.

" Es justicia,

" E'xmo Señor,

" THOMAS SUTCLIFFE."

This memorial was presented shortly after I received the decree of the 30th of October, and I got no answer, until I published all the other memorials and documents cited in them ; as well as the last I had sent in to government.

I published one thousand copies, and they were distributed as soon as printed. I took several copies to government on the 18th of December. The next day, my memorial was sent to me with the following decree.

" Santiago, December 19th, 1838.

" The many and multiplied attentions, that the actual state of war, in which the nation is engaged, require, does not at present permit government to take this memorial into consideration ; but they will do so, as soon as circumstances have changed.

" Rubric of his Excellency,

" RAMON CAVAREDA."

I now had clearly and fully justified my motives for having requested my retirement, and compensation for my services, as well as a remuneration for the many losses I had sustained, in the performance of my duty in Juan Fernandez. Therefore, as I was convinced that it would be imprudent to leave, at a time when I well knew that my services would be required ; I gave a further proof of my adhesion and attachment to Chile, by sending in a memorial, wherein I made a voluntary offer of my person and services, so that government might employ me as they should think convenient; but, an evasive decree led me to perceive that it would be impolitic to remain any longer in Chile, or whilst the administration of General Don Joaquin Prieto continued. Therefore, having completely deprived my calumniators of the power to tax me with having left the republic at a time that the war called upon the services of every soldier, I sent in a memorial, stating, that as my services were not at present required by the republic, I requested leave of absence, until circumstances should allow me to return, and follow up my claims, which was granted.

Lieutenant-General Don Manuel Blanco did me the honour to accept my power of attorney, and take charge of my documents, in order that he might reclaim the compensation, in the event of my remaining in England.

I published the memorials cited, and as a finale, I also added the decree respecting the laws of the press, to show the public that Latapiatt, and others, whom I had exposed, had not found it convenient to accuse any of my publications, in order to justify themselves; also, that the proper authorities had not acted according to the tenor of the decree, by suspending Latapiatt and the " commandante de armas" from their functions.

Previous to quitting the capital, I took leave of the most of my friends, personally, and am proud to state, that many expressed their regret at our parting ; but, almost all of them justified my mode of proceeding, and my having embraced such a golden opportunity, for the purpose of visiting my relatives and friends in Europe. I cannot refrain from stating, that I had the pleasure of leaving my old friend, General Borgoño, reinstated in his rank, although he was appointed to the intended mission to Spain.

I had the satisfaction of receiving many letters from my friends on the eve of my departure, of which I shall insert one from General Blanco, together with my farewell to the Chilians.

" Santiago, January, 17th, 1839.

"Señor Don Thomas Sutcliffe.

" My Esteemed Sutcliffe,

" In answer to your appreciated of yesterday, I wish you a good voyage, and every happiness.

"I can never forget the attachment and loyalty you have shown towards my person in one of the most critical circumstances of my public life, and whilst the lowest passions had risen against me, under the shade of an ungrateful government.

" Preserve this testimony of my gratitude, ' reconocimiento,' and be assured, that at all times, and at any distance, you may depend upon the esteem and friendship of your,

" MANUEL BLANCO ENCALADA."

MY FAREWELL.

" Being about to retire from Chile, I am impelled by sentiments of gratitude, that will ever accompany me, to adopt this mode of bidding farewell to those worthy Chilians who have favoured me with their friendship and esteem, during a residence of sixteen years in this country, as well as a tribute to them of my most sincere and grate-

ful thanks for the many favours I have received, and offer
my services, should they consider me of any utility; for I
will, in any part I may reside, feel the greatest pleasure in
having an opportunity whereby I may return their kindness, with unequivocal proofs of the unalterable profession
of my esteem.

"In order to satisfy the desires of many who have professed an interest in my concerns, and are desirous to learn
what are the motives that have compelled me to retire from
the military service of this republic, I published on the
14th of last month the documents in circulation, and to
which I have now added others, where may be seen, without the necessity of commentators, a chain of misfortunes
and vexations, that have not only obliged me to retire from
the army, but from a country in which it would have been
my greatest happiness to have passed the rest of my days.

"THOMAS SUTCLIFFE."

" Santiago, January 10th, 1839."

THE END.

GLOSSARY.

Acta, act or decree of congress, or any municipal, or military assembly.
Alcade, chief municipal officer.
Alameda, public promenade, or avenue of trees.
Alfalfa, a species of clover.
Adobes, bricks dried in the sun.
Animas, spirits of the dead.
Albricias, thanks, or rewards for good news.
Alojamiento, place of rest or lodging.
Aguardiente, ardent spirits.
Arriero, muleteer.
Arroba, weight of about 25 lbs.
Arroba, measure of about seven gallons.
Arribano, native of the southern frontier.
Angelito, angel, or dead infant.
Almofrez, leather case to carry bedding in.
Atento servidor, *A. S.*, attentive servant.

Blanco, white.
Bahia, bay.
Balsa, raft, or float.
Banos, baths.
Bolas, missile of three balls.
Blanco toro, raw spirits.
Brasero, chafing-dish.
Bayle, dance.
Baguales, wild horses.
Bando, the act of publishing a decree.
Beata, sanctified person.
Bochinche, tumult.
B. S. M., I kiss your hands.

Cabo, cape.
Cacique, Indian chief.
Cazadores, light infantry.
Cazadores a caballo, light cavalry.
Canada, water course.
Cabildo, municipality.
Cabildante, municipal officer.
Cura, curate,

Cedula, decree.
Chingana, dancing-house.
Chinas, trulls.
Cerro, hill.
Chilena, Chileno, Chilians.
Casas Matas, dungeon of Callao.
Cazuela, a stew of meat or fowls.
Corral, cattle-pen.
Chacara, small farm.
Chica, country wine.
Chicha manzana, cider.
Charke, dried beef.
Charke-can, a favourite Chilian mess.
Consulado, court of commerce.
Cuesta, road over a mountain.
Capa, Spanish cloak.
Chiripa, Indian garment.
Concepto, reputation.
Capataz, overlooker or driver.
Consejo de guerra, court-martial.
Corte marcial, military court of appeal.
Corte suprema, supreme courts.
Compadre, a relative through baptism.
Corredor, gallery, corridor.
Conjurador, exorcist, one who lays evil spirits, or drives away locusts, or other vermin that annoy the agriculturist.
Cavallo, horse.
Chili, Chile.

Don, Spanish title.
Doctor, Dr., collegiate title.
Dado de baja, cashiered
D. S. S. S., from your obedient servant.
D. S. S. A., from your true friend.
Dios que a v., God preserve you.
D. G. A. V. M. A. God preserve you many years.

Espanoles, Spaniards.
Estanco, monopoly.
Estancia, grazing farm.
Estanciero, grazier.
Estero, rivulet.

2 o

Escaveche, pickles.
Exercicios, penitential devotons.
El pueblo, the people.
Fanfarron, vain boaster, braggart.
Fanega, a measure from 150 to 200 lbs. weight.
Fiscal, attorney general.
Frayie, Fr., friar, monk.
Frigoles, French beans.
Fuerte, fort.
Farolero, one of the Spanish faction.

Guasso, or *huasso*, a countryman of Chile.
Gaucho, or *llanero*, a countryman of Rio de la Plata.
Granadero, grenadier.
Granadero a caballo, heavy horseman.
Grassa, fat.
Godos, Spaniards, or their partizans.
Gringoes, Europeans, not Spaniards.

Hacienda, La, the treasury.
Hacienda, Una, an estate.
Haciendado, landed proprietor.
Habilitador, purveyor.

Insurgente, American patriot.
Indio, India, Indians.
Jefe, a chief, or field officer.
Intendencia, provincial court.
Intendente, governor of a province.
Junta, state committee.
Isla, island.
Juez Fiscal, attorney-general.

Laguna, lake.
Lasso, a missile made of hide to catch cattle with.
Lomas, small hills.
Lavaderos, gold washings.
Longo, head.

Mayoral, overseen,
Mago domo, head servant.
Malone, Indian foray.
Machi, Indian sorceror.
Moeetones, Indian warriors.
Marco, mark, eight ounces.
Matanzas, place of slaughter.
Mate, herb of Paraguay.
Monteneros, Guerrillas.
Montanas, a range of woods at the base of the Andes.
Montes, woods.

Montas, heaps of gold dust found in lavaderos.
Mantas, garment.
Maturango, Spaniard.
Ms. As. many years.

Negro, black.
Nuestro Senor, our Saviour.

O'Higginista, partizans of General O'Higgins.
Oupellas, Indian ornaments.
Onza, an ounce or doubloon.

Padrino, godfather, defender.
Philopolitas, patriots.
Pipiolos, liberals.
Poncho, square mantle worn in South America.
Puente, bridge.
Puerto, port.
Porteno, native of a sea-port.
Porteno de Valparaiso, native of Valparaiso.
Parla, Indian palaver or conference.
Plaza, square.
Principal, principle.
Patio, court.
Pella, lump of pure gold.
Pepita, lump of gold found in a lavadero.
Pilon, horse without ears.
Peon, labourer.
Pulperia, a shop where spirits, liquors, and provisions are retailed.
Pelucones, aristocracy of Chile.
Pulque, wine.
Porrata, impressment of horses, &c.
Pueblo, El, the people.
Pasteles, pastry.
Patria, our country.
Patriotos, Patriotas, patriots.
Patria la vieja, first epoch of the revolution of Chile.
Pinones, Araucanian pines.
Punta, point.
Prieto, a dark colour
Plata, Plata, ahi viene la mosca, money, money, here comes the fly.

Quarto, a room.
Quartel, barracks.
Quadra, a measure of four acres.
Quebrada, ravine.
Quinta, villa.
Quintal, one hundred pounds.

Q. B. S. M., who kisses your hands.

Ramada, shed.
Rodeo, a gathering of cattle.
Rodeos, cattle pens.
Ravel, a fiddle with three strings.
Rancho, hut.
Rio, river.
Restaurador, restorer.

Santo, saint.
Senor, Sir.
S. E., your excellency.
S.S.S., your faithful servant.
S.S , your servant.
S.S.A., your faithful friend.
Sobriquet, nickname.
Sierra, mountain.
Serrillos, hills.
Saya, petticoat.
Socabon, adit of a mine.

Trabaja, V. mi amigo, que los pueblos no siempre son ingratos, preserve my friend, the people are not always ungrateful.

Temblores, Terramotos, earthquakes.
Taita, father.
Tertulia, evening party.
Trilla, harvest.
Trajes, costumes.
Tajamar, a parapet on the sea side, or banks of a river.
Tintorrillos, pettyfoggers.
Trapiche, water-wheel.
Toqui, Indian Generalisimo.
Toupa, Indian ornament.

Ulmen, Araucanian noble.

Vado, ford.
Villa, town.
Vaquero, herdsman.
V. B., approval.
Vara, Spanish yard.
V. S., your lordship.
Vendimia, vintage.
V. E., your excellency.

Yeyua, mare.
Yegua tordilla, warm punch..

ERRATA.

LONDON: FISHER, SON, AND CO., PRINTERS.

CPSIA information can be obtained at www.ICGtesting.com
Printed in the USA
BVOW04s1129120514

353266BV00016B/398/P